AUGUSTUS

AUGUSTUS

Pat Southern

London and New York

First published 1998
by Routledge
11 New Fetter Lane, London EC4P 4EE

Simultaneously published in the USA and Canada
by Routledge
29 West 35th Street, New York, NY 10001

Typeset in Garamond by
Florencetype Ltd, Stoodleigh, Devon
Printed and bound in Great Britain by
Biddles Ltd, Guildford and King's Lynn

British Library Cataloguing in Publication Data
A catalogue record for this book is available
from the British Library

Library of Congress Cataloging in Publication Data
A catalogue record for this book has been requested

ISBN 0–415–16631–4

This one is for Annis, all those years ago

CONTENTS

FIGURES

PLATES

(between pages 130 and 131)

PREFACE

This is a book about a man – an extraordinary man who might not have become extraordinary if he had not lived in extraordinary times. No biography can be written without taking into account the social, economic and political background and the times through which the individual lived, but Augustus poses several particular problems. Despite his talent for self-advertisement his character is only rarely revealed. Portraits of him abound, most of them contemporary and some of them reverential and posthumous, but in all of these portraits he is perpetually young and vigorous, never allowed to age even when he reached his seventies. Thus the real person was deliberately veiled, screened from public scrutiny by an orchestrated façade that was not necessarily false, but which was tailored to circumstances, and adapted accordingly when circumstances changed. The longevity of the man himself and his early entry into political life automatically ensure that the subject will be a large one, and this is compounded by the fact that Octavian-Augustus did not simply act against a background, or within the confines of the political development of the state; for most of his life he was the embodiment of the state. This means that a biography must also become a history of the transformation of the Republic into the Empire, a task which would require many years and at least 20 volumes to complete properly. Full debate of all issues is impossible in one volume, and would become monotonous or even misleading. As the saying goes 'L'art d'ennuyer est l'art de tout dire'. The phrase loses some of its panache in translation, but none of its meaning: 'the way to bore people is to say everything'.

The amount of modern literature is staggering – around 250 items in a bibliography published in the 1970s, and a vast growth has taken place since then. Most of the papers and books dealing with the Augustan age are quite specialised, covering one or two aspects of political, social or economic history, suggesting solutions for specific problems, or describing particular works of art or literature, and their relevance to political themes. The entire corpus is too vast to survey, though in fairness, Kienast can be said to have achieved it in his book on Augustus, with clear text and monumental references. The author makes no claims to the sort of completeness for which Kienast aimed. The main purpose of the present volume is to tell the story of Augustus in chronological sequence; it is primarily a biography and not a discussion of the finer details of administration. The text can be read as an entity without reference to the notes, or alternatively the notes to each paragraph can be used as a sort of starter pack to find further information. In dealing with a subject so thoroughly documented in secondary literature, a selection must be made in order to simplify matters, but simplification entails disregard of some specialisms and of much detail. For this reason, the art and literature of the Augustan period are only cursorily surveyed in this book; these subjects have been covered by experts whose in-depth studies render any further additions redundant. Besides, the art and literature reveal only one facet of the man, and it is to the man that this book must give its attention. Even when limited to these human parameters, the task was daunting even to the ancients. Velleius Paterculus, writing in AD 30, encapsulates the problems faced by anyone trying to write about Augustus: 'To tell of the wars waged under his command, of the pacification of the world by his victories, of his many works at home and outside of Italy would weary a writer intending to devote his whole life to this one task. As for myself, remembering the proposed scope of my work, I have confined myself to setting before the eyes and minds of my readers a general picture of his principate' (*Compendium of Roman History* 2.89.6. Loeb translation by Frederick W. Shipley).

ACKNOWLEDGEMENTS

My thanks to all those people who have helped me in my studies of the Romans, and particularly in the writing of this book. I owe an unpaid debt to the late Charles Daniels, who always made time to listen, and without whose encouragement I would never have written anything. Similarly there is another as yet undischarged debt to Professor Anthony Birley, whose assistance has been invaluable in saving me from errors, and whose expenditure of time and patience is limitless. As for illustrations, the talents and patience of Graeme Stobbs are very gratefully acknowledged; from graffiti-laden scraps of paper he produces maps and drawings at prodigious speed. The staffs of the libraries of the University of Newcastle upon Tyne, the Society for the Promotion of Roman Studies, and of the Newcastle Literary and Philosophical Society inter-library loan department, have all performed above and beyond the call of duty. I am grateful to the following museums, which kindly supplied photographs: the British Museum, London; Kunsthistorisches Museum, Vienna; Louvre Museum, Paris; Ny Carlsberg Glyptotek, Copenhagen; National Archaeological Museum, Athens; Römisch-Germanisches Museum, Cologne; Vatican Museum, Vatican City.

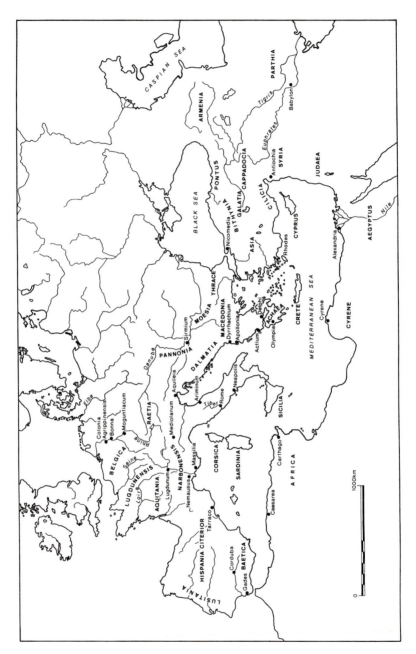

Map 1 Map of the Roman world at the end of Augustus' reign

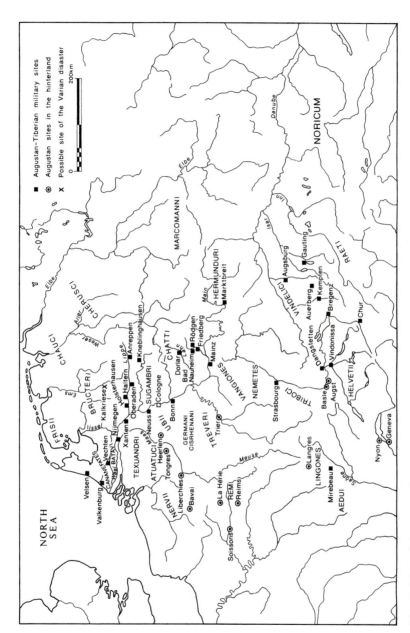

Map 2 Map of Augustan Germany

1

OCTAVIUS TO OCTAVIAN

The man who can justifiably be called the founder of the Roman Empire, the heir and successor of Julius Caesar and the Master of Ceremonies as the Republic was transformed into the Principate, was born simply Gaius Octavius, on 23 September 63 BC, in Rome. His family origins were relatively humble and therefore obscure. The Octavii were new men (*novi homines*) from Velitrae (modern Vellitri), a Volscian town about twenty-five miles south-east of Rome. The family entered the ranks of the Roman Senate only with Octavius' father, also called Gaius Octavius, who was praetor in 61 BC. A more spectacular background would have been better documented, or at least more firmly imprinted upon living memory, and it would therefore have been more difficult, when the time came to create the legend that surrounded him, for Augustus to refashion himself, or diplomatically to forget certain events and features of his life. His early obscurity was useful to him when he came to power, for the Princeps was impenetrable by design, and by implication he was almost perfect. All human failings, save for the acceptable anecdotal foibles, were expunged from the record. 'Accentuate the positive' might have been a principle established by Augustus when he composed the *Res Gestae*. When the propaganda machinery was in full flow, a little fictionalised biography entered the legend, connecting the Octavii of Velitrae with the family of the same name from Rome, whose lineage went back to the time of the wars with Hannibal. This connection is not proven beyond doubt, and in any case, even the Octavii of Rome were never as important as the Augustan propagandists would have us believe. To many people, noble ancestry is comforting and more acceptable than humble origins, and throughout history efforts have been made to find the relevant antecedents for parvenu leaders who found themselves in positions of power after the upheaval of civil or external wars.[1]

But all this came later and was retrospective. Gaius Octavius, sometimes also known as Thurinus, was the son of Gaius Octavius and his second wife, Atia. The elder Gaius had been married first to Ancharia, by whom he had a daughter, called Octavia Major, to distinguish her from her half sister Octavia Minor, born to Gaius and Atia. The Octavii were wealthy equestrians, who ran their banking business at Velitrae, and were members of the aristocracy of the town, which became a Roman colony in the fifth century BC. Suetonius says that there were many indications that the Octavian family was a distinguished one at Velitrae. A street in the most busy area of the town was named after them, and there was an altar consecrated by an Octavius whose claim to fame derived from his prompt improvisation during a sacrifice to Mars. He was interrupted, so the story goes, by news that troops from a neighbouring town were about to attack, so he quickly gathered the entrails of the sacrificial beast, offered them to the god in their unprepared state, went off to battle, and won. Such was the legend. In the event of his failure, of course, he would have gone down in history as an unprincipled, sacrilegious type whose fate should be a warning to all. The people of Velitrae were so pleased with the action of Octavius that they decreed that henceforth all sacrifices to Mars should be conducted in the same manner, and the remains of the sacrificed animals should be offered to the Octavii.[2]

The association with Velitrae was ineradicable, so deeply rooted that many people were prepared to state that Octavius, the future Princeps Augustus, was born there, but it is certain that he was born in Rome, at the Oxheads (*ad Capita Bubula*) on the Palatine Hill, not far from the *Sacra Via*, which runs from the bottom of the Palatine to the Senate House in the Forum Romanum. Octavius' father had first entered the Senate when he was appointed quaestor, perhaps in 70 BC. The primary necessity for entry to the Senate was wealth, and this the Octavii possessed from their banking business and their landed interests, so that by 70 they had accumulated the necessary sums (400,000 sesterces, increased to 1,000,000 or 1,200,000 in the early Empire) to enable Gaius Octavius to embark upon his senatorial career. When the child Octavius was two years old Gaius Octavius senior was elected praetor, having followed the usual career of military tribune, quaestor, then plebeian aedile.[3]

The stepping stones to political eminence in Republican Rome did not consist solely of possession of a sizeable fortune and successive tenure of the various military and civilian posts that preceded the consulship. It was absolutely vital to seek connections with eminent men. Above all it was necessary to marry well, thus forming alliances with the most influential families. This is what Gaius Octavius did in 65 when he chose Atia as his second wife. She was well connected, being the daughter of Atius Balbus from Aricia, and his wife Julia, the sister of Julius Caesar, who at that time was a rising politician. Although he was related to Pompeius Magnus through his mother, Atius Balbus had not profited from this relationship to become an influential man. It was Caesar who was rapidly gaining that distinction, so from the young Gaius Octavius' point of view the pre-eminent family connections were with the Julii, and this fact would have been impressed upon him from the moment he was born. Though he scarcely saw Julius until he was in his teens, he would have been fully aware of him via his mother.[4]

The events of 63 BC, when Octavius was born, brought Cicero to prominence. Cicero was consul in that year, and never afterwards let anyone forget that he had saved the state when he secured the condemnation of Catiline and his fellow conspirators. During the debates in the Senate about the punishment of Catiline, Gaius Julius Caesar spoke against execution of the conspirators, and he later criticised Cicero for having authorised the death penalty. Caesar had just become Pontifex Maximus, and was also engaged in ardent 'left wing' politics, typified by his prosecution, in partnership with the tribune Titus Labienus, of Gaius Rabirius for his part in the death of the tribune Saturninus, nearly four decades earlier. The point at issue was the sacrosanctity of tribunes, which Caesar milked for all that it was worth, not simply to ensure the future health and safety of tribunes, but primarily to ensure his own political importance and popularity. Caesar was becoming a force to be reckoned with, but at the moment he could not hope to stand alone. Later, when he allied himself to M. Licinius Crassus and Pompeius Magnus, he would lay the foundations of the road that brought his great nephew to supreme power.[5]

As a young child, Octavius possibly knew more of Julius Caesar than he did of his own father, whom he cannot have known very intimately. From the end of 61 until late in 59 the elder Gaius was absent as governor of Macedonia, where he conducted himself with credit, at least in the opinion of Cicero. The sources do not inform us that he took his wife and children with him. Shortly after his return, on the threshold of a consular career, he died suddenly before he could present himself as a candidate for the consular elections. Thus from the age of four until he was about six or seven years old, when his mother married again, Octavius was fatherless. During these formative years, he was educated by Atia, or so Tacitus says in his *Dialogues*, when he compared the older, and in his opinion better, methods of child rearing, as exemplified by Cornelia, the mother of the Gracchi, Aurelia, the mother of Caesar, and Atia, the mother of Augustus. By the time that Dio took up the theme, the stories of Octavius' childhood had passed right through hyperbole to emerge as fabulous legend. Stories proliferated, mostly consisting of prophecies of a glorious future: for example, it was said that both his mother and his father, and also various senators, saw Octavius in their dreams, usually accompanied by omens which clearly prophesied that he would one day rule the world; in more modest dreams it was foreseen that he would reorganise the state. Dio says that Caesar took the boy under his wing, and ensured that he was educated suitably for world rule. This is retrospective padding. Octavius was educated, certainly, and he may have learned much from Caesar, but it is questionable whether he was given lessons in world domination, which is what is implied by Dio's statement. More prosaically Octavius would have been educated as were other Roman boys. He was trained as an orator, in both Latin and Greek. Suetonius asserts that Augustus could neither speak nor write Greek with any fluency, but he is contradicted by the elder Pliny who says that he could. Concerning his later education, Dio tells us that Octavius was put through military service, and instructed in politics and the art of government. There is no solid evidence for this, only the retrospective assumption that somewhere along the way Octavius had learned all these things. As a young boy he could not have learned anything at first hand from Caesar, since the two probably did not meet until Octavius was 15 or 16 years old. In the year when Octavius' father died, Julius Caesar was consul, and in the following year he left Rome to take up his post as proconsul of Gaul. It is not known how closely Octavius followed the career of his great uncle, but as a young child he could scarcely have been unaware that Julius was consul. As the years went by, he would know that his great uncle was steadily gaining fame for himself during the conquest of Gaul. Octavius would also know that Caesar's daughter Julia was married to Pompeius Magnus, and that the wealthy Crassus was somehow associated with these two men. A very young child cannot be expected to be politically aware, but he would hear the names and titles, and make something of the information as he grew up.[6]

After the death of her husband, Atia was eligible for remarriage, and her connections with the Julian family would enhance her marital value. Since noble alliances were of paramount importance, without doubt Caesar himself would have expressed keen interest in her future. Any potential suitor would need to be vetted by him, even at a distance. At best, a new alliance might be of assistance to him, and at worst he would need to ensure that he would not be compromised during the rest of his political career. While Caesar was still in Gaul, but doubtless with his sanction, Atia was married for the second time, in 57 or 56, to L. Marcius Philippus, who had just returned from his term of office in Syria in time to stand for the consular elections. He was duly elected consul for 56. Philippus trod a careful path between factions in Rome: allied on the one hand to Caesar, he was also attached on the other hand to the powerful elite known as the *optimates* by the marriage of his daughter Marcia to Cato. He remained on the sidelines of the political scene, and if he did not distinguish himself, neither was he completely extinguished; he neither antagonised nor actively supported either party, and diplomatically remained neutral during the civil war between Pompeius and Caesar.[7]

During the late Republic the Roman political scene was dominated by three men, acting in concert in a combination misleadingly known to modern scholars as the 'First Triumvirate', a title which bestows on the loose alliance a permanence and a sophisticated organisation that it never possessed. In order to place the union of Caesar, Pompeius and Crassus in context it is necessary to review the chief events of the previous fifty years and more, for it was not simply the latest round of civil wars that formed the inheritance of Augustus when he put into effect his so-called restoration of the Republic. For many years before the conflict between Caesar and Pompeius, the Republic had reeled and recovered from successive wars, riots and disturbances. Some scholars would place the beginning of the end as far back as the wars with Hannibal, or with the agrarian legislation of Tiberius Gracchus in 133, while others find the cause of collapse in the Social War in 90, or the prolonged struggle between Marius and Sulla. These were significant and successive stages in the history of Rome, leading to the extraordinary commands and the growth of personal power that characterised the late Republic. When Sulla made his infamous march on the city it was the first time that a Roman magistrate had secured control of the government by means of an army, and furthermore he was not brought to trial for the murder of his opponents. He secured the command against Mithridates in the East, but the war was prolonged and while he was absent his opponents regained control in Rome. On his return, he was appointed Dictator for an unlimited term, with supreme powers, which he used to suppress his enemies with brutal determination. After he had set the state in order according to his oligarchic tenets, he laid down his powers and retired. But the rot had set in; his measures to secure the state did not long survive him, because he himself had set the example of how to obtain and wield power. Thereafter, personal interests, shifting allegiances, and extraordinary commands became more common. Individuals could now gather power into their own hands supported by their armies, and the Senate was quite unable to resist. The career of Pompeius illustrates the point. He raised a private army to fight for Sulla in 83; some years later he defeated the popular leader Sertorius, then obtained the consulship, in spite of being well below the minimum age and without having held any of the qualifying offices. The fact that he had his army behind him was extremely persuasive – and a lesson for the future. Pompeius duly became consul. He then set about reversing what Sulla had done. Most notably he restored the powers of the tribunate, an office which he utilised soon afterwards to pass the necessary legislation to obtain his special commands. After his consulship he did not seek a province, but his commands against the Mediterranean pirates, and then against Mithridates in the East, were much more glorious than the mundane governorship of a province.[8]

Pompeius did not receive his commands without opposition, which was still not subdued when he returned to Rome in 62. Even so, he did not march on the city at the head of his troops. Rather than embroil the state in civil war, Pompeius laid down his command and disbanded his army. Perhaps he thought that the weight of his prestige would be sufficient to persuade the Senate to co-operate with him, but for three years he could make no headway. His arrangements for the newly conquered Eastern provinces, and for the client kingdoms, were debated endlessly, with ratification always deferred; authorisation for his promised distribution of land to his soldiers was not forthcoming. His accumulated prestige was deliberately eroded, and since there was no tremendous danger from which the state needed to be saved, he could not recover his pre-eminence by dashing off to do something heroic. Undoubtedly competent on the military battlefield, on the political battlefield he was beginning to look foolish. Disgusted and at his wits' end, he threw in his lot with Caesar, whose election to the consulship in 59 owed much to Pompeius' support. Bibulus was elected as Caesar's colleague, which reveals that the combined weight of Pompeius, Caesar and Crassus, who were still secretive about their alliance, was not yet influential enough to control the elections entirely. Caesar quickly neutralised Bibulus' feeble opposition, leaving the field clear for the promotion of the personal designs of each of the members of the three-man combine. The arrangement was one of mutual support; Caesar needed Pompeius for his political stature, because his own standing did not yet equal that of the greatest soldier in Rome. Pompeius needed Caesar because he required an energetic consul with few scruples, who would push through the necessary ratification of his plans. Crassus joined the group for reasons which are less clear. He was the only serious rival to Pompeius, and their rivalry persisted for life, but Crassus could not afford to let the alliance of Pompeius and Caesar eclipse his own political standing. All these three men were concerned, first and foremost, with their own interests.[9]

In 59 Caesar forced through legislation with scant regard either for Bibulus or the finer points of law. At the end of his consulship, he had shackled the opposition. He cemented the alliance with Pompeius by arranging a marriage in the spring of 59 between the latter and his daughter Julia; it seems to have been a successful arrangement, and a marriage with more affection than a political arrangement warranted. For the time being, it was hardly noticeable that the 'Triumvirate' existed. Relations between the three members eventually broke down while Caesar was engaged on the conquest of Gaul. Pompeius found himself isolated and attacked. Crassus did not help him. Having severed some of his aristocratic connections, Pompeius had only a narrow choice of allies, and was thrown once more into the arms of Caesar. In 56 the three met at Luca to thrash out their difficulties and make plans for the future. Pompeius and Crassus were to be consuls for 55; they were more certain now of their grip on the elections. Caesar obtained, via the *Lex Pompeia Licinia* passed when the two took up their consulship, an extension of five years on his command in Gaul. After their joint consulship, provincial commands would follow for Pompeius and Crassus. Pompeius received command of Spain, but did not leave Italy, choosing instead to govern his province via subordinates, a novel arrangement, and an important precedent. Crassus received the Parthian command, where he came to grief in 53. His death, combined with that of Julia in 54, has been highlighted as the reason why the unofficial alliance broke down, leading to an inevitable rift and then civil war between Caesar and Pompeius. Gruen has challenged this conclusion, pointing out that there was no reason why political co-operation could not have continued, and that it was neither Crassus nor Julia who welded the three men together. After Julia's death, Caesar offered Octavia, sister of Octavius, in marriage to Pompeius. The great man refused her and looked elsewhere; this need not mean that he was turning away from Caesar entirely, but it was a significant move, indicating that Pompeius intended to go it alone or change direction. Whatever the reasons behind the declining relations between Caesar and Pompeius, conditions worsened after 53, eventually leading to war. It is certain that Crassus' death loosened his political alliances; most important, it left his clients without a leader. One of Crassus' sons died with him at Carrhae; the other, Marcus Crassus the younger, was a confirmed Caesarian. Many of Crassus' followers joined Caesar, thus creating an imbalance between him and Pompeius.[10]

From the age of eleven to fourteen, Octavius would witness and take note of the political manoeuvring at Rome as it became increasingly obvious that a war between Caesar and Pompeius was brewing. As a close relative of one of the chief protagonists, it would hardly have been possible to remain neutral, because even the most mundane family affairs took on a political flavour. Octavius made his first public appearance at the age of eleven when he delivered the funeral oration for his grandmother Julia, the sister of Caesar. Family connections and solidarity would feature largely in this performance. He would have known that Caesar had also made a similar funeral oration for his aunt Julia, the wife of Marius, at a time when connection with Marius was downright unhealthy, if not actually lethal. Funeral speeches were as much political gestures as they were acts of piety. They were historic occasions, when busts of famous or not so famous ancestors were displayed, and their noble deeds recalled. In making his speech for his grandmother, Octavius would necessarily have been conscious of his family history, and in this connection would have taken note of the current exploits of his great uncle. He could not have been indifferent to the debate that centred on the termination of Caesar's command in Gaul, and the legislative technicalities that surrounded it. The major problem was that Caesar needed the consulship immediately after his proconsulship, so that he could step from one appointment to the next without giving up his *imperium*. Any gap between the Gallic command and the consulship would leave him at the mercy of prosecution by anyone who cared to bring a charge against him, and throughout his career, especially during his consulship in 59, he had made so many enemies and behaved in such a way as to give them all plenty of scope to prosecute him for any one of his dubious acts. It was not necessarily true that anyone would dare to prosecute him, nor was it a foregone conclusion that Caesar would be condemned if anyone did so. It was a thinly disguised excuse to preserve power intact and uninterrupted, but Caesar was not prepared to give up or to compromise. He therefore desired to be allowed to stand for the consulship *in absentia*, and in order to obtain this concession he required collaborators in Rome. The best method was to have a tribune propose that he should be a candidate without having to appear in person. As sole consul in 52, Pompeius did co-operate with Caesar, but then passed a law, the *Lex Pompeia de iure magistratuum*, requiring candidates to present themselves in person. This has been interpreted either as double dealing or as forgetful incompetence; Gruen suggests that in fact it was perfectly acceptable for Pompeius to pass this law, since it did not affect Caesar, whose case, examined and sanctioned by the people, would be regarded as a legitimate exception. Pompeius simply wanted to ensure that the practice of standing for the consular elections *in absentia* did not become a habit.[11]

Next came the *Lex Pompeia de provinciis* which stated that there should be a five-year gap between the tenure of a magistracy at Rome and the government of a province. This meant that the men who were currently in office in Rome would not be the ones who were eligible for provincial governorships the following year, which in turn meant that until the first five years had elapsed, governors would have to be chosen from among the ex-consuls and ex-praetors who were qualified for, but did not necessarily aspire to, this sort of appointment. Thus Cicero was obliged to become governor of Cilicia, very much against his will, because for Cicero the only possible life was in Rome itself. More pertinent to Caesar's problems, it would not now be necessary to wait until a magistrate had completed his current term of office before sending him to take over in Gaul; any of the available pool of men of consular rank could be appointed to succeed Caesar the moment his command expired, thus exposing him to a short term as a *privatus*, when he would almost certainly be prosecuted and would definitely have to give up his *imperium*. Once again there was no very determined effort to oust Caesar from his position, since Pompeius inserted a clause into this law to safeguard him, treating him as a legitimate exception.[12]

Pompeius himself was, as sole consul, also a legitimate exception. His position has been described as both anomalous and unprecedented, and it was not entirely to his credit that he had achieved it in a time of upheaval. He had employed his usual tactics of not actively seeking office himself, but allowing others to agitate on his behalf while he waited until the situation became so intolerable that in the end the Senate was forced to ask him to take up the reins of state. In the constitutional difficulties of 53, the Senate did not favour any of the candidates for the consulship, and cancelled the elections for the consulships of 52. Disorder prevailed, and the supporters of Pompeius insisted that he should be made Dictator; others clamoured for the joint rule of both Pompeius and Caesar. The senators reacted badly to this last idea, and hastily reached a political compromise proposed by Cato; they appointed Pompeius sole consul, which was a contradiction in terms and an exercise in careful terminology in order to avoid a more emotive title. Octavius perhaps took note of the extent to which the Senate would tolerate the reality of power, provided that it was decently masked by appropriate titles that retained a veneer of legality. Whatever the title bestowed upon him, it had to be recognised that Pompeius was the only man apart from Caesar who could restore order, but the Senate shrank from appointing him Dictator. Too many could remember Sulla. Apart from the constitutional and legal limitations that distinguished the powers of a consul (who was subject to tribunician veto) from the comprehensive powers of a Dictator (who was not) it was almost purely an argument of semantics. With the accumulation of powers accruing to him, and by dint of his prestige and *auctoritas*, Pompeius was Dictator in all but name. He was chief magistrate at Rome, without a colleague, and he was at the same time governor of Spain, employing deputies to govern for him. He had access to armed force, if he so desired, while still consul; this was quite unconstitutional, since the consuls were supposed to lay down their military powers when they entered the city. If Octavius learned much from Caesar, he surely learned one or two useful lessons from Pompeius, and from the interaction between Pompeius and the Senate. If not handled too arbitrarily, and allowed to exercise some power, or at least to imagine that they could do so if they wished, most senators were tractable enough.[13]

In 51 it was rumoured that Caesar intended to enfranchise the Transpadane Gauls, which would increase his *clientelae* immeasurably, and men at Rome began to worry. The consul M. Marcellus challenged the enfranchisement, precipitating agitation to recall Caesar, who was not yet ready to return to Rome. He had just defeated Vercingetorix, and the siege of Alesia was over, but the war was nowhere near conclusion; he would need much more time to settle affairs in Gaul. If his five-year term agreed at Luca were to be taken seriously it meant that his proconsulship would not terminate until the early months of 50; it is unlikely that the *Lex Pompeia Licinia* contained a clause that specifically recorded a terminal date. Even though Marcellus' attacks became more pertinently directed towards Caesar, any discussion of his recall was deferred until 1 March 50.[14]

The termination of Caesar's command was always the crucial point. Caesar himself later claimed that he had been allowed to stand for the consulship in 49 for election to office in 48. This does not sit well with the evidence, but, for reasons which can only be guessed, Caesar did not choose to stand for the consular elections in 50. From then onwards, the support of Pompeius for Caesar steadily waned. He rejected the idea that Caesar could hold *imperium* in his province and be consul at the same time, despite the fact that he had set the precedent himself. Gruen affirms that 'one cannot divide Rome into Caesarians and Pompeians even as late as the year 50', but despite the absence of a definite polarisation of factions, there was already a growing body of resentment against both dynasts. All attempts at compromise were blocked by the tribune Curio, who swept aside suggestions in order to propose a compromise of his own, namely that both Pompeius and Caesar should lay down their commands simultaneously. The Senate voted 370 to 22 in favour of the motion, and the people displayed unequivocal enthusiasm for it, but the proposal was never implemented, despite its obvious popularity. The *optimates* were determined to block Caesar, and the one sure method of achieving their aim was to bring Pompeius into their own camp. As part of the plan, Gaius Marcellus inflated rumours that Caesar was about to invade Italy, and as consul he theatrically entrusted Pompeius with the safety of the state. Pompeius took command of the troops in Italy and began to talk of war. It was the only way to preserve his pre-eminence and his partisans. Affairs were rapidly coming to a head. Some attempt at negotiation was still feasibe, but all proposals failed. Pompeius was prepared to accept Caesar's offer to give up his armies and provinces, except for two legions and command over Illyricum and Cisalpine Gaul, but the consuls would not agree to this proposal. Next, Curio brought a letter from Caesar, suggesting that he would give up his command if Pompeius did the same, but he added threats that if Pompeius retained his armies, he would not give up his own, and instead he would avenge the wrongs done to him and his country. This incendiary talk was seen as a declaration of war. Appian documents the succeeding uproar. The Senate appointed Lucius Domitius as Caesar's successor, declared Pompeius protector of Rome, and Caesar an enemy of the state. The tribunes M. Antonius and Q. Cassius were thrown out of the Senate House, and instantly made their way to Caesar disguised as slaves. Ever alive to the value of inflammatory propaganda, Caesar showed the tribunes to the troops in their dishevelled condition, explaining that after all their heroic deeds the only reward that the Senate thought fit for the soldiers was to label them public enemies. This was his sole means of justifying what was none the less a *putsch*. It was also very effective.[15]

After the battle of Pharsalus and the defeat of Pompeius, Caesar declared for posterity that 'they would have it so', thus placing all the blame on the enemy and exonerating himself from any intention to start a war. He may not have been exaggerating unduly. Motives for the civil war between him and Pompeius derived as much from the machinations of other self-interested parties as from the will of either of the generals, but the situation quickly escalated to the point where neither party could back down. Caesar insisted that he was forced into war, that he fought for freedom from monopolisation of power by a faction, and that his prime concerns were defence of the constitution and the rights of tribunes. In reality it was a struggle for personal survival with powers intact. Survival *per se* was hardly important. For the Romans fear of death was far outweighed by fear of loss of prestige and *dignitas*. The state had become too small for both Pompeius and Caesar; neither could subordinate himself to the other, and given that both of them stood at the head of a complex and widespread series of alliances that formed powerful factions, the inevitable conflict could not be confined to the purely personal sphere.[16]

Caesar crossed the Rubicon, the river that marked the boundary of his province, beyond which he could not legally travel at the head of troops, at the beginning of January 49. He moved so fast that he took Rome by surprise. Pompeius was quite unprepared to meet Caesar in the field, and since he was far too good a general to be unaware of this fact, or to risk fighting a battle before he was ready, he retreated to the south, finally leaving Italy altogether. He embarked at Brundisium, and sailed across the Adriatic to Dyrrachium where he gathered his army and those senators who remained loyal to him. Deprived of an army to fight, Caesar spent a few days in Rome. He would be in a great hurry, and very busy, but it is not impossible that he and Octavius met at this time. Even if they did not meet, Octavius would watch and learn. One of Caesar's first acts was to seize the treasury (*aerarium*) to finance his immediate needs. This money had been lodged there long ago in the history of the Republic, after the disastrous invasion of Italy by the Gauls. The money was dedicated to the defence of Rome against a similar threat, and anyone who removed it, for any other purpose than for making war against the Gauls, would find himself under a public curse: there may have been at least the hint of a smile on Caesar's face when he pre-empted criticism by pointing out that since he had defeated the Gauls, he was presumably exempt from the effects of such a curse.[17]

The few senators who had remained in Rome probably did not put up much resistance to Caesar, but this is understandable, since he was backed up by thousands of battle-hardened troops who would not hesitate to execute whoever their general pointed out to them. There were some arrangements to be made for the defence of Italy and neighbouring provinces before Caesar could leave Rome. He left Marcus Antonius in charge of troops in Italy, appointed his adherents to commands in Sicily, Sardinia, Illyricum and Cisalpine Gaul, and then turned first to Spain, where Pompeius' legates, Petreius and Afranius, commanded armies. Caesar declared that he was going to meet an army without a leader, and he would then go to Dyrrachium to meet a leader without an army. After initial reverses, he defeated the lieutenants of Pompeius at Ilerda in August 49.[18]

On his return to Rome, Caesar was supreme, but not everyone was cowed by his power. Cicero recounts popular demonstrations against Caesar in the theatre in the spring of 49. Otherwise, as the war in Spain progressed, and when Caesar turned his attention to Pompeius himself, it was business as usual at Rome. The praetor Lepidus proposed that Caesar should be made Dictator, and the Senate agreed. Utilising this office to obtain what he wanted quickly and without fuss, Caesar made appointments of magistrates and priests for the following year, then he abdicated, since as Dio pointed out, he already possessed all the authority and functions that he could possibly require, backed up as he was by his armies. He was elected consul for 48, and left Italy on 4 January that same year for the war against Pompeius. He did not return to Rome until September 47. After his defeat at Pharsalus, Pompeius fled to Egypt, where he was murdered by a nervous palace staff, who thought to please Caesar and avoid a Roman war on their own territory. There was already a war between Cleopatra and her brother Ptolemy, and when Caesar arrived in pursuit of Pompeius, he took charge, remaining in Egypt long enough to stabilise the political situation there. This was highly relevant to Roman interests, since most of Rome's corn supply could be found in Egypt; as a potential acquisition this ancient kingdom was far too valuable to ignore. Once he had established Cleopatra as Queen, Caesar conducted a campaign against Pharnaces in the East. In the meantime, in Rome, Octavius assumed the *toga virilis* on 18 October at the age of fifteen. This was a public, formal ceremony, during which boys laid aside the *toga praetexta* that marked their youth, and became officially enrolled as adult citizens. The normal age was seventeen, which was also the age when military service began, and the legal age at which a man could be prosecuted. In the early Empire, the lowering of the age of the assumption of the *toga virilis* was regarded as a distinction of honour, and Augustus' grandsons Gaius and Lucius assumed it at the same age as Octavius, at fifteen. Nicolaus of Damascus gives Octavius' age as only fourteen when the ceremony took place, but the evidence from Suetonius weighs against this. According to Dio, the ceremonial dressing was marred by a potentially bad omen, which Octavius turned to good account. While he was putting on his tunic, the seams came apart and it fell to the ground. With great presence of mind, Octavius said 'I shall have all the senatorial dignity at my feet.' The story is most probably a later interpolation, but it is not at odds with Octavius' character, since it illustrates a quick mind working at its manipulative best.[19]

Though he was now officially a man, Octavius was still subject to parental discipline, according to Nicolaus; Atia seems to have retained strict control of her son, not allowing him to go out except on legitimate business, and making him sleep in the same apartment as before. No adolescent resentment is recorded, but that would be in defiance of the legend. One can only speculate whether ambition already smouldered under the surface of this strict control, waiting with calculated patience for an opportunity to burst into flame. If he harboured such feelings, Octavius controlled them well; self-control was his hallmark in later life, and he seems to have regretted bitterly the few occasions when he lost it. Perhaps he began to practise it whilst still very young. Shortly after assuming the *toga virilis* he took up his first official tasks. Nicolaus tells us that the people elected him to one of the preisthoods, as *pontifex* in place of Lucius Domitius Ahenobarbus who had died. Behind this bland statement lurk a covert fact or two which were not emphasised in Nicolaus' narrative. The election was at the request of Julius Caesar, and therefore not quite so spontaneous as Nicolaus suggests, and Domitius Ahenobarbus had not simply died but had been killed at Pharsalus. Nicolaus glossed over these reminders of the Civil War between Pompeius and Caesar, concentrating instead on the glorification of his subject. The office of *pontifex* was a high honour, and one which Octavius took very seriously. He was conscientious in the performance of his duties, though according to Nicolaus he had to undertake them all after dark because, being a remarkably attractive youth, this was the only way that he could avoid the unwelcome attentions of women, thus preserving his chastity.[20]

Julius Caesar returned to Rome in September 47, and remained until the end of the year. He had been appointed Dictator for the second time, after the battle of Pharsalus, probably with fuller powers than before, but with a fixed term of office, due to expire in October 47. The exact details are uncertain, but he seems to have relinquished the Dictatorship at the prescribed time. He was elected consul, with M. Lepidus as his colleague, for 46. Since he was not due to take up office until 1 January, and had probably renounced the Dictatorship the previous October, it might seem that he was potentially powerless, but in reality he was still supreme because he had not relinquished his proconsular *imperium* and the command of his armies. Technically, he could not wield proconsular power in the city, and was supposed to lay down command of his troops the moment he crossed the *pomerium* or city limits, but somehow no one thought to raise the legal niceties with him. Secure in his position as first man in Rome, he threw himself into the task of restoring the state. There was much to do, and for Caesar it was a race against time because he could not postpone for very long the impending war against the remnants of the Pompeian armies in Africa. In a great rush, he restored order in the city, conducted elections of the magistrates for the last few months of 47, and tried to ease the parlous economic situation which had been the direct cause of rioting in Rome. Marcus Antonius, Caesar's master of horse (*magister equitum*), was currently out of favour because he had been far too brutal in quelling the riots. It was not only the civilian population who were discontented. Caesar's veteran soldiers, assembled in Campania for the coming African war, decided that they had fought long enough without the just rewards that had been promised to them but had never yet materialised. It is human nature, after throwing all energies into something for sustained periods without much tangible profit, to look up once in a while and ask 'Why am I doing this?' Caesar showed no sign of ever stopping, and by now the soldiers wanted a deadline. When their discontent came to a head, they marched on Rome to confront Caesar. He met them calmly, listened to their requests for discharge, and then addressed them, not as *commilitones*, fellow soldiers, but as *Quirites*, citizens, and with that one word brought them back to unswerving loyalty. Whether or not Octavius was present, he could not fail to have heard the story. It is not too fanciful to suggest that Caesar elaborated upon it over dinner, or at some other occasion, and Octavius would have learned a valuable lesson in man-management. Caesar called the soldiers' bluff, and they knew him well enough to realise that he would go ahead without them, recruit new troops and probably still win the war against the Pompeians in Africa, thus depriving the original war-weary Caesarians of the victory and the booty.[21]

It can never be known whether Caesar took the time to discuss the political and military situation with Octavius, but he did take the time to promote him, by having him appointed *praefectus urbi*, city prefect, during the celebration of the *Feriae Latinae*. This was a religious festival dating back to the conquest of Alba Longa during the early Republic. All the magistrates, including the tribunes of the plebs, left the city to perform the ceremonies at the Alban Mount, and in the intervening period the priests took over the official functions of the consuls. The office of prefect of the city was originally created to oversee public order in Rome while the magistrates were absent. It was a purely honorary appointment, but since the holder of the office became token head of the government for one or two days, he would be under the public eye and marked out for greater things in the future. The duties were primarily to conduct legal business. According to Dio it was quite usual in Republican times for adolescents to be appointed to the office during the celebrations of the *Feriae Latinae*. It was only in the reign of Tiberius and later Emperors that the permanent city prefect was created, fulfilling much more important and extensive functions, quite separate from the duties carried out by the prefects of the *Feriae Latinae*, who continued to be appointed during the Empire, alongside the usual *praefectus urbi*. In the late Republic, the tasks would not be too onerous, and would provide valuable administrative experience.[22]

The career structure followed by most Romans embraced both civil and military posts, usually in a predictable succession. It was considered vitally important for Roman youths to gain experience of military affairs as soon as possible, so Caesar proposed that Octavius should accompany him on his expedition to Africa, where he planned to make war on the Pompeians. Unfortunately Octavius was constantly plagued by ill-health, and was unable to take advantage of his great-uncle's offer. The continual illnesses documented throughout Augustus' life defy clear explanation. The precise medical conditions have not been described, and in any case, the illnesses may not have sprung from the same cause; viruses and food poisoning may have been to blame on some occasions, and there were probably some periods of total exhaustion and possibly sunstroke. On this occasion Atia protested, and Caesar did not pursue the matter so as not to endanger the boy's fragile constitution. He could not wait to fight the war, but perhaps he thought he could afford to wait to take the young man under his wing.[23]

14

Caesar left Italy in December 47 and was absent for seven months. He won the battle of Thapsus on 6 April 46 and the news reached Rome on the 20th, but after the battle there was much to occupy the victors, so Caesar remained in Africa until July 46. The Senate granted him fresh honours, more extensive than before. A festival of thanksgiving to last for forty days was voted to him after the news of the victory reached the city. It was decided, possibly by popular election, that he should be Dictator for ten years and *praefectus morum* for three years. The latter appointment was something new; it was clearly derived from the powers of the censor, and presumably gave him the means of controlling the membership of the Senate. More extravagantly, a statue of Caesar with a globe at his feet was erected in the Capitoline Temple, with an inscription reminding onlookers of his divine descent from Venus. Very soon after the erection of this statue, Caesar had the inscription removed, so it is known only from secondary reports by ancient authors, whose own sources are not established. The text and even the language are unknown. Although Latin would have been the obvious choice, some authorities insist that the inscription may have been in Greek. It seems to have described Caesar as *divus*, or the equivalent in Greek, implying that he was a living god, and not just of divine descent. Perhaps he thought that this was going a little too far, or even that it was tempting fate, begging the gods to put him firmly in his mortal place. Some authors suggest that the opposite is true, and that Caesar was disgruntled because it was not enough for his ambitions; but one may wonder what earthly honours were left to Caesar after deification whilst still alive. More honours may have been voted to him in addition to those listed here, but he may have refused them. Dio says that he includes in his list of honours only those that Caesar accepted, which does suggest that some discretion may have been exercised in choosing which to take on and which to reject.[24]

Octavius was closely associated with Caesar from the summer of 46 onwards, and Nicolaus of Damascus makes much of this association. He may have been influenced by the material included in Augustus' *Memoirs* which possibly also laid great emphasis on the connection with Caesar at this point in Octavius' career. The *Memoirs* were written at a comparatively early stage, before Augustus had become the elder statesman in his own right. Later in his life he played down the Caesarian antecedents to his long reign, but in the early days he used the association to enhance his reputation, almost as a prop, since by reminding the relevant people of Caesar he won their support. As a youth he accompanied his great-uncle everywhere, to the theatre, to banquets and other social gatherings: he received military decorations (*dona militaria*) and even rode behind Caesar's chariot in the triumph celebrated after the African war, despite the fact that he had played no part in it. He developed a certain influence with the great man, if Nicolaus is to be believed, but naturally he employed it only for the benefit of others and not for his own gain. People approached him to intercede on their behalf with the Dictator, but Octavius was careful not to ask for favours at inopportune moments, thus displaying the intelligent diplomacy that he scarcely ever lost throughout his life. In one instance, he was particularly successful when he intervened on behalf of his friend Marcus Vipsanius Agrippa, whose brother had been taken prisoner while fighting on the Pompeian side in Africa. Caesar was known to be ill-disposed towards these particular captives since many of them had fought against him in more than one war. On occasion he allowed himself to be persuaded to release one or two of them, so Agrippa's brother went free. Significantly he did not reach the same heights as Marcus Agrippa himself; Octavius perhaps knew where favours had to stop. The chief interest of the story lies in the fact that he and Agrippa were not simply acquaintances at this time, but firm friends, and had no doubt been so since their schooldays.[25]

During the long hot summer of 46, Caesar turned his attention to the many administrative tasks left unfinished because of the wars. Among the most famous was the reform of the calendar. The old calendar was based on a lunar reckoning, and every two years an extra month had to be inserted to keep the record straight. This intercalation had been grossly neglected in the turmoil of the civil wars, so that the seasons no longer matched the months that were normally associated with them. Caesar introduced a calendar based on a solar year, still in use nowadays, with 365 days to each year and one extra day inserted every four years. In order to adapt the Roman calendar to this new way of reckoning, it was necessary to lengthen the year 46 by a total of 67 days, so that the seasons lined up with the months again; Caesar had already added the extra lunar month in February, but that was not sufficient, so he added two more between November and December. In the summer Octavius was entrusted with the direction of the theatrical productions designed for the benefit and entertainment (one might also add distraction) of the populace. He attended all the performances, and at the end of his tasks fell ill, probably as a result of sunstroke. Suetonius notes that Augustus could never withstand the effects of the sun and never went anywhere without a hat; possibly he had learned this precautionary measure the hard way, and as a youth had for a short while scorned the protective value of hats. Whatever the ailment he was dangerously ill. It is recorded that Caesar was extremely concerned, on one occasion leaping up from his dinner to go and sit by his young kinsman's bedside. Octavius recovered, but not in sufficient time to accompany Caesar to Spain, where the elder son of Pompeius Magnus had assembled a large anti-Caesarian force. The threat was serious, so Caesar left Rome at the end of the year without allowing enough time to conduct the elections of the magistrates for 45. As a temporary measure Caesar was appointed sole consul. Since he was already Dictator, he scarcely needed the powers, but this may have been a political stopgap, or at least a deliberate ploy to defer the decisions about who should or should not become consul until he returned.[26]

As soon as he was well enough, Octavius set out on his own initiative to follow Caesar, accompanied by a few friends, among whom no doubt Agrippa was included. This was the first time that Octavius showed his mettle, for it was no light undertaking to travel alone to a distant theatre of war without considerable armed protection. He seems to have arrived too late to witness the battle of Munda, but the details are obscure. Suetonius and Velleius Paterculus simply inform their readers that Octavius followed Caesar to Spain, and Dio is slightly misleading in that he makes it sound as though Octavius was with Caesar throughout the whole campaign. Nicolaus of Damascus does not mention the fighting at all, as he surely would have done if his hero Octavius had played even the smallest part in the battle of Munda. He lays more emphasis on the conversations that Caesar held with his great-nephew, when they discussed current problems and Caesar asked for his opinion, which he gave intelligently, concisely and without straying from the point. This incisive judgement seems to have been one of the most prominent features of the young Octavius, who skil-fully avoided saying too much or too little, just as he avoided either offending or becoming too closely involved with people who might later compromise him. He was aware even then that every deed, every word, contributed to the formation of his reputation, and once a word was spoken or an action performed it could not be undone, so he was careful to confine his actions and his utterances to those areas where they might conceivably count for something. According to Nicolaus, Octavius was already giving no little thought to the foundations of a good reputation at home. There is no reason to doubt this, no matter that Octavius perhaps did not foresee at this stage the heights to which his reputation would eventually climb. Nicolaus' text more than likely derives, in written or oral form, from Augustus himself, and ideally it presents to the world the portrait of the young Octavius as Augustus wished him to be portrayed. Looking back on his early behav-iour, Augustus would be in a better position than anybody else to recognise his own most pertinent and salient traits, without which he could not have survived, let alone achieved anything significant.[27]

Caesar remained in Spain until June 45, attending to the administration of the provinces, and perhaps quite consciously laying the foundations for future Imperial government. He settled time-expired veterans, and Spanish tribesmen who had fought loyally for Rome, in newly founded colonies and in existing cities, especially harbours and ports on the east coast of Spain, which were then elevated to colonial status. While he and Octavius were at New Carthage an embassy arrived from Saguntum. They were desperate to clear their city of certain charges laid against it, and chose Octavius as their spokesman. He reasoned so well and so modestly with Caesar that he effected the pardon of the Saguntines, thus earning their undying grati-tude. Nicolaus details more of the same adulation about Octavius' modesty, charm, intelligence, and his influence with Caesar, but all these points have already been made and it would appear superfluous, if not sickening, to repeat them. On the journey back to Rome, Marcus Antonius joined the party in northern Italy, and travelled in Caesar's carriage, while Octavius travelled in the next carriage with Decimus Brutus. Clearly Antonius was now back in favour, and it would be interesting to know the main topics of his conversations with Caesar at this point, but they have not been recorded. Nor have the conversations of Octavius and Decimus Brutus; they were presumably very circumspect, polite and convincing, which would perhaps have gone some way to explaining how Octavius managed to convince Decimus that he was fighting disinterestedly for the Republic when they joined forces against Antonius at Mutina, after Caesar was assassinated. Before the main party reached Rome, Octavius left to proceed more quickly to the city. He was met by a young man claiming to be the grandson of Marius, who wanted to persuade Caesar to recognise his family connections. The man was an impostor, but he had collected a large following, influential and popular, and potentially riotous. He even approached Cicero to defend him on some charge or other, but Cicero had refused to be drawn into close association with him, even though he seems at first to have believed in the Marian connections of the pretender. In fact many people had been taken in by him, so presumably the new Marius was quite plausible. Octavius avoided a potentially embarrassing situation, neither recognising the claims of the false heir, nor receiving him, until Julius Ceasar as both head of the family, and more importantly, head of state, should return and pronounce judgement on the matter. Cautious as always, he kept all avenues open; he did not reject Marius out of hand, thereby inflaming the populace who supported him, and perhaps creating irretrievable difficulties for himself if the man should prove to be genuine and to gain favour with Caesar; nor did he accept him, which would have offended the nobility and probably alienated Caesar. It would have been quite easy for an eighteen-year-old to succumb to external pressure, and to have blundered unwittingly into a compromising situation, but Octavius' cautious reserve was a prudent survival technique and the product of an astute mind, one which perhaps weighed the evidence more deeply and thought further ahead than many others.[28]

Before he entered the city, Caesar went to one of his estates, at Labici, south-east of Rome. There he wrote his will, according to Suetonius, in September 45. He left a quarter of his estate to his male relatives Lucius Pinarius and Quintus Pedius, and the other three-quarters to Octavius, whom he adopted in a clause appended to the will. Once written, the will would be lodged in the temple of the Vestals, and none of the contents would be revealed until after Caesar's assassination in March 44. It cannot be known whether Octavius had any knowledge of what was contained in it, and so his degree of surprise, when he found himself heir to Caesar in more senses than the purely financial, can only be guessed. In September

45, no one could have predicted that Caesar's ascendancy would be over in less than six months, and most especially no one could have imagined that the resultant vacancy would one day be filled by a taciturn youth who was constantly ailing.[29]

At the end of 45 the Senate could not do enough to honour Caesar. There were religious ceremonies, games and races, and the dedication of yet more statues in his name. A new temple was to be built to *Libertas*, and a new palace was to be erected on the Quirinal Hill for the use of the Dictator. The month Quinctilis was to be renamed July to commemorate him. He was permitted to wear triumphal clothing on official occasions, and a laurel wreath at all times. Such exaltation was gratifying enough, and served to underline Caesar's supremacy, but honours by themselves would have been quite empty and almost meaningless without the real powers that were willingly voted to him. He was to be Dictator for ten years and consul for the same period. He was granted the use of Imperator as a hereditary name, and held yet another triumph, though not without opposition from the tribune Pontius Aquila, who pointedly remained seated instead of rising to greet him as everyone else did. Caesar was annoyed, but confined himself to irritable sarcasms, and otherwise left Aquila alone. He had harped upon the theme of tribunician sacrosanctity more than once, and had never been ashamed to use his defence of it to support his actions. More pertinently, tribunician sacrosanctity had been granted to Caesar himself, so it would have been more than just ironic if he had indulged himself in vindictive punishment of a tribune simply for opposing him. In any case he had no need for such demonstrations of power. He had complete control of the finances and the armies and could appoint whoever he desired to any of the magistracies, though he prudently declined to appoint all of them. Under this heading, a tidy compromise was reached by a law of the tribune Lucius Antonius, granting Caesar the right to recommend half of the candidates for all the magistracies except the consulship, but even that office was almost entirely under his control, as demonstrated by the fact that the consuls of 44 were to be Caesar and Marcus Antonius. In practice this apparent reluctance to appoint all the magistrates was short-lived. Since it was rapidly becoming clear that for the security of Roman interests, or as sceptics have suggested, to provide an excuse for Caesar to extract himself from an impossible, self-generated situation, more wars would have to be fought against the Dacians and the Parthians, and since the command was readily voted to him, Caesar also accepted the right to appoint all magistrates for the next three years, by which time it was thought that the wars should have been satisfactorily concluded. Thus Rome would be in the hands of Caesar's henchmen until his return, and through them he could continue to direct Roman affairs.[30]

With regard to Octavius, Caesar began to promote him by modest stages. By a law of the tribune Lucius Cassius, Caesar was authorised to create new patricians, and among others he elevated Octavius. At some time towards the end of 45, he sent him to Apollonia on the coast of Macedonia to complete his education, along with a few friends, such as Agrippa, Maecenas and Salvidienus Rufus. He took with him Apollodorus of Pergamum as one of his teachers; this was the man who taught him how to exercise patience and self-control. The choice of the region and the city of Apollonia cannot have been made purely for its opportunities for erudition; had that been the sole aim, then surely Athens would have been the first choice. It was not merely coincidental that five legions were stationed in Macedonia, and according to Appian, many of the officers were regular guests of Octavius, who took part in training the troops. Military experience was just as important as academic pursuits, and up to now Octavius had received little in the way of military knowledge. As part of his preparations for the Dacian campaign, Caesar designated Octavius *magister equitum* in place of Lepidus. This appointment, apparently never actually taken up, has been the subject of debate by various authors who have doubted that such a responsible office could have been given to someone so young and inexperienced as Octavius. Appian says that the office was an annual one that Caesar passed around among his friends, which creates the false impression that the office was one of little importance and could be given to almost anyone. In that case, there should be no problem about allowing Octavius to fill the role, but Appian's statement is not to be taken at face value since there was considerable importance attached to the appointment. Marcus Antonius had been *magister equitum* when he quelled the riots in Rome, some said too brutally. Lepidus, who preceded Octavius as holder of the office, was not an insignificant figure. Attempts have been made to explain away the appointment of Octavius on dubious linguistic grounds. In Greek, the terms for *magister equitum* and *praefectus urbi* are easily confused, so it can be argued that there must have been some misunderstanding between the appointment of the sixteen-year-old Octavius as city prefect during the celebrations of the *Feriae Latinae*, and his later and possibly erroneous designation as master of the horse. More recently, the case has been restated that Caesar did indeed designate Octavius to be his *magister equitum*, despite the silence of authors such as Suetonius on this important issue. The implications of the appointment are enormous, and have great bearing on the adoption of Octavius as Caesar's son. At the very least, such a public honour underlined Caesar's interest in the boy, but what cannot be discerned is how many people besides Caesar knew that this interest in Octavius extended as far as making him his heir to his property and his name. Caesar's intentions may or may not have been known to Octavius himself before he left Rome at the end of 45, but the official story implies that he had no inkling of it. Tradition states that when he had been at Apollonia for only a few months, news was brought by a slave of Atia that Caesar had been murdered. Few other details were known, and it was only when he arrived in Italy that Octavius learned of the adoption, which entitled him, if he so wished, to style himself Gaius Julius Caesar Octavianus. This combination of names followed the customary Roman fashion, indicating that Octavius had been adopted into the family of the Julii Caesares from his original family of the Octavii. But Octavius completely ignored the last of these names, laying great emphasis from the very beginning upon his connection with Gaius Julius Caesar. He immediately began to style himself as such. Any author who writes of the future Augustus is constrained to point out that neither of the names by which he is known in age-old tradition were those which he used of himself, but he was content to let the name Augustus play its part. The private man behind the official façade did not let the mask slip very often, and his mask was at first that of Caesar. Thus 'Octavianus' was never used by the young man himself, and in fact he would have taken exception to it. But this name is so deeply embedded in modern consciousness that it seems mere pedantry to insist on the use of any other. The name Octavian has the advantage of distinguishing the first Augustus from the original Gaius Julius Caesar, who was brought down by his assassins on the Ides of March 44, at the base of Pompeius' statue.[31]

2

CAESAR, SON OF CAESAR

It is to Octavian's credit, and a tribute to his cautious common sense, that on receiving the news of Caesar's assassination he did not march into Italy at the head of the Macedonian legions, as some of his colleagues at Apollonia allegedly urged him to do. The officers and men were ready to follow him if he so commanded, but he declined the offer. He had decided to return home immediately, possibly in some trepidation since he could not know for certain the exact circumstances in Rome. The messenger sent by his mother had left the city immediately after the murder of Caesar; anything could have happened in the interval, and even now the situation could be steadily worsening day by day. There was every possibility that Octavian and his friends may have been in some personal, physical danger from any one of several sources, most especially if the conspirators were in power and had determined to eradicate all Caesar's most prominent allies and family members by proscriptions.[1]

In these circumstances, it would have been easy for Octavian to persuade himself that he required at least a substantial bodyguard for support and protection when he landed in Italy. But that could have precipitated a tremendous over-reaction. It would not have been appropriate to show his hand too soon, and would have been an ineradicable false move, a blunder, even, if it turned out that he was not under any threat. So he took only a few friends with him, M. Vipsanius Agrippa, and most probably Maecenas, and landed uneventfully on the Italian coast, about twenty miles south of Brundisium, avoiding the main port in case the troops there were hostile, or there was a price on his head which unfriendly persons might be eagerly waiting to collect. He travelled on foot to the small town of Lupiae, where he was no doubt relieved to hear that he was not in any danger. He went on to Brundisium, and found there letters from his mother and stepfather, informing him of his inheritance of the most part of Caesar's fortune and of his adoption as Caesar's son. Philippus advised him to refuse the adoption, in order to guarantee for himself a quiet life. The advice was probably well-meant, and not entirely self-seeking, though it could be interpreted as a craven plea to Octavian to avoid embroiling his family in a power

22

struggle that could engulf them all, and was almost certain to erupt if he tried to assume even a small part of Caesar's political influence. Octavian wrote back to say that he intended to accept. It would have been uncharacteristic of him to do this without careful deliberation. In Brundisium, if not before, Octavian probably took stock of his situation.[2]

With regard to his own reputation, despite Nicolaus' assertion that the young Octavius took care to create a good impression of himself in Rome, the contemporary record is virtually silent about Caesar's teenage greatnephew until after the assassination on the Ides of March 44. Thoroughgoing sceptics might suggest that Augustus, once he had achieved unassailable power, exercised a rigorous retrospective censorship, which may even be true of the period of the Triumvirate and his association with Antonius, but was probably quite unecessary for his early life; as a boy it is likely that he was a nonentity. The surviving account of his youth is no doubt exaggerated, not only written with the benefit of hindsight, but refashioned and adjusted as well. This is not to say that there was any widespread fabrication or suppression of information, only an elaboration of certain elements which probably went unnoticed by Octavian's contemporaries. Posterity has accepted his presentation of himself as Caesar's understudy, but at the beginning of the performance, in Act I so to speak, there were too many large personalities in centre stage for any of the cast to pay attention to the teenage Gaius Octavius. Coupled with his lack of years, this comparative anonymity could be turned to advantage. If he had not yet earned an excellent reputation, neither had he earned a bad one, so he had nothing to stain his name and no foolish acts to live down. Therefore his modesty, good sense, and calmness would not be interpreted as contrary to his nature. There was nothing to contradict. He maintained a bland exterior, displayed no inordinate ambition for outright personal power, and proceeded with caution but not timidity. In the light of his later ruthlessly determined actions, it is impossible to see in this early behaviour anything other than a studied role-play. If such it was, he put on an act of great plausibility, allaying suspicions all round. Cicero was relieved to find that Octavian had not arrived with troops to try to effect an immediate *coup d'état*, but he sounded the first note of dismayed suspicion when he learned that Octavian was determined to take up 'that inheritance' (*illum hereditatem*). They encountered each other at Cumae when Octavian came to stay with his stepfather Philippus, whose villa was next to Cicero's. Octavian's unassuming diplomacy gave nothing away. Cicero wrote to Atticus on 21 April that Octavian was devoted to him (*mihi totus deditus*), and the next day he wrote: 'Octavius is here with us on terms of respect and friendship. His people call him Caesar, but Philippus does not, so I did not, either. I hold that it is impossible for a loyal citizen to do so. We are surrounded by so many who threaten death to our friends ... What do you think will happen when this boy comes to Rome?' Reading between the lines, Octavian had shown no offence at being addressed as Octavius and not Caesar, even though it may have irked him; he had not insisted that all comers should use his new name, but at the same time had not discouraged those who did. If he had not attempted to silence the incendiary talk of vengeance for Caesar, neither had he succumbed to it. Later he declared his intention of avenging his great-uncle, but at this time he was playing a careful and watchful game, keeping silent, preparing to carry out his plans in his own way. He had struck the right note and the correct pose from the start: in effect, a superlative performance. As manipulator and scene-setter, psychologist and actor, he was rapidly becoming expert, and would rarely if ever lose his way.[3]

In addition to making an assessment of his own situation, Octavian would need to take into account both a character study of his great-uncle, and an analysis of the events leading up to the fateful Ides of March. During his stay in Apollonia, Octavian was probably kept informed, by Atia if by no one else, of Caesar's activities, and of the reactions of the Senate and people to his steadily accumulating power. He would have known of the wide-spread fear that Caesar intended to make himself king, and of the nervousness that this would instil into nearly everyone in Rome. Even now, modern scholars still debate whether or not Caesar wanted the title *Rex*, and whether he desired to set up a hereditary monarchy, which involves distinctly related, but different, concepts of such enormous import. Added to this is the suspicion that Caesar wanted to be made a god while still alive, which complicates the hereditary factor, especially when the comparison is drawn with the type of divine monarchy common in the East, and especially in Egypt. The divinity question is dealt with more fully below, along with the debate about the deification of Caesar (pp. 61–63), where it is argued that divine honours were accorded to the Dictator while he was alive, but full deification was to be put into effect only after his death. Thus there are several problems all bound up with the monarchical tendencies of Caesar, and in equating them without the attendant discussion of all the implied nuances, some confusion can result. As to the question of whether Caesar desired to be king, with the title *Rex* and all the ancient emotional baggage that such a name carried with it, the evidence can be interpreted in two different ways and used to support either of two diametrically opposed opinions. The famous tale of the festival of the Lupercalia, when Marcus Antonius offered Caesar the crown, has been used to illustrate the theory that in reality Caesar desired it very strongly but was discouraged by the lack of popular approval; Plutarch calls the incident an experiment which failed, indicating that Caesar wanted to test public opinion, and would have accepted readily if only the people had shown the slightest enthusiasm. It must be borne in mind that Antonius might have acted purely on his own initiative and therefore the whole episode may have come as a surprise to Caesar. But it matters little whether or not he was prepared for it, because it is still quite uncertain whether he would quickly have seized the opportunity to assume the crown if the people had approved, or whether he greeted the incident with horror, privately thinking something along the lines of 'God protect me from my friends!' Alternatively, in collusion with Antonius, Caesar may have engineered the event in order to disarm his critics by demonstrating that he definitely did not want to be king; if so, then that experiment failed also, because it merely increased suspicion, hydra-like, instead of putting an end to it. Thus it is possible to argue on the one hand that Caesar was genuinely averse to being called *Rex* and was therefore an unfortunate victim of escalating events manufactured by his enemies, or on the other hand that he schemed to try to extract from the people by a shabby and crude scenario what he wanted the most.[4]

Monarchy denotes literally the rule of one person, so in this sense Caesar was already a *de facto* monarch in that he had absolute sole power. In this case the debate concerns the possibility that this had been his aim all along, from birth almost, and whether or not he intended to give up or share his power when all his administrative measures were completed. If he never intended to step down, then the debate extends to a secondary factor, whether he intended to create a hereditary monarchy, no matter what his exact title should be, *Rex* or otherwise. Some scholars are quite adamant that it would not have been possible for Caesar to bequeath his political power, but this is a judgement based on earthly reality and pedestrian precedent, and Caesar was not bounded by such puny restrictions. Although a realist, in his determination he was never a man who discerned where the possible shaded off into the unachievable. A hereditary element had already entered the scene when the Senate granted him the title Imperator as a name that could be passed on to his descendants; according to Dio both this and the office of Pontifex Maximus were heritable. The truth of the heritable nature of Imperator and of the priesthood has been questioned, and it is not beyond the bounds of possibility that the whole story is a fabrication or a misunderstanding, incorporated into Dio's narrative because by his day the facts fitted the customary situation of the Emperors. On the other hand it is certain that Caesar considered the name Imperator and the office of Pontifex Maximus supremely important, as attested by his ostentatious use of them on his coins and on inscriptions. It cannot be denied that there would have been considerable advantages for Caesar's successor in the acquisition by inheritance of these significant titles. Augustus utilised the name Imperator much more effectively than ever Caesar had done, but he had the grace to wait until the holder of the highest priestly office, Lepidus, was dead before assuming it himself, even though the people clamoured for him to become Pontifex Maximus. It is quite feasible that Caesar entertained hopes of handing over the trappings of power to Octavian, and that he hoped to survive long enough to introduce further hereditary factors, step by step, backed up by legislation sanctioned by an increasingly partisan Senate. Being a realist, his calculations most probably included the possibility that he would not be allowed to survive, in which case he perhaps knew enough of his great-nephew to be confident that he would fight to retain his inheritance, in the social, economic, and political sense. Caesar was too much the man of politics to ignore the political situation, both present and future, when he made his will. As Syme points out, on this matter there can be opinion but no certainty. In any case, argument about what Caesar intended is purely an academic exercise, and is perhaps not quite so important as what actually happened. The facts are that Caesar was assassinated and eventually by dint of determination and a favourable combination of circumstances, Octavian succeeded him. As a youth, Octavian was in a much better position to know what was in Caesar's mind for the future of Rome, but even this is not of prime importance, except that it would be of assistance to modern authors if it were possible to discern to what extent Octavian and Caesar had collaborated. If Octavian knew all along that Caesar intended that he should succeed him, then this merely explains rather prosaically his tenacity of purpose in pursuing his goal. If the adoption took him by surprise, then this tenacity is all the more remarkable, and reveals a degree of opportunism that does not sit comfortably with the later Augustan legend of selfless devotion to the state.[5]

Octavian cannot have failed to take heed of the lessons of the last few months of Caesar's Dictatorship. He would probably have understood that Caesar was a man in a hurry, who was eager to push through all his plans without the dragging delay of senatorial debate; it was notorious that Caesar merely presented ideas to the Senate and then called them decrees, and that the names of witnesses who had not even been present at the meetings of the Senate somehow found themselves attached to these so-called decrees. Caesar had neither time nor patience for more leisurely, tactful dealings with the Senate. He saw clearly what must be done, and set it in motion without bothering to disguise his all-embracing power. Perhaps he was aware that no matter how pressing, sensible and vital his plans were for Rome, the senators felt offended if there was no chance to debate and contribute ideas; if he was aware of it he shrugged it off with characteristic disdain. He possessed a keen intellect, almost amounting to genius, that even his enemies could not deny. He thought in terms of the whole Roman world, whereas the senators shared the customary blinkered and monolithic vision which was limited to the city of Rome, excluding everything else. Through his intelligence and penetrating discernment Caesar made people nervous, as Cicero's letters to and from his friends attest. No one knew how to behave for fear of being wrong, or simply displeasing the Dictator. People began to mistrust each other in case harmful gossip was repeated about them, or sentiments that they had not expressed were invented for them. It is hardly surprising that a rigid paralysis set in. Even though Caesar's policy of *clementia* may well have sprung from genuine motives, it alienated him because it meant that everyone, quite literally, was at his mercy, never a position that anyone finds acceptable. It engendered not only fear but deep resentment. Nicolaus of Damascus devoted several paragraphs to this topic, listing all the various categories of men who resented Caesar although he may have treated them well. The passage is interesting because it may well have derived from Augustus' *Memoirs* and if so it represents his own thoughts on the matter, formed either with the benefit of hindsight after some reflection, or even contemporary incisive judgement which he never afterwards saw any reason to change. For those who opposed or feared Caesar, it was presumably the final straw when in February 44, allegedly after some hesitation, Caesar accepted the title *Dictator perpetuo*, which meant that there would be no limit to his term of office and even less likelihood that there would ever be an end to his domination. Thus the events of the last months of 45 and the first part of 44 comprised a whole catalogue of situations to be avoided if ever Octavian found himself in a similar position of power.[6]

He cannot have deluded himself that claiming his full inheritance would be a simple matter, not least because posthumous adoption really only extended to inheritance of property, sometimes on condition that the legatee adopted the name of the legator. This is much less than the legally approved, full adoption as Caesar's son that Octavian required, so the matter would have to be fought out in court. On the other hand he probably reasoned that he would be fooling himself if thought that by modestly retiring into private life he could avoid conflict. There were too many men with vested interests in Caesarian politics to allow such a potentially useful figurehead to slip through their fingers. It was no part of the new Gaius Julius Caesar's plan to be manipulated by others for the satisfaction of their own ends. Once he had made up his mind, he was consistent in his purpose. He never doubted his inheritance, and sounded a positive note from the beginning, ensuring that no one else should doubt him. Retrospectively too, he laboured the point: Nicolaus of Damascus never let slip an opportunity to insert a word or two into his narrative about the inheritance, at times blatantly, reminding his audience that Octavian was the one to whom power had been bequeathed, and at times subliminally, as for instance when the soldiers declared that they would protect Octavian's inherited rights. Octavian's insistence on being called Gaius Julius Caesar, and later *divi filius*, and his constant striving to remind all and sundry of his connection with Caesar, might seem unecessarily heavy-handed, but he knew from the first moment that if he accepted the inheritance at all he had to accept it in full, with all that it implied; there could be no half measures. His rise to power would of necessity have to be rapid. He could not reasonably hope to step in at the exact point where Caesar left off, but he would need legitimate office somewhere near the top of the range of the career pattern. The steady progression through the various magistracies was definitely not for the new Gaius Julius Caesar. Like Pompeius before him the ideal situation would be to enter the Senate with a high rank before he could be eliminated. The intermediate goal would be to obtain a precarious security via a magistracy and a limited freedom of action, always with one eye on the unwritten constitution of the *res publica*. Strictly speaking, Rome had no constitution in the modern sense. Public business, which is precisely what *res publica* means, was conducted according to custom, framed by a series of laws which could be added or subtracted as necessary, so there was a considerable amount of flexibility in the way in which the system worked. This had both advantages and disadvantages. The absence of an over-restrictive rigidity meant that it was fairly easy to adapt to new situations, but it also meant that the system could be exploited by men who were more interested in personal advancement than in the Roman state. Bending the rules of the game had been established practice for some time, often mollified by a clever use of words, as when Pompeius had been sole consul, a contradiction in terms which nevertheless satisfied the niceties of the rules. A rise to power via constitutional means was a sound insurance policy for the future. If Octavian could achieve his aims without using military force and without antagonising the Senate, then so much the better. His initial intentions to work through the Senate are attested in his letters to Cicero, written at the end of October. These letters are no longer extant, but their contents were duly reported by Cicero to Atticus on 4 November 44. It would be a dangerous path to follow, because if his plans went awry then the next alternatives were either the immediate use of force or imminent elimination. Once embarked upon this path, Octavian could never turn back; in pursuing it he proved himself flexible, adaptable, shrewd, eminently realistic, and totally ruthless.[7]

What he needed most were three things: money, trusted agents, and knowledge. All three were to a large extent inextricably intertwined, in that none of them could be obtained or retained without the other two. Octavian seems to have solved the problem of raising immediate funds without much difficulty, indeed he never seems to have lacked money, but its origins are not very well documented. Landed interests will have supplied quite considerable wealth, but the amount of money that Octavian had at his disposal when he began to raise recruits in the late summer and autumn of 44 indicates that he must have tapped other sources of supply. Dio sweepingly and unhelpfully asserts that Octavian had large numbers of soldiers and a great deal of money, which is stating the obvious. Nicolaus of Damascus says that he used the money from Caesar's war chest saved up for the Parthian campaign, which Octavian had sent for before he left Apollonia for Italy. Exactly when this money arrived is disputed. He could hardly have carried it all with him, especially since he reached Italy with only a few friends (and presumably their slaves) so as not to attract attention.

Nothing would have attracted attention quite so quickly as large heavy boxes with an interesting chink of coin. Almost as an afterthought, Nicolaus adds that Octavian also received a year's tribute from Asia, a staggering concept that the author does not elaborate upon. The amounts of money will have been extremely large and it was perhaps best not to dwell on the subject, since that tribute ought to have been paid to Rome and not to an individual. Nicolaus hastens to add that Octavian took only what was Caesar's, and paid the rest into the public funds. This sounds suspiciously like an exercise in retrospective self-justification. The money may in truth have been paid into the treasury at some unspecified time, perhaps not too closely associated with the reception into Octavian's coffers: it is highly likely that Octavian regarded it for the time being as a loan, so that the borrowing and the eventual discharge of the debt were probably separated by a number of years. Another source of money is described obliquely by Appian, who explains that once he arrived in Italy men began to flock to him, among them soldiers who were convoying money to the provinces and men who were bringing money into Italy from other places. It is not stated directly that Octavian appropriated this money, but it is a permissible assumption that if it was offered then he would accept gracefully. Likewise he could begin to sound out the Caesarian networks of freedmen and equestrians; these were not men of great political standing, but financiers and bankers whose names are in large part unrecorded. Men such as these would probably supply most of Octavian's immediate needs.[8]

One of the most important, if not *the* most important, of these men was Cornelius Balbus, who was one of the most influential and trusted members of Caesar's entourage. Octavian arrived in Naples on 18 April, and next morning he received Balbus. The meeting cannot have been coincidental. Communications will have been set up long before. Octavian told Balbus that he was determined to accept the inheritance, and presumably they discussed the advantages and pitfalls of doing so. Balbus went straight from his interview with Octavian to visit Cicero, who relayed the news in a letter to Atticus. Balbus was extremely wealthy, notoriously so; he was already wealthy before he met Caesar, which was no doubt one of the main reasons why Caesar cultivated him. He was also the patron of his native city of Gades (modern Cadiz) in Spain, and of Capua in Italy. He owned sumptuous palaces and gardens, and at his death he bequeathed 25 denarii to every citizen of Rome. He had started out as a protégé of Pompeius, and had become secretary and much else besides to Caesar; he knew many men among Caesar's friends and enemies and stepped carefully among them all. He earned respect, not all of it grudging, for his integrity in dealing with people: he did not gossip or pass judgements. There is no evidence at all to indicate what kind of service he rendered to Octavian, only some evidence that he was supremely useful in that he was rewarded with the suffect consulship in 40. This might sound routine and not significant, but he was not a Roman and not a noble, and the honour was correspondingly great. The fact that there is no inkling of his activities is perhaps only to be expected, for even if they did not border on the nefarious, it is most probable that they were never intended for public consumption. Balbus was so close to Caesar and so ubiquitous that it is quite improbable that Octavian did not know him already. All that had to be established on 19 April 44 was whether they were compatible and could be of mutual benefit to each other. At this stage in the proceedings, Balbus was the better known and more influential of the two. It has been pointed out that a great leap of faith was required to discern Augustus behind the young Octavian, more so in 44 BC than in modern times. It is not known whether Balbus was capable of forming such a prescient view of Caesar's heir, but he did not come down on the side of Antonius against Octavian, which perhaps speaks for his foresight. In any event, it is without doubt that whatever the outcome and duration of his association with Octavian, Balbus would have devoted some serious 'quality time', as the modern idiom describes it, to planning his escape routes with his fortune intact. Potentially, Balbus could have been a dangerous adversary. If he proved not to be friendly to Octavian, he knew so much that it would probably have been necessary to remove him permanently. This only emphasises his importance. The supply of money will have been only one aspect of his usefulness to the young Caesar, as to the previous one; it is highly likely that he operated a wide network of agents who performed all sorts of other services. Agents are not synonymous with clients. The latter flocked to Octavian from among Caesar's *clientelae*, but these were overt in their support of Caesar's heir and were politically orientated. Agents were different. They were not overt and were only marginally political, and by the very nature of their calling they were anonymous. Octavian needed men from all walks of life, soldiers, slaves, equestrian businessmen, possibly some women too, all of whom could go abroad unsuspected and gather information, or whisper into the ears of potential supporters who needed just a little encouragement to bring them over to the young Caesar. This sort of activity is either directly attested in the ancient sources, or implied by reading with close attention. For instance it is documented that Octavian's agents subverted Antonius' troops by distributing leaflets among them. If this is to be taken absolutely literally, then someone had to compose the words with care; there were presumably workshops where the leaflets were copied out, printing machines not having been invented, and men to collect bundles of them for distribution where they would be most helpful. The organisation of such a venture requires reasonable numbers of personnel, who must be trustworthy and dedicated, in order to carry out their tasks clandestinely. Without such men, success in military or political affairs would have been well-nigh impossible. They therefore had to be gathered quickly. When he arrived in Italy, Octavian brought with him only a small entourage. Once landed on the coast, he sent some men to Brundisium to find out if he was in any danger, but the numbers with him cannot have been large. Anyone who wants to lie low cannot afford to trust many people, and cannot advertise his presence by a large following. When he was certain that he was not to be arrested or lynched, the process of collecting useful men could begin. In Brundisium, and in most of the towns he came to on the way to Rome, more and more people came to him; Appian says that many of them were unknown to him, and therefore he did not know whom to trust. Other men besides himself had networks of agents, longer established than his own, and all eager to know what he was going to do next. Balbus perhaps assisted him in sifting the pure from the dross, and the well-disposed from the downright dangerous.[9]

Meanwhile, what was happening in Rome? In Brundisium and on the way home Octavian would gather more information. He would learn, perhaps with incredulous contempt, that the murderers of Caesar had laid no plans to take over the city, and in fact had made hardly any plans at all except how to despatch his great-uncle. The rest of the news was not encouraging, and probably gave him pause for thought. Rome was now in the hands of the consul Marcus Antonius, Caesar's lieutenant and colleague, whom the conspirators had spared, much to Cicero's openly declared disappointment. Antonius had restored order, no mean task in the circumstances. He had temporarily won over the Senate by proposing that the Dictatorship should be abolished, and instead of pursuing the conspirators he had come to terms with them. He even managed to solve the conundrum posed by the murder of Caesar – namely, that if he had been killed unjustly, then all his acts were valid, but the murderers should be brought to trial, for if they were allowed to go free it implied that their actions did not constitute a crime but a perfectly justifiable tyrannicide, and in that case all Caesar's acts were invalid. Antonius pointed out that if in strict accordance with having come to terms with the conspirators he then took the next logical step of declaring Caesar's acts null and void, then there would be no magistrates and no effective government, and many men who had received their provincial commands at the hands of Caesar, or places in the Senate, would now be unemployed. Cicero suggested that there should be a general amnesty, which timely compromise was immediately put into effect. Even so, the conspirators felt it safer to leave the city, and Antonius did nothing to stop them. Brutus and Cassius lurked in Italy, while others went to the provinces assigned to them by Caesar. An uneasy peace reigned while Antonius grew more and more powerful. He had persuaded Caesar's widow, Calpurnia, to relinquish to him all her husband's papers, and the Senate played into his hands by agreeing that all the Dictator's acts, including those that he merely intended, should still be valid. This gave Antonius free rein to promote ideas of his own which he said had originated in Caesar's notes. Since he had purloined the services of Faberius, one of Caesar's secretaries, many people thought that the two of them must be acting in nefarious collusion, and consequently they doubted the authenticity of Antonius' statements but could not prove any illegality. Antonius probably had no further ambitions at this stage apart from remaining alive and intact; he was moderate in his suggestions and energetic in keeping the peace, but anticipation of what he might do, and distrust of his motives, contributed to a bad press, both from his contemporaries and later authors. As a military man, he had already made his mark with Caesar's troops, and now he displayed considerable talents as a demagogue when he delivered the funeral oration for Caesar, immortalised perhaps not too far from the truth by Shakespeare. If Antonius managed to gain control of the soldiery and the populace he would be a formidable danger to the die-hard Republicans in the Senate. All this was especially exaggerated by Cicero, who was determined (almost to the exclusion of any other idea) to stir up opposition to Antonius, seemingly without having stopped to think that if Antonius had so desired he could have had all Rome in his pocket on 16 or 17 March, and once having won he need never have let go.[10]

For Octavian, confrontation with Antonius was almost inevitable, not least because Antonius probably saw himself as a more worthy and much more capable military and political successor to Caesar than a teenage boy with no experience in either of these spheres. More importantly, though he worked hard to restore order and could not be said to be totally self-seeking, Antonius had begun to arrogate power to himself and was not disposed to share it. He had many rivals among Caesar's long list of henchmen, such as his newly appointed consular colleague Dolabella, the consuls-elect for the following year, Aulus Hirtius and Vibius Pansa, and the new Pontifex Maximus, Lepidus, who had been chosen to succeed Caesar in this important office. The Caesarians had not unanimously accepted the overlordship of Antonius, so he found himself potentially in danger from all sides. He had reached a point where he could not back down and retire into private life even if he had wanted to, because he would not have survived. As consul he was relatively secure, especially since he had built up an armed bodyguard allegedly 6,000 strong, but when his office expired he would need to step straight into a proconsular command, preferably with a large army and preferably close to Italy, so he would not lose his dominant influence; it was known by the end of May that he was beginning to manoeuvre to exchange his assigned province of Macedonia, which was of no immediate use to him, for Gallia Cisalpina, which had already been assigned to one of Caesar's assassins, Decimus Brutus. In addition Antonius was determined to keep control of the Macedonian legions, so he began to arrange for their transfer to Italy. It was quite clear that Antonius had no intention of sinking into obscurity after his consulship ended, and even more clear that it was not part of his future plans to subordinate himself and become the willing ally of Caesar's adopted son. The first clash came when Octavian tried to claim the money left to him in Caesar's will. Antonius would not, or could not, pay – most likely because he had spent it. He was suspected of using much of it to pay off all his substantial debts; this may be partly true, but on the one hand he would have required large sums for all sorts of purposes in order to carry on some semblance of government, and on the other hand Caesar's own accounting had not been too scrupulous about the divisions between his private fortune and the public funds. It is perhaps a little unfair, then, to accuse Antonius of pursuing nothing but a policy of embezzlement for his own ends.[11]

While Antonius had an established following, family connections, consular power, an armed bodyguard and a proconsular command awaiting him, Octavian had little except his name at this stage and had to build on this meagre foundation. Perhaps because of this, Antonius did not take him very seriously, and his later taunt that Octavian owed everything to his name is not far short of the truth, but Antonius might have added that he owed much more to his determination to keep his name despite obstacles put in his way. Octavian came away from his first interview with Antonius without gaining anything, financially or otherwise. He immediately set about gathering enough cash to pay out of his own pocket the per capita sums decreed to the people by the terms of Caesar's will. Generosity to the populace was merely a by-product of Octavian's plans. The disbursement was a political manoeuvre, and in its execution it was designed to resolve two problems at once. Much of Caesar's property had been acquired by dubious means by buying up estates of proscribed or banished persons, and though the purchases had been carried out legally, and Octavian could produce deeds of sale, many men were prepared to take him to court over possession of these estates. Initial judgements went against him, so he began to sell the property at the lowest prices, to put a stop to future litigation, and then used the money to distribute among the people. When the proceeds of the sales proved to be insufficient, he asked his relatives Pedius and Pinarius for their shares of Caesar's fortune, and began to sell the property of his real father Gaius Octavius as well. All this was at least in part a calculated risk. Octavian was not facing destitution, nor was he in truth depriving himself of the very means of existence. The sales of property were undertaken for political purposes. Naturally he did not do this in the utmost secrecy, and naturally popular sympathy flowed in his direction. Popular sympathy was a very powerful tool which Julius Caesar had used to great effect, and Octavian was learning very rapidly. By implication Antonius emerged as the villain of the piece, for having reduced the poor young man to such straitened circumstances. The first round of the war of words had been won by Octavian.[12]

Self-advertisement and connection with Caesar, and above all his declared intention to avenge Caesar's death, were Octavian's prime concerns. It soon became the prime concern of Antonius to block all attempts by Octavian to establish this connection. The struggle was not purely personal; Antonius had devoted considerable effort to keeping the peace after the Ides of March, coming to terms with the conspirators while not entirely obliterating the memory of Caesar, and on the whole he had balanced the two delicate elements very well. Though he had abandoned much of the conciliatory policy on his own account and was busily establishing Antonian politics in place of Caesarian politics, the arrival of Caesar's heir upset the balance disastrously because it revived the inflammatory Caesarian tradition, the deleterious effects of which Antonius had tried to suppress. Since he made no secret of his moral obligation to avenge the death of his adoptive father, Octavian's deliberate advertisement of his Caesarian connections threatened to split the already disjointed state and to undermine Antonius' position as neutral pacifier and sole merchant of Caesar's ideas. On each occasion that Octavian displayed his Caesarian colours either literally or metaphorically, Antonius blocked him, usually by indirect means, by instructing his circle of tribunes to pull the necessary strings. Minor examples included Octavian's attempts to remind the people of Caesar at popular festivals. At the *Ludi Ceriales* in May, he endeavoured to put on show Caesar's golden chair, decreed to him by the Senate, but Antonius prevented him from doing so. In July Marcus Brutus, urban praetor, absent from Rome by special dispensation of the consul Antonius, organised and financed by remote control the Games of Apollo. The populace was very disaffected with the conspirators after their assassination of the people's hero, and by the provision of lavish entertainment Brutus hoped to win back some popular support. The attempt was a dismal failure. Octavian leapt at the chance to outdo him. With the help of Caesar's friend Gaius Matius, recruited to Octavian's cause, he arranged and financed the *Ludi Victoriae Caesaris*, games in honour of Venus Genetrix to celebrate Caesar's victories. These games lasted for ten days, and while they were performed a comet appeared each evening, soon labelled the *sidus Iulium* (literally translated, 'the star of Julius' signifying that Caesar had become a god and had been transported into the Heavens). This may have been a rumour that originated with Octavian himself, but even if it was not one of his own fabrications he seized upon it with energetic zeal. He placed a star on Caesar's statues and used the symbol on coins, all of which supported his claim to be the son of a god (*divi filius*). In private he conceived of the comet as a sign for himself, as he confided to one of his closest friends. It required courage to act as he had been doing, so he grasped at signs as superstitiously as anyone else embarking on dangerous or arduous projects.[13]

A more serious power struggle than bickering over games and shows came when Octavian tried to ratify his adoption by a law of the people (*lex curiata*). Antonius appeared to be doing everything in his power to put the law into effect but behind the scenes he instructed his tribunes, no doubt bought with ready cash, to do everything in their power to block the ratification. Appian invents a speech for Antonius, in which the latter points out that since it was only by his efforts that Caesar's acts were ratified, including the adoption of Octavius in his will, then in fact Octavian is entirely in debt to him, Marcus Antonius, and should be grateful. If Antonius ever expressed such a sentiment, then it was just a blustering demonstration of strength, probably tinged with a slight regret that he had not suppressed this clause in Caesar's will. The technicalities of the adoption cause modern scholars considerable problems, mostly because the legal position is quite unknown. While the adoption of members of the extended family or even of non-relatives was an established procedure in ancient Rome, the method by which Caesar adopted Octavius by naming him in his will is unusual. Testamentary adoption almost certainly did not have the same validity as an adoption arranged while both parties still lived. Recorded examples of adoption after the death of the adoptive parent are too rare to extrapolate any information, nor do the legal texts have anything to say on the matter. Syme dismissed testamentary adoption altogether, declaring that it simply did not exist. If this is so, then it explains why Octavian was so persistent in having the adoption established and ratified by law. He began proceedings as soon as he arrived in Rome in May 44, but thanks to Antonius he made no progress. It was not something that Octavian was prepared to overlook. It has already been stated that he had no doubt in his own mind that he was the heir of Caesar in all aspects of the inheritance, economic, political, military and filial. The soldiers and many of Caesar's *amici* accepted him without question, but this support was not sufficient without due process of law. Though he was thwarted by Antonius in 44 and had to concede defeat, when Octavian became consul in August 43 it was almost his first act to have the *lex curiata* passed. Whether this was simply excessive caution or the fulfilment of a legal requirement cannot be known, but it amounts to the same thing; Octavian wanted the world to know exactly were he stood on the issue. One of his problems may have derived from the unclarified status of any natural sons of Caesar, born to him during his lifetime or after his death. The tribulations caused by the pretender Marius may have been made a deep impression on Octavian when he returned from Caesar's war in Spain. Many people had believed Marius' claims, so Octavian needed to remove all doubt as to who had inherited Caesar's name and fortune. More threatening still was the existence of Caesarion, the son of Caesar and Cleopatra. He and his mother had returned to Egypt after the Ides of March, but though they were far away from Rome, Cleopatra was not necessarily benign, nor was she a shy and retiring wallflower. She had made no secret of Caesarion's parentage, as indicated by the name she had given him, and she was hardly likely to recede into the background now that Caesar was dead. Octavian presumably had met her and, more importantly, made his assessment as to her ambitions and character very early in his life. His perception of Cleopatra as an enemy no doubt arose equally early; he may have given way to the simple human emotion of jealousy because she claimed much of Caesar's attention and had given him an heir. When Antonius began to link his fate to hers, Octavian probably did not have to summon a passionate hatred of Cleopatra in order to persuade the Romans to go to war. There may well have been enough dislike already festering to obviate the need for more. In 44 and 43, he had to act quickly to establish himself. The possibility that Octavian was not the first and only choice as Caesar's heir would not make a firm foundation for the assumption of power based on possession of Caesar's name. Schmitthenner investigated these possibilities, and his overall conclusions are not favourable to Octavian who is accused of shady dealings; it has been pointed out by more than one author that Caesarion was permanently removed as soon as Octavian was in a position to do so, after the battle of Actium and the fall of Alexandria. While this murder can be seen as a purely practical measure to put an end to any potential rebellion in the name of Caesarion, it also had the advantage of obliterating Octavian's most eligible rival.[14]

The fluctuations of Octavian's relationship with Antonius are variously documented according to the individual bias of the ancient authors, with the result that the details of some of their interactions are obscured, a situation compounded by the fact that chronological sequences are not established beyond doubt. None the less a broad general pattern emerges. Among a welter of petty divisions among the state, a triangular power struggle evolved from the inability of the three main protagonists to act in concert. Antonius was intent on retaining personal influence without antagonising the conspirators and thus precipitating war. The Senate, and the conspirators themselves, who had dispersed, did not want Antonius at any price, but could not risk open war with him because they were quite unprepared; there was no senatorial army waiting at the gates of Rome, while Antonius had access to Caesar's troops who were only too willing to avenge their general. It would take some considerable time for the various conspirators to gain control of the provincial armies that were left open to them. Octavian, the third contender for power, had no official position and was not supported by law, but he had to be taken seriously by virtue of his name and inheritance, his influence among the populace and with the troops, including the veterans settled in Italy, so the Senate did not relish the thought of acting alongside him, or even worse, under his domination. The situation would deteriorate rapidly if any two sides sank their differences and combined against the third. For the Senate, it was unthinkable to allow Octavian and Antonius to combine forces, a sentiment expressed in a letter from Cicero to Atticus, written at a time when he was wondering if Octavian was to be trusted. Cicero wanted neither Caesar's heir nor Antonius, but he knew that the two must be kept apart at all costs. For the Caesarian troops and veterans, an alliance between Caesar's lieutenant and Caesar's adopted son was the preferred option because then they would not have to choose sides and fight each other. The confusion of the soldiers and their torn loyalties are nicely documented in the pages of Appian when he describes in two juxtaposed passages the troop-raising activities of Antonius and Octavian. The military tribunes made two attempts to heal the rift and reconcile Antonius with Octavian. After the first reconciliation, performed in public on the Capitol, Octavian assisted Antonius in persuading the people to pass the necessary law for the exchange of provinces (*Lex de permutatione provinciarum*) so that Antonius could relinquish his command of Macedonia and take up the governorship of Gallia Cisalpina. Since this would entail ousting Decimus Brutus from his proconsular command, the Senate was hardly likely to agree to this proposal, so Antonius went directly to the people. Octavian was not perhaps quite so interested in assisting Antonius as he was in removing Decimus, one of the assassins of Caesar, from a position of power. The means was never as important as the end result to Octavian.[15]

The rift between Antonius and Octavian broke open again when one of the tribunes died in office, and Octavian was suspected of wanting to become tribune in his place. Since he had been made a patrician by Caesar, Octavian was ineligible for the post, which traditionally was reserved for plebeians, though there were precedents in the recent past for such a change of role, for example when Clodius had himself adopted into a plebeian family in order to circumvent this formality. The episode is puzzling, because, as Syme points out, Octavian could easily have purchased the services of tribunes by bribery in order to achieve whatever it was that he wanted; possibly he felt that he had not yet gained enough influence to do so, or Antonius may have had all the available tribunes firmly in his pocket, so Octavian may have felt that the only answer was to become tribune himself rather than trust uncertain characters. Later in his reign he placed great emphasis on his tribunician powers, so the possibility that he really did intend to become tribune should not be dismissed. Appian says that Octavian favoured Flaminius for tribune, but the people declared themselves ready to elect Octavian himself. If this is not a complete fabrication to start with, it is highly likely that this declaration of the people was not exactly a spontaneous expression; it smacks of undercover work by Octavian's agents. Octavian as tribune would have been anathema to both Antonius and the Senate. Neither of them could bear to contemplate it, because Octavian would probably have used the office to bring the conspirators to trial. In the event it was a non-starter. Octavian did not become tribune. Shortly after this, a rumour took hold that Octavian had tried to infiltrate and subvert some of Antonius' bodyguard, with the purpose of assassinating him. The Senate gave eager credence to this story, but Appian sounds a note of common sense when he points out that Antonius was more useful to Octavian alive and well as a check on the power of the conspirators. But it was too late for common sense. Hostile manoeuvring began. Antonius went off to Brundisium to meet the legions just arriving from Macedonia, where he found the troops not fully committed to him. These men had known Octavian while he had spent a few months in Macedonia, and so Antonius suspected him of subversion but could not find the agents responsible for it, which speaks for the integrity of Octavian's networks. Octavian himself began to raise an army, going first to Casilinum and Calatia, where some of Caesar's veterans were settled. These towns were situated on either side of Capua, where it will be remembered that Cornelius Balbus was patron; it is therefore likely that Balbus and his friends had already been hard at work in the region for some time, canvassing for Octavian. In any event the subversion of the Macedonian legions and the troop-raising activities were not sudden innovations to meet the potential threat of Antonius. The prospect of Antonius at the head of an army must have been foreseen, and planned for accordingly. There were only two alternatives in this situation; either Octavian must conclude an early alliance with Antonius, but from a position of strength, or he must declare his open hostility. In either case he needed an army of his own, ready, equipped, and waiting. It was the timing which was crucial: Octavian cannot have been blind to the need for troops, but he required some reasonable excuse to raise them, so he had to wait until some action on Antonius' part provided him with the excuse that he needed. Antonius had gone to meet his four Macedonian legions (there were five in total, but one was left behind to garrison the province) to prepare to take them northwards for the coming campaign to wrest Gallia Cisalpina from Decimus Brutus, but such was the distrust of him in Rome that it was an easy task to spread the fear that he might use them to march on the city itself instead of going to his province. At first, before distrust of Antonius had reached such a peak, Octavian could pretend that he was simply taking precautionary measures to protect himself against Antonius; a month or two later he would be able to claim, via Cicero's speeches, that by his timely action in raising troops he had saved the state from Antonius' worst excesses.[16]

November 44 was a dangerous time for Octavian. Antonius was on his way back from Brundisium, in a towering rage at the subversion of his Macedonian legions, and he was fully prepared to have Octavian declared *hostis*, an enemy of the state and an outlaw. The possibility that he might succeed could not be discounted. Octavian had no legally sanctioned position. He was merely a young man at the head of a private army, a *dux privatus* as Pompeius had been when he raised troops for Sulla, but when Pompeius raised troops the circumstances were very different in that a war was being fought. Octavian could not fall back on such a convenient excuse. There was a risk that he could be accused of being a rebel, since by gathering an army he was likely to precipitate a war against the legally appointed consul Antonius. His army was probably about 10,000 strong, perhaps not properly equipped, but the men were veterans who had fought under Caesar, experienced and loyal. Octavian marched 3,000 of them to Rome, after first sounding out Cicero, who was at Puteoli, for advice on whether to march to the city, or to station himself at Capua to await the arrival of Antonius, or to go to meet the Macedonian legions marching up the coast, many of whom he considered loyal to himself. Cicero thought that in Rome Octavian would gain the upper hand with the support of the mob, and possibly even some of the 'good men' in the Senate. But the time was not yet right for Octavian. In his letter to Cicero he offered himself as the champion of the Senate, as the general who would save the state from Antonius, but Cicero did not co-operate. He refused to go to meet Octavian as the latter requested, since he knew that it could not be done in secret and was therefore subject to all manner of risks. Cicero had been absent from Rome since September, when he had clashed violently with Antonius and produced the first of his speeches which came to be known as the *Philippics*; he was not yet ready to make his reappearance in the Senate. Thus Octavian was entirely on his own, and according to Appian his attempt to stir up the soldiers in Rome was not successful because the men were reluctant to fight against Antonius. He had misjudged the situation rather badly, trying to rush things because Antonius' threat was very real and he could not afford to wait. Perhaps this was the origin of his famous saying *festina lente*, make haste slowly. His haste this time had led him to commit the gross and highly illegal error of occupying the Forum with armed men. It revealed how far he was prepared to go, and lacked the saving grace of success. The only remedy was to disappear for a while. Octavian went of to Arretium, the native region of his friend Maecenas, and then to Ravenna to raise more troops.[17]

In some danger from Antonius and out on a limb, Octavian needed senatorial backing, and he had no time to lose in seeking and obtaining it. An alliance with Cicero was one way to get it. He had corresponded with Cicero for a while, explaining at the end of October that he wanted to act through the Senate, and trying to encourage the orator to return to the city to save the republic a second time. Such flattery is blatantly obvious and Cicero no doubt saw through it, but eventually, in the middle of November 44, he did return to Rome and took up the reins of state again. In the meantime, Antonius had returned from Brundisium, summoning the Senate for 24 November, apparently having briefed one of the ex-consuls to move that Octavian should be declared *hostis*. Just before he was due to attend the meeting of the Senate, he heard of the defection of two of the Macedonian legions. In the nick of time, the *legio Martia* had gone over to Octavian, followed shortly afterwards by the *legio Quarta*, so Octavian's investments in subversive agents had paid off handsomely. Antonius tried to remedy the situation, but in the end he did not pursue Octavian further and decided to leave Rome before his consulship expired. He set off for his province of Gallia Cisalpina, where Decimus Brutus, an assassin of Caesar, had already installed himself. Antonius made short work of him, forcing him into Mutina (Modena) and laying siege to the town.[18]

The short-lived alliance between Octavian and the Senate, linked by Cicero, was formed against Antonius. Appian depicts the alliance as a mere façade on both sides. Octavian pretended to be serving the senators in order to achieve power; the senate had no army to use in defence of Decimus Brutus against Antonius, so for the time being they were content to let Octavian march north to Mutina. The consuls-elect, the Caesarians Hirtius and Pansa, would not be able to take up office until 1 January 43, and in any case it would take some time to raise a new army under their command. Octavian had no official standing as yet; the soldiers proposed that he should be made propraetor, which would very properly place him in a subordinate position to the consuls. Cicero could not propose this measure until the next consular year began on 1 January, but he prepared the ground when he made his speech on 29 December (the third *Philippic*). He was already thinking of himself as the saviour of the state, cleverly utilising the services of the young Octavian, deluding himself that he could control him; he repeatedly included this self-perception in his correspondence and his later speeches. He paved the way for adulation of the new Caesar and spread the propaganda that by his admirable and timely efforts in raising troops at his own expense he had saved Rome from the fury of Antonius. On 1 January in the fifth *Philippic* Cicero made three proposals which were of great importance to Octavian, and a fourth proposal concerning his army. Firstly, Octavian was to be propraetor with the fullest powers, as though the appointment had been a regular one. This entailed granting him *imperium* without which, Cicero explained to an audience who knew it perfectly well, no military affairs could be conducted and no army legally raised and held together. Secondly, Cicero proposed that Octavian should be made a senator, and thirdly that he should be allowed to stand for any office as if he had been quaestor the year before. The quaestorship was the lowest ranking magistracy, and there were age limits on eligibility for any office, a fact which this proposal consciously ignored. In effect it would mean that Octavian was to be treated as if he was already over thirty years old, and Cicero devotes a long passage to expounding the theory that to discriminate against youth was not always the wisest policy, enumerating among his examples of successful young men the inevitable story of Alexander the Great. Cicero vouches for Octavian's integrity, with the statement that he knows all the young man's thoughts and feelings. Perhaps he really believed that he did know Octavian, or perhaps he was just using the statement as a device to sway the Senate, while fully aware that he had been allowed to see only what Octavian wanted him to see. Cicero was astute and intelligent – except where his vanity was concerned. If he believed that he knew Octavian and could control him, then his astuteness is eroded and his penetrating intelligence is questionable, and on the other hand, if Cicero had been taken in by Octavian's avowed intent to serve the state through the Senate, it says a great deal for Octavian's manipulative and convincing acting abilities. To a modern audience furnished with the benefit of hindsight the whole episode becomes tragi-comic; as the play unfolds, an eminent old statesman imagines that he is using a younger man to save the state under his guidance and for the glorification of his career, only to be used himself as the instrument that launched a career far greater than his own.[19]

With regard to Octavian's troops, Cicero proposed that the Senate should find land for the veterans, guarantee to pay whatever sums the young Caesar had promised the soldiers, and grant them exemption from service after they had been discharged. These provisions, and also the proposal that Octavian should be allowed to stand for office as though he had already served as quaestor, were insurance policies for the future, and probably originated around a discussion table, with Octavian outlining what he wanted and Cicero pruning the list to an acceptable form for the meeting of the Senate where he would put across the ideas. The immediate brief was to assist Decimus Brutus against Antonius, and not yet to lay the foundations for Octavian's further career, but he had already thought ahead. Is it too fanciful to imagine Octavian, accompanied by Agrippa and Maecenas, Salvidienus Rufus, Gaius Matius, and Caesar's financiers Balbus and Oppius, thrashing out the details of what they wanted from Cicero and making alternative plans in case the project did not follow the desired path? They needed Cicero, for the time being, because they had no senatorial party of their own. All that had to be done was to convince him that Octavian hated Antonius more than he hated Decimus Brutus. For Octavian was not just an individual in search of destiny; he was a corporate entity, a committee whose goal was firstly survival and secondly the highest point that their corporate efforts could reach in the government, though they probably had no fully elucidated conception at that moment of precisely what that point would be. This is not to detract from Octavian's own capacity for caution and wide-ranging forethought; rather it testifies to his ability to inspire loyalty in others and to make the best use of their talents.[20]

On 1 January, when Cicero made his important speech placing Octavian's army on a legal footing, Octavian himself was marching towards Mutina. On 7 January he took command of his army in his official capacity and thereafter he celebrated this date as the anniversary of his military command (*dies imperii*). At the end of his reign, looking back on his achievements, Augustus regarded this as the crucial moment. The *Res Gestae* opens with the phrase 'At the age of nineteen on my own initiative and at my own expense, I raised an army with which I successfully championed the liberty of the Republic when it was being oppressed by the tyranny of a faction.' Thus he presented the best possible interpretation of the civil strife which no one could have forgotten; without naming Antonius he interpreted his own part in the struggle in general terms as defence of the Republic. The idea was not new; Cicero inserted the theme into as many sections of the *Philippics* as he could, though always taking care to mention the name of the man from whom Octavian had saved the state. In Rome debate had continued until 4 January about the situation, and in the end victory went to the moderates who suggested that before war was declared against Antonius an embassy should be sent to him to ask him to give up the province of Gallia Cisalpina and hand it over to Decimus Brutus. Cicero opposed this but it was carried despite his urgings to the contrary, so war was deferred for a while. Antonius' reply was that he would give up Cisalpine Gaul in exchange for the Transalpine province, which he could govern for five years. He also asked that all his acts should be ratified. This was not at all unreasonable, and certainly not as unreasonable as Cicero had predicted, so he had to work very hard to keep up the opposition to Antonius. He was successful, eventually, and so war was declared. It was decreed that military dress should be worn, and the consuls were empowered to save the state. Cicero failed to persuade the Senate to declare Antonius *hostis*, but for the moment that was just a personal failure, and he could fall back on the consolation that the war might yet remove Antonius permanently. On 20 April the news reached Rome of the battle of Forum Gallorum, fought on the 15th near Mutina, between Antonius and the consul Pansa; the latter had been injured, and was later to die of his wound. There was an immediate panic in the city because it was thought that Antonius' victory was more complete than it actually was. Rumours began to circulate that Cicero was aiming at the Dictatorship, and he underwent a disturbing few hours before the true report of the battle arrived. Antonius was in no position to march on the city. Then it was proposed by the city praetor Marcus Cornutus that civil dress should be resumed to indicate that peace was restored, and that there should be public thanksgiving. Cicero replied that it was too soon to give up military dress, since Decimus Brutus was still under siege, but he agreed to the proposal for public thanksgiving, which he suggested should last for an unprecedented fifty days, in the names of all three generals, whom he styled Imperators. Octavian had not actually fought in the main battle; his task had been to protect the camp, so it was somewhat eulogistic to elevate him to the same level as the consuls, but Cicero probably saw no harm in it. After all both consuls were still alive at this point, and Octavian was a minor personality as far as the Senate was concerned.[21]

All this changed dramatically when the second battle of Mutina was fought on 21 April, resulting in a disaster for Antonius and the death of the consul Hirtius. Antonius decided to withdraw across the Alps into Gaul. To the uninitiated it seemed as though Antonius was finally defeated, and all that was required was to pursue him. The Senate rejoiced, and Octavian's position became very awkward. He was left alone, now that Hirtius was dead and the other consul, Pansa, was wounded and soon to die. Octavian was now forced to co-operate directly with Decimus Brutus, who had murdered Caesar, a task which he avoided on one pretext or another for as long as possible. He had been praised by Cicero when the Senate needed his services and his army; now that the danger was averted, he was made to feel unnecessary. He was granted only an ovation for his part in the Mutina battle, while Decimus Brutus was awarded a triumph and placed in overall command of the consular armies. A commission was set up to distribute land to the veterans, but Octavian was not included on it, and the payments supposedly guaranteed to his soldiers were not forthcoming, two factors which perhaps were deliberately calculated to embarrass him and undermine his military support. And probably at this time he was informed of Cicero's clever pun concerning him: *laudandum adulescentem, ornandum, tollendum,* which means the young man should be praised, honoured and immortalised, which comes closest to translating the pun. *Tollere* can mean to raise up, and also to remove by death. It was characteristic of Cicero that he could not resist such a brilliant play on words, and significantly, when Decimus Brutus wrote to tell him that Octavian knew of his turn of phrase, he did not deny authorship of it; in his reply to Decimus he merely burst out for a sentence or two against Labeo Segulius who had discussed the subject with Octavian. The original informant is not known. Decimus Brutus' letter, written on 24 May, begins with the news that he had heard the story before, so it was already current by mid-May. It is perhaps relevant that it was also known by mid-May that Octavian was thinking in terms of the consulship. He had expressed no emotions about Cicero's description of him, and according to Decimus it was Labeo Segulius who brought up the subject, even though Octavian already knew of it; Octavian's reply was that he had no intention of allowing himself to be immortalised. On the surface he thought very little of the matter; underneath that surface there may have been other thoughts. The possibility that he had trusted Cicero is slight; if he had inherited anything at all from his contact with Julius Caesar it ought to have been an ability to survive whilst trusting scarcely anyone, even for an instant. But there may have been an element of disappointment, world weariness, and anger, which he did not reveal. The normal human reaction would have been to bluster, tell friends all about the problem in a raised voice, write indignant letters, and fume in private. Not so the cool and calculating Octavian. Such behaviour would wreck the game he intended to play. He knew for certain now that he could hope for nothing from the Senate without coercion, and that his relationship with Cicero was at an end, but after all there was no need to let either of these two parties know that he knew. He merely noted their sentiments, and waited.[22]

Another significant piece of information in Decimus Brutus' letter of 24 May is that although he had been ordered to do so, Octavian would not give up Pansa's legion. Not only was Octavian persistently failing in the pursuit of Antonius, he was also keeping his troops together. For the time being it served his purpose to pretend that he could not control them, with the unspoken sub-text that since the senators had not paid them, nor allowed him to oversee the settlement of the veterans, they had only themselves to blame. The *legio Quarta* and the *legio Martia* would not move if they had to serve under Decimus Brutus; no doubt Octavian had spared no pains to remind them that Decimus had murdered Caesar. The rest of the troops were steadily working themselves up about the lack of pay, and the exclusion of their young commander from the land commission, so that their interests were not being represented by the one man who could help them, and then there was that terrible thing that Cicero had said about him. Octavian was letting his troops do all the agitating for him while he pretended that he could do nothing about it. In June, Plancus, the governor of Gallia Comata, wrote to Cicero, full of surprise that the young Caesar had not sent his army to help him and Decimus against Antonius, but by the end of July Plancus had finally begun to penetrate what was in Octavian's mind – namely, that while he had consistently promised to march each time he was asked to do so, he was merely stalling for time because he had set his goals somewhat higher. That same month the soldiers sent an embassy of 400 men to Rome to demand from the Senate the consulship for their young commander. Naturally the senators refused, probably after they had stopped laughing. Octavian had waited long enough to achieve his aims by constitutional means, and by co-operation with the Senate. Antonius was far away at the moment, but it was a certainty that he would be back, most likely with the other Caesarian provincial governors in alliance with him, and backed by their armies. In the interim, before Antonius gained too much power, it was time to act. Octavian gathered his eight legions and marched on Rome.[23]

3

CONSUL AND TRIUMVIR

In the summer of 43 the Roman world was rapidly polarising into two hostile portions: Caesarians in the West and the 'Liberators' in the East. Antonius had retreated into Gaul, but he was far from beaten. By the end of May, Lepidus as governor of Gallia Narbonensis had succumbed to the inevitable and joined him. In his correspondence, Lepidus had prevaricated and protested his loyalty to the Senate for as long as he could, waiting to see what would happen. He had no real taste for combat with Antonius, and no inclination to sacrifice himself and his army to no purpose. His soldiers were already fraternising with the enemy, and Antonius himself walked right up to his camp unopposed. Lepidus explained himself politely to the Senate, and made peace with his rival, insisting that it was the mood of his troops and his impossible situation that compelled him to join Antonius. Senatorial disgust with his actions prompted them to declare him a public enemy (*hostis publicus*) in June. His property was forfeited to the state, and his sons forbidden to hold office. Lepidus cannot have made his decisions lightly, despite many accusations, both contemporary and modern, that he vacillated through weakness of character. Antonius was already *hostis* as a result of Cicero's unstinting efforts, so the two Caesarians now shared a common status which threw them together for better or worse; they had nothing to gain by negotiation with the Senate, and nothing to lose except their lives by fighting. Antonius was now in command of a swelling force of auxiliary troops and eventually about twenty-two legions, three of them raised on the initiative of P. Ventidius Bassus, who had miraculously led his little army northwards through Italy, avoiding battle all the way; he crossed the Apennines, and reached Antonius just as he was retreating into Gaul. The opposition to Antonius and Lepidus comprised the joint armies of L. Munatius Plancus, governor of Gallia Comata, and Decimus Brutus. Technically, the troops of the young Caesar were also part of the opposition, but Caesar was determined to sit still and do nothing, a fact which Antonius presumably noted with interest. Immobile in Hispania Inferior, C. Asinius Pollio also waited upon events, another fact of which Antonius was doubtless fully aware. Of these main protagonists, Decimus Brutus was the odd one out. He had been party to the murder of Caesar; all the rest were Caesar's men. It was only a matter of time before an immense power bloc formed in the West, armed and ready. The only questions were how soon could Antonius emerge at its head, and in what position would Octavian find himself when that happened.[1]

In the East, the conspirators were also arming. After leaving Rome, Brutus and Cassius had been assigned to the administration of the corn supply in Sicily and Asia, which would have conveniently removed them from the scene of action without granting them any real powers. They had refused these tasks, officially because they found them degrading, but in reality because the duties assigned to them offered no security. For that they were forced to aim higher, at provincial government and command of troops. At first it seemed hopeless. The Caesarian colours were successfully displayed by Antonius' consular colleague Dolabella, appointed governor of Syria as part of Caesar's provincial administrative plans. He did not travel directly to his province, but moved via Macedonia and Thrace into Asia. He defeated and killed Trebonius, the proconsul of Asia appointed by the Senate and authorised to collect money and troops on behalf of Brutus and Cassius. Like Antonius and Lepidus, Dolabella was declared *hostis* by the Senate, and by degrees his fortunate beginning turned into a less fortunate progress. The situation gradually changed in favour of the conspirators. By a combination of good luck and good management, Cassius established himself in Syria before Dolabella arrived. A minor war was already in progress between the Caesarians and their opponents. Caecilius Bassus, locked up in Apamea with one legion, was under siege by the six legions of Staius Murcus and Marcius Crispus, when Cassius arrived. The siege was raised and the three commanders and all seven legions sank their differences and joined him. Queen Cleopatra sent four legions from Egypt under the command of Aulus Alienus to aid Dolabella, but they never reached him. Faced with a choice of fighting their way to him against seven legions, or simply joining those seven legions, it probably took them a very short time to arrive at their decision. Cassius already had a high moral standing in the East, because after the battle of Carrhae, as Crassus' quaestor, he had saved the situation in Syria. To this high moral standing he added great physical strength, since he now commanded eleven legions.[2]

Meanwhile, in Greece, Brutus had assembled a following. He raised troops in Macedonia and formed them into legions, then campaigned in Thrace, where he recruited auxiliary soldiers. His next move was to gain control of the lucrative province of Asia. As the conspirators and the Senate gained in strength and daring, so the position of the Caesarians declined in the East. The provinces were reassigned; Brutus was recognised as governor of Macedonia, though he had established himself there illegally and violently. Some time later Cassius was confirmed in his tenure of Syria. Ironically, these arrangements reflected the exact provisions which Caesar had made for these areas. Marcus Antonius had installed his brother as governor of Macedonia, but no sooner had Gaius Antonius arrived than Brutus blockaded him in Apollonia, leaving him alone for the time being since he would provide a valuable hostage and therefore some bargaining power. Cicero thought otherwise, influenced by an unreasoning hatred of Marcus Antonius; he wrote to Brutus that a little salutary severity went a long way as an example to others, so he should kill Gaius immediately. Less hysterically and more usefully, Cicero proposed that Brutus should be charged with keeping safe all Macedonia, Greece and Illyricum; the proposal was immediately adopted. This extended command, coupled with that of Cassius in Syria, ensured that almost all the East was under the control of the conspirators. They also controlled the sea, by means of the fleet of Sextus Pompeius who offered his services and was officially accepted as an ally, with power over all the coastal areas. This arrangement was ratified by the Senate on 20 March 43. Despite their strength, the conspirators made no move to invade Italy. Brutus steadfastly ignored the demands of the Senate and the exhortations of Cicero to come to Rome and defeat Antonius. Instead he eventually marched to join Cassius. The final chapter was the suicide of Dolabella, trapped in Laodicea with little hope of rescue or even survival. The Caesarian cause was extinguished in the East, but the news did not reach Rome until the end of the year.[3]

The options open to Octavian in June and July 43 were difficult but crystal clear. An alliance with Brutus and Cassius was out of the question, anathema to him and his troops. He had already rejected the idea of co-operation with Decimus Brutus, but he could not afford to broadcast this decision just yet. It suited his purpose to allow everyone to imagine that he could not persuade his troops to follow Decimus, while all the time Decimus marched further and further away, thus removing any immediate obstacle to the projected march on Rome, for which Octavian had doubtless been prepared for some considerable time; it was not the sort of plan to be made on the spur of the moment. It had become increasingly obvious by now that he could entertain no further hope of working with the Senate, so his initial use of that body to gain official status was now redundant. If he waited until Antonius made a move he could not guarantee that he would be taken up a second time as the champion of the Senate, even with limited and temporary powers – and in any case ranging himself against Caesarian forces under Antonius and Lepidus was an illogical, false position for Caesar's heir to occupy. More importantly if he waited for Antonius to take the initiative it would be too late. He had no powers except military force, and that force was now quite inferior to that of Antonius. He would find himself marooned and powerless, caught between the two millstones of the Senate on the one hand and Caesar's capable understudy on the other. He would be ground down to nothing, welcome to neither party. Everything pointed towards an alliance with Antonius. Left entirely to his own devices he could not even hope to withstand the conspirators, let alone defeat them. If he was to survive, an alliance with Antonius was imperative; indeed it was the most natural choice. But as a youth of nineteen, with a waning political influence and not enough legions to match Antonius, Octavian would have been very much the junior partner. All that he would achieve by alliance with Antonius at this juncture would be to exchange his expendability with the Senate for an equally expendable status with Antonius. The consulship, temptingly and very conveniently vacant, was the ultimate and optimum goal. He would have laughed to scorn the doubts expressed by Plancus in a letter to Cicero, where he grumbled that Octavian had set his heart on an almost worthless consulship of a few months' duration, when he could instead have been acquiring glory for himself by fighting the enemies of the Republic. Octavian was not concerned with status for its own sake. He knew perfectly well what he intended to do with his consulship of a few months. It was a means to an end, like so many of his actions or inactions. He used it merely to get what he wanted, and then once these aims were satisfied, his subsequent disinterest in the office is demonstrated by the readiness with which he surrendered it to Ventidius as part of the arrangements made when the Triumvirate was formed.[4]

As consul, Octavian would gain temporary ascendancy over the Senate, long enough to annul its influence and its danger to him, and at the same time he would be in possession of constitutionally based power that would elevate him to a bargaining position with Antonius. He would be able to legalise his adoption by Caesar, thereby establishing himself as *patronus* of Caesar's extensive *clientelae* and wealthy freedmen, as well as becoming legal owner of his property. As Caesar's son, he would be obliged to avenge his father's death, and as consul he would be able to outlaw the conspirators, the first stage on the road to complete annihilation of anyone who had the remotest connection with Caesar's murder, a long-term aspiration to which he was totally dedicated. Octavian's soldiers stood to gain too, if their commander became consul. They would receive their promised payments, and many of them thought no further than this during their march on Rome. Realising the value of outright bribery and unscrupulous enough to use it, the Senate belatedly despatched envoys to the troops, promising them money; Dio indicates that they actually sent a portion of the cash, and Appian says that Octavian gave orders to chase away the convoy bringing money in case some of his soldiers were beguiled by new-found wealth and forgot the main purpose of their march. Then came the offer for Octavian to stand for the consulship *in absentia*; Caesar's ghost would have found that quite amusing. Neither the army nor its young general were fooled, and pressed on towards the city. Among other things, Octavian was worried that his mother and sister might come to some harm if he delayed. He did not know for certain if they were safe, and had perhaps heard rumours that the Senate had ordered a search for them. Rome was put into a state of defence. The two legions summoned by the Senate from Africa had arrived, along with 1,000 cavalry, and there was another legion, originally raised by Plancus but left behind in the city. That amounted to three legions with no significant commander and no time to engender any sense of unity, against eight unified legions under a commander to whom they had every reason to remain devoted. The three legions joined the eight legions, which was a foregone conclusion to anyone with an ounce of sense. Even after all this, the Senate enjoyed a brief resurgence of hope when they heard that two of Octavian's legions had turned against him; they met hurriedly by night and sent officers to levy troops in Picenum, one of whom was Marcus Aquilius Crassus, who was captured before he reached his destination. He was publicly pardoned by Octavian the consul, and a short time later coolly proscribed by Octavian the Triumvir. It is permissible to wonder why the Senate was taken in by the false rumour that Octavian's legions had deserted him; even if it had been true, it still left him with six legions which had fought together against five which had not. Perhaps it was just wishful thinking elevated into belated action, but by their persistence in trying to resist by armed force the senators showed their hand, thus revealing to Octavian the precise value of their feelings towards him.[5]

On Octavian's arrival in Rome, as his army approached the Campus Martius, six vultures were seen and hailed as a truly favourable omen; it was compared to similar omens observed when Romulus founded the city. Good fortune also smiled on Octavian's mother and sister, who were discovered safe and sound, having taken refuge with the Vestals. The family was safe, and could not now be exploited as hostages to ensure Octavian's co-operation. Starting as he meant to go on, Octavian made the Senate keep its promise to the soldiers to pay them the amounts suggested by Cicero. The first instalments were delivered before he was elected consul. This was Octavian's capital investment for the eventual creation of his monarchy; the handouts to the soldiers amounted to roughly ten times their annual pay. Thus the precedent was set, and the memory of cash payments survived for over two hundred years, when the legionaries, who had probably read their history books, tried to persuade Severus to pay them the same amounts; he refused; perhaps miraculously, he also survived. The consular elections for the remainder of 43 duly took place, in a convoluted but constitutional fashion. The proper procedure in the event of the deaths of both consuls was for the Senate to appoint an *interrex*, but this entailed calling for the resignation of all the patrician magistrates, many of whom were not in the vicinity of Rome. A novel procedure was adopted instead, constitutionally anomalous, but providing a veneer of respectability. The city praetor arranged for the election of two men temporarily endowed with consular powers to preside over the real elections. While they were held, Octavian withdrew from the city so as not to interfere with the freedom of choice of the people. Dio points out how ridiculous this was: Octavian's physical presence was neither here nor there, but his power was all-pervasive, all-persuasive, irresistible. Aged nineteen, Octavian was elected consul on 19 August, the month which the Romans knew as Sextilis, until many years later they renamed it in his honour.[6]

Octavian's consular colleague was his kinsman Q. Pedius, whom Dio outspokenly labels subordinate. Pedius may not have been the first choice as colleague. Syme speculated that Octavian may have desired the election of Publius Servilius Isauricus, to whose daughter he had recently been betrothed. Roman contemporaries thought that Cicero was to be consul, either by his own wish or by invitation of Octavian. Cicero's ambitions in this direction are neither attested nor refuted. Marcus Brutus was told in May that Cicero had actually become consul, but he distrusted his sources. Octavian may still have been prepared to co-operate with Cicero, and through him with the Senate. There was no overt quarrel between them; he had not broken off all relations with either party, and had apparently never said anything in public in recrimination for his shabby treatment at the hands of the Senate, nor had he acknowledged that he had heard of Cicero's alleged remarks about him. What he had done was to demand the consulship in an arbitrary fashion, which of course offended corporate sensibilities, but he had not made specific personal enemies, and had therefore kept his options open. More realistically he may have hoped to utilise the prestige of Cicero to add authenticity to his acts. It is a possibility that cannot be entirely discounted, but Octavian was leaning so far towards Antonius at this time that even if he was simply trying to hedge his bets it could only have complicated matters to try to maintain smooth relations between two such diametrically opposed forces. In the event, Cicero was eclipsed when Octavian became consul, and he was too astute to fail to recognise the facts. He retired eventually to his estates at Tusculum.[7]

When Octavian took up his office as consul and stepped onto the Rostra to address the people, yet more vultures made a timely flight over the Forum – so timely that it is tempting to wonder whether they had just been released from a cage somewhere close by. Such manipulation of superstition is not out of the question; the main purpose would be to emphasise the connection with Romulus, and to rely upon fate was haphazard to say the least; sometimes nature required a little assistance. Without delay, Octavian set about his main business. He distributed the remaining instalments of cash to his soldiers. To neglect that duty would be to court disaster and lose all future credibility with the army. He also paid the outstanding legacies still not settled from the terms of Caesar's will. The source of the cash is not stated. Dio says that he appropriated public funds but pretended that he paid for everything out of his own private fortune. Appian agrees that he used public funds but does not exactly accuse him of deceit; he hints at supplies from Caesar's circle of freedmen. Probably both are correct; there need not be one single source for Octavian's wealth, and

Caesar himself had confused public and private money. In Octavian's case, the task in hand was far more important than scruple. Next, he turned to his own needs. His adoption as Caesar's son was at last ratified by a *lex curiata*, so now Octavian was legally entitled to call himself Gaius Julius Caesar, as indeed he had insisted upon for the past fifteen months. The law declaring Dolabella *hostis* was revoked; Antonius and Lepidus would have to wait a little longer for the laws against them to be repealed. A special court was set up for the trial of the murderers of Caesar, in their absence. The assassins themselves were indicted and prosecuted for their part in the murder, but the net was spread wider than that, to include some men who were prosecuted for the possession of information about the conspiracy, even though they were nowhere in evidence when the crime was committed. Sextus Pompeius was included in the prosecutions, one of the chief accusers being Marcus Vipsanius Agrippa, presumably acting on the advice of Octavian. A single day sufficed to pass judgment upon all the conspirators and their satellites. They were all found guilty, which meant that not only were they outlawed but also their property was forfeited to the state. A lone voice spoke up in favour of Marcus Brutus, that of Silicius Corona, who boasted of his bravery. Octavian did not retaliate, thus gaining a reputation for clemency. For the time being his play-acting as the implacably just but reasonably merciful consul seems to have been credible; there were no sudden departures for the camps of Brutus and Cassius from the ranks of those to whom Octavian extended his mercy. The consequence was that men such as Silicius Corona and Aquilius Crassus felt no alarm and remained in Rome long enough to meet their ultimate fate at the hands of the Triumvirs when they were proscribed. Perhaps they did not realise the acute qualities of Octavian's memory for names and faces, attitudes and deeds, nor the extent to which he was capable of concealing his emotions and ambitions when it was neither politic nor convenient to display them. His restraint was formidable; his ambitions yielded to the immediately practical, and otherwise remained on ice, until the time was ripe.[8]

The conspirators were now technically outside the law, and in illegal possession of armies in the provinces that they had taken over by force. But the charge of illegality was only the first step; by itself it was not sufficient to deprive Brutus and Cassius of their commands, and Octavian could not contemplate making war against them until he possessed more troops. Therefore if he could come to an arrangement with Antonius the combined weight of their joint armies would bring the goal nearer, especially since Antonius' qualities as a general were far from negligible. The time for bargaining with Antonius was approaching, though not yet to be overtly admitted. Leaving Pedius in charge of the city, Octavian marched north, ostensibly to make war on Decimus Brutus, offering assistance to Antonius if he so required. There may have been one other event to attend to before Octavian could leave Rome to go to meet Antonius. At some date not specified, but while he was still consul and therefore between 19 August and 17 November, his mother Atia died. It may have been the ordeal of going into hiding during her son's march on Rome that contributed to her death, but it is nowhere documented how or why she died. Octavian gave her a splendid public funeral with all honours. His grief is not recorded, and it would be uncharacteristic of the resolute and calculating young man to allow it to interfere with the task in hand. It is possible that with the death of his mother, the last restraining influence on his conduct was removed; he need not now feel that he was answerable to anyone. He may also have felt that he had lost everything that mattered, his own father long ago, Julius Caesar, and now his mother. Consequently, from then on, more than ever before, he may have felt that his goal in life was all or nothing, and no savagery or personal risk was beyond him.[9]

While Octavian was on his journey, his colleague and kinsman Pedius managed to persuade the Senate to revoke the laws declaring Antonius and Lepidus outlaws. It was no secret any longer that there would be some sort of alliance between the three Caesarian leaders, and that this union spelled danger for Brutus and Cassius, but the Senate was in no position for last-ditch heroics. The ground had been well prepared for an understanding between Antonius and Octavian. Before the battles at Mutina, Antonius had sent his famous letter to Hirtius and Octavian, known to us from Cicero's shredding of it, clause by clause, in the Senate. Despite Cicero's criticism and personal abuse, the letter showed that Antonius had a firm grasp of reality, a feature which Octavian no doubt stored in his memory for later use. After the initial defeat of Antonius, Octavian had returned captured officers from Antonius' army with messages of friendship, and whenever he came upon Antonian stragglers he either enrolled them in his own army or simply let them go free. He did nothing to prevent Ventidius from joining Antonius, possibly because his troops would not march against Ventidius, or more likely because the complete destruction of Antonius was not likely to prove beneficial in the long run, since it would leave Octavian to face the Senate and the conspirators with no allies. Better to let well alone at that moment; Antonius in retreat was preferable to Antonius either totally defeated or overwhelmingly victorious. In the period after Mutina, both had made use of the respite to fortify themselves. Octavian had achieved the consulship and legitimate power. In July Antonius had been joined by Asinius Pollio with two legions. Shortly afterwards, persuaded by Pollio and also common sense, Plancus joined Antonius as well, leaving Decimus Brutus vulnerably exposed with six new and untrained legions and four experienced ones whose energies had been sapped by near starvation at Mutina. Decimus' hour had almost come. He was deflected from his retreat towards Ravenna and Aquileia by Octavian's northward march, so he turned northwest to aim for the Rhine. The inexperienced recruits left him and joined Octavian, and the rest of his army drifted away to Antonius.

Accompanied by only a few horsemen, Decimus was captured and killed by a Gallic chieftain; some said it was done on the orders of Antonius. It hardly mattered; outlawed thanks to Octavian's pursuit of Caesar's murderers, deserted by his troops, isolated and in the wrong part of the Roman world, Decimus could not have survived.[10]

For the first time in a year, Octavian and Antonius met face to face, to hold their conference on an island in the middle of a river, probably near Bologna (ancient Bononia). Only Appian says that the meeting took place at Mutina, but even though it meets the criteria of the river with islands in the middle, Mutina would have been redolent of the recent conflict, so it is more likely that Bologna was the venue, as all the other sources state. Antonius had many clients in the city, which adds some weight to the argument. Wherever the meeting took place, the results are more important than the location because they changed the course of Roman history, if not the history of the world. The stage management was public and ostentatious, bordering on the ceremonial. The protagonists approached the river with five legions apiece, then advanced to the bridge with 300 men as bodyguards. Lepidus went ahead to search the designated island, then waved his cloak when he had ascertained that all was safe. They all took up positions on the island and sat down, with Octavian in the centre as befitted his rank as consul. In full view of everyone, but out of earshot and therefore enjoying complete privacy, they began to forge the union of three Caesarian leaders known to the modern world as the second Triumvirate. The so-called 'first Triumvirate' is a convenient modern term derived from analogy with the later alliance, and is used to describe the agreement made in 60/59 between Gnaeus Pompeius Magnus, Gaius Julius Caesar and M. Licinius Crassus. This earlier arrangement was an unofficial merger of interests, not sanctioned by law, and the participants were not styled *Tresviri* or Triumvirs. The closest analogy for the titles adopted by Antonius, Octavian and Lepidus derives from the Dictatorship; both Sulla and Caesar were each in their turn legally appointed *Dictator rei publicae constituendae*. Using almost the same formula, the members of the new alliance were appointed *Tresviri rei publicae constituendae*, with powers confirmed for five years. Two lessons had been learned from the career of Julius Caesar. The use of the title Dictator was a sensitive issue, and had been abolished by Antonius soon after Caesar's assassination. The Triumvirs possessed powers of a blatantly dictatorial nature, but avoided the mention of the actual word. They also avoided the slightest hint of the depressing notion *'perpetuo'* by limiting their office to a five-year term. It took two whole days to come to the final agreement, and the results were thorough. The Triumvirs were to hold equal power to the consuls, which meant in effect that they would be superior to all other magistrates. They were to be empowered to make laws; to nominate magistrates and provincial governors; and all three of them were to be appointed to a province, or, as it turned out, more than one area of Roman territory grouped together as one command, with control of troops. Since their territories were extensive, and they could not be in all places at once, they would govern their provinces by proxy as Pompeius had governed Spain, and like Pompeius they would hold power at Rome at the same time, but with the significant difference that Pompeius was limited to one year of office as consul, while the powers of the Triumvirate were confirmed for five years. Antonius demanded Cisalpine and Transalpine Gaul, thus metaphorically flexing his muscles as the senior partner; control of the two Gauls allowed him to retain control of Italy. Lepidus drew Gallia Narbonensis and Spain; Octavian was to command Africa, Sicily and Sardinia. There were advantages and disadvantages for Octavian in this allocation. His provinces would have to be fought for and won. There was a civil war in progress in Africa, and the security of the islands was threatened by the naval power of Sextus Pompeius. On the other hand the struggle would be well worth the effort because the provinces were rich in grain production, a supremely important factor at this stage since Rome did not yet control Egypt and the wealth of agricultural produce that came with it. Whoever controlled the corn supply also controlled Rome, so it was tantamount to handing the city to Octavian, if he could win the necessary battles.[11]

Before they could make any progress at all, the Triumvirs had to attend to their armies; they could not afford to neglect their troops if they hoped for military success. Octavian as consul announced to the soldiers the main features of the new alliance, which were written down, signed and sealed. News of the intended proscriptions was not broadcast, so the Triumvirs could be said to have lied by omission. In order to pacify the armies and keep their spirits up, the Triumvirs marked out eighteen cities in the most productive areas of Italy for the settlement of veterans. It was an outright and shameless bribe, and there were great upheavals when the time came to redistribute the lands and properties, but the soldiers were necessary in a way that the small landowners were not, so the Triumvirs were willing to tolerate such disruption of civilian life as a more viable alternative to the potential risk of armed insurrection; it was expedient and the lesser of two evils. The actual execution of the settlement of veterans fell to Octavian. It was not an easy task, but like the winning of his provinces the operation would yield benefits if properly carried out. The veterans would look to him as their benefactor, thus providing him with a ready power base in Italy and a counterweight to the influence of Antonius in the north, where he controlled most of Gaul. Thus, although Octavian faced difficulties in his allotted tasks as Triumvir, the gamble probably did not deter him; the stakes were high, but so were the rewards, and they were directly and consistently focused on Rome and Italy.[12]

The finer details of the tripartite alliance penetrated to a more personal level. Octavian was to relinquish the consulship to Ventidius, a sacrifice which probably cost him very little, since he had already derived what he wanted from his brief tenure of the office. Marriage ties were proposed to bind the Triumvirate together. Octavian was to be betrothed to Clodia, the daughter of Antonius' wife Fulvia by her previous marriage to Clodius. Octavian played safe; he readily broke off the existing betrothal to the daughter of Servilius Isauricus, but did not enter into full marriage with Clodia, maintaining that she was too young. Lepidus' son was betrothed to Antonius' own daughter. Lepidus is usually considered the 'sleeping partner' in the Triumvirate, but as Pontifex Maximus and a member of the aristocracy he brought high patrician and religious status to the alliance. Cicero noted all the sterling qualities and his family connections in a speech to the Senate, at a time when it still hoped that Lepidus would remain loyal to the Republic. Though he was eventually relegated to a negligible position, Lepidus was indispensable in the early years of the Triumvirate; he was consul in 42, and he lent his legions to the war effort, three to Octavian and four to Antonius, keeping three for himself for the control of Rome and Italy while Antonius and Octavian made war against Brutus and Cassius.[13]

This ultimate ambition was not forgotten. Octavian was implacably dedicated to the destruction of Caesar's assassins, and though Antonius had initially favoured reconciliation, he too recognised that the time for compromise was long past. Civil war with Brutus and Cassius was now inevitable, and consequently there could be no half measures. All opposition must be annihilated, either by warfare or by any other means. Accordingly, after the official Triumviral programme was announced to the troops, and the soldiers went off to celebrate, the Triumvirs retired together for a private conference to produce in cold blood a list of those whom they wished to eliminate by proscription. A preliminary list of seventeen names, including that of Cicero, his brother and nephew, was sent to Pedius in Rome. Many more names were added once the Triumvirs reached Rome and their powers were confirmed by law, but most of these names were presumably discussed now at the private meeting on the island. This was nothing less than authorised multiple murder, and the fact that Rome had seen it all before is no excuse. Ancient and modern authors alike have been reluctant to place too much blame upon Octavian for his share in these murders. Suetonius maintains that Octavian held out against the idea for some time and then gave in, but once he had given in he proved more zealous in the end than the other two Triumvirs when the proscriptions had begun. Dio excuses the young Caesar because he was outnumbered and overwhelmed by his colleagues, and since he never did anything comparably cruel in his later career this post-Triumviral reticence can be taken as proof that he was not really vicious. Modern authors too have decided that Octavian's cruelty was merely assumed in order to achieve his immediate aims. This rather misses the point; to a man about to die as a result of the proscriptions, it could have been of little comfort to know that Octavian was not really cruel, and to those who witnessed the proscriptions but survived, it was no comfort at all to know that this cruelty was merely assumed in order to meet a specific aim – one simply never knew when it might be assumed again. It is remarkable that with the passage of time combined with a fortunate series of events and careful manipulation of the legend, Octavian managed to exonerate or at least gloss over his share in the proscriptions. Antonius played into Octavian's hands at every turn. His reputation as a profligate was already embedded in Roman consciousness, and he did not take sufficient care in the choice of and control of his associates, whose activities reflected badly upon him. This was a matter that Octavian understood by instinct and perhaps by observation and analysis of the entourage of Caesar: there was no question of allowing friends, close colleagues, clients or agents, to act as anything other than synchronised cogs in the machine, otherwise the whole machine would cease to function. Antonius was too liberal, too easy going and perhaps too human, and his machinery collapsed. Finally, of course, Antonius had the consideration to be dead, so he takes all the blame for the dreadful acts of 43–42. Plutarch talks of Octavian defending Cicero and then finally sacrificing him to the blood lust of Antonius. These stories cannot possibly be anything other than fabrications. The Triumviral discussions took place in private. No one except the three participants can have known who said what, or why he said it. Information about the widespread proscriptions was not prematurely divulged to anyone, and even the announcements to the troops did not breathe a word of the intended massacres, which came as an unexpected shock to all parties. Seemingly no one had read between the lines to predict that this is what would happen; many people who might have escaped while Octavian went to meet Antonius remained in the city long enough to become victims. Octavian was extremely fortunate in that he outlived his two associates, and over a long period, fortified by the advantage of having brought peace, he could mould and influence the official record. Antonius was cast as the arch-villain long before he ever came to Actium, so after this preliminary blackening of his name while he still lived, the burden of guilt could quite credibly be offloaded on to him after his death. The unpalatable truth is that Octavian had as much of a vested interest as either Antonius or Lepidus in the removal of many people, both real or imagined enemies. He had good reason to eliminate Cicero, who would perhaps in turn have eliminated him if it had been necessary; it is significant that Cicero did not deny that he had said that the young man must be 'immortalised', and it must not be forgotten that Cicero's real triumph was to save the state by having the death sentence passed on Catiline and his associates, a policy which Caesar had advised against at the time. Octavian probably did not mourn Cicero, though much later, as Augustus, he acknowledged the great qualities of the statesman when it was safe to do so. Some scholars hold the opinion that Octavian himself had few enemies, and that after the publication of the first seventeen names both the elimination of Octavian's opponents and revenge for Caesar's death were properly and fully effected. This is nonsense. Octavian had as many enemies as Caesar had, or, to define the problem more closely, as many enemies as he thought Caesar *may* have had, which is infinitely wider in scope. Truth and reality would play little part in the schemes of one who did not even consider taking any chances. Octavian knew the gruesome alternative and did not shrink from it, and though it has overtones of sacrilege to say so, as much blame attaches to him as to Antonius or Lepidus for the proscriptions of 43 and 42. The proscriptions divided the entire state. Each and every class was affected, families and friends, masters and slaves, parents and children, soldiers and civilians, rich and poor. Appian and Dio catalogue the few personal sacrifices and displays of loyalty, and the very much larger number of betrayals and shameful acts of cowardice. Not many people behaved with dignity or grace, and when the episode was all over there would be many who entertained dark memories which they would rather forget. This explains in large part why and how Augustus was successful in drawing a veil over the worst of the Triumviral crimes. In 36 after the defeat of Sextus Pompeius, he ordered all documents concerning the years after the Ides of March to be destroyed. If there was any protest it was not recorded, or if record of it was made then that was also suppressed. A new beginning was necessary for many people, and held almost universal appeal; destruction of records was equivalent to purging the memory of the past, which faded as Augustus' long reign progressed. He survived as head of state for another five decades and used the time with great success to rewrite himself, emphasising his many worthy achievements and using their brilliance to mask the shadows cast by the events on the road to power.[14]

It has been affirmed, probably incorrectly, that the main motive for the proscriptions was financial, for the properties of the proscribed could be seized and sold. The Triumvirs were obviously desperate to raise cash, as evidenced by their later measures to force people to yield up a percentage of their total wealth. This enforced taxation, coupled with the sale of properties of their victims, has perhaps masked the intentions of the Triumvirs. It has been suggested that they were perfectly content to allow some men to escape to join Brutus and Cassius, or to be rescued by Sextus Pompeius, because the Triumvirs were not interested in the removal of persons, only in separating them from their cash. This was indeed the fate of many of the proscribed, who conveniently left their properties and fortunes behind, a circumstance of which the Triumvirs took immediate advantage since they were not averse to gaining wealth in this way. But it was merely a fortuitous by-product; the real aim was dispersal of enemies by fair means or foul. During the first days of the licensed killing, the city was sealed off to prevent the escape of the intended victims, so in these instances removal by death was quite decidedly the primary aim, and the financial profit was merely a gratuitous bonus. Kienast is surely right to point out that the financial motive was secondary, and the driving necessity behind the proscriptions was eradication of opposition. The Triumvirs made no secret of this. Their proclamation of 28 November, as reported by Appian, contains an unequivocal statement of intent to sweep aside all their enemies once and for all. Even if Appian can be accused of misquotation or embellishment of the original Triumviral proclamation, the total eradication of opposition was a concept that presumably found acceptance among his listeners and readers. He quotes the final toll as 300 senators and 2,000 equites, which has been repeated and accepted by some scholars, despite the discrepancy in Livy's account where it is stated that the victims numbered 130 senators. Attempts to reconcile the two figures are doomed to failure because the numbers of victims simply cannot be confirmed. The total of 300 senators is an almost incredible but possibly significant figure. It is in fact the entire Senate of pre-Caesarian days, and amounts to one-third of the inflated Senate that Caesar left behind. This is not to make the claim that it was the entire pre-Caesarian Senate that was eliminated, but it demonstrates how ruthlessly and comprehensively the Triumvirs planned the removal of their enemies. Absolute accuracy is perhaps not so important as the ideology behind the proscriptions, which basically concerned the long-term survival of the Triumvirs themselves and the security of Italy while Antonius and Octavian fought the coming civil war in the East. For this purpose the Senate had to be brought to heel. Caesar's deliberate policy of *clementia* had not worked, nor had he been saved from assassination by swelling the ranks of the Senate with his own men. There had already been a thinning of the upper echelons of the Senate; some men of consular rank had died, others had been killed in the first round of the civil war with Antonius in Italy and with the Caesarians in the East. The proscriptions can be interpreted as an additional form of culling, the effects of which were severe because the Triumvirs each had their own circle of enemies, only some of whom mutually overlapped. In addition, it was not only individual senators that had to be removed, because individuals by themselves were not always dangerous. It was the power blocs formed by the networks of alliances that represented the worst threat to the Triumvirs, so in many cases the friends, families and associates of the proscribed senators were also targeted. The equites who fell victim to the purge may not have posed any direct threat to the existence of the Triumvirs, but as the satellites, business agents, and financiers of senators, they were naturally eradicated with them. It was essential to remove each power base very thoroughly, from senatorial figurehead right down to loyal bankers and assiduous agents. Only by so doing could the Triumvirs eliminate the potential regrowth of dangerous pockets of opposition. The Triumvirs even proscribed members of their own families. Lepidus proscribed his brother Aemilius Paullus, who had been instrumental in having him declared *hostis*. Antonius included his uncle, Lucius Caesar, in the lists of victims. It may be significant that both these men escaped death. It may have been intended all along that they should do do, perhaps because the inclusion of their relatives in the proscriptions was merely a gesture to demonstrate just how seriously and ruthlessly the Triumvirs intended to pursue their aims.[15]

Though their position was new and constitutionally unprecedented, and their power was extensive and arbitrary, the Triumvirs were anxious to remain as far as possible within the existing framework of the Republican administrative machinery: however, they had no intention of limiting themselves to what it was possible to achieve by remaining passively within the bounds of that framework. Rather, they considered what they wanted to put into effect and then found a way of adapting the law to conform to their needs – much as Caesar and Pompeius had done in the past, but now the precedent was employed more ruthlessly and rapidly. The Triumvirate was formally constituted by the *Lex Titia* passed by the tribune P. Titius on 27 November 43. The five-year term was extended by a few days so that the terminal date was to be 31 December 38, a date which is attested epigraphically. The renewal of the Triumvirate after that date is fraught with difficulties, but in 43 a second term may not have been foreseen. Immediate worries about the probable duration of the Triumvirate were no doubt subsumed by the serious affair of the proscriptions. The first list of seventeen proscribed men had already been published, and on 28 November, the day after the Triumvirate was established, another list of names was posted up in the city, followed by a third and longer list some time later. Just before or possibly during the ensuing panic, the consul Pedius died; he perhaps believed that the first seventeen victims were the only ones to be proscribed, and thus met his end in a state of shock. The cause of his death is not established. Of the original seventeen proscribed, the most illustrious victim was Cicero who was killed on 7 December. He made arrangements to flee, and in fact could have escaped to the camp of Brutus or Cassius if he had so wished, but he may have lost heart after his brother and nephew were killed in Rome. His vacillation can be interpreted as cowardice, but it may have derived from a stubbornly heroic attachment to Italy, conflicting with a sense of duty which compelled him to join Brutus. He met the soldiers bravely at the end. Antonius ordained that his head and hands should be nailed to the Rostra in the Forum. It was a reminder that Cicero had delivered his speeches there, and a salutary lesson that he had met a gruesome end for having done so. It is possible to understand Antonius' extreme hatred because his stepfather had been executed by Cicero in 63 as a member of the Catilinarian conspiracy, and secondly because in all the personal and political jibes of the *Philippics*, and no doubt in private conversations, Cicero had deliberately provoked Antonius beyond endurance. But Antonius would have earned much more credit for himself if he had limited his venom to a speech of his own and then allowed Cicero a decent funeral.[16]

Rapid and forceful removal of enemies represented only half of the necessary measures to establish the Triumvirate. There could be no guarantee of security for the Triumvirs unless they could also assume immediate control of the government of the city of Rome and the provinces. The consuls and the provincial governors constituted one of the most serious potential threats, and unlike the tribunes, who constituted an equally damaging but different source of opposition, they could not be so easily bought and manipulated. The consulship was the first office to be organised to the Triumvirs' satisfaction. For what remained of 43, P. Ventidius and C. Carrinas, both of whom were Antonius' men, were to be consuls in place of Octavian who resigned and Pedius who was dead. The consuls for the ensuing years were designated now, those for 42 being Lepidus and Plancus. They were to be succeeded by P. Servilius Isauricus and L. Antonius in 41, followed by Asinius Pollio and Gnaeus Domitius Calvinus in 40. Each candidate for the most important offices had to be chosen with care, and it was important to fill all the offices for some time to come so that Antonius and Octavian could rely upon peace and quiet behind them while they waged war in the East. The government of the Western provinces was divided up between the Triumvirs themselves, and then exercised via delegates, much as Pompeius had governed Spain while remaining in Rome. For the time being, the Eastern provinces were closed to the Triumvirate. Minor provincial offices and city magistracies in Rome were redistributed as the proscribed victims vacated them, until it became virtually a free-for-all, with appointments offered as rewards or sought as favours. The method of appointment did not matter, since the end result was that most provincial commands and city magistracies would be held by Caesarian partisans. The Triumvirs perhaps did not control absolutely all the appointments; some magistrates were probably still elected, but the survival of the elections is debatable, and even if elections did take place they may have comprised only a rather nervous but formal ratification of Triumviral wishes. Traditional forms and procedures were not abolished, but it would require an enormous act of faith, then as now, to maintain that after 27 November 43 the Republic was alive and well.[17]

The financial situation was chaotic. Brutus and Cassius had diverted the taxes of the Eastern provinces to their own use, thus depriving the Triumvirs of the greatest source of ready cash. The Western provinces were never as wealthy as their Eastern counterparts, and in any case they were almost exhausted. Italy itself had to bear the brunt of the Triumvirs' expenses, which were monumental in scale and immediate in the need for settlement. Payment for the troops was always the most pressing consideration, and preparations for the coming war were just as urgent. The one went hand in hand with the other; if no pay was forthcoming the soldiers would hardly be co-operative when it came to making war overseas against Romans like themselves. The sales of confiscated estates did not produce much more than a small percentage of the required sums, because people were reluctant to buy the properties of the proscribed. It has been argued above that the desire for financial profit was not the main reason for the proscriptions. The Triumvirs may have expected very low returns from the disposal of estates, and the sales of many of them to soldiers, who were the only ones who dared to buy them, may have been an end in itself in order to keep at least a portion of the troops contented. Since the confiscations were not highly profitable, other sources of cash had to be found. Antiquated taxes that had not been levied for years were revived, and new taxes were imposed. The consuls of 42, Lepidus and Plancus, levied a percentage tax on wealth, and instituted a system of self-assessment whereby each person estimated his own contribution, which naturally led to charges of attempts to defraud the government and then to more confiscations by way of punishment. This wealth tax even extended to women, 1,400 of whom were singled out for contributions. Under the leadership of Hortensia, the daughter of Cicero's old rival Hortensius, and with the support of Octavian's sister and Antonius' mother, the women pointed out that since they were not allowed to vote or to take part in government, sequestration of their resources was unfair, especially after many of their husbands, fathers and sons had been killed or driven away. They declared themselves ready to make voluntary contributions should there be any threat to Italy or to Rome, but they particularly objected to being asked to provide resources to fund a civil war. The Triumvirs were not pleased by their revolt, but next day they reduced the original list to 400 names. After this attempt to raise cash had been partly thwarted, there remained the temple treasuries. In this there was nothing new; generals of all epochs before and since have robbed temple treasuries to fund wars, but the Triumvirs brought particular opprobrium upon themselves because they seized the personal savings of individuals entrusted to the care of the Vestals.[18]

During the last days of 43 Plancus and Lepidus held separate triumphs, respectively for successes in Gaul and for negotiations with Sextus Pompeius. Then they took up office as consuls for 42. On 1 January the Senate and magistrates took a solemn oath to maintain the acts of Caesar the Dictator, an unequivocal return to the status quo of 44, where all the Triumvirs could pick up the threads of government at the point where Antonius the consul left off. After confirming Caesar's acts in the earthly sphere, the Triumvirs also confirmed his presence in the heavens. All three men stood to gain from the enrolment of Caesar among the gods, but none more than Octavian, who soon began to call himself *divi filius*, a calculated advertisement that he was the son of a god. This was unprecedented and daring, and an unequivocal declaration of his intention to rise higher than most other men. Precisely when he began to use the name is disputed; he had no reason to be coy about it and no reason for tactful delay. There is evidence to suggest that he had already adopted it by 40: a series of coins bearing the legend *Divi Juli F* and portraying both military standards and agricultural implements has been dated to the period of the land settlements just after Philippi, a context that is most apt in view of the appearance of the symbols of the military and agricultural equipment on the coins. This date has been disputed, but at present it cannot be proved conclusively that Octavian adopted the title *divi filius* any earlier than 40. It is worth pointing out that it is unlikely that he wasted two years before he realised the advantages inherent in the name. As a further honour to Caesar it was decreed that a temple to *Divus Julius* should be built in the Forum on the site of Caesar's funeral pyre. It was finally dedicated in 29. The cult of *Divus Julius* was propagated actively; it was established in Italy by the *Lex Rufrena*. Scholars are divided over the relationship between the divine honours awarded to Caesar just before his death and the deification in 42. Part of the argument hinges on whether Caesar intended to set up a divine monarchy on the pattern familiar in the East. For some authors it is quite obvious that this was indeed his goal, while others point out the dearth of contemporary evidence from such writers as Cicero, who would surely have had something witty and damning to say if he suspected Caesar of such a scheme. It is possible that the question of monarchy, divine or otherwise, is a modern confusion, quite peripheral to the main issue of divinity. A more sensible and indeed down-to-earth suggestion is that the divine honours awarded to the living Caesar and his deification after his death were linked from the beginning, and were always intended to be so, in that his divinity was recognised but he could not actually become a god until he was dead. In this case, the Triumvirs were simply bringing to fruition the process begun by law while Caesar was still alive, thereby doing justice to his memory. There is support for this in the narrative of Dio, who treated the divine honours and the deification of Caesar as a continuous development; for him the divine honours granted to the living Caesar comprised a necessary evolutionary stage in the creation of the dead *Divus Julius*. It is difficult to discern how much Dio's view may have been attributable to influences from his own times, when deification of the Emperor was a fully established and normal procedure unless the Emperor in question had been particularly obnoxious. Depending upon the acceptance or rejection of Caesar as divine monarch, the intentions of Octavian with regard to the cult of *Divus Julius* are interpreted very differently. For some, Octavian was the rightful successor to Caesar, and as the conscientious adopted son he wished only to honour the memory of his father. It could also be said that Octavian ruthlessly exploited the divinity of his ancestor in an opportunistic bid to enhance his own power. In either case he profited. Divine ancestry was not an uncommon claim among the Roman aristocracy, and all the Triumvirs utilised the system at one time or another, chiefly by means of their coinage where they advertised the family mythology of the Antonii, the Aemilii, and the Julii. In the East Antonius was equated with both Hercules and Dionysus. Caesar himself claimed descent from Venus. Octavian's claim was much more direct. Ostentatiously rejecting divinity on his own account, he rose to power via Caesar's divine image instead. It was all the more effective because his relationship was not to a mythical goddess from a remote age, but to a real person from the recent past. The audience who would be most appreciative of this relationship would naturally be the army.[19]

It has been argued that deification removed Caesar from the mortal realm of envy and hatred, and that Octavian was concerned to drive a wedge between the image and the memory of Caesar the Dictator and that of the new, improved, and infinitely more marketable divine Caesar. Gradually the latter obliterated the former, until Augustan literature could ignore Caesar the Dictator altogether. If he is mentioned at all, it is usually when the worldly and authoritarian aspects come to light, but this is seldom seen. The establishment of the division between the Dictator and *Divus Julius* was necessarily a slow process, and the emphasis must be on the gradual element in the transformation. In January 42, too many people remembered the earthly Caesar the Dictator and Caesar the general. The Triumvirs had just declared all his acts valid and binding, so however hard Octavian tried to focus attention on *Divus Julius*, and so to distract attention from the Dictator, for some years the true image would remain. Indeed it was important that it did not yet fade entirely, because it was the most influential tool in playing upon the loyalty of the army. The sling bullets used by Octavian's army at the siege of Perusia were inscribed *Divum Julium* and the watchword of the army was *Divus Julius.* This was as much a declaration of intent to the outside world as it was a reminder to Octavian's own army, though it served both purposes well enough. The propagation of the idea of Caesar as a god, powerful and protective, would inspire confidence in the soldiers, but at the same time it was important that they should also remember him as a man, on the basic human level of their balding general who braved anything and everything to lead them to victory. By implication this meant that the depersonalisation of Caesar could not yet be absolute. The sheer utility of all this was quite undisguised and served its purpose until 29, when Octavian finally dedicated the temple to *Divus Julius* in the Forum in Rome. Throughout the Triumvirate and even for some time after the battle of Actium, Octavian's purpose was to advertise and execute vengeance for Caesar's death and to establish a solid and sacrosanct foundation for his own power. After he had eliminated his rivals and achieved a steady increment in his power and prestige, Octavian placed less emphasis on *Divus Julius* and more on his own position as Princeps. In the same proportion, though his reliance upon the army was no less permanent and total, it became less overt.[20]

The army was at the core of events of 42, but it was Antonius and not Octavian who quite rightly emerged with all the laurels. The sources, even the favourable Augustan ones, all concur in describing to a greater or lesser degree Octavian's lack of success. He sent Salvidienus to oust Sextus Pompeius from Sicily, which was designated one of Octavian's own provinces, but the sailors and soldiers under Pompeius were more experienced and easily drove Salvidienus off. Perhaps the experience and strength of Sextus had been underestimated. The project had to be shelved because the campaign against Brutus and Cassius was beginning, and this took precedence over winning back Sicily. When Octavian and Antonius crossed the Adriatic with their combined strength of twenty-eight legions, finally arriving at Philippi, Octavian's performance earned him no credit. He was ill, and at first remained behind at Dyrrachium, but followed Antonius for compelling reasons. If Antonius were to be defeated, Octavian would have to face the conspirators alone, which would have been potentially disastrous. On the other hand, an independently victorious Antonius would present different but hardly less formidable problems. So Octavian and Antonius faced Brutus and Cassius at Philippi, where the conspirators had dug themselves in with mountains on one flank and a marsh on the other; in front of them they had built a fortified line, which Antonius pierced only with difficulty. The battle of Philippi actually comprised two battles, the first a stalemate and the second a victory for Antonius. In the first battle, Antonius captured the camp of Cassius, while Brutus was doing the same damage by capturing the camp of Octavian. There are variations on the story of how Octavian avoided capture and death; in his *Memoirs* Augustus claimed that he was given warning in a dream of one of his friends that he should stay in the battle line, even though he was ill. This he did and thus was not in the camp at the time of its capture. It may be true; stranger things have been known to happen in wars. But even Agrippa and Maecenas do not deny that Octavian hid in a marsh at some point during the fighting. Augustus never made any claim to have been a great soldier, and perhaps he merely upgraded the scene from bog to battle line to satisfy posterity. His personal courage should never be in doubt, nor should it be doubted that he was genuinely ill at Philippi, though his ailments remain a mystery. After the first battle, there was an immediate return to the status quo, because neither side could afford to hang on to their gains. The event that tipped the balance was the unnecessary suicide of Cassius, who was discouraged because he thought that Brutus had been defeated. Reliable and accurate information might have saved the day, but now Brutus was alone. He knew very well that his best option was to wait, secure in a defensive position, well supplied by the fleet which disrupted the communications between Rome and the Triumvirs and sometimes captured their convoys. In the end, if Brutus had simply waited long enough, Octavian and Antonius would have been forced to move to find food. The situation was an echo of the campaign in 48, when Pompeius knew that he could outwit Caesar for the same reasons, but like Brutus he too was a victim of the Republican system. They were both of them subject to the constant nagging of insubordinate subordinates, and though they were both single-minded they were neither of them sufficiently autocratic to master their fire-eating colleagues. After an interval of about twenty days, Brutus risked battle, and lost. His camp was captured and held by Octavian, while Antonius and the cavalry pursued Brutus himself, who conveniently committed suicide. The survivors of noble rank fled, some of them to join Sextus Pompeius, others elsewhere, and for the time being dispersal was as good as death in battle since it meant an end to armed and united opposition to the Triumvirs. Octavian put to death everyone who had been a party to the murder of Caesar. Stories were told of his inflexible cruelty, and his lack of interest in even the most harmless relaxation of ferocity. He refused proper burial to at least one of his victims, and displayed complete lack of compassion when a father begged to die in place of his son. Octavian told them to play *mora*, a game of chance, or to draw lots as to who should die. He executed the father and then the son committed suicide; the two deaths were regrettable, but the deaths were not the most lamented aspect. Octavian's cavalier treatment of the two men stirred deep emotions; perhaps he thought it just retribution for the cold-blooded murder of his adoptive father, who had shown mercy but never been granted the chance to plead for his life. Implacable and indifferent, Octavian probably despised the men who pleaded with him for mercy of any description. In two years he had not grown weary of vengeance, and his unfeeling anger may not have been founded on mere play acting. The possibility that he entertained entirely genuine and completely undiminished hatred for the murderers of Caesar should not be dismissed. If nothing else, he was consistent.[21]

The ancient historians recognised the momentous importance of the battle of Philippi because it marked the transformation of the Republican form of government into that of the Triumvirate and then the Principate, or as Appian describes it without mincing words 'the form of government was decided chiefly by that day's work, and they have not gone back to democracy yet'. Dio's conclusion is starker in its judgement: 'What else can one say regarding the contestants on both sides than that the vanquished were Romans and the victor was Caesar!' But though that was the logical conclusion with the benefit of hindsight, the young Caesar's victory was not yet complete, and would not be complete for several more years. After the battle, according to Suetonius, the soldiers saluted Antonius as Imperator, but reviled Octavian. If this is not complete fabrication it may indicate the work of Antonius' agents against Octavian, and it may have influenced the way in which Octavian dealt with the machinations of Lucius Antonius and Marcus Antonius' wife Fulvia, who stirred up the events culminating in the Perusine war two years later. At any rate, it is highly unlikely that either of the two Triumvirs trusted each other. They parted on a theoretical basis of equality, but in the practical sense Antonius was the acknowledged superior. He remained in the East, where there was much to do, and Octavian returned to Italy with the discharged veterans whom he now had to settle on the land. On the way back to Rome he was so ill that rumours began to circulate that he was dead or dying, rumours which disquieted him sufficiently to prompt him to send messages ahead to Rome proving that he was still alive and on his way there. He arrived at Brundisium and was forced to lodge there for a while in order to recuperate, delaying his arrival in Rome until early in 41. He would need all his strength to perform the tasks that awaited him in Italy and the provinces, which had been reshuffled once again. Allegedly on the basis of Caesar's original plans for Cisalpine Gaul, this area now ceased to be a province. It made perfect sense to integrate it into Italy, utilising the Alps as the northern boundary. Beyond this boundary, the tribes were not wholly subdued or pacified, and could not be counted on as allies; it would require several more years and the talents of several generals, and ultimately the skills of Tiberius and Drusus, before Roman control of the Alpine passes was established. Lepidus was now relegated to the background as far as his political power in Rome and in the provinces was concerned. The official reason for reducing his influence was the suspicion that he was in regular and possibly nefarious communication with Sextus Pompeius, a charge which gained some credence owing to his past record of co-operation with the younger Pompeius. Gallia Narbonensis was wrested from Lepidus and given to Antonius, who already commanded Gallia Comata and had control of all the Eastern provinces as well. Octavian promised Lepidus command of Africa, provided that he could eventually demonstrate his loyalty to the Triumvirate. In exchange Octavian took over Lepidus' erstwhile province of Spain, which was almost wholly in the hands of Sextus Pompeius. Salvidienus was despatched to the province with six legions to win it back for Octavian.[22]

The most urgent task in Italy was to settle the veterans on lands promised them at the outset of the civil wars. Though there were some deserted farms and some remnants of state-owned lands in Italy, there was nowhere near enough to settle the vast numbers of veterans. The total is unknown and much disputed. A recent modern estimate is that 46,000 men required settlement, a figure which includes not only the veterans from the legions which had fought at Philippi but also those from Africa and the Western provinces. The important point is that the settlement involved the displacement of farmers who made a modest living from the land, and their substitution by soldiers whose relationship with the plough and knowledge of animal husbandry was tenuous. On the whole it was neither a social nor an agricultural success, but it is difficult to discern any viable contemporary alternative. The structure of the Republic and the Roman way of life did not allow for equivalents to the modern job-creation schemes that have traditionally mopped up veterans from more recent armies. It was a task in which Octavian could not possibly please anyone, and this may be the reason why Lepidus did not seem to have agitated to play a larger part in government and in fact meekly acquiesced in the loss of his provinces. He probably did not want to become embroiled in this unpopular and disruptive settlement programme. He certainly did not render any assistance to Octavian, and nor did the consuls Lucius Antonius and Servilius Isauricus. Lucius, in fact, did everything in his power to hinder progress, playing off one side against the other, seemingly with no clear programme of his own in mind to substitute for the state of affairs in Italy. The farmers who were evicted to make room for the soldiers naturally complained because they had lost their means of subsistence; the soldiers complained that they had not received what was promised to them, so there was sufficient discontent in the air to fuel Lucius and Fulvia's campaign against Octavian, whose popularity sank like a stone. In response he divorced Clodia and sent her back to her mother, indicating that he was not now connected in any way to Fulvia or to her entourage.[23]

Though the veteran settlement was a thorny problem, according to Appian the tact and diplomacy exercised by Octavian initially resolved some of the difficulties. Appian ascribes the disturbances caused by Lucius Antonius to jealousy on behalf of his brother because Octavian was reaping all the praise whilst Antonius, the real victor of Philippi, was absent. This may be a distortion of the truth. Octavian's relationship with the veterans was not always smooth. The soldiers quickly turned against him when his actions did not conform to their desires. They nearly lynched him when he ejected one of their colleagues from the rows of seats reserved for the equestrians at the games. The seats were assigned to the equestrians by law, so Octavian had of necessity to uphold the law even if the offender was a soldier from the armies to which he owed his elevated position. Since the man in question disappeared for a while, the rumour spread that he had been taken away and executed, so the soldiers rioted, baying for Octavian's blood. Then the soldier turned up unharmed, in the nick of time. All this in the space of a few moments revealed the volatile fickleness of the mob and the soldiery, and the fragility of any relationship with them that was not constantly and assiduously groomed. It was a valuable lesson, duly noted by Dio. The soldiers had become arrogant and greedy because they had realised their value to the Triumvirs. Appian says that Octavian indulged them with gifts and money, and by this means he earned their affection if not their respect, so the Antonians reasoned that they must pry the veterans away from Octavian before he became supreme. Accordingly Lucius opened hostilities by insisting that the veterans of the Antonian legions ought to be settled by Antonius' own agents and not by Octavian, which gave rise to the notion that perhaps Octavian had not treated the Antonian troops as impartially as he should have done. Octavian tried to heal the rift that Lucius had created; unexpectedly, perhaps, he authorised Antonius' chosen agents to oversee the settlement of his troops. Lucius was temporarily thwarted on that particular issue because Octavian's ready compliance ensured that he now had not a leg to stand on so he had to think up some other scheme for the discomfiture of the young Caesar.[24]

Disarmed by Octavian for the moment, Lucius changed tactics and went on to take up the cause of the dispossessed landowners. The unknown quantity behind all this is the extent to which Antonius himself connived at the scheming of his brother and his own wife. He has his defenders, ancient and modern, who claim that he was quite ignorant of what was going on in Italy, but Octavian could never be certain that his Triumviral partner was innocent. He could not accuse Antonius directly, but he no doubt reasoned that if he lost his grip on the soldiers and the populace alike, and allowed everything to get out of control, then that might provide the motive for recalling Antonius to restore the law and order that he, Octavian, had ignominiously let slip. The ploy had been used before, and if it was successful this time, when everything was in chaos, then Octavian would be finshed for ever, except to survive as a satellite of Antonius, either totally obliterated or perhaps just effaced but magnanimously forgiven for his failures; allowances would be made for his youth, ill health, and inexperience, and a complete block put upon his further career. Antonius could then abolish the Triumvirate, assume the consulship, restore the constitution (after a fashion) and keep control of Rome and his provinces, well within the legal framework that was so necessary for success. Octavian would not be able to emerge again except by making war on Antonius, which would mark him out as the unconstitutional ambitious but guilty party and destroy all his credit. Then there was the very real possibility that even if he risked all that, he would lose. It was a dangerous time for Octavian. The involvement or otherwise of Marcus Antonius did not affect the immediate situation to any degree; it did not really matter whether Antonius had instigated the disturbances via his wife and brother, or whether he merely condoned their scheming while he remained aloof, or indeed whether he was completely innocent and not embroiled in the matter at all. In the end it was inevitable that Octavian would have to fight it out on Italian soil. There were attempts at reconciliation. In Dio's narrative all the credit goes to Octavian for attempting to negotiate, but this is largely because Octavian is portrayed as a prototype Augustus, already part of the legend, wise and authoritative with right on his side. Appian says that the attempt to bring about a reconciliation was made on the initiative of the soldiers. The first meeting between Octavian and Lucius Antonius was held at Teanum, but the proposals put forward were never put into effect. What was revealed was that the struggle was really about the conflict between the powers of the consuls and the legally sanctioned, but technically unconstitutional powers of the Triumvirs, with Octavian as the main target. Lepidus was already neutralised and Antonius was sitting on the fence, inscrutable, distant, and as yet unimpeachable. Each side began to prepare for war. The legions tried to arrange a meeting at Gabii, between their own representatives, Octavian, and Lucius Antonius. Octavian attended the meeting, but Lucius and Fulvia boycotted it, remaining in Praeneste where they had fled because of their supposed fear of Octavian.[25]

The war began with sporadic outbreaks of violence. In order to guard his rear, Octavian sent one legion to Brundisium in case reinforcements arrived from the East, which indicates how little he trusted Antonius. He recalled Salvidienus Rufus who was marching to Spain with six legions to make war on Sextus Pompeius; he placed two legions under Lepidus to protect Rome; he recruited as many troops as he could, and he put M. Vipsanius Agrippa in command of whatever soldiers he could muster in the time available. Though Agrippa had long been associated with Octavian, from early schooldays onwards, this is the first time that he emerges as the trusted military lieutenant, and he aquitted himself with credit, thus laying the foundations of the partnership that shaped the Empire. Lepidus did not perform so well, and failed to stop Lucius marching into Rome. At least he avoided bloodshed, and he took refuge with Octavian. With Rome at his disposal, Lucius made a speech declaring that he would restore the authority of the consulship and abolish the Triumvirate; this meant of course that he would eliminate Octavian and Lepidus, and bring in Marcus Antonius on the side of respectable government. Lucius was well received, hailed as Imperator, and given a command against an unnamed enemy. He swept out of Rome intending to stop Salvidienus in his tracks as he came south on the Via Cassia. Instead he miscalculated and manoeuvred himself into a trap between Salvidienus and Agrippa, who managed to get behind him and started to close the gap, cutting his communications with Rome. Lucius had no choice but to turn aside. He aimed for Perusia nearby and shut himself up there, hoping to be relieved by Antonius' lieutenants Asinius Pollio and Ventidius, who commanded armies in the two Gauls, and possibly by Plancus, who was at Spoletium with an army of veterans. The plan misfired because Antonius had not declared his intentions to his legates, and they were uncertain as to how they should react. Plancus did not make the slightest effort, and Pollio and Ventidius moved only very slowly and possibly very reluctantly. In the meantime Octavian built up siege works around Perusia, and while he gradually starved the city into surrender, he and Agrippa marched on Ventidius and Pollio, who did not stand and fight. There was no decisive battle; the two Antonian generals removed themselves, crossed the Apennines, split up and went their separate ways, Ventidius to Ariminum, and Pollio to Ravenna. It was only a matter of time now before Perusia fell to Octavian. Lucius gave in at the end of February 40. He was allowed to go free, and so were his men, because punishment of the soldiers could result in retribution from Marcus Antonius. Plancus escaped with Fulvia to join Antonius, and eventually Ventidius followed. Other senators and some of the leading citizens of Perusia were not so protected. Octavian put many of them to death; the war had been between him and Lucius, but anyone who had assisted Lucius could be considered an enemy. The usual tales of unemotional cruelty attach to these acts. It was said that he sacrificed his victims on an altar to *Divus Julius.* As for Perusia, the citizens were not punished, but the town was given up to the soldiers and during the pillage went up in flames.[26]

4

THE DECISIVE DECADE

During the ten years that elapsed between the fall of Perusia and the capture of Alexandria in 30, Octavian gradually established himself in a position of power. Though he began his account of his achievements (*Res Gestae*) with the raising of the army at the age of nineteen, Augustus was reticent about the details of what happened next, passing in three chapters from a narrative of specific events to a general account of his victories, triumphs and honours. It is impossible to discern how he regarded the years which were so fruitful and formative. Looking back on them, he would be able to pick out the significant trends and relevant turning points, while the less portentous events would recede into obscurity. Going forwards through those years with no guarantee of ultimate success, he would not be able to evaluate the situation quite so clearly; the salient factors would be tenacity of purpose combined with flexibility of method. There were more roads than one towards his goal, and it is possible that that goal was not clearly defined at first. His rise was not rapid, nor steady; he met with hindrances and disappointments, but he possessed a superhuman patience and a dogged determination that enabled him to surmount difficulties and defeats which might have discouraged less obdurate people. He experienced more than one narrow escape from personal danger both on the political scene and in military action; like a cork, he sometimes briefly sank below the surface, but rapidly came back up, buoyant and unsinkable. Though he had youth on his side, its advantages were neutralised by his frequent illnesses, some of them serious enough to threaten his survival; but despite his ailments he managed to appear at the right place at the right time when it mattered. These efforts cost him a great deal sometimes, but he showed indomitable will-power and courage that impressed his contemporaries. He built on this foundation shrewdly, and where he lacked certain qualities he used the skills of other people to fill the gap; indeed, much of his success can be laid at the door of his associates, in whom he inspired a loyalty that scarcely ever wavered. That may have come about either because of his personal charm, or in some cases loyalty may have derived from the prospect of the rewards that he could offer if he remained at the helm. Of his original group of friends, only Salvidienus proved doubtful, and he was executed for reasons which are obscure. Octavian already operated at the head of a network of clients and agents, consisting of those he inherited from Caesar and those he acquired for himself. Very few of these are recorded; the unsung majority yield to the more famous names. In the military and naval sphere, Octavian could rely on his friend Agrippa, without whom it is possible that the world would never have known Augustus; and Maecenas rendered excellent service in the diplomatic sphere. These two men are inextricably associated with Octavian, but their contribution to his success cannot be measured precisely. Augustus was not afraid of acknowledging their useful-ness and his reliance upon them, and even after their deaths he still made reference to them as his companions and guides. When the scandalous affairs of his daughter Julia became known, he so far forgot himself that he expressed his anger in the Senate, furious that the matter should be a matter of public discussion. The cool, calm exterior had given way to an outburst of emotion, which he immediately regretted, adding that if Agrippa or Maecenas had been alive they would never have allowed him to display his feelings for all to see.[1]

Marcus Vipsanius Agrippa sprang from humble origins, and first encoun-tered Octavian while still a boy. His name crops up now and then during Caesar's supremacy, so it seems that his association with Octavian was fairly constant, and that he was a firm friend. He came to prominence in the Perusine war, where in a modest way he demonstrated his capacities as a general, undertaking independent tasks very competently. He was sent into Gaul after the troubles with Lucius Antonius were over, and there he enjoyed considerable success, being the only general of his day, besides Caesar, to cross the Rhine. It was presumably his loyalty to Octavian that led him to refuse a triumph on his return from Gaul, at a time when Octavian himself had made only a very poor showing against Sextus Pompeius. Such self-effacement is a rare quality, and Agrippa was rarer still in that he never seems to have agitated for supremacy throughout his long association with Augustus. Velleius Paterculus sums him up: 'he was well-disciplined in obedience, but to one man only'. When Augustus was dangerously ill in 23, and not expected to recover, it was Agrippa to whom he chose to delegate tangible authority by handing over to him his signet ring, thus probably offending Marcellus, Augustus' nephew, who was generally consid-ered to be the most eligible candidate to follow in Augustus' footsteps. Agrippa was granted an independent *imperium* in 21; that much is certain, but discussion still goes on as to the exact nature of this *imperium*. There are those who suggest that it was *imperium aequum*, or power equal to that of all other governors of the provinces, and there are scholars who are convinced that Agrippa was granted *imperium maius*, or power that was greater than that of all other governors, to enable him to act freely and give orders to whomever he wished. If this was so, then Agrippa's status was indeed high, and the honour and responsibility very significant. But there are serious reservations about this problem. If it is correct, as has been argued, that *imperium maius* did not exist, and that *imperium* was always *imperium* no matter what the circumstances, then all argument must face redundancy, or at least early retirement. Agrippa's position is not greatly diminished by this theory; in fact it is enhanced, for if there was no such *imperium maius* then Augustus did not possess it either, and so Agrippa was not held back, one rank behind Augustus as some have suggested, but was his equal in nearly all respects. This is underlined by the bestowal upon him of *tribunicia potestas* for a five-year term in 18, and for a second five-year term in 13. The only difference between him and Augustus was the duration of the power; Augustus held it for life, while Agrippa was restricted to five years. It is possible that he would have received such grants continually, but he held his second five-year tribunician power for only a very short time before he died in 12. The grant of *tribunicia potestas* was a signal honour, not granted to anyone else except Tiberius. Augustus' debt to Agrippa was not a secret, and rewards were not lacking, but, significantly, Agrippa's name occurs in the *Res Gestae* only when it is necessary to acknowledge him as consul. Otherwise every achievement is credited solely to Augustus himself. Agrippa would have expected nothing else. His achievements earned him credit among those who knew him well, and he was content with that; glory was reserved for Caesar Augustus. Dio reports on Agrippa's opinion of his place in life; if it is an invented speech, it does at least fit the known facets of Agrippa's character. In a nutshell, he regarded himself as a facilitator, who eased the path for his master without exceeding the bounds of permissible glory for himself.[2]

The family of Gaius Maecenas hailed from Arretium. He was a member of the equestrian class, and according to Velleius was content to remain so. The high-flying senatorial career held no attractions for him; he was talented in other directions. Whenever he was called upon to take action, he displayed an almost sleepless energy and was capable of an intuitive foresight; equally, when there was occasion for it, his love of leisure and academic pursuits consumed him to the exclusion of all else. Though he was not a soldier, Maecenas was present at the battles of Mutina and Philippi, and from 40 onwards he was entrusted with a variety of diplomatic missions on Octavian's behalf without being endowed, or perhaps encumbered, with any form of office or magistracy. Though he played a great part in public life his exploits are less public than those of Agrippa, since for much of the time he either worked in the background or carried out confidential missions which have remained confidential. He attracted a circle of literary and scholarly writers, and used this influence in the cause of Augustus, but not just on the normal scale for the aggrandisement of one man; it was the entire state that was lauded and promoted via that one man. At some time before 23, Maecenas married Terentia, a sister of A. Terentius Varro Murena. He divorced her in 12, allegedly because of Augustus' overwhelming interest in her. It was thought for a long time that A. Terentius Varro Murena, consul designate for 23, was involved in a plot with Fannius Caepio to assassinate Augustus, but it seems certain now that the Varro Murena implicated in this mysterious affair was a different man, namely L. Licinius Varro Murena, who defended Marcus Primus and lost his case (see below, pp. 120–1). Some opprobrium may have fallen upon Maecenas because of his relationship to the family, but it is probably just inflated rumour. The scandal, whatever it may have been, was said to have destroyed his relationship with Augustus and brought about his fall from favour, but it has been argued recently that there was no quarrel at all, merely a change of roles whereby Maecenas set up the literary circle and its productions, and Augustus gradually took control of it himself, when he had time to pay attention to that side of political life. It is established that Maecenas withdrew from public life, though a specific date cannot be ascertained. After 23, he played little part in government, perhaps because his diplomacy and tact were no longer needed, or because he wished to enjoy life after the initial turmoil. He died in 8, four years after the death of Agrippa.[3]

Many other men served Augustus as well and as loyally as these two, but Agrippa and Maecenas were long-standing friends whose attachment developed very early, well before it became clear that by following in the wake of their friend Gaius Octavius, great-nephew of Gaius Julius Caesar, there might be substantial rewards to be picked up here and there. The loyalty of Agrippa and Maecenas was to the youth Octavius, not to his position or rank. Immediately after Caesar's death, there was no indication that Octavius rather than Antonius would be the eventual successor to the Dictator, so the creation of an entourage would require forethought and persuasion. Octavian used his time in Rome as Triumvir very well; in 37, when he met Antonius and Sextus Pompeius for negotiations, he brought with him Vergil, evicted from his ancestral home in Mantua because of the veteran settlements, and Horace, who had been on the losing side at Philippi. The literary circle was already forming; so too was the administrative and military community. The names of the various Augustan generals, legates and officials have come down to us from Appian, Dio, Suetonius, Tacitus and other sources, investigated and documented for modern readers by Sir Ronald Syme, whose line of enquiry about Augustus depicted the man himself through the medium of his contemporaries. Apart from his Caesarian connections, Octavian's circle was limited at first, not perhaps in numbers of personnel, nor even in wealthy individuals, but definitely limited in terms of noble power and influence. What was lacking until the first few years after Perusia was a senatorial faction such as the strong and influential alliances that Octavian had helped to destroy in the Triumviral proscriptions. His first attempt to ally himself to the leading families was not a success. He married Scribonia, who was related to Sextus Pompeius (she was the aunt of Sextus' wife). He married her in the hope that he would be able to use the connection to make peace with Sextus, and thereby create an alternative power bloc to counter the prestige and power of Antonius. Even if all he could achieve was to keep Pompeius and Antonius apart, it would be better than nothing. As an alliance, it served its purpose temporarily; as a marriage it was a disaster. Scribonia was much older than Octavian, almost old enough to be his mother; she had a son who was very nearly as old as Octavian. Though this sort of age gap need not prohibit a successful relationship, in this case the two were hardly compatible. When it became clear that war with Pompeius was no longer an option but a necessity, Octavian waited until the birth of his daughter Julia, and on that same day he divorced her mother. He had already met Livia Drusilla and allegedly fallen in love with her; the story is one of the few perceived truths about Augustus that survives unsullied from ancient times, accepted probably because of wishful thinking and sheer relief that he was susceptible to at least one human passion. He was quite undeterred by the fact that Livia was already married, the mother of one young son, and pregnant with her second child. Since she was very obviously pregnant, there could be no doubt about the paternity of the child, and this put few hindrances in the way of the divorce, to which the compliant husband Tiberius Claudius Nero readily agreed. Octavian married Livia with what has been termed indecent haste. Genuine affection was not a necessary feature of Roman marriages, but this match seems to have been one of the exceptions. It cannot be denied that the marriage was extremely advantageous to Octavian, so he would probably have gone ahead with it without the least trace of affection. It was a definite bonus that he liked her, but the prime consideration was the fact that Livia was well connected and through her Octavian began to attract leading men to his cause.[4]

Family connections, the importance of which cannot be overstressed, would not have sufficed by themselves to keep Octavian in the foremost ranks of society. The decade before Actium saw a gradual accretion of his powers by a combination of good fortune and an alert, optimistic attitude, which enabled Octavian to seize upon every strand of power and hold onto it with a limpet grasp once he had obtained it. He increased his territorial commands, and with them the size of his armies, until he was equal in strength to Antonius. Equality in military and political power was necessary for survival, but in a society that was interested only in supremacy that very equality invited rivalry and suspicion. After the Perusine war, Octavian was one among four contenders for power. Lepidus still counted for something; Sextus Pompeius was undoubted master of the seas, and Antonius controlled all the East with its resources immediately to hand. The political system could not accommodate all four of them indefinitely, even if they had been able to operate exclusively within their own domains, without encroaching in any way on the territory or preserves of the others.

There was mutual distrust on the one hand, as well as shared expedients on the other; if expediency ruled for the time being then there was the danger of coalition between any of the parties, which upset the balance. Ever watchful, Octavian concentrated first and foremost on surviving, while at the same time he took advantage of every opportunity to discredit and eventually remove the rivals who obstructed his rise to sole power. This is not to imply that he mapped out his course in advance and then engineered events to fall in with his plans, though with hindsight it probably seemed as though that was exactly how he progressed. This is the slant that Tacitus gives his account, under the guise of weighing the good and bad points of Octavian's metamorphosis into Augustus. Accusations of intent to establish one-man rule are permissible, provided that it is realised that as events fell into place Octavian adapted himself as he went along, and dealt with failures as well as successes. He utilised circumstances but did not control his fate. In the early days he did not possess sufficient influence to put a superhuman plan for supremacy into operation. Though he may all along have kept his eyes firmly on the distant goal of personal rule, he could not possibly have dictated the stages by which he intended to achieve it. He could probably have elbowed his way to a thinly veiled dictatorship very rapidly if he had so desired, but that went against common sense and would merely have served to attract enemies from all directions. Experience and precedent had proved that such a course would have been glorious but also brief. Besides, Octavian was much more subtle than that. Pompeius Magnus had shown how expedient it was to wait to be asked to save the state; Octavian turned it into an art form. He became expert at transferring the blame for any disturbance onto his opponents, while presenting himself as the innocent injured party. From his early attempts to come to some sort of understanding with Antonius and Sextus Pompeius he learned how to sway the people and the soldiers. He was not successful every time, but mistakes can teach as much if not more than successes. He was forced to succumb to popular pressure to make peace with his rivals on more than one occasion, and found that the soldiers would not always unquestioningly march with him against Antonius, because they did not necessarily view him as an enemy. When the time came, therefore, Octavian set about turning him into one, not directly, for that would have been too crude, but indirectly via Cleopatra. When war was finally declared, it was against her, a foreigner, who was represented as the greatest threat to Rome since Hannibal, a compliment, in its way, to Cleopatra's intelligence and importance. Antonius was the main rival, but he was a Roman and it would not be considered proper to target him as the enemy at first. He was included in the pre-war campaign by implication because of his association with Cleopatra. There is some doubt as to whether he had actually married her in 37, or whether he had merely participated in some kind of ceremony which could be construed as a marriage by the people of Egypt. If he had married her, then he had done so bigamously because he had not at that time divorced Octavian's sister Octavia; he had also committed an illegal act because marriage with aliens was forbidden by Roman law. The actual form of his association with Cleopatra is hardly important, compared to the use that Octavian was able to make of it. It looked like a marriage with a foreigner, and it looked especially threatening when Antonius acknowledged Cleopatra's children. The threat was of course to Octavian, but he managed to convert it into a threat to the supremacy and even the survival of the Roman people. This was the root of the matter. The marriage by itself was bad enough, but the strong hint of dynastic succession, combined with Cleopatra's supposedly insatiable desire for world domination, proclaimed disunity of the Roman world for generations to come. For the moment, the time was not quite ripe for Octavian to seize upon all this and magnify it without also appearing to think purely of his own interests. Antonius had done him no personal harm, and in Rome his standing as military commander and politician was undiminished. Apart from his potentially illegal and threatening marriage, it required a few years for Antonius to provide Octavian with enough material to use against him. But waiting was not a problem to Octavian. His maxim *festina lente*, make haste slowly, was applied to himself as rigorously as he applied it to his associates. He also used to say that a thing was done quickly enough that was done well enough. Patiently he bided his time until an insidious campaign of name-blackening, not to mention vilification, finally bore fruit. He exaggerated, elaborated, and distorted, but his stories retained an element of truth. Accusations of deceitfulness and outright lies have been made against him, but typically cannot be fully substantiated; his method was more usually to give his opponents an inch, wait for a suitable turn of events, and then on their behalf to take the proverbial yard himself. By the time he made war on his enemies he had usually brought about a situation where the people and the soldiers were practically begging him to do so. He did not always win battles, but he won wars. He did not enter into such things without due consideration, often saying that wars should not be undertaken unless the chance of gain outweighed the fear of loss, but once committed he was absolutely tenacious of his purpose. It took him three years to defeat Sextus Pompeius, and almost coincidentally he neutralised Lepidus at the same time, bloodlessly, but none the less decisively. Five years later it was the turn of Antonius. The battle of Actium, so important in modern histories as a terminus or a beginning, and both lauded and reviled in ancient literature as the birth of a new era, was actually something of a damp squib when it was fought. It was the preparation, long and thorough, focused and determined, which made it so decisive. Antonius was extinguished, and there was no one to take up his cause. Though Octavian's career was by no means smooth or easy after 31, he was in sole charge. It remains to examine how he arrived there.[5]

77

When Perusia fell, Lucius Antonius was allowed to go to Spain, where he was closely watched by Octavian's agents. He eventually died there, not inconveniently perhaps. Another convenient death, very soon after the fall of Perusia was that of Calenus, the governor of Gaul and one of Antonius' men. Octavian took control of the legions of Calenus' command on the pretext that he was simply taking care of Antonius' interests. The control of Gaul was a necessary adjunct to the control of Italy, and if he had learned nothing else from Caesar, Octavian could hardly have failed to absorb this fact. The importance of Gaul to his own command in Italy, coupled with the immediate placement of his own commanders in the legions of the unfortunate Calenus, rather gives the lie to his claim that he was concerned to protect Antonius' interests. He had at least one eye on his own ambitions and security, which seemed at this point to include strengthening himself against Antonius. He uprooted and sent to Antonius those men whom he distrusted, and dispatched Lepidus to Africa with six legions whose loyalties were suspect. Finally he placed Salvidienus in command of Gaul. On his return to Rome, the news was not encouraging. Antonius had allied with Sextus Pompeius and Domitius Ahenobarbus, who had collected a fleet after Philippi and played understudy to Sextus ever since. Not only had they allied, they were now besieging Brundisium, because the town had locked its gates against them. It mattered very little whether or not Octavian had ordered the town and garrison to do so; the hard fact was that it had happened and now another civil war seemed imminent. But the soldiers were tired and had little inclination to fight each other; war was averted by negotiation. Maecenas acted as envoy for Octavian, and Pollio fulfilled the same role for Antonius. The neutral L. Cocceius Nerva interceded on behalf of both Triumvirs. The resultant treaty of Brundisium, agreed in autumn 40, redivided the Roman world more or less in recognition of the status quo. Antonius held the Eastern provinces, and Octavian's portion was the West. His provinces encased Italy on both sides, Gaul and Spain on the West, and Dalmatia or Illyricum on the East. Marriage ties were proposed to bind the Triumvirs together. Fulvia had died suddenly in Greece, so now Antonius was free to marry. Octavian suggested that Antonius should be wed to his sister Octavia, and his suggestion was accepted. Pompeius was confirmed in his possession of Sicily, less from magnanimous motives than recognition of how difficult it would be to take it from him. He had hoped for more, perhaps to take the place of Lepidus in the Triumvirate, and his failure to gain anything became a sore point that festered for the next four years. Domitius Ahenobarbus was sent to govern Bithynia. The negotiations were rounded off with sumptuous feasting; Octavian entertained Antonius in Roman style, while Antonius entertained Octavian in Eastern fashion. The staunch adherence of Antonius to the East would have been noted by Octavian, and stored for later use. After the feasting the two journeyed to Rome, to meet with a joyous reception from the people.[6]

The Triumvirs attended to business. Connections with Caesar were reaffirmed. Antonius became *flamen divi Juli*, priest of the cult of the divine Julius, and as attested on an inscription, Octavian began to style himself *Imperator Caesar divi filius*, using *Imperator* as a *praenomen*. The earliest attested use of the title on the coinage is in 38, but Octavian may have begun to employ the name immediately after the treaty of Brundisium to underline the connection with Caesar. Cornelius Balbus was made consul, presumably as a reward for his unrecorded services to Octavian; it is not certain whether this was an *ad hoc* decision made from a position of strength, or whether his name had always been on Octavian's list of promotions for the year 40. Salvidienus was summoned from Gaul and executed, after Octavian had laid the case before the Senate and obtained the *senatus consultum ultimum*. The execution was thus legally sanctioned, but the crime and the charge remain obscure. The ancient sources declare that Salvidienus had been on the point of deserting to Antonius when it seemed certain that civil war was about to break out, and Antonius had informed Octavian as a demonstration of goodwill. But the fact was that Salvidienus had not mobilised, there had been no war and now the two main antagonists were reconciled. Salvidienus' crime perhaps had more serious undertones than that of a mere turncoat. He could have used his position in Gaul to deny the province to both Octavian and Antonius alike. Perhaps he had been acting a little too independently, and the Senate as a body would be very sensitive about independent commanders with armies in Gaul. Playing on this sensitivity, Octavian went to considerable lengths to arraign Salvidienus before the Senate, thus converting him from merely a personal enemy into an enemy of the entire state. Whether he was justified or not cannot be known, but he had made several statements in one by having Salvidienus properly tried and executed. He had managed to imply that the state was more important than the Triumvirs and their personal rivalries; that the Triumvirs would protect the state, and that in order to do so, they would not hesitate to punish any of their erstwhile friends who posed any sort of threat. It was very neat. Octavian replaced Salvidienus with Agrippa, whose exploits earned him real credit and the offer of a triumph, which he refused.[7]

The rejoicing in Rome was short lived, ending as soon as Sextus Pompeius began his blockade of Italy, deliberately disrupting the food supply. He was still supreme in the Mediterranean, and disappointment that he had not gained more from the treaty of Brundisium prompted him to show his strength in a series of raids on coastal towns. Popular pressure was brought to bear on Antonius and Octavian to put a stop to the blockade which threatened to cause famine in Rome. The food supply was always a sensitive issue, but never more so than now, when civil wars, the proscriptions and the disruptions resulting from the veteran settlements had all contributed to the destruction of Italian agriculture. Riots broke out. Octavian tried to calm the mob, and was stoned for his efforts. He bore it stoically, and Appian makes his hero Antonius responsible for rescuing Octavian by authorising the timely intervention of his troops. Since Octavian had no fleet and Antonius could contribute only a few ships, the only alternative at the moment was further negotiation with Pompeius. After an abortive attempt to reach agreement, the protagonists finally met in the summer of 39, and agreed upon the treaty of Misenum, the terms of which gave Pompeius control of Sardinia, Corsica and Sicily, with the promise that he would be given the Peloponnese at a later date, thus removing territories from both Octavian and Antonius. Most important, Pompeius was to guarantee Rome's corn supply, and was excluded from basing troops in Italy. As reward for his compliance he was admitted to the college of augurs, and he was to be consul in 38. The Triumvirs designated the consuls for 35 to 31, having already decided on those for 39 to 36. To mark their confidence and goodwill, they declared an amnesty for all those who had fled to Pompeius for refuge; the men who now returned to Rome would provide a fertile recruiting ground for Octavian's party. At the end of the negotiations, Pompeius entertained the two Triumvirs to dinner on board his flagship, nobly resisting the suggestion of his admiral Menas that it would be a good idea to cut the cables and sail away with two illustrious prisoners, and quietly dispose of them.[8]

Perhaps unaware that they had narrowly avoided such an untimely end, the Triumvirs went their separate ways. Antonius attended to the problems of the East, having taken care to have all his arrangements confirmed in advance by the Senate. He was probably mindful of the example of Pompeius Magnus, whose eminently sensible administrative arrangements for his Eastern conquests were debated out of existence and into futility. Octavian could have influenced the decisions of the Senate, so obviously Antonius was taking no chances with either of them. In Antonius' absence, Octavian used his position in Italy to great advantage, steadily building a faction, extending his influence and consolidating his power. Antonius may have had many agents acting on his behalf in Rome, but there was no substitute for being there in person, to react immediately to events and to monitor changing moods. It was Antonius' misfortune that he was absent, increasingly identified with things Eastern and non-Roman, and not brilliantly successful in his campaign against the Parthians. If he had won splendid victories, Octavian would have had to put a lot of effort into portraying Antonius as an enemy. As it was, while Antonius became increasingly Easternised, Octavian upheld Roman virtues and brought his wars to successful conclusions with the aid of his generals. Administration in Rome was theoretically in the hands of both Triumvirs. They were still concerned with appearances, but could only disguise very thinly the fact that they were using constitutional means to bring about unconstitutional results. In 39 they had all their acts ratified from their first day of power, so that any charge of illegality could be countered with the retrospective senatorial sanction of their deeds. Also in 39, according to Dio, more than two consuls were chosen for the first time, without the excuse that one or both consuls had died or been removed from office. In 38 no less than sixty-seven praetors held office. This would be an excellent method of rewarding men for their loyalties and services, granting them experience in administration and furthering their careers all at one stroke. It is speculated that some of these praetors, whose names are not known, would be proscribed men returning under the terms of the amnesty declared at the treaty of Misenum. More important, the advancement of their careers would be owed to Octavian, so that when the final break with Antonius occurred, they may not have had to think long and hard about where their loyalties lay.[9]

The treaty with Pompeius was almost a dead letter from the first day. War broke out again very soon, and occupied most of 38. Pompeius had not received the Peloponnese as had been promised, so it is possible to blame Antonius for the non-co-operation and therefore label him the true instigator of the war. This is quite unfair, because if Pompeius had really wanted the Peloponnese he could have gone there and fought for it, but he chose as an immediate and more effective alternative the usual blockade of Rome's food supply, prompting the usual riots in the city in response. Octavian began to act. He divorced Scribonia and married Livia on 17 January 38. Next he put into operation his plan to invade Sicily, striking at the heart of Pompeius' domains. The attack was to come from several sides at once, and theoretically stood every chance of success. Menas, Pompeius' admiral in command of Sardinia, had just deserted to Octavian, bringing three legions with him. He was placed under C. Calvisius who commanded one wing of the fleet, the other wing being under L. Cornificius. Unfortunately, Octavian proved no match for Pompeius, and was defeated in a battle off Cumae. Several ships were destroyed, and what made matters worse was the destruction of the surviving ships in a storm next day. His losses in the first skirmish were so heavy that Octavian was forced to ask Antonius for help. The latter was at Athens, with work of his own to attend to in the East, but he sailed to Brundisium as requested. When he arrived, Octavian was not there, so he did not wait, for which Octavian reproached him later. Antonius returned to Athens, where Maecenas pursued him to try to persuade him to meet Octavian. His entreaties were combined with those of Octavia, who seemed to have some influence over her husband at this stage. The meeting eventually took place at Tarentum in 37, probably in summer, though the exact date is not given in the ancient sources. The only clue is that it was too late for Antonius to begin the Parthian campaign by the time the negotiations were over, which would mean that the conclusion was reached anywhere between the late summer and the early autumn of 37. The terms of the agreement were favourable to Octavian. Antonius was to hand over to him 120 ships with their crews, in exchange for 20,000 soldiers which he needed for his forthcoming Parthian campaign; but in the end he never received them. The rest of the negotiations concerned the Triumvirate, which had officially expired on 31 December 38. Technically the Triumvirs had held power illegally since that date by virtue of their supreme military force, without even any pretence at a legal or constitutional infrastructure. This had not inconvenienced them nor diminished their authority, and so confident were they that they now renewed the Triumvirate for a further five years, seemingly without the immediate benefit of an appeal to the people or the formality of a *lex*. Octavian attended to this formality later on, observing the proper procedure by having a law passed which presumably retrospectively ratified the arrangement that the Triumvirs initially made by themselves, for themselves. The reality of the situation had an obvious part to play, and explains why the Triumvirs found it so relatively easy to remain in power. At the time of the meeting at Tarentum, Pompeius was strangling Rome, and Octavian was prepared to stop him; in the East Antonius was about to deal with the perceived threat from the Parthians. The concession which Octavian made to the law was to style himself, after 37, *Triumvir rei publicae constituendae iterum*; Antonius did not bother with this nicety. In the *Res Gestae* Augustus glossed over the little hiatus between 31 December 38 and the conference of 37, simply describing his term as Triumvir as ten consecutive years. It is the description 'consecutive' that causes the problems, leading to the assumption that the second term of the Triumvirate was back-dated to run from the expiry date of the first five-year term on 31 December 38, thereby establishing the new terminal date of the second five-year term as 31 December 33. There is some confusion over Appian's statement that the second five-year term did not expire until 32. It is a highly contentious issue, raising the question of Octavian's constitutional position in 32. If they had ceased to be Triumvirs at the end of 33, it is puzzling why Octavian and Antonius decided to be consuls in 31, thus leaving a gap of one year without legal sanction or any official position. The complications of the years 32–31 will be discussed below in their chronological context.[10]

While the conference at Tarentum was progressing, preparations for the next stage of the war against Pompeius had already begun when Agrippa returned from Gaul at the end of 38. He was consul designate for 37; that was perhaps sufficient honour to satisfy his ambition. Perhaps time was pressing as well. For several reasons he decided to forgo his triumph; the ancient sources declare that he had no wish to reflect badly upon the failures of Octavian. Agrippa set to work to build another fleet. He built an artificial harbour called Portus Julius by joining the Lucrine lake to lake Avernus, hitherto separated from each other by a narrow strip of land. He probably had to dredge the Lucrine lake to make it deep enough for shipping. There he trained the crews. Manpower was evidently a problem. Of these crews, 20,000 were slaves specially freed for the purpose of training them as rowers. It is firmly embedded in popular imagination, and reinforced by novels and films, that the rowers on the galleys were slaves, but this is erroneous. (Superlative film though it is, and eleven Oscars notwithstanding, *Ben Hur* has led people astray.) Agrippa planned with forethought; he is credited with the invention of the *harpax*, a grappling hook that could be used to haul enemy ships closer and thereby hold them and destroy them. The idea was not new, but it seems that Agrippa made certain innovations which improved on the original. His catapults could shoot the hooks for a much greater distance, and he managed to cover the ropes immediately behind the hooks with a protective wooden shield which prevented the enemy crews from cutting them away so easily. Meanwhile, as the crews tried to detach the hooks, Agrippa's men could winch the ships closer, and then board them. Shipbuilding and training went on all through 37 and the first half of 36. By the summer of that year, Octavian and Agrippa were ready. The plan of campaign was again centred on Sicily. Lepidus was brought into the attack this time; his task was to approach Sicily from the south with his legions from Africa. Statilius Taurus was to approach from Tarentum, and Octavian himself from Puteoli. The date chosen for the attack was 1 July, the month named after Caesar. Only Lepidus managed to gain a foothold in the island. A storm broke out on 3 July and drove Statilius Taurus back to Tarentum, and the same storm wrecked Octavian's ships. The damage was extensive and took a month to repair. While this was being done, Octavian toured the Italian colonies to engender support and recruit soldiers to his cause. Maecenas was sent to Rome to dispel fears that Sextus Pompeius was about to take over the city, evidently with the gods on his side, because they sent opportune storms to save him whenever he was under threat. In August Octavian resumed the offensive. It was hoped that he would be able to ferry his legions into Sicily while Agrippa held off Pompeius' fleet. Part of the plan worked, and three legions were eventually encamped on the island while Agrippa fought a naval battle off Mylae. It was not decisive. Pompeius withdrew, but then fell upon Octavian before he had managed to bring all his troops across the sea into Sicily. Octavian put Lucius Cornificius in command of the three legions that he had already landed on the island, and decided to engage Pompeius at sea. The result was the destruction once again of Octavian's ships, with potentially more disastrous consequences. Octavian only narrowly avoided death and reached the shore accompanied by a sole companion. It was probably the lowest moment of his career. He was physically exhausted, and morally dejected. He could not know that Agrippa was safe and sound, because he was forced to conclude that Pompeius' attack on his own ships meant that Agrippa had been defeated. He had no idea what had become of the three legions that he had deposited on the island, now that Pompeius was free to attack them too. It must have seemed that all was lost. Personal rescue came from the troops of M. Valerius Messalla Corvinus, who revived and looked after the young commander who had once placed his name on the proscription lists. From Messalla's camp, Octavian sent messages to Agrippa, and to L. Cornificius. The news was cheering; all was not lost, because these two commanders had joined up and taken Tyndaris, one of Pompeius' bases. The next stage was to attack other towns, especially Messana. Deprived of land bases Pompeius would have little choice left except to uproot himself and establish his operations elsewhere, or risk everything on a naval battle, which up to now he had always won. This was what he did, and he came to grief at the battle of Naulochus in September 36. His ships were sunk, burnt or wrecked. He fled to Antonius, but instead of following a direct course he also sold his services to the Parthians, rendering himself suspect to all Romans, especially Antonius, whose sympathies were not likely to lie with anyone who made common cause with his main Eastern enemy. Any chances of future negotiations were thus blocked for Pompeius, who was eventually killed, either on the orders of Antonius himself or of Antonius' legate Plancus.[11]

After Pompeius fled, peace was at hand for Octavian, but it was not achieved before a slight hiccup in Sicily. When Messana surrendered, Lepidus asserted himself, accepting the surrender in his own name without waiting for the arrival of Octavian. This action and his subsequent demeanour strongly indicated that he was aiming at the domination of Sicily if nothing more, and he obviously thought that command of twenty legions would guarantee his success. When Octavian did arrive, Lepidus dictated terms – namely, that he should go away again and leave the island for good. It was ill-advised. The soldiers would not fight, mostly because they saw no end to the battles and there was no promise of huge rewards when one Roman commander set himself against another. Most likely they had been well and truly briefed by Octavian's agents. At any rate they deserted Lepidus and all that Octavian had to do was to sit and wait. After a suitable interval he walked into Lepidus' camp, where he was greeted by the spectacle of his Triumviral colleague begging for mercy. Octavian was merciful, and sent Lepidus back to Italy, his power broken for ever. Lepidus' Triumviral powers were formally abrogated, but he was left in office as Pontifex Maximus. For the rest of his life he was kept under virtual house arrest. The punishment fitted Octavian's judgement of Lepidus. Had there been anything to fear, Octavian would have executed him, finding some way of doing so with legal backing, just as he had found a way of ridding himself of Salvidienus. The next problem, immediately consequent upon the first, was a near mutiny of the troops in Sicily. There were more than forty legions encamped on the island, all eager for discharge or some tangible reward for their share in the victory. According to Appian it was Octavian's troops who were most troublesome, but this need not be a sinister development, indicating a sudden withdrawal of loyalty or sympathy. It was natural that the soldiers who were the most ardent in his support should now seek from him some especial mark of favour. Octavian promised to reward everyone commensurately with their share in his victories. Of those who had fought with him from the beginning at Mutina, Philippi, and Naulochus, he released 20,000 men immediately and sent them back to Italy. The centurions were granted the status of town councillors in their home towns, and the right to wear purple-bordered cloaks. Appian includes the story of the rebellious centurion Ofillius, who dared to argue with Octavian and then permanently disappeared. The sinister disappearance brought everyone into line. For the men who would promise to stay with him, Octavian hinted at monetary rewards and the prospect of great wealth in the coming foreign wars in Illyricum, where fractious tribes were causing trouble. Lastly he purged the army of slaves and undesirables, restoring runaways to their owners and executing all those slaves whom nobody claimed. It was cruel but necessary. No one would follow a man who was lax about this sort of thing; rank and distinction had to be preserved after all.[12]

The Senate and the people of Rome welcomed Octavian as a hero, ready to shower him with honours. The most important and also most controversial is the award of tribunician power. There is confusion in the sources, none of which give exactly the same information. Debate centres on whether Octavian was endowed with full tribunician power at this moment or whether he was simply granted the personal sacrosanctity of a tribune and the right to sit on the tribunes' bench at meetings. Octavian himself counted his tribunician years from 23, which seems to support the argument that he received the full *tribunicia potestas* only then, implying that he could not have possessed all the attributes of tribunician power from the beginning. Dio complicates the issue by making three entries under this heading; according to him, Octavian was granted only the sacrosanctity of a tribune in 36, full power in 30, and then again in 23, which leads to all sorts of theories that Octavian either refused one of the offers, or accepted it and laid it down again before finally adopting it in 23. It is unlikely that he was granted full tribunician power in 36; if he had possessed such power then it is strange that he did not count his tribunician years from that date, and it is quite improbable that having been offered such a useful tool at some time before 23 he would have refused it. He could never guarantee that it would be offered again without a great deal of background coercion. The other alternative that has been suggested – namely that he accepted it, relinquished it, and accepted it again – relinquished it, and accepted it again – would have been equally uncharacteristic. It may be that Dio was trying to say that Octavian achieved full tribunician power by gradual stages, for which the details have been lost; such a process would have been more characteristic of Octavian's approach to such matters. For the time being, honours were abundant and were probably quite sufficient for his purpose. Agrippa was not forgotten, being the first Roman, according to Velleius, to be awarded the *corona classica* or *navalis*, a golden crown with representations of ships' beaks incorporated into its design. Octavian was granted the right to wear a laurel wreath, which he used to advantage by depicting himself on the coinage adorned with a wreath. The comparison with Julius Caesar would have been quite clear. In an attempt to please him the people voted death to Lepidus, but Octavian refused. It would have invited all kinds of retribution to execute the Pontifex Maximus in cold blood. The time for that had passed when Octavian allowed Lepidus to return to Italy. If he had so wished at that juncture he could have divested Lepidus of his priestly office and then used the will of the people as a valid excuse to rid himself of a potential troublemaker. There was no need for such drastic measures. He had already made the judgement that all he had to do was watch Lepidus closely. It was a good beginning to be acknowledged as merciful, and it went some way towards wiping out the memory of his appearance in Rome as Triumvir at the end of 43. The importance of Octavian's victory over Pompeius cannot be too strongly emphasised; it brought him tremendous credit, especially for the way in which he had absolutely refused to be beaten, returning to the task again and again, grimly determined, until he won. Even more important, it was successfully presented as a corporate victory, won on behalf of the people, not a personal vendetta to eliminate an enemy who stood in his way. Thus far Octavian could avoid the charge that he was intent on establishing dictatorial autocratic rule. The food supply was secured, and the special taxes, levied by various means to fund the war, could at last be rescinded. All Octavian's actions after Naulochus were positive, and for the good of all. He did not confine his plans to the city of Rome, but embraced all Italy in his schemes; during the next few years he put into operation what can only be described as a proactive welfare programme. While the finer details were worked out over a protracted period of time, it is highly likely that the broad general outline was established after Naulochus, taking the long-term view. It would not have been difficult to pinpoint the areas where improvements were desperately needed. All that was required was time and personnel, sometimes employed quite unconventionally, for instance when Agrippa, who had already reached the consulship in 37, became aedile in 33, and began to overhaul Rome's water supply, sewage system and other public works. In Italy, agriculture had suffered dreadfully in the civil wars and during the settlements of the veterans. The devastation was noted in contemporary literature, for example in Vergil's *First Eclogue*, and in the *Georgics*, where the uncompromising portrayal of the bleak and suffering countryside has been interpreted as evidence that since Octavian did nothing to suppress such information and comment he had clearly opted for a free style of patronage rather than a stultifyingly restricted control of poets and writers. His policy was more likely the result of common sense. The state of Italian agriculture simply could not be ignored. To control writers in such a way as to make light of the problem would have been ludicrous and would have caused a complete dearth of confidence in Octavian. In allowing or even encouraging Vergil to describe the countryside as it really was, in his own terms, was one way of acknowledging the problem quite openly, with the unspoken implication that since he knew all about it the young Caesar intended to make amends.[13]

The land settlements for the veterans after Naulochus involved little dispossession of existing farmers, since the acquisition of land was made as far as possible by cash purchase, instead of by enforced evictions. Dio asserts that public land was used where available, and it quite possible that farms given to soldiers in the earlier settlements were now vacant again. Some men were sent to Gaul and settled there. This time Italy was to be treated with more care, and that care was to be demonstrated ostentatiously, not only in the matter of veteran settlement but also in terms of general welfare. Octavian sent Sabinus to deal with the brigands who had grown powerful and dangerous in Italy during the unrest of the past few years. Within twelve months it was safe to travel again, so successfully did Sabinus eradicate the problem. Thus the food supply, protection of property, and personal safety were unequivocally taken under Octavian's wing. It remained to give some attention to the ruling classes, to integrate them into the scheme of things. Administration of public affairs was now partially restored to the magistrates, with the promise that the Republic would be fully restored when Antonius came home from the East. The positive side to this promise veiled the negative aspect, which was that Octavian did not intend to relinquish his accumulated political and military influence while Antonius still held power in the East. But for the purposes of public relations, it seemed as though Octavian was merely unwilling to act alone, without deference to his colleague. The status quo could be prolonged on this basis, and the onus for bringing it all to a successful and peaceful conclusion rested with Antonius. Octavian's accommodating attitude was meanwhile underlined by his decree that all documents relating to the period of the proscriptions were to be burned or otherwise destroyed, to demonstrate the fact that there was to be an end to civil wars, heralding a splendid new beginning, full of hope. It was permissible to draw a line and start again. Even so, at the end of 36 Octavian cannot have felt that peace would be universal and long-lasting. Foreign wars there would be in any number, but that was acceptable for Romans. What was not acceptable in 36 was the slightest hint that there might be a struggle to the death with Antonius, who had on each occasion helped Octavian when asked to do so, and who was trying to establish Roman supremacy over the Parthians by making war on them, carrying out the task that Caesar had set himself in 44. The time was not yet ripe to call Antonius an enemy, so there was no choice but to call him friend, and celebrate the end of civil war.[14]

Foreign wars being eminently welcome to Romans, both Antonius and Octavian waged war outside Italy, for a variety of reasons and with varying degrees of success. Octavian's track record as a general had been less than spectacular; he required some measure of *kudos* to match that of Antonius, whose military reputation and ascendancy were still very strong. Octavian chose well. The Roman province of Illyricum, not yet properly pacified, would provide an excellent theatre of war for his troops (see Figure 4.1). If the sources are to be believed, he had already planned for this war before he had tidied up after the victory over Pompeius. One of the methods by which he quelled the mutiny in Sicily was to promise rich rewards in Illyricum for any soldiers who would remain with him. It has been pointed out that this was pure charlatanism, shamelessly employed to induce the soldiers to follow him; Illyricum was not the place to find rich rewards, at least not in the modern sense. Perhaps soldiers of the first century BC had a different conception from ours of what was to be classified as a rich reward. Politically and strategically, Illyricum was ripe for attention. It lay across the road to Macedonia, which route it was vital to secure, and there was the advantage that the inhabitants could be represented as a threat to Italy. Some time ago they had attacked Tergeste (modern Trieste). They had defeated Gabinius in his campaigns of 48–47, and had captured some standards, so there was a revenge motive as well. Apart from that, there was really no excuse for the war, as Dio rightly commented. It is not difficult to discern the real reason for making war in Illyricum. Under the guise of attending to the welfare of Italy, Octavian could keep his army together, training the men via the experience they would gain in rugged terrain against an expendable army. By employing his troops in this way he absolved himself of the necessity of discharging them, thus avoiding the risk of converting them into veterans who needed land. By removing them from Italy he did not need to worry about unemployed and troublesome soldiers, profitlessly idling their time away, fomenting discontent, harrassing the citizens, and eating the vital food supplies that he had just secured for the people of Rome. Attempts have been made by modern authors to imbue these Illyrian campaigns with a grand strategic design. It has been postulated that the master plan was to secure Roman domination up to the Danube, or alternatively that Octavian wished to block any projected invasion by Antonius via the land route into Italy, or even that he desired to secure the route because he planned to launch an invasion southwards against Antonius. These considerations are not relevant to Octavian's immediate purpose. He needed somewhere to base himself and his army, not too far from Italy, where it was not too difficult to wage war but difficult enough to enable him to emerge with the appearance of a successful general. Provided that he did not meet with total disaster, the results of the wars were not of extreme importance. He gained no territory, but that did not matter. In 35 he moved against the Iapodes and besieged their stronghold of Metulum on the river Colapis (Kolpa or Kulpe). At one point during the siege the soldiers wavered in crossing a bridge, or as some sources have it, a ramp from a siege tower. Octavian tried to rally them, but the structure collapsed

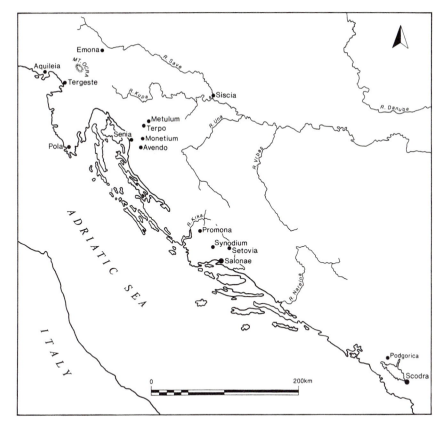

Figure 4.1 Octavian's campaigns in Illyricum

and he was injured, fortunately not too seriously. The demonstration of courage could yield nothing but good results, binding the army more closely to him and enhancing his reputation as a general. Next he destroyed Segesta (modern Siscia, or Sisak, south-east of Zagreb) at the point where the Kolpa joins the Save. He returned to Rome, intent on pressing forward during the following year, but in 34 he turned aside and attacked the Dalmatae, or Delmatae, destroying the strongholds of Promona and then Synodium, appropriately for Roman ideals of revenge, for this was near the place where Gabinius had been defeated. At the beginning of the year 33, Octavian returned once more to Rome to take up his second consulship, which he laid down immediately in order to attend to the war. In the spring the Dalmatae surrendered, along with other tribes. The war was over, and Octavian's reputation much improved. His capacity for self-advertisement had not abated. He had impressed the army by his conspicuous personal bravery; he had been wounded twice, eradicating the suspicion that he was always ill at crucial moments, perhaps by design to avoid sharing in the hardships of the troops. Not as celebrated as Caesar, he was none the less a fully fledged leader of soldiers. At home it remained to impress the senators and the people. He read out an account of his achievements in the Senate, including for greater effect a long list of tribes that he had conquered. He brought back the rescued standards that Gabinius had lost, and housed them with appropriate ceremony in the newly built Porticus Octavia, which was only one of the buildings which he and his associates had already begun in order to beautify and embellish Rome. So much for the Roman people. On a personal note he postponed the triumph that was voted to him, displaying a suitable modesty, but he was not so modest that he could afford to acknowledge the contributions of Agrippa, active in Illyricum from 35 to 34, or of Statilius Taurus, who took over from 34 until 33. Acknowledgement was reserved for a later time when Octavian had become Augustus and was secure in his sole rule. For the time being, rewards came in a different form. Taurus had been granted a triumph over Africa in 34, before being appointed to his command in Illyricum, and Agrippa's position was already assured as second man in Rome. He never sought tangible proofs of Octavian's approval, content to remain chief assistant. The Illyrian victories were earmarked as Octavian's own, at a time when he needed to stand out. He made little enough of them in the *Res Gestae* because by the time he wrote of his achievements these wars had receded into the background, overshadowed by more momentous events. In his earlier *Memoirs* he devoted much more attention to them. Appian used this work to produce his account of the wars, so the details come down to us at second hand, but derived from Augustus' own words.[15]

Antonius' great project was the invasion of Parthia, for which he had been preparing for some time, interrupted by Octavian's demands for assistance. His military preparations were accompanied by a necessary preliminary overhaul of the administration of the entire East, which he carried out over a prolonged period from 39 to 36. He divided the area into a series of client kingdoms ruled by men who were well disposed towards Rome. His administrative arrangements were undertaken with care and good sense, so that when Octavian finally emerged supreme he made adjustments and fine tunings, but did not find it necessary to make very many radical alterations, retaining most of the new territorial boundaries that Antonius had redrawn and confirming many of the new kings and princes in their powers. While Antonius made all his political preparations, in 38 Ventidius fought with great success against Pacorus, the son of the king of Parthia. He had attacked Syria, so Ventidius' campaign was fought with right on the Roman side. He was granted a triumph as reward. Thereafter the Antonian generals Sosius in Syria and Canidius in Armenia maintained the status quo. The foundations for the Parthian campaign were well laid, but the campaign itself was not the resounding success that Antonius had dreamed of. It began very promisingly in the spring of 36, while Octavian and Agrippa were still training their crews and preparing for the resumption of hostilities against Sextus Pompeius. At this point Antonius could afford to rest on his laurels, his reputation intact, his plans well made, and his army loyal. His timing was impeccable. A considerable schism had arisen in the Parthian court, where the new ruler Phraates had killed off all his relatives and divided the nobility, some of whom rebelled against him. There could be no more propitious time for a Roman offensive. Unexpectedly, success eluded Antonius for several reasons. He advanced too quickly, attempted a siege which he was forced to abandon, and in the ensuing retreat he lost a great part of his army. His qualities as a commander, resourceful and energetic in adversity, were never more in evidence, but such qualities, commendable though they were, could in no way substitute for victory, endless booty and the return of the standards lost by Crassus. The details of the Parthian campaign belong to the history of Antonius rather than to the history of Augustus, who eventually achieved by patient diplomacy what Antonius had failed to achieve by armed invasion. When Antonius reached safety he summoned Cleopatra to his aid; it is to her credit that she set sail in winter, regardless of the risks, to meet the tattered remnants of the Roman army, bringing with her vital supplies of food and clothing. For the next two years (35–34) Antonius turned his attention to Armenia, always the buffer between Parthia and Rome. Without a battle, Antonius seized King Artavasdes and imprisoned him, then occupied the whole country and issued commemorative coins with the proud legend *Armenia devicta*, to indicate that he had conquered the land. Octavian put it about that this victory was nothing but a sham, dishonourable and discreditable to Rome. He would probably not have achieved very much by this political slander if that had been where it all ended, but Antonius compounded his own situation at the end of 34 by holding a victory parade which so resembled a Roman triumph that he seemed to be making a mockery of it. This had sacrilegious undertones, because all spoils of victory were traditionally to be rendered as an offering to Jupiter Optimus Maximus on the Capitol Hill in Rome, and here was a Roman general masquerading as the new Dionysus, rendering them instead to foreign gods in a foreign country. Worse still, either at the same time as his parade or shortly afterwards, Antonius disposed of various territories (which were not indisputably his to distribute) as gifts to Cleopatra and her children in a ceremony which became known as the Donations of Alexandria. Cleopatra was to rule over Egypt, Cyprus and Coele Syria, and Caesarion, her son by Caesar, was now declared *rex regum*, king of kings, and recognised as heir to Julius Caesar. The children of Antonius and Cleopatra were to divide between them Libya, Cyrene, Phoenicia, Syria, Cilicia, and Armenia. To this list was added Media and Parthia, a slightly presumptuous addition since neither territory was yet conquered. There is some doubt as to the immediate effect of these measures in Rome. Defenders of Antonius declare that there was hardly a ripple, until Octavian stirred up the opposition for his own personal gratification, to justify his campaign against Antonius.[16]

There will probably never be any decisive proof that Antonius and Cleopatra entertained the huge ambitions for world domination that have been attributed to them. They have their defenders and slanderers, neither of which opposing factions can be entirely vindicated in their beliefs. History must be content with what finally happened, relegating motives and what-might-have-been to the background. A vexed question, quite apart from what motivated all the central characters, is the extent to which Octavian shaped the contemporary view of the events preceding and following the battle of Actium and the fall of Alexandria, and how much of our perception of the whole is the product of a post-Actian justificatory rewriting process. Cleopatra definitely had the interests of Egypt and its dependent territories in mind, but how far she intended to extend her influence is unknown. Her proprietorial interests in the Near East stretched at least as far as the lucrative commercial activities of Judaea and Arabia, where she took over certain productive areas with profitable businesses, and then magnanimously leased them back to the rulers, Herod and Malchus, who had been installed by Antonius. Some credit is due to Antonius for the fact that he did not relinquish control of the entire Eastern world to Cleopatra, however infatuated he may have been with her; he still kept a stern Roman head on his shoulders. It is not possible to state categorically whether or not Cleopatra ever uttered the words that she was reputedly fond of repeating: 'When I dispense justice on the Capitol'. Her ultimate design may or may not have been to dominate the whole Roman world, but that is the reputation that Octavian built up for her, based on actions of hers and of Antonius' that played into his hands. The behaviour of both Antonius and Cleopatra would plausibly bear the interpretation that Octavian put upon it, and the cumulative effect, accrued over a period of time and culminating in 32, allowed Octavian to portray not only himself but also Rome as the injured party. His real design was to remove Antonius, but by going off at a tangent and targeting Cleopatra he could stir up Roman emotion more effectively. For a while the war of words and emotions remained on the personal level. Antonius' treatment of the worthy and blameless Octavia gained much sympathy for Octavian. In 35, he sent his wronged sister to Antonius with 2,000 soldiers (far short of the total of 20,000 that had been promised), but Antonius repudiated his wife and sent her home. He did not finally divorce her until 32, but the delay only counted against him, especially since Octavia herself refused to divorce him, despite the excellent grounds he had given her. Accused of immoral behaviour, Antonius wrote the famous letter to Octavian, reported by Suetonius, the gist of which was that both of them were free to associate with any woman they liked, including Cleopatra, because after all sex was only sex and meant nothing, and moreover Octavian was not as virtuous in this department of life as he claimed. Personal abuse of this sort was standard practice; perhaps Antonius thought that this was as far as it needed to go, forgetting, or perhaps never realising, that he was dealing with an unscrupulous, devious, clever and ambitious politician. Perhaps he thought his position in the East secure and quite unassailable. Perhaps he simply underestimated Octavian's strengths. His agents presumably informed him of the change of direction of politics at Rome, if indeed such a change was detectable. It may be that historians have sought to push too far back in the retrospective search for the degeneration of relations between Antonius and Octavian. It has been pointed out that in 33 when he ought to have been feverishly preparing for war, Antonius had not even begun to move his legions from their positions in the East, and that he seemed to have no intention of fighting Octavian. It is said that at the beginning of 33 when he took up his consulship Octavian made a virulent speech against Antonius, but at least one author has relegated this speech to the beginning of 32, and it may be that Octavian, who was concentrating on ending the war in Illyricum and then on his civic regeneration programme all through 33, had not yet fully revealed his hand. Antonius may not have been as undiscerning as he has been judged; there may have been little to discern.[17]

Octavian's position in 33 gained strength every day. At the end of the wars in Illyricum, he was the hero of the people and Senate. He was granted a triumph which he stored up for use in the future. He had built up a coterie of generals who had held triumphs over Africa and Spain, though the number of generals who 'triumphed' over Spain only serves to emphasise the difficulties of subduing that country. Octavian and his victorious generals then went on to beautify Rome, restoring old buildings or erecting new ones, in most cases temples to the gods or public amenities that benefited the populace. According to Velleius Paterculus, Octavian directed this building work by dropping unmistakable hints to his generals, so the embellishment of Rome was not so spontaneous nor so voluntary as it sounds. Agrippa arranged entertainments for the people, showered them with free gifts, and provided them with baths. As praetor, he had gained some experience in the technicalities of water supply, and all through 33 as aedile he continued his sterling work, not only repairing sewers and aqueducts but more importantly setting up maintenance schemes to ensure that his extensive work would never be needed on such a scale again. Rome had stopped living hand to mouth, not only in the nutritional sense but in most aspects of life. There was now someone in charge who saw further ahead than the traditional but truncated annual offices held in Rome, which hampered rather than facilitated the kind of continuity that Octavian tried to foster. There had never been any such corporate, closely administered schemes for building and repair works, supervision of the provinces, security of the individual and property. Piecemeal government had given way to planned, co-ordinated, all-embracing influence. It would never fully return to the old order of things, and yet there was no sharp break with tradition. Octavian was careful to regenerate old Roman virtues and customs, to appeal to the old gods, to reaffirm *Romanitas*. On this foundation, in the crucial year 32, he was ready to begin hostilities with Antonius. The consuls for 32 were the two Antonians, Gaius Sosius and Domitius Ahenobarbus. Against this potential opposition, Octavian's arsenal was perhaps merely psychological rather than physical; his political status is the source of endless debate. The terminal date of the Triumvirate is not established beyond doubt, though the balance of scholarly opinion tilts in favour of an expiry date of 31 December 33. This poses an immediate problem in assessing Octavian's political and legal position in 32. There is no explicit elucidation in any of the ancient sources. There are several options. It has been argued that Octavian was still Triumvir because the second five-year term of the Triumvirate had been dated from the beginning of 36, and did not therefore expire until the end of 32. For this there is not the slightest proof. Alternatively it has been suggested that the actual date was quite irrelevant, since Octavian was *de facto* Triumvir and remained so until he abdicated formally. Thirdly, there are those who believe that in 32 the Triumvirate was a dead letter and Octavian was thrown on his own resources. It is quite likely that even contemporaries were not sure of the details. In any case legality had in some measure yielded to power and influence, which Octavian had steadily built up via his naval and military successes, the elimination of his immediate rivals, and the active building schemes and public works in Rome. In the city and in Italy it is likely that he had no official powers whatsoever; outside Italy he still held his proconsular *imperium* over Gaul, Spain, Africa, Sicily and Sardinia. His provincial commands did not cease with the Triumvirate, and as commander of several provinces with large numbers of troops at his disposal he could have browbeaten the Senate and people into obeying his every whim, confident that few people would be inclined to argue with him. But those days were over. Octavian needed another prop besides his armies and naked military force, which throws into sharp relief the oath of loyalty to himself (described below, pp. 96–7) sworn by the peoples of Italy and the Western provinces. The oath did not confer any legal powers or definite status upon him, but it gave him a firm social and psychological basis for his future actions.[18]

All that has survived is some notification of what happened. It was said that the consuls had received a despatch from Antonius, which they suppressed. In this document, Antonius allegedly asked for ratification of his acts, which he did not require, since he had extracted legal sanction from the Senate and made himself secure well in advance before he began his Parthian campaigns. But that was not all, for the document contained details of the Donations of Alexandria and the disposal of territories in favour of Cleopatra and her children, which the consuls thought too damaging to reveal. The tale should be treated with a grain of suspicion. On 1 January Sosius made a speech denouncing Octavian, proposing something that the tribune Nonius Balbus vetoed. The problem is that it is not known what it was that he vetoed. It is likely that Sosius demanded the instantaneous resignation of Octavian and the renunciation of all his powers. No one knows what was proposed, nor whose interests were served by the tribune's veto. It may be that Octavian kept Nonius Balbus close to hand to protect his position should need arise, or, alternatively, Sosius may have primed the tribune to extricate him from a tricky situation should everything start to go wrong. Octavian was not in the city at the time; he returned a few days later in spectacular fashion, entered the Senate with an armed guard, and sat between the two consuls to emphasise his determination and strength. He declared that Antonius should come to Rome, and lay down his powers formally; an offer that was not capable of fulfilment and clearly not meant to be taken seriously, except as metaphorical chest beating and a delaying tactic on the part of Octavian. Considerable orchestration no doubt went into this, not without some risks. Success was by no means assured, and failure at this point would have involved Octavian in further dubious activities just to stay alive, but since his plan worked, and the consuls took fright and fled to Antonius, the illegal nature or otherwise of his venture could be conveniently forgotten. Polarisation was now complete. Everyone who wished to go to Antonius was allowed to do so; it is estimated that 300 senators fled, but this figure is nowhere firmly attested. It derives from the assumption that there were about 1,000 senators in total, and then depends upon the subtraction of the 700 that Augustus said remained loyal to him. Reciprocally, Antonians who began to imagine themselves better off elsewhere than with Antonius now came to Rome. Two of these men, Titius and Plancus, are said to have revealed to Octavian the whereabouts of Antonius' last will and testament, which they had witnessed. Dio says that they gave to Octavian the name of the man who held it; tradition says that the will was lodged with the Vestals, which would be the more normal arrangement. Wherever it was, Octavian obtained it, and read it out in the Senate. He calculated very finely, confident no doubt that his own shocking display of unscrupulous behaviour would fortunately be obliterated by the even more shocking sentiments in Antonius' will. Octavian has been accused by modern authors of fabricating the whole or parts of the will. He opened it in complete privacy, and may have forged sections of it, but this is to ignore the practicalities of doing so. If the conjecture is true, then he did so very plausibly, building on Antonius' known character and deeds. But there was probably no need to fabricate anything. He probably had only to rehearse and put on a good performance in the Senate. The emphasis was on Antonius' connections with the East, and by implication with Cleopatra. The final ignominious clause was that Antonius wished to be buried in Alexandria. It seemed that another Empire was growing in the East, dominated by Cleopatra, doubly distasteful to the Romans because she was both foreign and female. War was declared against her. Octavian unearthed some venerable ancient ritual that involved casting a spear into a patch of land that substituted for enemy territory, thus making visible and thereby inevitable the intention of the Romans to make war on their enemy. Antonius was not declared *hostis* at this time, but the formality was quite superfluous. Octavian had achieved what he wanted.[19]

A year went by before the battle of Actium was fought on 2 September 31. Octavian put the year to good use. He dropped the title Triumvir, whereas Antonius continued to use it until his death. Such a blatant demonstration of power was not appropriate for Octavian. He had to persuade the ruling class and the populace that not only did he intend no harm, but that he was acting positively on their behalf, with their best interests always at heart. The Senate backed him in the declaration of war against Cleopatra, but senatorial backing did not by itself raise, clothe, feed, and train armies. New taxes were necessary. Riots ensued. Octavian retaliated before sympathies for his cause dissipated and dwindled. He took the extraordinary step of administering an oath in all parts of the Roman world under his dominion. Exact chronology now evades elucidation. Dio relates the reading of Antonius' will, the declaration of war against Cleopatra, and then the taking of the oath to Octavian. Cautious as Octavian usually was, it is possible that he took the precaution of bolstering himself up by means of the oath before he began to stir up the Senate and people against Antonius. This is the chronology that Syme preferred, but it is not established beyond doubt, and it has even been suggested that the oath belongs to a period of retrospective self-justification *after* Actium. The oath was one of loyalty to Octavian as leader of the 'crusade' against Cleopatra. The actual text is lost. It may be that this oath evolved into the regular oath of allegiance to each of the Emperors on his accession, taken by the whole populace, including senators, equestrians, civilians and soldiers. In 32 the most useful precedent was the military oath sworn by soldiers to their commanders, so it is likely that the form of words in the oath to Octavian resembled this more regular formula. Whatever the words or form of address, Antonius' clients were absolved; for instance, the whole town of Bononia where Antonius had many partisans was not coerced, and was held up as an example of Octavian's fair treatment. Many years later Augustus described it thus: 'All Italy swore an oath of allegiance to me of its own free will (*sponte sua*) and chose me as the leader in the war in which I won at Actium.' The description 'of its own free will' perhaps requires some slight modification; Suetonius was sceptical about it. However it was engineered, and whenever it was administered, it gave Octavian moral support for the war. He divested Antonius of all powers, and usurped his place as consular colleague for 31 by substituting Valerius Messalla, who had rescued him when he was ship-wrecked in the naval war against Pompeius.[20]

In the East, Antonius bestirred himself. He wintered in Greece, where he defended the coasts by stretching out along them most of his legions under the command of Canidius. His main strength was in his naval forces, so he seems to have placed all his reliance upon a decisive naval battle. But his old vigour had gone; no wonder that men said he had been bewitched by Cleopatra. He had manoeuvred himself into a predicament where he was forced to defend a long coastline with too many landing places, and he failed to prevent Agrippa from taking Methone. Octavian occupied Corcyra almost unopposed. Antonius did little to retain command of his lines of communication, and when Octavian moved to the peninsula of Actium (see Figure 4.2), he followed but achieved nothing, except to make an unsuccessful attempt to blockade him. Sosius risked a naval encounter with Agrippa and lost. The surviving record is very brief, much too obscure to retrieve the details of a campaign that occupied several months, but ultimately it is certain that all the odds were stacked against Antonius when he failed to achieve anything very rapidly against Octavian. It was all or nothing, instantaneously, and Antonius lost by his delay. In the ensuing stalemate, desertions began. Antonius' forces were never totally united, especially since the presence of Cleopatra was bitterly contested, and Antonius stubbornly refused to send her away. When he finally decided to fight it was noted that he ordered the crews to carry sails, which he said were necessary in case he had to pursue a fleeing enemy, but in view of his subsequent action in leaving the scene of the battle it is easy to accuse him of planning to run away. Without putting up too much of a fight, he and Cleopatra broke away from the fleet and sailed back to Alexandria, accompanied by about forty ships. They left the rest of their fleet to the mercy of Octavian. There was no heroic, hard fought battle, but there was an undeniably complete victory. The two principal enemies were still at large, but that hardly mattered because most of their troops had deserted them. Unlike Caesar after Pharsalus, Octavian could afford to be more leisurely in his approach to Alexandria. He intended to spend the winter on the island of Samos, but was forced to return to Italy, in response to the entreaties of Agrippa and Maecenas, who had been sent on ahead. Octavian arrived at Brundisium to find that most of Rome had come to meet him there, which was a tremendous honour; only two praetors and the tribunes had remained behind to deal with day-to-day administration. The problems that Maecenas and Agrippa had been unable to solve concerned the veterans, who were restless and potentially troublesome. Peace in Italy had been hard won and Octavian could not afford to have it disturbed. Rewards or occupations, or both, had to be found for the soldiers. Octavian adopted several measures at the same time. He pensioned off some of the men, settled some of them on land allotments, or sent them to new campaigns. He sold his

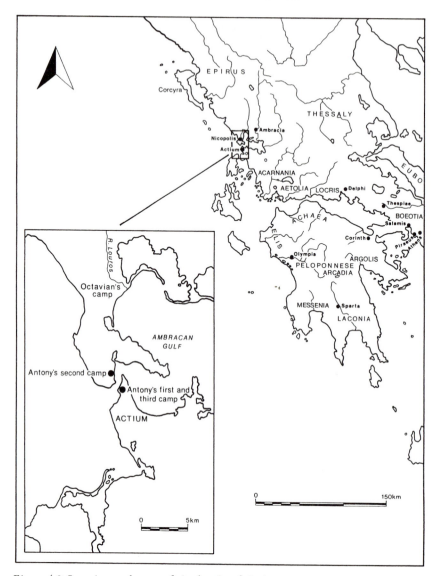

Figure 4.2 Location and map of the battle of Actium

own property to raise the money to pay them or to buy land for them, a ploy which earned him considerable credit. He was soon able to fill his coffers again when he had captured Alexandria and turned Egypt into a province. There may have been another problem to attend to at this time, though its context is disputed. The son of Lepidus raised revolt against Octavian at some time while he was in the East; some authorities date the conspiracy to autumn or winter 31, while others prefer to place it

98

in the period after the fall of Alexandria in the following year. The vigilance of Maecenas rooted out the plot before it could be put into effect. Appian tells us that Maecenas sent the young Lepidus as a prisoner to Octavian at Actium, but corroboration for the tale is lacking. Firm evidence for the date is not perhaps as important as the knowledge that Maecenas had established an inner ring of personnel acting as what might best be described as a private news agency, or a preventive and pre-emptive police network. Within a short time, thirty days after he had landed at Brundisium, Octavian set off to return to the East. He passed through Corinth and approached Egypt from Syria, while Cornelius Gallus advanced from the west. There was surprisingly little resistance. Antonius risked a battle, but his soldiers deserted in droves. His end was now inevitable. Not only his end, but also Cleopatra's. Alexandria fell to Octavian on 1 August 30. Antonius and then Cleopatra committed suicide. The absolute accuracy of the details recorded by ancient authors, and relayed via Shakespeare through films and plays, is not important. Something along those novelesque lines is entirely possible. Marcus Antonius has his niche in history, romantic or serious, and probably everyone in almost the entire western world has heard of Cleopatra.[21]

5

EMPIRE BUILDING

With the fall of Alexandria and the deaths of Antonius and Cleopatra, all serious military and political rivals to Octavian evaporated. Antonius' troops joined him, and the wealth of Egypt was his for the taking. It has been said that he desired to capture Cleopatra alive in order to march her through the streets of Rome in his triumphal procession. Perhaps he entertained such thoughts in a brief fantasy, but in the end it was far more convenient that Cleopatra died in Alexandria, whether by her own hand or with some unsought assistance. Octavian honoured her last wishes and buried her next to Antonius. He could have been much more vicious and refused her an honourable burial, but it would have earned him no credit and served no real purpose. He confined his implacable ruthlessness to the execution of Caesarion and Antonius' son Antyllus, who might have proved embarassing rivals if they had been allowed to go free. The other offspring of Antonius were brought up by his widow Octavia.[1]

After fourteen years of political wrestling, wars, devious planning and struggle for mere survival, Octavian was now alone and supreme. For the time being at least, his ascendancy was assured. He was consul, the armies looked to him as leader, Agrippa and Maecenas were in Rome, playing the parts of caretakers and sentinels and much else besides, fulfilling several tasks at once. But ascendancy is fragile and fickle. Achieving it is only the first step. Maintaining it is much more diffficult. The story of how Octavian did so is nothing less than the history of the transformation of the old-style Republican government of Rome, Italy and the provinces into the Roman Empire. In such a vast scenario, individuals are relegated to the background, while events and trends take centre stage. The story becomes one of the Augustan age, rather than a biography. Like the god Janus, Augustus looked both backwards and forwards in time, and to explain what he achieved necessitates explaining what went before, as the Republic became the Empire. The study of that complicated period must recognise certain significant features and events which serve as turning points. The procedure facilitates analysis of the subject, by slicing the whole into a series of manageable sections, but it obscures the possible alternatives that present themselves constantly in real life. The key dates that have emerged, 27, 23, 19 and so on, give the impression that the Empire was pre-ordained, ingeniously planned, all its parts assembled with the precision of a Swiss watchmaker and then set in perpetual motion once wound up. The thematic approach, so essential to an understanding of the inception of the Roman Empire, only serves to enhance this impression. The chronological approach is beset with problems, not least the lack of firm dates for certain events, and also because over the wide extent of territory that comprised the Empire, simultaneous developments took place which render a linear account more complicated. It is much more convenient to study the reign of Augustus under separate headings, such as the provinces, the frontiers, the army, the city of Rome, art and architecture, literature, administration, the Senate and equites, the Imperial family. The development of all these factors can then be pursued individually, from antecedents to finished form. Logical though it is, such a narration of related facts, isolated from contemporary developments and compressed together in a way which obscures the long passage of time, contributes to the general impression of Augustus as conscious founder of the Empire, with an enlightened vision and a single plan, unfolded in progressive stages. At the end of the year after the fall of Alexandria, Octavian no doubt knew in broad general outline what he wanted to achieve, but he could not have predicted how, if at all, he would be able to put it into effect. The foundation of the Empire was not a deliberate act but a series of developments, and moreover it was a long, slow process, involving cautious reconnoitring, some sidestepping and backtracking, and above all constant vigilance. The fantasy game of 'what if' is time consuming and ultimately unproductive, but it is salutary to remember that Octavian's rise to sole power was not a foregone conclusion, nor was his tenacious hold on it once he had achieved it. If illness or assassination failed to carry him off physically, there was always the threat of political manoeuvring. He had to be vitally aware of what men were thinking, and if possible pre-empt their actions or meet them half way. It would have been difficult to topple him from power altogether since he commanded large numbers of seasoned troops, and he had already demonstrated that he would not hesitate to use them to protect himself, but above all in these new times of peace he had to avoid being put into the position of having to do so. He needed to retain power, but without appearing to have usurped it. Augustus later insisted that he reached and remained in his supreme position by 'universal consent' (*per consensus universorum potitus rerum omnium*) which is a much wider concept than the oath of loyalty to himself that Octavian engineered throughout Italy and the provinces. It is also a more acceptable basis for power than the mechanical application of the law, which can place a man at the head of the government and maintain him there, but cannot make people accept him emotionally. Augustus carefully glossed over the tangled matter of how and on what legal basis he arrived at complete control of the state. He had dropped the title of Triumvir, and the Triumvirate had expired, either at the end of 32, or possibly at the end of 31, but it can be argued that the debate about the legal termination is quite useless, because until Octavian formally laid down his powers as Triumvir then he still exercised Triumviral authority, even if he did not draw attention to this fact. By the time he wrote the *Res Gestae* the memory of the events of the Triumviral period had faded, and indeed had been positively encouraged to fade. Even in 30, it was not a phase of which Octavian wished to remind people.[2]

Nevertheless, firm resolve to remain in control was already apparent in Octavian in 31 and 30. Some of his responses to embassies from Eastern cities have survived, attesting to his attitude and intentions. He expresses himself in the first person, and invites further embassies and petitions to himself. Thus in the days before and after Actium he was making decisions on his own account, like a monarch. This is neither the language nor the stance of someone who intends to step down from power. The retention of power brought with it an interminable, daunting labour. Virtually every aspect of Roman life needed some degree of attention and repair, but Octavian did not shirk the responsibility. If he ever contemplated simply resting on his laurels and walking away, which is doubtful, he probably realised in the next instant that he could not bear to watch if anyone else took charge. He believed in himself as the right man for the task, and set about making others believe in him too. He had been marked out by Caesar as his successor, which he took to mean that it was his duty to finish off in his own fashion what Caesar had begun.[3]

It was not too difficult to enumerate the tasks that faced him. The one overriding problem that beset Roman politics was a lack of continuity, because of the continual change of magistrates all largely pursuing their own ends. The Roman world was a collection of territories only just emerging as an Empire, so there was a considerable task facing Octavian with regard to the provinces. Like Caesar he viewed the Empire as a whole, recognising the need not just for conquest and exploitation for the glory of Rome but also for integration and consistent administration. All this would take time to achieve. Transport and communications would be a vital part of provincial, indeed for Italian, administration, and would benefit from a single guiding hand instead of sporadic and piecemeal development. To guard the newly won provinces and to conquer new ones, the army would play a vital part, and would require much reorganisation. There were far too many troops under arms in 30 after the fall of Alexandria; many men would have to be discharged, which entailed finding land or pensions for them. Some legions would still be needed to protect the provinces, and in the longer term Octavian presumably bore in mind the need for the creation of a standing army, regularly recruited, serving for a specified length of time, and properly catered for after retirement. The time-served veterans who had been settled on the land were not toothless old men who had served for a number of years. They had joined to follow one man, whether that man were Caesar, or Antonius or Octavian himself. They joined for the duration of the campaigns, and then required settlement; it was quite obvious that it would be much more convenient to have men sign up for several years, because in that case there would be plenty of time to make arrangements for their retirement, which would in itself aid recruitment and relieve the anxieties of the provincials and the Italians about penniless veterans marauding their homes.[4]

In Rome and Italy there would be much to do in the way of repair, both in the cities and in the devastated countryside which had suffered in the wars. The city of Rome required above all a regular, dependable food supply, and clean water, and both these matters had already been taken under the wing of Octavian or Agrippa, but not in any permanent sense. The city administration needed to be placed under a properly organised scheme; there was no centrally directed police force or fire service, for instance. Socially, the ancient Roman customs and the old religion had suffered serious lapses during the wars, and both required revitalisation. Confidence had to be restored, and a purification before Rome could go forwards. But in order to move on, certain changes must be made, and that would be the most difficult task of all. Octavian could probably see more clearly than anyone else where changes would be necessary to allow Rome to grow to Empire stature. Caesar had seen it but he had tried to move much too quickly. It was all a question of balance, to manoeuvre the Senate and people into believing that in fact the changes were their own ideas, and that Octavian was merely the facilitator. Above all the Senate would have to be handed tactfully. Too harshly repressed, or too fiercely pushed into the background, the senators would feel resentful and then give up hope. Octavian could never place them in a position where they felt they had nothing to lose, or else he would meet the same fate as his great-uncle at a rather earlier age. He had to induce them to think that it was all worth while, but at the same time he had to retain his own pre-eminence as the sole source of benefits and advancement. Influence rather than overt strength would be the order of the day. For the rest, a new social mobility was required, which would allow people to advance upwards throught the social scale, or at least to imagine that they could do so if they exerted themselves in the service of Rome and Octavian. This implied that noble snobbery must be overcome, because only then would it be possible to utilise the talents of everyone and to appoint as far as possible the best qualified man for each task, instead of choosing from a restricted pool of mostly self-interested nobles who might one day emulate Octavian by raising an army and challenging him. That above all had to be prevented.[5]

The vast majority of people required safety for their persons and their property, protection from enemies both local and foreign, some guarantee against famine, the promise of economic success, and to be allowed to get on with their own lives. This meant that the erstwhile image of Octavian the Triumvir, ruthless against everyone who happened to stand in the way of whatever it was that he wanted, had to be decisively shed. The potentially universal threat implicit in such unbridled power had served its purpose and was now an embarrassment, so Octavian had to set about obliterating that image and substituting a new one. He had to appear benign and liberal, with the correct balance of fairness to the innocent and implacable ruthlessness to the guilty. This meant that there had to be clear rules as to how far anyone could go in his search for personal pre-eminence, which in turn necessitated the establishment or the refinement of the career structure, in which men must be subordinated without knowing that they were subordinated. One way of achieving this was never to accept permanent office for himself, even though retirement was not included in his vocabulary. The myth of terminal dates must always be kept alive, hence his powers, slightly variable but always supreme, were granted in blocks of years, five or sometimes ten at a time, so that it was possible to review the situation on a regular basis. Octavian probably remembered very starkly that Caesar did not survive for more than a few weeks after accepting the appointment as *Dictator perpetuo*.[6]

Explicit clarity as to his powers was deliberately never achieved. In his replies to the embassies from the Eastern cities, he carefully styled himself consul, as was right and proper. But he and everyone else knew that he was much more than that. The secret of success, which was probably very clear to him even in 30, would be to avoid the use of extraordinary titles, particularly those that implied arbitrary force, whilst at the same time concentrating on self-advertisement in its more positive forms. From 32, when he dropped the title Triumvir, until the end of his life, Augustus observed these simple principles. The *Res Gestae*, written in retrospect, is a model of circumspection, not to say circumlocution by simple omission, or by refusing to name the source of his power in technical terms. It would have been of enormous assistance if somewhere in the *Res Gestae* he had described precisely whether he held consular or proconsular powers at certain times in his career; a lot of ink would have been spared for other debates. But these words find no place in this work, nor in any other. New words were fashioned out of strictly traditonal forms, bland words lacking any hint of coercive force. He claimed to be merely the first man in the state with no powers greater than any of his colleagues, eventually adopting the title Princeps, one with a long history and established usage, acceptably free from military or political taint, with an archaic nobility about it. Augustus broadened and ennobled the word, until it was all-embracing, extended into another realm. Instead of *imperium* the word he chose to describe his influence was *auctoritas*, a concept that defies complete elucidation in English translation. Authority conveys only some of its meaning, and confuses the issue somewhat because 'authority' has connotations of an official appointment or magistracy, or some kind of qualification earned via a properly approved scheme, probably with the award of a uniform or a rolled-up parchment at the end of it all. Augustus wanted none of these official connotations; he was the experienced elder statesman, benignly dispensing accumulated wisdom to lesser beings.[7]

It is not too fanciful to suggest that Octavian mulled over all these salient points at the end of the year after Alexandria fell. This is not to say that he decided upon his course of action and the choice of titles then and there, but innate caution and the lessons he had learned from Caesar and his fate were probably his guiding lights. He would see quite vividly what had to be done, and while focusing on the ends he would wait his time and continually adapt the means. If he waited for the correct moment to introduce ideas, his actions would not seem to have sprung from the unfeeling mind of an autocrat. There may have been many plans which he never brought to fruition because of lack of suitable opportunity. He would be limited by all manner of constrictions, among them unavoidable circumstances, financial considerations, and on occasion vociferous or covert opposition, though it is possible to overestimate the influence of the latter, using opposition to explain each and every action or reaction throughout Augustus' reign.[8]

Octavian was still in the East, wintering on Samos, when he entered on his fifth consulship in January 29, with Sextus Apuleius as his colleague. In Rome on 1 January, the Senate gratefully confirmed all his acts, which relieved him of the necessity of fighting for recognition, as had happened to Pompeius Magnus when he returned from his Eastern campaigns. On 11 January, the doors of the temple of Janus were closed, signifying that Rome was at peace, for it was the rule that while she was at war the doors remained open day and night. The definition of war and peace perhaps requires a litle refinement; it did not seem to matter that there were battles going on all over the Empire, against the Treveri in Gaul, who had brought German allies in on their side, and against the Cantabri and Astures in Spain, and against tribesmen in other areas. These peoples posed no serious threat to Rome herself, and, as Dio affirms, there was nothing to say about them in Roman opinion. The closing of the temple doors was said to be the honour that pleased Octavian best. It suited the image that he wished to propagate, as the bringer of peace. But the ongoing labour did not end with peace. The reorganisation of the provinces and most aspects of government could not be delayed. The organisation of the East claimed Octavian's first attentions. Egypt was made into a province, thus securing its valuable corn supply for Rome and the Royal Treasury for Octavian (Figure 5.1). Cornelius Gallus, who had marched from the west towards Alexandria while Octavian approached from the east, was made governor of the new province. He was not a senator, being of equestrian rank, but this did not deter

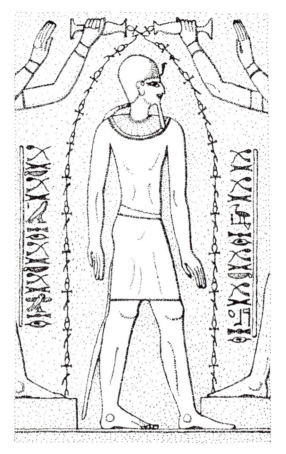

Figure 5.1 Augustus as Pharaoh, from Temple K, Philae, Egypt. After Taylor (1931, 144). Redrawn by Graeme Stobbs

Octavian from employing him in this new role. It has been debated whether this was an *ad hoc* decision made on the spur of the moment, using, as it were, the immediate tools that were to hand, or whether it was a calculated measure adopted with considerable forethought. Whatever the means by which Gallus was made Prefect of Egypt, the post went to equestrians ever afterwards. If Octavian had made a mistake in his choice, he did not choose to alter it, even when three or four years later Gallus seems to have overstepped the mark and after a mysterious sequence of events was obliged to do away with himself. If this unfortunate development was in any way associated with Gallus' rank rather than his personality, that would have been the time to rethink the governance of Egypt, but Augustus, as he then was, did not do so. Besides, decisions made on the spur of the moment do not suit Octavian's cautiousness. However convenient it may have been to employ Gallus simply because he was on the spot, it would not have been difficult to find someone else to fill the post, even if he had been forced to wait until that person could reach Egypt. An equestrian Prefect of Egypt, responsible to himself alone and not the Senate, answered Octavian's purpose very well, and continued to answer it throughout his reign. If he had offered the senators one sniff of Egypt, candidates would have been queuing up outside his door. It would have been very easy to reverse his decision, but the outcome was that the Prefecture of Egypt became one of the ultimate equestrian career goals. Senators were forbidden to enter the province without express permission from the Emperor.[9]

By remaining in the East Octavian allowed time for everything to settle down, both in Rome and in the Empire. Dio recounts how he waited until a dispute between Tiridates and Phraates of Parthia had been resolved, refusing to interfere even though he was asked to do so. He then negotiated with the victor, Phraates, and gained credit in Rome for his arrangements. Later, he tried to advance the cause of Tiridates, by assisting him in his efforts to usurp the Parthian throne, but after the failure of this attempt, friendly relations with Phraates were again restored (see below, pp. 126–7). The Eastern cities clamoured to honour him, with games and spectacles, and even worship. At Ephesus and Nicaea, the chief cities of Asia and Bithynia respectively, he permitted the Roman inhabitants to build temples to Rome and the divine Julius, and for the non-Roman citizens of Pergamum and Nicomedia, he authorised the dedication of temples to Rome and to himself. Careful not to offend either Roman sensibilities or provincial zeal, he included Rome in his personal panoply. The Eastern peoples readily adapted to the worship of a living individual. Octavian readily adapted to the honour. Nearer home the honours were exalted but of a more earthly kind. They fall into categories of monumental, distinction in dress and in name, adulatory celebrations, and useful privileges. He was decreed two triumphal arches, one in Rome and one at Brundisium, along with numerous other images and architectural monuments. Prayers were said for him and thanksgiving voted for his victories. Dio recounts how the consul Valerius Potitus, successor to Sextus Apuleius, offered sacrifices in person and in public on Octavian's arrival, a signal honour not accorded to anyone alse. A triumph over Cleopatra was voted, and then another over the Egyptians, by which was meant Actium and Alexandria. Antonius was never mentioned by name in the victory celebrations, but his monuments were pulled down and his name obliterated. His birthday was declared *nefastus*, unlucky and unfit for the transaction of public business. Octavian's birthday on the other hand was honoured with public holidays and celebrations, and he was given permission to wear a triumphal crown at all festivals. The name Imperator, which he had been using on coinage of the Triumviral period, was now confirmed as his by right. By the *Lex*

Saenia of 30 he was granted the right to appoint patricians, just as Caesar had been, and to which privilege Octavian owed his own promotion. In the *Res Gestae*, Augustus did not refer to the law but documented the fact that he created new patricians in response to a request from the Senate and the people.[10]

One of the honours which he refused was the formal greeting of the entire populace when he came home. It was normal for a man's friends and family, and clients and anyone else who was interested in him, to come out of the city to greet him when he returned after a tour of duty abroad, winning glory for Rome. This time there had been no occasion for the citizens to decide whether to do so, because the Senate had ordered it. Probably for two compelling reasons, Octavian declined the distinction, one reason being that it was no distinction at all when performed under compulsion, and could damage his reputation, and secondly it was a tiring process, like an extended audience, so that he would be under observation all the way home at a time when he was frequently under par if not actually ill. Consistently thereafter, Augustus often returned to Rome unexpectedly at night, so as to arrive home in privacy and calm. No doubt to underline his supremacy he did not return to Italy until August 29, ready to celebrate his triple triumph on three separate days, the 13th, 14th and 15th of August, over Dalmatia, for the victory at Actium and the defeat of Cleopatra. In accordance with Roman custom, he would not enter the city until the day of his first triumph, and he whiled away some of his time in the company of Maecenas and Vergil, who read the newly completed *Georgics* to him. As a gesture to spare the Italian cities from unnecessary expense, he did not accept the *aureum coronarium* or money tribute that had evolved from the custom of sending gold crowns to the generals celebrating a triumph. The cities had suffered devastations and deprivations during the wars, so Octavian relinquished the honour, gaining credit for his generosity while at the same time tacitly acknowledging the impoverished condition of the citizens; he would need their support in the future. The displays of his three triumphs will have required considerable orchestration, involving large numbers of personnel, as anyone will know who has organised the simplest village May Day festival. It testifies to Octavian's ability to direct events from a distance via such men as Agrippa and Maecenas, who held no official posts at this time. The festivities also required superhuman stamina; Rome in August can be exhausting, even to natives. The triumphs were the apogee of Octavian's military career. He would never celebrate another, which may have been as much by accident as design, but it fitted in with his policy of reserving the highest privileges for himself. If he did not celebrate another triumph, then by example he could quell the soaring ambitions of others. The family of Octavian featured in the triumphs; his sister's son Marcellus, and Livia Drusilla's son Tiberius rode with him, both teenage boys who had not played a part in the wars, but spectators would no doubt remember that the youth Octavius had accompanied Caesar in a triumph in which he himself had performed no warlike deeds. It may have been just after the triumphs were celebrated that the famous incident took place recounted by Macrobius, who dates it to Octavian's return to Rome after Actium. Among those gathering to congratulate him there was a man carrying a raven; good mimics as these birds are, this one said clearly 'Hail, Caesar, victorious commander.' Octavian was impressed by the raven's prowess, and paid 20,000 sesterces for it. Unfortunately the lucky vendor tried to cheat his partner of his share of the money, so the partner informed Octavian that he should demand to see the other raven that his friend had in his possession. It was produced and said 'Hail, Antonius, victorious commander.' Octavian took it in good part, but insisted that the partners should divide the 20,000 sesterces between them. On 18 August, Octavian dedicated the temple of *Divus Julius* at one end of the Forum, and the *Curia Julia*, the new Senate House, at the other. Then there were games and festivals, after which distractions, according to Dio, everyone forgot the wars and all the previous turmoil. After the euphoria there were also tangible rewards. Octavian paid all debts which he owed, and cancelled debts to himself. The Egyptian spoils allowed him to be more than generous, more even than lavish, with ready cash. He gave the soldiers bounties, and put into operation a massive settlement programme for the veterans. This time, the process was more sensitive, and did not seem to incur protest. He paid for lands himself, and did not confine the settlements to Italy. This time much of the Roman world was involved in the founding of colonies or upgrading towns and cities to colonial status. In some instances he gave the veterans cash pensions. Probably all those who had served under Antonius were pensioned off in this way. It has been estimated that he settled about 40,000 to 50,000 veterans in Italy, from a total of 25–30 legions. The remaining troops were redistributed and set to work, not all of it warlike; in Egypt, for instance, the soldiers were employed in cleaning out old canals and improving the water supply. These arrangements were not all completed overnight, but in broad general outline this was the plan that Octavian adopted from the end of 30 onwards.[11]

With Agrippa as colleague, Octavian entered his sixth consulship in 28. The main task now was to dismantle the Triumvirate and restore Rome and the provinces to a workable form of government. For the first time in very many years the two consuls remained in Rome or Italy for the whole year. It is recorded that Octavian shared the *fasces* (the axe and bundles of rods carried by lictors) with Agrippa, another sign that things were returning to normal, but the one problem with this statement is that it is not known how many lictors Octavian possessed to begin with. As Triumvir and consul he may have been allowed twenty-four lictors, which he now halved in order to grant twelve of them to Agrippa. A contrary school of thought is that he had always employed the usual twelve but now ceased to keep them to himself all the time, following the normal custom of sharing them with his consular colleague every alternate month. Whichever it was, the Romans heaved a sigh of relief that Octavian seemed bent on regularity and good order. This was quite unequivocal when he annulled all the acts of the Triumvirs, in an act that looked both backwards and forwards. It cancelled the horrors of the past and also proclaimed that there would be no return to such things. From a lofty and distant standpoint, Tacitus was to view it all far more sourly, because in seeming to release the Romans from their bonds Augustus actually tightened them further than ever. At the time, though, it was successful; it was precisely what was necessary, and having known worse things most people acquiesced. Confidence returned, the social order was repaired, religion was revitalised. Augustus boasted of restoring eighty-two temples, some at his own expense, but he also coerced people to share in the task. As consuls, Octavian and Agrippa were granted the powers of the censors (*censoria potestas*) without actually holding the office of censor. Using these powers, they carried out a census, which revealed that there were 4,063,000 registered Roman citizens. As with all statistics, there are reservations about what this means. Was it a figure limited to adult males, or were women and children included? The three censuses reported in the *Res Gestae* show a steady increase in the numbers of citizens, but once again there is a limit to the conclusions that can be drawn because the methods and criteria of taking the census are not known. Next, in order to purify the city and the people, the *lustrum* was carried out; there had been no such ceremony for over four decades, and it no doubt appealed to the emotions as much as any religious or practical sense. Another kind of purification was the *lectio* of the Senate. The undesirables who had crept in during the Dictatorship and the Triumvirate were weeded out. Some were persuaded to resign, then a list of names was posted up, this time not associated with anything so dire as the proscriptions. Partly it was an appeal to majority opinion, and partly a practical measure to reduce the Senate to a more manageable number. It was naturally interpreted as a movement to eradicate Antonians, and stories circulated that Agrippa and Octavian wore armour under their togas when attending the Senate meetings while the process was carried out. This is more likely hyperbole invented at the time, or by later authors. The adjustment of the Senate was not entirely one sided, since it is recorded that Octavian gave money to those men who were worthy to serve but could not meet the stipulated monetary qualification, and he created patricians to replace those noble families eradicated during the wars, which Augustus says he did in his fifth consulship; but it was surely a continuous process, and not something that could be solved all at once. At some time in 28, according to Dio, Octavian became *princeps senatus*, but it is possible that he already had the distinction by 29. By this means he was recognised as the leading senator of his day, and was permitted to speak first at meetings of the Senate. The honour was no small one, but it did not reach the dizzy heights of the title Princeps by which Augustus later became known; that was a much more robust demonstration of all-embracing supremacy.[12]

All this social, religious and political repair work was the preliminary to the so-called 'First Settlement' of the Ides (13th) of January 27, when Octavian as consul for the seventh time made a speech in the Senate giving back power to that body and thus restoring the Republic (res *publica restituta*, or *reddita*). Great controversy lurks behind those deceptively simple phrases. To contemporaries, it would seem that the restoration of the Republic did not make a momentous impact; there are few references to it as an event. But to the ancient authors who came after, this was the birth of the Empire and as time went by the portrayal of Octavian's actions in 27 gathered momentum. Describing the results, Velleius Paterculus crammed more superlatives into one paragraph than any of the panegyricists of the later Emperors proclaimed for their heroes. Dio's account of what Octavian actually said on the Ides of January is almost certainly fictional; the author employs a long speech, which would have taken some considerable time to deliver, to outline the foundation and functioning of the Empire. In reality, no one now knows what was in the speech, but it was likely that it was brief and delivered with well-chosen words. Suetonius says that Augustus used to write everything down to ensure that he said no more and no less than he intended, even when he wanted to talk to his wife. It is the sign of a busy man who does not want to have to remember all the salient points while pondering innumerable other matters, and in the case of his speech on the Ides of January he would not want to risk making any omissions or over-statements. Whether he read out loud from his script or rehearsed and put on a good act is not known and is largely irrelevant, except to affirm that the whole performance was certainly not a spontaneous gesture. All of Octavian's energies during his sixth consulship, possibly even during his fifth consulship in 29, had been directed to this end. At the end of his life, Augustus regarded it as an ongoing process, covering an extended timespan; he wrote in the *Res Gestae* that in his sixth and seventh consulships he transferred control of the *res publica* from his power to the Senate and people. Preparations had been carefully made. Before he gave his speech he had already discussed the matter with his closest associates, as Dio expressly states, but whether this was a discussion with his *consilium*, or a semi-official forerunner of it, remains to be established, since firm evidence of the functioning of the *consilium* at this early date is lacking. Suffice it to be said that he would not risk putting such an important motion before the Senate without first having sounded out the likely response. If the Senate had taken him at his word, risen in a body to congratulate him on his generosity and then rushed to take over the entire government, his position would have been a little uncomfortable. The timing was very important; it had to be done before his stranglehold on power convinced everyone that he was aiming at the Dictatorship like his adoptive father, and, even more important, before any other potential candidate began to imagine that he could run the Empire rather better. In other words he had to act while he was still in favour and indispensable. As for the plan, he was simply bringing to fruition what had been promised repeatedly in the past, to restore normal government, but whatever that was, probably no one could quite decide after the upheavals of the past. It has been described as launching a political programme that befitted reality, and it goes without saying that it was a programme that did no damage to Octavian but was also acceptable to the majority. As Syme points out, after the Dictatorship and Triumvirate the end result of the speech on the Ides of January was not at all displeasing. The senators coyly declined the government of the whole Empire. Graciously, Octavian accepted a compromise. He was to receive Gaul, Spain, Syria, Cilicia and Cyprus and Egypt as his *provincia* for ten years, which he would govern, in the fully evolved system, through *legati Augusti pro praetore*, men chosen by himself and given praetorian rank, no matter that they may have reached higher office than praetor; by this means the legates remained subordinate to him. One of the main consequences – indeed according to Syme one of the main reasons for the change – was that he ousted the proconsular governors from his provinces, and installed men who owed their advancement to him alone, which would provide some guarantee for their loyalty and obedience. As for the rest of the provinces, the Senate would govern them as of old, sending out ex-praetors and ex-consuls, who were all called proconsuls whatever their previous status, and who in some cases would command armies. Octavian did not take over all the armed provinces nor all the troops, but it is possible that as consul he could exercise overall command of the armies; this point has been debated for some time, since Augustus carefully never elaborated upon the theme with any specific description. The thorny question, debated for ages without solution, is Octavian's exact status, and that of the provincial governors of the senatorial provinces. Some authors have decided quite categorically that Octavian held *imperium proconsulare* and so governed his provinces as any other governor, except that he chose to do so through legates. His proconsular power was not valid in the city, but while he was consul he would not be inconvenienced by that. Other scholars have decided that from 27 until 23 he was governor by consequence of his status as consul with *imperium consulare*, which allowed him to make decisions for his own and other provinces. Dio insists that from the very first after the reorganisation of 27, Augustus issued orders to proconsular governors of senatorial provinces, and the inscription from Cyme seems to support this since the phrase 'on the orders of Augustus' is unequivocal, but even here nuances of interpretation can negate the evidence if, as some authors believe, the orders stemmed from superior influence rather than legally based powers. If it is true that he could make decisions and give orders to provincial governors, then it was only in 23 that he needed to make changes to these arrangements because he then ceased to be consul and so required proconsular powers to continue to govern his own provinces, coupled with *imperium maius* or powers greater than all other governors in order to be able to direct affairs. Some scholars have re-examined the proconsular powers of Augustus, and concluded that there was no such thing as *imperium maius*; this theory maintains that Republican precedent allowed only for *imperium aequum*, which curtails the extent of Augustus' authority and has great import for his status when he relinquished the consulship in 23. The precedents had been set in the recent past, as for instance when Pompeius Magnus obtained his command against the Mediterranean pirates and was granted the necessary powers, for a limited time, to give orders to governors in the territories surrounding the Mediterranean; but this was for a specific and narrowly defined purpose, even if it did affect very large areas of the Roman world. Augustus needed something more, but could never admit to permanence. The theory that Augustus exchanged the consulship for proconsular powers is a neat solution that may well be correct, but the flaw in the argument is that no one could have expected that he would be consul every year for the full ten years of his provincial governorship. Undisguised monopolisation of power in this way was contrary to all the careful and painstaking measures to place temporal limitations on each of his official appointments. It can be argued that although his public image was one of obedience to the laws and the old traditional customs, he was privately determined that he should always be consul; Suetonius says that he tried to obtain the agreement of the Senate that there should be two other consuls besides himself, which indicates very strongly that he had no intention of relinquishing the office. Even if he was prepared to leave the question of the consulship permanently open, playing it by ear, as it were, it would have been quite uncharacteristically lax if Augustus had not established at the beginning exactly how he was to govern his provinces for the next decade. No one can prove or disprove any of the theories about the *imperium* of Augustus in 27. As with so many aspects of his reign there is only passionate belief.[13]

There may have been further items on the agenda on 13 January, but that can never be ascertained. It may be that the single most important factor had been dealt with, and that was what Augustus meant by restoring the *res publica*. There was a pause while the Senate considered what to do next to honour Octavian. This too was probably guided if not totally orchestrated in advance. It would not be acceptable if the rewards were inadequate, or embarrassing or compromising in some way. There was an interval of three days before the Senate responded. The time lapse may have been due to shell-shock on the part of the senators, or to wrangling over the correct honours and adulation. Lacey has simplified the matter by pointing out that the day following Octavian's speech in the Senate was Antonius' birthday (14 January), which had been recently declared *nefastus*, so no public business could be performed; on the next day (15 January) there was a religious festival which would have limited the time available for a meeting of the Senate. Therefore it was only on the 16th that the Senate could award appropriate thanks and honours. Munatius Plancus proposed that henceforth Octavian should be known as Augustus, a word which is connected to augur and augury and therefore has a somewhat religious flavour, and indeed is also connected to *auctoritas*; it had a good pedigree, did not denote an official appointment, was suitably elevated but politically harmless. It is reported that Octavian toyed with the name Romulus, but rejected it because of the regal connotations. Romulus had been that dreaded concept, king of Rome, and Caesar had come to grief on account of the suspicion that he intended to elevate himself to such a rank. There were many other tangible honours, deeply significant for the Romans. It was decreed that Augustus' house doors should be decked with laurel, and that he should be awarded the *corona civica* for saving the lives of citizens, a strange irony when it is remembered how many citizens had been proscribed by the same person now being honoured. He took the award seriously, though, because he was now promoting himself as saviour, so he placed the legend *ob cives servatos* on his coins, underlining the life-saving attributes he wished to advertise.[14]

What happened in 27 is not fully understood despite the availability of some documentation. Even more obscure is what Augustus himself felt and thought. Of the political developments we are allowed to glimpse a little; of the person, the private man, there is nothing. Did he go home to celebrate, feeling that he had 'arrived' as the modern idiom expresses it, or did he take it all unemotionally in his stride, knowing that there was still a long way to go? Livia may have been party to his thoughts, and no doubt Agrippa knew them too. The rest of the family remain in the shadows. Augustus was not yet forty, and had been married to Livia for over ten years, and yet there had been no children born of that marriage. His daughter Julia was growing up, but he seems to have regarded her merely as a political negotiating tool, or a surrogate heir provider. His sister's son, the teenage Marcellus, was the favourite, if not yet, then very soon; Tiberius and Drusus, the sons of Livia, were perhaps regarded as runners-up. His private family life remained private, by design and vigilant determination. For one thing he probably needed the refuge of privacy; when he needed to seclude himself to work or simply to be alone, he retired to a room at the top of the house, which he called 'Syracuse' or his workshop. In general, for public consumption, the ordinary, mundane, not to mention sordid human details were not the images he wished to project. For some time now, via the poets and artists, he had been founding the legend. There have been several studies of all aspects of the image of Augustus; it would be needlessly repetitive to go over this ground again when it has already been dealt with by experts. The image is important, but it is not the person;

it is the persona, in the psychological sense of the word, which is only a part of the whole being. In literature Augustus was the hero, with all the right attributes; the audience for these messages would not be the wide popular market but the educated and cultivated upper classes. Monuments and statues were available for all to see as a constant reminder of the man who had brought peace, but these visible messages would need to be augmented regularly or their impact would fade. People very quickly become accustomed to their surroundings and cease to notice what has always been there; only tourists take real interest in statues, and even then pass on to the next one within minutes. The way to impress the people was to give them civic amenities along with their food supply and personal protection, and to ensure firstly that the provenance of all these bounties is well known, and secondly that such benefits flow out in a regular stream without too many long intervals. Realists know that all the successes of a lifetime can be negated by one failure if the effect on the majority is deep enough. Cromwell and Napoleon both said of the crowds who came out to cheer them that the very same crowds would turn out and cheer just as loudly if either of them were on the way to execution. When Augustus left Rome in the summer of 27, he began the repair of the Via Flaminia, from Rome to Ariminum (modern Rimini). He also repaired nearly all the bridges on this route, except two, one of which was the Milvian bridge on the outskirts of Rome. Presumably it had been kept in good repair, and now Augustus placed a statue of himself as a reminder of who was responsible for this work. He encouraged other generals to spend their resources on similar public works. While Augustus was absent, the city would have been alive with building projects, left for the supervision of Agrippa, throughout 27 and the next few years. Dio groups the buildings together for ease of explanation, so it is not certain that all those that are described within the context of a certain year do in fact belong to that year. Some of the buildings had already been completed, such as the white marble temple of Apollo next to Augustus' house on the Palatine, dedicated in 28, and possibly the family mausoleum which may have been built at the same time. It was well to be prepared for death, because Augustus was so often ill, and he would not be happy with anything less than a monumental tomb. On the whole he was probably well pleased with what had happened in 27, but in life there are always disappointments. In July of that year, M. Licinius Crassus, grandson of the Crassus who had died in Parthia, held his triumph for his exploits in Moesia in 29–28. It should have been a cause for celebration, but instead left a sourness on the part of the *triumphator* and Augustus because Crassus had failed to realise that the old Republican tradition of great generals returning from the wars and demanding recognition had been permanently monopolised. He claimed the title of Imperator, and also the rare honour of *spolia opima* awarded to those few generals who had personally killed an enemy leader in battle, whereby in a prestigious ceremony the victorious Roman would dedicate the spoils of war, usually the dead man's armour and weapons, in the temple of Juppiter Feretrius on the Capitol. Perhaps Crassus meant only to serve the state with honour, with Rome permanently at the forefront of his mind and himself a close second; but it was an ominous sign, which Augustus could not countenance. Though he held his triumph, somewhat belatedly, Crassus did not realise his wish to dedicate his spoils in the temple of Juppiter Feretrius. The reasons are obscure. The orthodox version of the story places Augustus in the centre stage, publicly challenging Crassus' claim and preventing him from attaining his ambition. The method by which Augustus was supposed to have achieved this is tenuous to say the least. By a dubious argument concerning the status of the last known man to claim the honour, named Cossus, it was revealed that *spolia opima* could be awarded only to those generals who had been in supreme command, acting under their own auspices. It was deemed that Crassus did not qualify on that heading, and so Augustus squashed his demand for the *spolia opima* and also, according to Dio, he purloined from Crassus the title Imperator, maintaining that the victory was his because Crassus had been acting as a subordinate under the auspices of Octavian, as he then was, as commander in chief. In this version of the problem, the matter then becomes rather wider than the prevention of bids for supremacy by upstart rivals; it concerns the question, not hitherto plainly answered, of who is really in charge. If Octavian's powers extended to provinces other than his own, then it seemed that the old Caesarian domination had returned under another guise. The Crassus 'crisis' has been interpreted as one of the main factors, if not the only one, that precipitated the settlement of 27, when Octavian was forced into making the gesture of returning the provinces to the Senate and thereby 'restoring the Republic' almost as a by-product of saving his own skin. This view has been challenged after a re-examination of the evidence by J.W. Rich, who argues that Crassus did indeed adopt the title Imperator, despite Dio's assertion to the contrary. More important, the mechanisms by which Augustus could deny Crassus' claim are dubious, as the story related above plainly reveals. A more realistic interpretation is that Augustus and his chosen friends worked informally behind the scenes to persuade Crassus not to go through with his plans. Thus the ideology of the crisis theory is no longer tenable, and Crassus' connection with the settlement of January 27 is negligible. On the other hand, the ideology of Octavian is not refuted; he held the monopoly on supremacy, and whether he put Crassus in his place by official or unofficial means, that much was made absolutely clear. It probably irked him somewhat that he was forced into the position, so early, of having to make this so glaringly obvious. If he had given way to Crassus the floodgates would have been opened for the next man and the next, until the competition for first place led to a repetition of the wars of the 40s. That was, on balance, a worse prospect than spoiling the carefully groomed image of Augustus as merely first among equals, with no coercive powers in excess of anyone else. The myth was exploded, but no one seemed to protest. The memory of the Dictatorship and the Triumvirate, still painfully vivid, no doubt silenced any adverse reaction.[15]

Augustus did not remain in Rome to witness Crassus' triumph. He went to Gaul, and then to Spain to carry on the war there, perhaps taking Marcellus and Tiberius with him. While he was absent, the affair of Cornelius Gallus, the first prefect of Egypt, played itself out. Considerable mystery attaches to this story, which is not fully explained. It is not even securely dated; Dio chronicles it under the year 26; Syme redated it to the end of 27. It seems that Gallus had overstepped the mark, like Crassus perhaps. He had campaigned in Egypt as far as the First Cataract of the Nile, and had not been shy of recording his exploits, but it is not certain that he had demanded excessive honours like Crassus. The only ascertainable fact is that he lost favour with Augustus, and when the Senate charged him with treason, he committed suicide. The question is, what treason had he committed? Dio says that he spread malicious gossip about Augustus, but unless he had declared himself by some action or had tried to subvert other men to join him in a plot, it seems unnecessarily violent to condemn him for gossip. It is counter-productive to stamp out freedom of speech when the current programme is to propagate an atmosphere of confidence and trust. The facts will always be obscure. Did Gallus fall from favour first, and then succumb to the jackals in the Senate who seized their chance to prosecute an abandoned *eques* hated by the higher ranking members, or did he commit some crime against Augustus, who then set in motion or sanctioned the prosecution at the hands of the Senate? Suetonius relays only the charge of ingratitude against Gallus, an indication perhaps that he did not know the details of the case any more than modern scholars do. If that was Gallus' only crime then the judgment was very harsh. Gratitude cannot be compelled, and the realist in Augustus will have known that. Officially he thanked the Senate, and in private he grieved over the incident. He did not immediately reverse his decision as to the post of Prefect of Egypt, but installed another equestrian, Aelius Gallus, with instructions to campaign against Arabia and Ethiopia to bring them to terms and establish boundaries. The purpose of the Arabian campaign has been reanalysed in connection with the political and diplomatic wrangling with Parthia. It is suggested that Gallus' operations were co-ordinated with those of the usurper Tiridates, who crossed the Euphrates with Augustus' blessing, if not actual backing, at the same time as Gallus marched into Arabia. Thus Parthia would be threatened from two sides at once. Ultimately the Arabian campaign was a failure, and Tiridates managed to establish himself for only a very short time before being ejected (see below, pp. 126–7).[16]

There is little evidence for Augustus' movements in 26, except that he was in Spain, campaigning against the Cantabri, and directing affairs from abroad. It was rumoured that he was going to make an expedition to Britain, perhaps in emulation of his father Julius Caesar, but this may be only wishful thinking on the part of the Roman populace who desired that he should take Roman arms to the ends of the earth. Augustus had enough to concern him in maintaining the provinces he already had, and as Strabo points out, somewhat dismissively, there was no reason to invade Britain and go to all the trouble of annexing and administering it because the British chiefs had made alliances with Rome. A simplistic view, perhaps, but despite excuses laid at his door, such as exiled British rulers appealing to him for reinstatement, Augustus never did succumb to the temptation to invade Britain. Apart from a brief description of the Spanish campaigns, Dio concentrates on Rome, where in September 27 Messalla Corvinus held his triumph. A new honour was bestowed on Messalla in 26 when he was made prefect of the city, but his appointment lasted only six days, and then he gave it up, perhaps in response to hostility from the Senate. Once again, mystery surrounds the matter. It may have been an experiment which was made too soon for Roman taste. Augustus tried again after a suitable interval. Some time later, the city prefect became a regular appointment, with responsibility for policing Rome and command over the urban cohorts to give him the means to do so, but that was in the future. In the past, the city prefect had been installed only when both consuls were absent, and in 26 Statilius Taurus, consular colleague of Augustus, was still in Rome. It is not likely that the protest originated from Taurus in a fit of jealousy, which isolates the Senate as the objecting body, if there were objections at all. There may have been some practical purpose behind the appointment that is now lost to sight, since it would be unlike Augustus to award the post as an empty honour; there were many baubles which he could have offered Messalla instead of an office which was a glaring anomaly, and which might compromise him. It does not seem to have been considered that Messalla might have been given a specific task to perform, possibly relating to some kind of police work, which he performed in six days, rather like a mini version of Pompeius Magnus' rapid sweep of the Mediterranean when he cleared the sea of pirates.[17]

Agrippa's position in 26 has not been clarified. He had received some important marks of distinction, such as the blue pennant awarded him after Actium, which complemented the honours that he won after Naulochus. His high standing could not be in doubt, but he was not consul and had no other magistracy. He did not accompany Augustus to Spain. His building programme will have occupied much of his time and energy, but seemingly he had no province and probably could not hold proconsular rank after his consulship. The term *provincia* did not originally denote a territorial area; it meant strictly a task, as in 'Not my province' meaning 'That job is nothing to do with me.' As Rome expanded and took in more territory, the tasks given to the retiring magistrates also had to expand to enable government of these new areas to be carried out, so the same word was applied to the government of a province as had been attached to the performance of special duties in Rome. It is not recorded that Agrippa's special *provincia* concerned building work, so the conclusion is forced on scholars that he was merely a *privatus* at this time. Unwilling to accept this, some authors have postulated that he must have been given some special command or rank in 27; Lacey's theory is that he was made prefect of the fleet with responsibility for the Mediterranean coastal areas (*praefectus classis et orae maritimae*), the precedents for which were Pompeius Magnus' command against the pirates, and Sextus Pompeius' brief overlordship of the seas during the civil wars. For this there is not the least shred of evidence, but it is entirely possible that Agrippa was given some official post which has escaped the notice of the ancient authors. Meanwhile the conquest of Spain was dragging on. Augustus fell ill at Tarraco and had to conduct the war through subordinates. He regarded the conquest as complete, but in fact it took a few more years and Agrippa's talents to achieve it. Spain is a difficult country, the graveyard of many a Roman general's reputation, and described, many centuries later, as a country where large armies starve and small ones are defeated. It has been said that Augustus' illness may have lasted all through the latter part of 26 and all of 25, and this may have been what prompted him to arrange the marriage of his nephew Marcellus and his daughter Julia in a bid to produce heirs. If so, the hope was a little far-fetched. It is biologically impossible to hurry the production of heirs and advance their growth, and it is hardly likely that any notice would have been taken of an infant if Augustus died. It is more probable that this marriage was always a project that he had in mind and he was merely waiting for Julia to arrive at the right age. More cynically, his actions of 25 and 24 can be seen as the preliminary to the rearrangements of 23. When he returned home at the end of 25 he held no triumph but announced that he would give 400 sesterces each to 250,000 citizens, significantly the same figure that he had paid out in 29 when he did hold triumphs. Thus the people were not deprived of their rewards, even when the pomp and circumstance were absent. On 1 January the Senate confirmed by oath all Augustus' acts since 29, and Dio affirms that he was now dispensed from all the laws, which cannot be taken as literal truth. He was exempt from some of the laws, but not from the whole. At this stage the Senate and people would not have been ready for such an arbitrary position. In 24, Marcellus and Julia were married, with the faithful Agrippa presiding over the ceremony because Augustus was ill. Whether or not the dynastic tendencies were feared just yet is not known, but it was plain that both Marcellus and Tiberius were favoured members of the family who were destined for higher things. Marcellus was to be aedile in 23, as though he had been quaestor already and therefore eligible for the other magistracies. Tiberius was permitted to stand for office five years before the legal term, and was to become quaestor in 23. It was prudent to advance these young men in echelon, rather than simultaneously, in case offence was caused at such overwhelming determination to favour the family and not promising aristocrats of other households. If it was taken for granted that Marcellus was the appointed heir, Augustus surprised everyone when he succumbed to an even more serious illness early in 23. It was thought that this time he would die, and he gave his signet ring to Agrippa, and an up-to-date account of the administration of the provinces and the finances to his consular colleague Piso. If he died at this point, he knew that only Agrippa could continue from where he left off, and only Agrippa would have the stamina and determination to do so, with the backing of the armies, if such extreme measures were necessary. Indeed Agrippa was the man who could keep the armies united under his command and so prevent their subversion by anyone else with ambitions. Marcellus was too inexperienced, and Augustus knew it. Later, when he had recovered, the story goes that he came under some criticism about his successor. He offered to read his will in the Senate to prove that he had not named anyone; that is, he had not named a successor to his powers and political standing, like a monarch. Purely family matters were not at issue here, but as a consequence of his status Augustus had progressed beyond ordinary families, and whatever arrangements he made would have great bearing on the future of the Roman world. Despite the speculation, both ancient and modern, that Marcellus was to be the heir, it seems that Augustus did not adopt him, and refers to him in the *Res Gestae* as *gener* (son-in-law), and not *filius* (son). The offer was not taken up, and for the time being the subject of the succession was closed.[18]

In July 23, having recovered from his illness thanks to the ministrations of his Greek physician Antonius Musa, Augustus gave up the consulship. One school of thought maintains that he did so in response to a crisis, exacerbated by his illness in 23. The so-called crisis is related to the trial of Marcus Primus and the subsequent condemnation of Varro Murena (probably L. Licinius Varro Murena, and not, as previously thought, A. Terentius Varro Murena) and Fannius Caepio. The absence of hard facts allows for a multiplication of opinions as to the nature and even the date of the so-called conspiracy. Marcus Primus had been governor of Macedonia, and had made war on Thrace without authority. He was charged and brought to trial, possibly at the end of 24 or early in 23. He declared that he had acted on the orders of Augustus, and then Marcellus. Macedonia was a senatorial province, so if Augustus had issued orders without explaining to the Senate his pose as first among equals was demonstrably false. He came to court and declared on oath that he had issued no such orders. Varro Murena, defending Primus, made it clear that he did not believe this. None the less, Primus was condemned. There are so many possible permutations that it would be tedious to enumerate them all, but among the possibilities there was either a scheme to discredit Augustus by employing Primus as an innocent dupe or Augustus himself had miscalculated and been found out. The latter does not seem credible; if he had wanted to direct affairs in a senatorial province there were more acceptable and equally persuasive means of doing so that would surely have met with success. He could have prepared the ground by emphasising the dangers from Thrace and had the senators eating out of his hand, ready to give the command to him or to anyone else whom he indicated to them. It has been assumed that after his failure in court, Murena began to fester and plot revenge, and then joined forces with Fannius Caepio, who for reasons unknown was already scheming against Augustus. The conspiracy was discovered and the guilty parties executed. That is the publicised version of events. The reasons and the details are lost, if indeed they were ever known to more than a few people. Dio recounts the Caepio–Murena conspiracy under the year 22. Some modern authors prefer to date both the trial of Primus and the discovery of the conspiracy to 23, so that the affair precedes and precipitates the so-called second settlement made in that year. The evidence, such as it is, about the Primus trial and the conspiracy has been re-examined and it seems that the chronology can be reversed. The settlement was probably already completed when the problems arose with Murena and Caepio, and it could even be said that the conspiracy was a result, not a cause, of Augustus' rearrangements. The truth will probably always be unattainable. The opposition theorists interpret many of Augustus' rearrangements as grudging reactions to pressure, rather than proactive measures properly planned. It may be true that Augustus was determined to be consul for ever, or at least for as long as he could get away with it, but it was less and less of an excusable necessity now that there was no serious external threat and no internal discord likely to lead to war. His monopolisation of the office excluded others from ever attaining it, and without this experience of government and the elevated rank the senators were no doubt beginning to feel deprived of the chances of advancement. The small use that he made of the men of consular rank in his own entourage and in his provinces also frustrated the prospective candidates. No one likes to think that promotion is blocked, even if the person being blocked has no intention of rising any higher. Recognising this, Augustus may have made an attempt to retain his powers as consul, whilst still opening up avenues for senators to further their careers, by proposing that there should always be two colleagues when he was consul himself. Suetonius gives no date for this proposal, which is often associated with the events of 19, but the context of 23 is the most likely, representing an attempt at compromise before finally giving up the consulship in return for other powers. He was consul again only as colleague of his adopted sons, and it is probable that once he had taken the decision to relinquish his monopoly he did so with resolution, and did not risk beseeching the Senate for favours in 19, despite the popular demand that he should be consul. Since no one can know what was in Augustus' mind, theories as to why he relinquished the consulship can never be more than unproven opinions. It is certain that he would not have done so without first ensuring that there was an alternative source of power ready for him to assume. He lost powers and privileges if not rank when he resigned from the consulship. As a partial exchange for his consulship he now received, for a limited term, *imperium proconsulare*. There is great controversy over the extent of these proconsular powers. If he was granted *imperium proconsulare maius*, as some authors have stated, then his authority exceeded that of all other provincial governors; but this conflicts with Augustus' own assertion that he never held any powers greater than those of his colleagues. For various reasons, some modern researchers believe that there was never any question of *imperium maius* either for Augustus or for Agrippa; in this case, then, Augustus received *imperium proconsulare aequum* or proconsular powers equal to all the provincial governors, and therefore had to rely upon prestige, influence and the undefinable persuasive power of his *auctoritas* if he wished to interfere in the government of provinces not directly under his control. *Imperium aequum* was much more compatible with Republican precedent and held no distasteful connotations of domination. Augustus strove to avoid such blatant declarations, even though it was perfectly obvious that in reality he did dominate the state. In three respects he departed from his Republican predecessors, who were usually granted such extraordinary powers solely to enable them to carry out a specific task or a strictly defined series of tasks; they did not normally receive a command that extended to all the provinces at once, and they were obliged to lay down their powers when they crossed the *pomerium* on their return to Rome. None of these restrictions applied to Augustus, except that his proconsular powers were set within a temporal limit, which meant that they had to be renewed at intervals. Otherwise he was elevated to special status, since he was not limited to the performance of any special task, and could exercise authority in all the provinces at all times within his temporal limit of five, or on occasion, ten years. He was also granted the exceptional privilege, by a special legal enactment, of exemption from having to lay down his powers when he crossed the *pomerium* on his return to Rome. Without this enactment he would have been obliged to enter Rome as a mere *privatus*; he could of course rely upon the intimidating weight of prestige and influence to protect him for a while, but he had seen in the past how easily prestige could be eroded, descending very rapidly into powerlessness. Prestige was good. Laws were better.[19]

Proconsular *imperium* was only one prop for his authority; he needed another, which he found in tribunician powers (*tribunicia potestas*). This too was confirmed by a law. Dio's account links this to the Latin Festival, which would date it to June or early July. If this is correct, the assumption of the *tribunicia potestas* and the relinquishing of the consulship were timed very finely. The statement that Dio makes – that Augustus was made tribune for life – is erroneous, since Augustus was never tribune but held the powers of a tribune. The problems associated with the *tribunicia potestas* have already been discussed (above, pp. 85–6). It remains uncertain as to whether he had already been granted full tribunician powers prior to 23, either all at once or by accepting them in gradual stages from 36 onwards, or whether he had only the sacrosanctity until 23 and so assumed all the powers now. The separation of the powers from the actual office was new and revolutionary; the recent bestowal of censorial powers on Augustus and Agrippa while they were consuls is not a valid precedent because they exercised this power via the consulship, and not independently. Augustus thereafter counted his tribunician years, often abbreviated to *trib. pot.* on inscriptions and coins, from 23. He was not elected every year, and had no need to be, but perhaps his aversion to accepting anything in perpetuity prompted him to subscribe to the appearance of annual renewal. He was not subject to the veto of other tribunes, but could veto any proposals in the Senate. The mere fact that he could do so seems to have obviated the need for him to exercise his authority, and it has been suggested that one of the principal reasons for assuming the tribunician powers was to keep the nobles in check with the threat, that if necessary, he could revert to popular politics and achieve what he wanted without reference to them. In turn, it was his guarantee to the people that the nobles could not oppress them, which was a nice balance of control. He made use of the tribunician powers to introduce legislation, but did not make use of the powers of veto. Later Emperors did so on a limited basis. The *tribunicia potestas* became the foremost Imperial title, the *summi fastigii vocabulum*, the title of supreme eminence, as Tacitus describes it. The successor to the throne was often marked out by bestowal of tribunician powers; those who shared it with Augustus were Agrippa and Tiberius, but for a limited term only, in keeping with the policy of continual renewal rather than permanence. Augustus had arrived at the most successful basis of Imperial rule, and had managed to do so without inventing anything too disturbing or too outlandish. His powers were rooted in Roman custom, but tailored to fit the circumstances. The institutions established in 23 endured for many years throughout the reigns of several Emperors. Had there been a flaw, or the slightest loophole, it is to be supposed that someone would have noticed and made the necessary amendments.[20]

At some time during the year 23, perhaps before Augustus resigned as consul, Agrippa went to the East. It was said even by contemporaries that he removed himself in a fit of pique because of the favours shown to Marcellus, or that he did the tactful thing and allowed Augustus to groom his chosen successor in peace and quiet. If this far-fetched theory were even remotely based on truth then it is difficult to explain why Agrippa did not return to Rome when Marcellus died unexpectedly, probably at the end of 23. It was a year particularly noted for plagues, so Marcellus' death is probably not as suspicious as Robert Graves has depicted it in *I, Claudius*, even though Dio includes the tale that Livia was suspected of doing away with Marcellus because Tiberius had not been so favoured with promotions. Augustus' hopes for the future were dashed, but he still could count on his daughter Julia, now a widow and soon to be married to Agrippa when he returned to Rome in 21. Thus the *novus homo* Agrippa was elevated to high position in the household of the Princeps, which contradicts in large part those sources who state that Agrippa was banished, and in disgrace, in the latter half of 23. In fact, after the death of Marcellus, Maecenas commented that Agrippa had been raised so high that there were only two alternatives left in dealing with him: either he married Julia or he would have to be eliminated. It requires only a little imagination to hear the languid drawling tone, and to picture Maecenas, half joking, half serious, perhaps disinterestedly filing his nails, or more likely having his nails filed for him. He and Agrippa supposedly disliked each other, but Maecenas was right in that Agrippa had been raised very high, and disgrace, banishment, or piqued self-imposed exile in 23 are all totally at odds with Agrippa's position in the East. Josephus, writing much later, says that he had charge of the whole of the East, acting as the deputy of Caesar for the lands beyond the Ionian Sea. Dio describes the command in more limited terms, confining it to Syria, but Agrippa based himself elsewhere and seems to have had freedom to travel where he liked and do as he liked, so he was certainly not under a cloud and probably did command a wide area, perhaps in an experiment to share the burden of Imperial administration. Augustus was convalescing during the second half of 23, and he was older now, turning 40 at the end of the year. Whilst this hardly makes him a geriatric, his perception of the Empire had probably undergone some adjustment since the days of Actium and Alexandria. The hard work involved in administering it, while at the same time being ever-vigilant about his standing in Rome, could not fail to take its toll. One possibility worthy of consideration is that Agrippa went to the East to prepare the ground for Augustus' own mission to the Parthians. It has been suggested that relations between Rome and Parthia had degenerated in 24 because of Augustus' involvement in the attempted usurpation of the Parthian throne by Tiridates, which had failed. The situation would have been sensitive and tense, so Agrippa's brief would have been to monitor developments, keep Augustus informed, and to react quickly wherever and whenever it became necessary. But there was more to it than that. The East had been Antonius' preserve. To the cities of the East, Octavian was the victor and they were the defeated subjects. If they could have escaped from this position they probably would have done so with alacrity; it was a volatile and unstable region, ripe for some enterprising general or Eastern potentate to stage a coup, with access to troops and rich resources. The East as a whole required careful handling, constant alertness, and a reliable intelligence service. Agrippa was the only man whom Augustus could trust, and the only man with sufficient knowledge, courage and authority to look after Roman interests in the East, and prevent anyone else from damaging them. As usual, there is controversy over Agrippa's powers. Some scholars are quite certain that he had been granted *imperium proconsulare* that was equal to that of other provincial governors, thus keeping Agrippa one stage behind Augustus himself, who it is argued held *imperium proconsulare maius* as suitable compensation for the resignation of the consulship. Others are just as certain that Agrippa held *imperium proconsulare maius*, just as it is supposed that Augustus did, and that therefore Augustus and Agrippa were equal partners in all respects. Another, more recent school of thought, denies the existence of *imperium maius* in any circumstances, which reduces both Augustus and Agrippa to *imperium aequum* and levels off and simplifies any argument about status, subordination or equality. A fragmentary document preserving part of Augustus' funeral oration for Agrippa tantalises scholars with the phrase 'it was enacted by law that no one should have powers superior to yours, no matter to which Roman territories you were sent'. The problems as always are several. First, there is no evidence of the date when this legal enactment was made; secondly, there is no inkling of the duration of the powers that were granted by it; thirdly, the phraseology is ambiguous and can be interpreted in two ways: on the one hand that Agrippa had greater powers than all other provincial governors, or on the other that he had equal powers, which still satisfies the spirit of what Augustus said, that no one held greater powers than Agrippa wherever he went. A recent solution, very tidy but unsupported by firm evidence, is that just after Augustus was granted *imperium maius*, Agrippa was accorded the same privilege for five years, renewed in 18 and again in 13; the last date is the sole notice in Dio's account of Agrippa's *imperium*. Another theory is that in 26 Agrippa was made prefect of the fleet with authority over the entire Mediterranean coastline, and under this command he went to the East in 23, then his position was redefined in 18. Walter Ameling's solution is simpler than most theories; he denies the existence of *imperium maius* and proposes instead that Agrippa held an independent command by dint of his *imperium proconsulare aequum*, that he was not dependent upon the superior powers of Augustus, and that this privilege was granted to Agrippa in 23 and retained until his death in 12. It has to be admitted that no one knows why Agrippa went to the East, nor what he did whilst there; it is known that he returned in 21, and was sent to Rome to restore order. He divorced his wife Marcella, Augustus' niece, and moved one degree up the social scale by marrying Julia, Augustus' daughter. With no official post, he remained in Rome until 20, when he went first to Gaul and then to Spain where in 19 he brought the province finally under Roman control.[21]

As Augustus was setting out for the East in 22, food shortages threatened to bring famine to Rome, and the usual response of the people in these circumstances was to riot. Augustus returned when it became clear that this was not simply a short-term disturbance. He was offered and refused the Dictatorship, which he probably regarded as a death sentence. The offer was reduced to an annual consulship, that could be constantly renewed in a similar fashion to his tribunician powers, but to accept that would negate all that he had achieved by giving up the consulship only months before. His refusal was quite spectacular, involving tearing of clothes, a descent to his knees, to beg the people not to force an offensive office upon him. Such histrionics to express a point of view were probably necessary in an age before TV closeups had been invented. He accepted instead the *cura annonae*, literally 'the care of the food supply'. He restored order and the regular supply of food apparently effortlessly, and quickly – in fact so quickly that he has been accused of having caused the shortage in the first place in order to make himself indispensable. The problem was presumably with the transport and distribution of food, not with the growing and harvesting of it. Once the crisis was over, a new senatorial committee was set up to oversee the distribution of the corn dole. Finally, Augustus travelled to the East and installed himself on the island of Samos, where he spent the winter of 22–21. He spent some time adjusting the boundaries and the actual rulers of the smaller Eastern states, and settled internal disputes, but the real target was Armenia, and negotiations with Parthia for the return of the lost standards captured in battle from Crassus in 53, Decidius Saxa in 40 and Antonius in 36. There were other issues at stake as well as this emotive one of the standards. Public opinion would have been satisfied to see Augustus mount an expedition to regain the standards in an all-out war of revenge, but he was not inclined to succumb to pressure. He wanted to avoid war with a power that was Rome's equal, and one which moreover would be fighting on its own ground, with an established and irritating track record of winning; underhanded scheming and then shrewd and subtle diplomacy took the place of boorish battling. It has already been suggested (above, p. 117) that Augustus may have hoped to avoid war but still achieve control over Parthia by installing Tiridates, or rather by allowing Tiridates to install himself with support in the shape of an expedition into Arabia conducted by Aelius Gallus from Egypt. When everything went wrong, Tiridates fled with the kidnapped son of king Phraates, and brought him to Augustus, who returned the young man to Phraates and sent Tiridates to live in Rome. That experiment had failed, but another opportunity soon presented itself of coming to terms with Parthia. In 20, while Augustus was still in the East, the Armenians erupted against their king Artaxias, and sent embassies to ask for the return of the king's brother Tigranes, who had been living as an honoured refugee in Rome for ten years. Marcellus was dead, so Augustus called upon his stepson Tiberius, who was now aged 21 and eligible for command. He was instructed to gather an army, probably from Macedonia and Illyricum, and march to Armenia with the intention of replacing Artaxias by his brother Tigranes.

As Tiberius approached, Augustus went to Syria, and the combined weight of Roman troops and the prestige of the Princeps soon calmed everything down, like oil on troubled waters. Tiberius encountered no opposition and installed Tigranes as king of Armenia – literally, since he put the crown on his head with his own hands. Phraates probably reasoned that this show of force had real substance behind it, and handed over the Roman standards. It is possible that there may have been some agreement as to mutual boundaries and recognition of the Roman influence in Armenia, which Augustus says he could have made into a province, but he resisted, emulating instead the custom of Roman ancestors and limiting himself to installing Tigranes as king. The arrangements made now endured as long as all these three main personalities survived. In 10, Phraates sent his sons to be educated at Rome, but in 2 he expired, perhaps a victim of an assasssin. Augustus was forced to intervene, and sent his grandson Gaius on a military expedition. In 20, this was far off, and the success of Tiberius' expedition and Augustus' diplomatic victory were exploited as if they had been successful wars. Dio thought that Tiberius reacted pompously, and his sceptical comments about Augustus' achievements are not in keeping with the adulatory phrases of the contemporary poets. Artists too were drawn into the scheme. The Prima Porta statue, for instance, has as its centre-piece on the breastplate the Parthian king returning the standards to the victorious Augustus. The standards themselves were taken back to Rome, and placed in the temple of Mars Ultor (Mars the Avenger), the temple vowed in 42 and finally dedicated in 2; the laying up of the standards was celebrated by Ovid. Slogans on the coinage spoke of Armenia captured (*Armenia capta*), and standards returned (*signis receptis*). Pictorially, they are unequivocal about Roman supremacy, since the coins show the subdued Parthian and Armenian just as Horace describes them 'on humbled knees'. Augustus was voted a triumph, which he did not accept, and a triumphal arch in the Forum. He was no doubt satisfied and pleased with his achievements. His own military prowess was negligible, and without Agrippa he would probably never have reached the heights that he presently occupied. The Parthian negotiations had involved the gathering of troops to settle the Armenian question and to make it absolutely clear that Rome controlled the interests of this important state on the borders of Roman and Parthian territory. Augustus had made the necessary show of force without making war, which as a moral victory could be portrayed as superior to and more intelligent and less wasteful than fighting. The procedure was calculated and seemingly painless, a very smooth operation indeed; but the reality may have been much more tense, causing Augustus both metaphorical and physical headaches. He had committed himself, when he opened negotiations with Parthia, to achieving some worthwhile result, but if Phraates had determined not to co-operate what would he have done next? As time went by, he would have looked more and more foolish, and the choice then would have been between a dignified withdrawal and loss of face, or open warfare, which he knew would be difficult if not disastrous. In the literature and as portrayed in the art and sculpture, it all seemed preordained, but the situation was probably one of extreme tension and uncertainty, not at all a suitable scenario for someone who allegedly suffered from liver problems.[22]

During Augustus' absence, affairs in Rome had not been smooth. The people reacted badly when Augustus resigned the consulship, especially since he underlined his decision by his refusal to accept the annual but perpetual version offered to him in the place of the Dictatorship in 22. The faith of the people in his ability to govern the state excluded other ordinary mortals, and for 21 they absolutely refused to elect more than one consul, hoping that Augustus could be persuaded to fill the vacant place. He was wintering on Samos and sent his refusal by letter. It would have the appearance of vacillation if he gave in after two years and accepted the consulship, and it would probably throw him into an unfavourable comparison with Pompeius Magnus, whose tactic had frequently been to sit tight until the Senate and people begged him to do what he had always wanted from the beginning. Agrippa was sent back to Rome as Augustus arrived in the East, but he could not prevent a repeat of 22–21, when in 20 the people again refused to elect a second consul for the following year. For 19, therefore, Sentius Saturninus became sole consul. Agrippa had gone to Spain, and Augustus was still in the East, so the Senate and the lone consul were left to deal with the exhorbitant demands of the praetor Egnatius Rufus to be allowed to stand for the consulship, whether for the next year in the normal way or for the vacant place for 19 is not certain. At any rate he was not legally eligible for either year, not having allowed for the prescribed time lapse between offices. His past successes with the populace seem to have gone to his head. He had performed excellently as aedile, gathering together at his own expense a fire brigade, something which Rome lacked, with which he put out several fires in the city. There was a precedent in that Crassus had also formed a fire brigade, but he used it to put out fires only if he could buy the property, so the only person who gained anything was Crassus. Egnatius Rufus was slightly more altruistic, but of course he was using his fire brigade as a vehicle for his own promotion, and the fact that some of the urban plebs were rescued and their houses saved was merely a fortunate by-product. That did not matter to the practical lower-class Romans, who refunded him for his expenses in maintaining his gang of slaves. At the end of his term of office, Rufus boasted that he handed over the city intact to his successor, indicating that others had not enjoyed quite such an unsullied record, which is only to be expected in a closely inhabited area with a large quantity of wooden buildings and no fire service. The ordinary inhabitants of Rome, always grateful for innovations which assisted them, elected Rufus to the praetorship. If he had been content with that, and had had the grace or good sense to wait until he was eligible for higher office, he may have survived to enjoy an esteemed career. As it was, with the people behind him, the Princeps absent and the most able lieutenant in Spain, he began to cause trouble. Sentius Saturninus refused his candidacy on perfectly reasonable grounds. The next stages are obscure, but resulted in the passing of the *senatus consultum ultimum*, the instant suppression of a popular riot before it began, and the condemnation of Rufus for an alleged conspiracy, followed naturally by his execution. The Senate had acted responsibly and showed itself capable and willing to defend itself against popular pressure, though whether the senators thought of their own interests or those of Augustus as the first priority is not established.[23]

The long stay in the East was not a sinecure for Augustus. Administrative work did not cease, though there is evidence for only a little of it. Dio's account contains details of the territories which he reorganised, and the curious statement that he wrote to the Senate to express his opinion that it would be wise not to extend Roman territory beyond what Rome already possessed in the East, and that he thought it best to leave the allied states to their own government. This may be an anchronism, for Dio was certain that Augustus consistently wished to retain the Empire within its limits, whereas this was his later philosophy, after the Varan disaster in AD 9. The source for Dio's information is unknown, but there may have been a small element of truth in the report in that Augustus perhaps wrote concerning one or two specific states, affirming that he did not wish his arrangements with the client kings to be disturbed. At this period expansion was still very much alive, as witnessed by the campaigns in Spain, the Alps, and in Germany. Rome was a world power, destined to rule the earth; her fame had spread as far as the Indian sub-continent. Trade with India was already established, and while Augustus was in the East an embassy arrived. There were many embassies arriving all the time, but none perhaps so splendid and outlandish as this one. The Romans saw tigers for the first time, and no doubt all kinds of luxurious goods were sent as presents. At Athens, Augustus reputedly witnessed a vivid self-sacrifice by one of the Indian sages, who was initiated into the cult of Demeter and Kore, and then immolated himself in the sacred fires. Augustus' response is not recorded. As the troubles of 19 proceeded in Rome, envoys came to him to ask him to take the vacant consulship. Instead, he insisted upon the appointment of one of the envoys, Quintus Lucretius, who had been proscribed long ago but had obviously escaped. It may be that Augustus intended to make a conciliatory gesture by appointing this man, but he would not take the consulship himself. Dio relates the troubles in Rome to the return of Augustus, but he probably did not rush home on account of the execution of Egnatius Rufus and the possibility that in his absence there would be a return to the days of the demagogues. In the autumn of 19 he set out for Rome, where more honours were voted to him. He declined most of them, except the foundation of an altar to Fortuna Redux, the goddess who presided over homecomings. Preoccupied perhaps with saving Augustus for the Roman world, she was not paying sufficient attention for Vergil, who had come to Athens to meet his patron and died at Brundisium on the return journey.[24]

PLATES

Plate 1 Bust of the young Octavian, aged *c.* 17. The portrait may not be contemporary; it is an idealised and possibly even a posthumous copy. Courtesy Vatican Museums, Vatican City.

Plate 2 Silver denarius of 44, showing the head of Caesar on the obverse, where he is styled Imperator and Pontifex Maximus. The reverse shows Venus Victrix, Caesar's divine ancestress. She holds Victory in her right hand. *BMCR* I 545.4152. © British Museum.

Plate 3 Bronze sestertius of 43. Octavian on the obverse as C. Caesar, consul and priest. On the reverse Julius Caesar is styled *Dictator Perpetuo* but is not yet deified, which means that the coin belongs to the period before November 42. *BMCR* II 404.74. © British Museum.

Plate 4 Gold aureus of 38, with the head of Julius Caesar on the obverse. Octavian calls himself *Divi Iuli filius*, and uses *Imperator* as a *praenomen*. Marcus Vipsanius Agrippa is honoured on the reverse as consul designate, his reward for his successes in Gaul. *BMCR* II 411.102. © British Museum.

Plate 5 Silver denarius of 31, depicting Octavian on the obverse and Venus Victrix
on the reverse, holding a helmet and sceptre. Her shield bears a star, and
the legend refers to Caesar *divi filius*. BMC 599. © British Museum.

Plate 6 Bronze sestertius probably of the period of the battle of Actium. Even in
31 Octavian did not allow the people and army to forget the divine Caesar,
styled *Divos Julius* on the obverse. BMCR II 413.106 © British Museum.

Plate 7 Gold aureus of 27 celebrating the fall of Alexandria in 30, signified by
the crocodile and the legend *Aegypt capta*. BMC 655. © British Museum.

III

Plate 8 Bronze head of Augustus cut off from a larger statue. Found beyond the Egyptian frontier in the Nubian city of Meroe where it had been taken as a trophy. © British Museum.

Plate 9 Gold aureus of 27. The head of Augustus is surrounded by the legend *Caesar cos. VII civibus servateis,* indicating that he had saved the lives of citizens. The name Augustus appears over the head of the eagle on the reverse. *BMC* 656. © British Museum.

Plate 10 Silver denarius probably of 18, celebrating the recovery of the Roman standards from the Parthians in 20. The moneyer P. Petronius Turpilianus, one of the *IIIVIRI monetalis,* depicts the goddess Feronia, an Italian deity of nature. *BMC* 13. © British Museum.

Plate 11 Sestertius made of brass, probably of 20. The obverse reminds people once again that Augustus was the saviour of the citizens. *BMC* 171. © British Museum.

V

Plate 12 The famous statue of Augustus found in a villa near the Tiber at Prima Porta. Augustus is shown barefoot, equating him stylistically with the gods and heroes. He is in military dress, and the scenes on the breastplate depict the Parthian King returning the standards to Augustus himself. Although the standards were recovered by diplomacy rather than military means, the emphasis is on military prowess. Courtesy Vatican Museums, Vatican City.

VI

Plate 13 Idealised head of Augustus. Courtesy Vatican Museums, Vatican City.

Plate 14 Part of a bronze equestrian statue from Greece. Courtesy National
Archaeological Museum, Athens.

Plate 15 Head of Augustus, veiled for making sacrifice to the gods. Courtesy
Römisch-Germanisches Museum, Cologne.

Plate 16 Wreathed head of Augustus displaying the calm, assured and noble authority typical of the fully developed Augustan portraiture. Photo Karen R. Dixon. Mittelrheinisches Landesmuseum Mainz.

Plate 17 Cameo of Augustus; the setting is an addition of the seventeenth century. Courtesy Römisch-Germanisches Museum, Cologne.

Plate 18 Sardonyx cameo of Augustus. The gold diadem is a medieval addition. © British Museum.

Plate 19 Gold aureus, probably dated to 12. Augustus wears an oak wreath and is styled simply Caesar Augustus. On the reverse, Marcus Vipsanius Agrippa is depicted wearing his mural and naval crowns, won as battle honours on land and sea. *BMC* 110. © British Museum.

Plate 20 Silver denarius of 12. Augustus on the obverse, and Julia, Gaius and Lucius on the reverse. *BMC* 106. © British Museum.

Plate 21 Produced late in his reign, this head of Augustus portrays him as the eternally youthful Princeps. No statues or busts of Augustus showed any signs of ageing even when he had reached his seventies. © British Museum.

Plate 22 Head of Livia in green basalt. It was previously thought to be that of Augustus' sister Octavia. Courtesy Musée du Louvre. Photo La Licorne.

Plate 23 Marble bust of Livia, a fourth century copy of the original of 27–23, found in Egypt. Courtesy Ny Carlsberg Glyptotek.

Plate 24 Wreathed head of Livia. Courtesy Römisch-Germanisches Museum, Cologne.

Plate 25 Statue of Livia as the goddess Ceres, or perhaps Fortuna. Courtesy Ny
Carlsberg Glyptotek.

Plate 26 Cameo of Augustus' daughter Julia. © British Museum.

Plate 27 The *Gemma Augustea* from the last years of Augustus' reign. The goddess Roma sits in the centre with Augustus to her left. All the symbols of Roman power surround him, the eagle under his seat, the oak wreath (*corona civica*) above him, the shield beneath his feet. The scene depicts a triumphal procession, perhaps that of AD 12, in which case the general descending from the chariot is Tiberius. The emphasis is on military successes; the whole of the lower level of the cameo is taken up with victorious soldiers and captured enemies. Courtesy Kunsthistorisches Museum, Vienna.

Plate 28 Portrait of Gaius Caesar from late in Augustus' reign, probably 2 BC to AD 4. © British Museum.

Plate 29 Tiberius depicted as a young man, though he was probably aged about 42 at the time the sculpture was executed. © British Museum.

Plate 30 Statue of Tiberius. Courtesy Vatican Museums, Vatican City.

6

TOTUS ORBIS TERRARUM

At his homecoming in the autumn of 19, Augustus was in a much stronger position than at any of his previous returns to Rome. The food crisis of 22, and his prompt, successful action in dealing with it, coupled with the clamorous insistence of the populace that he should always occupy one of the consulships each year, had only served to highlight his popularity and to demonstrate that when he was absent the state did not run quite so smoothly. Acceptance of Augustus' pervasive influence may not have been quite so universal as he liked to claim, but at least his power was assured, legally sanctioned, and preserved by a combination of determination, alert watchfulness, and the latent if reluctant use of force. Military strength was never mentioned, but no one could be in any doubt that should such a drastic measure prove necessary, Augustus would not have hesitated to use it. Precise definition of Augustus' powers is bedevilled as always by lack of any sources at all, or sometimes by conflicting information. It is certain that in 18 he was granted proconsular *imperium* for a further five years, along with Agrippa, who was also granted tribunician power for the same period, thus becoming Augustus' colleague on one of the five occasions when the Princeps asked for one. There is ongoing debate as to the precise extent of both Augustus' and Agrippa's proconsular power (see above, p. 122), and even more controversy over the powers granted to Augustus on his return in 19. Dio's statement that Augustus was granted 'a kind of consular power for life' has been contested for generations. Dio goes on to say that Augustus henceforth had the right to twelve lictors and to take his seat between the two consuls in the Senate, but the unresolved problem concerns the reality of the powers that Augustus received. It can be interpreted in two different ways. It may mean that Augustus merely took the honorary insignia of a consul denoting his special rank, but did not hold the power as such; or on the other hand he may have received full powers, in which case the twelve lictors and the special seat in the Senate would follow as a matter of course. Unfortunately Dio's source is unknown, and he is the only ancient author who relates these facts, so firm corroboration for what he says cannot be found, which leads to uncertainty, speculation, and therefore argument. Augustus himself makes the explicit statement that when he was offered the consulship every year for life (in 22), he refused the offer. The difference between the consulship and consular power would be sufficiently well known to the inhabitants of the Roman world, but the omission of any reference whatsoever in this context to a compromise made only three or four years later is almost an insult to people's intelligence. Likewise, it is strange that Suetonius, with his passion for classification of information into categories, did not mention the 'consulship for life' immediately following the statement that Augustus asked for two colleagues whenever he was consul himself. The idea was rejected, but if Dio is correct, and Augustus did eventually assume consular power, this would be the place for Suetonius to add a footnote that Augustus had only to wait a while before he realised his ambition in a slightly different form. But Suetonius makes no reference to it, and it is too simplistic to suggest that some tired-eyed copyist missed out the vital line that would have settled the matter once and for all.[1]

There are several scholars who believe that Augustus accepted the consular powers for life, thus reaching his apogee at this point, being now endowed with all the powers that he needed to control the Empire; it is usually pointed out that he had relinquished far too much in 23 by giving up the consulship because the *tribunicia potestas* and proconsular *imperium* could not compensate for all that he had lost, so it was merely the logical outcome that he should take up the consular powers again in an altered form without holding the actual office. If it is accepted that Augustus held *imperium consulare* from 19 onwards then it simplifies very considerably the problems relating to certain of his enactments and actions which cannot be attributed solely to any of his other powers. Those who reject the idea that Augustus assumed consular power for life are forced to find a way of reconciling Augustus' own assertion that he conducted the censuses of 8 BC and AD 14 by dint of consular powers. The usual solution is to interpret the consular powers in these two instances as special temporary grants made specifically for the purpose of conducting the censuses. The other aspects of consular power outlined by Dio, such as the use of twelve *fasces* and the right to sit between the consuls, must then be either rejected out of hand as errors of fact or construed as honorary grants with no more substance than supreme distinction. But empty honours cannot have been all that was implied here; the right to display all the insignia of the consuls was surely not curtailed by any limitation on his actions, even in theory, and in practice it would have required considerable fortitude to point out in a debate in the Senate that the opinions just expressed by that man sitting between the two consuls carried no weight, since he possessed only the honours and not the powers of the consuls. Augustus' influence, *auctoritas*, was fully recognised and very firmly embedded in senatorial consciousness without being defined too closely. Perhaps this is the key to the puzzle, in that neither Augustus nor the Senate ever progressed beyond a deliberate vagueness on the issue of consular powers and their duration. It must be admitted that it ran counter to everything else in Augustus' scheme of things to accept any office, or the powers of any office, for life. Suetonius may be mistaken in reporting that Augustus was granted permanent supervision of morals and legislation (*morum legumque regimen perpetuum*). This statement is not necessarily accurate, because Dio says that the grant was for five years only; in any case, supervison of morals, permanent or temporary, is not in the same league as consular power. Augustus does not elucidate this problem in the *Res Gestae*, and indeed it was never his intention to account for himself in minutely documented detail. But unlike his proconsular *imperium* which was renewed in 18 for a further five years, and then at successive intervals thereafter, renewal of consular power is not heard of, which absence of evidence proves nothing since it can be used to argue on the one hand that he never held consular power at all, or on the other hand that he did indeed adopt it for life, so there was of course never any need to renew it, which is why we do not hear of it. This spiral argument could run and run forever without resolution. It could be suggested that if in 18 Augustus did not feel that *imperium proconsulare* could be granted for life, nor even for ten years, then it was not the time to accept anything so inflammatory as life-long consular powers. He liked to progress imperceptibly, step by step, as Tacitus recognised when he described Augustus' gradual assumption (*insurgere paulatim*) of all the Imperial powers that later Emperors enjoyed. It was true that the people had begged him to be consul each year, so he was assured of their approval, but it was not the people who had murdered Caesar. That desperate act was to be laid at the door of the Senate, and hitherto Augustus had mollified the Senate by avoiding anything in his fusion of influence and real powers that hinted at permanence. Without further information there is only speculation on which to base any opinion. It is possible that Augustus and the Senate had reached agreement in conferences which have gone unrecorded. Scholars have noted that after 19 the two parties seem to have been reconciled, and the arrangements for the consulship in general and Augustus' consular power in particular may have been part of a compromise, a sort of package with more far-reaching effects than the establishment of Augustus' personal authority. Prior to 19, the consuls had been new men, all of them naturally acceptable to Augustus himself; the nobles had scarcely been allowed a glimpse of the consulship. After 19, there was a noticeable reversal of this trend; more and more nobles reached the consulship, to the near-exclusion of the new men.[2]

The nobility was now a mixed bag of ancient Roman families and new nobles elevated by Augustus from both Roman and Italian stock. Thus the composition of the aristocracy was broadened, but this was not enough. Without experience of the highest office the nobles would lose their influence at an alarming rate, and both sides knew it. Having demonstrated that he could exclude them from all further influence in the state if he so wished, perhaps Augustus felt that it was time to relax a little and permit a controlled resurgence of noble power. The old Republican nobility had suffered enormous losses in the two great civil wars, and had now been diluted by Augustus' own noble creations, but even though some of the nobility owed their advancement to him, Augustus probably did not trust them as a class, not for an instant, and so if he were to foster their advancement he would need to be certain that by doing so he could not be eclipsed himself. If he were to be toppled from his supreme position, the resultant vacuum would soon be filled by the usual Republican round of clever politicians turned victorious generals, warring on each other to retain their powers. A balance was necessary between obliterating the nobles altogether, which he could have brought about if he had so wished, and allowing them so much influence that they posed a threat to his survival. In 23 Augustus had demonstrated his willingness to renounce the consulship for ever, and for over four years he had survived intact. A grant of consular power at this juncture could hardly increase his influence to any dangerous degree because he was already indisputably supreme. The hypothetical compromise of 19 may have evolved from these considerations as an offer made by Augustus himself at a point where the nobles were fully cognisant of reality, frustrated, impotent, and willing to come to terms. If the offer of compromise originated with the nobles it signified only that they had given in and that Augustus had obtained what he needed, but it is much more likely that he met them half way and made the following proposal: he would not hold the office of consul, but to all intents and purposes he would have every appearance of *being* consul, and in return he would open up the much-sought-after magistracy to the nobility. As a guarantee for their good behaviour they were to know at all times who was in charge and to whom they owed their advancement. Tacitus' general statement that Augustus called himself consul (*consulem se ferens*) strictly belongs to the era when Augustus was endeavouring to thrust the memory of the Triumvirate into the background, but since Tacitus was trying to compress into one paragraph all the elements of fully evolved Imperial rule his phrase may have wider relevance, extending to the final panoply of Augustus' authority. There is no proof that this is what happened in 19, but the arrangement would have been very attractive. It would have the added advantage of calming the populace, who would no longer need to indulge in disruptive riots in order to realise their desire for Augustus to be consul. Exhaustion may have played a part. Augustus had waited a long time while the people fruitlessly demanded that he should be consul, while the nobles were made aware that they could not progress without his sanction and while the mutual distrust between populace and nobility worked itself to a climax. Now, and forever after, the two sides were held in check by one man, and each could progress assured of his protection. The waiting game had paid off handsomely.[3]

134

Augustus was now in his forties, already the elder statesman by dint of his long experience. He could afford to allow himself a certain degree of satisfaction, both personal and public. At home he was perhaps content. His extended family had not yet begun to give him too much cause for concern. Livia's role in his life is recognised as important but it is not elaborately documented. Dio gives her a voice and opinions of her own, which she undoubtedly had, but Dio uses her as a vehicle to present a point of view that is not necessarily hers, much as he uses Maecenas and Agrippa to present alternative constructions of Imperial government in Book 52 of his work. More telling is the inscription from Aphrodisias referring to Livia's interest in the people of Samos, which is admitted by Augustus. She was unsuccessful in persuading her husband to grant them their freedom as they had petitioned him, but this cannot have been the only occasion when she expressed an opinion. She asked for citizenship for a Gaul, but Augustus declined to 'prostitute' the citizenship, and instead liberated the man from all tribute since he could sustain financial losses better than the dilution of a privilege. There will have been many more petitioners who sought access to Augustus via his wife, but there is little information on the case histories, and none at all about Livia's autonomy in making decisions about which items to refuse on her own account and which to refer to her husband. Suetonius gives the impression that Augustus' relationship with his wife was rather clinical when he recounts the fact that Augustus used to write everything down, even when he wanted to talk to Livia, so that he would say no more and no less than he intended. On matters of state, and most especially on occasions when he could be observed and overheard, this may have been true; an *aide memoire* is useful for a man who needs to remember many things at once, and the dangers of uncontrolled garrulousness are very serious. A loose tongue can lead to distraction which wastes time or gets the speaker involved in all sorts of difficulties that he can well do without, and then there is the danger that people who overhear can go off with half-formed stories which become more elaborate at every repetition. In off-duty hours we are surely not meant to assume that he wrote down ordinary conversation, to remind himself to inform Livia that she looked becoming in her latest clothes, or that he had enjoyed his dinner. Augustus' public image is all that has descended through the ages, so that it is difficult to discern the man. In the glimpses that are afforded us, Augustus seems to have been subject to the same doubts, emotions, joys and angers as anyone else, which makes it all the more remarkable that he could overcome the human norms to emerge as an acknowledged super-being, and moreover sustain the act for so many years. The anecdotes about him belong mostly to the more relaxed time when his power was assured and he was older and more experienced; the earlier tales are reactive rather than self-instigated, though a witty response reveals the way of thought and self-possession of the individual just as much as an original statement. Augustus never seems to have been bothered by what men thought of him; he was self-sufficient, relied only upon himself in emotional terms if not in practical affairs, and had no illusions about humanity in general.[4]

Perhaps because he was self-sufficient he could take a joke at his own expense, as several anecdotes suggest. He possessed a sense of humour that was as cynical on his own account as it was on anyone else's. In his youth he had written, among other things, a tragedy about Ajax. Looking back on it later he cringed and obliterated it; in the Roman world writings were wiped away with a sponge, much as pencil marks can be removed with an eraser nowadays, so when a friend asked him what had become of his tragedy he said that Ajax had committed suicide by falling on his sponge. He was capable of making humorous gestures, as when he heard of an auction of the property of an equestrian who had fallen into huge debts, impossible to pay off. He instructed his agents to bid for the man's pillows, because if he could slumber on them while burdened with so many worries then they must be specially effective in inducing sleep. On those occasions when he was bested by intelligent people or ironic circumstances, Augustus laughed instead of getting angry. People seem to have been allowed reasonable access to him and considerable freedom of speech; witty or biting retorts are on record which brought him to down to earth, and sometimes made him change his mind. A Greek writer of epigrams used to approach him constantly, every time he came down the Palatine to the Forum, offering samples of his work in an attempt to gain financial rewards. Tired of the man, Augustus wrote some verses of his own and gave them to him, but the Greek turned it to his own advantage by telling him that he thought the verses were very good. He thrust some money into Augustus' hand, telling him that if had possessed more, he would gladly have given it to him. Augustus took the hint and gave in. He paid the epigrammatist 100,000 sesterces, probably aware that by the next day there would be a long line of versifiers queuing up on the Palatine as he emerged. In a circumstance of more serious consequence, a soldier asked for Augustus' support in a legal case, and in response Augustus chose a lawyer to act on the soldier's behalf. Not content with that, the soldier yelled 'Caesar, when you were in danger at Actium, I did not choose a substitute! I fought for you myself.' Augustus did the decent thing and acted as counsel. These tales reveal something of both the private and public image. Augustus was a hard-nosed realist with a full appreciation of the responsibility he owed to the state. His whole life was tailored to that end, rigidly controlled within the bounds of ordinary human experience. On his deathbed he acknowledged that it had all been an act, though a highly successful one, when he asked the assembled family and friends if they had enjoyed the show. The act was not always a sham, of course; it combined his own characteristics with a necessary performance of duty. His tastes were simple, his home life the embodiment of the old Roman virtues that he began to promote actively in the years after his return in 19. In so long a reign, if these simple tastes had been contrary to his nature, the strain would have told, and been revealed, but apart from his alleged penchant for deflowering virgins it is not recorded that he was ever discovered secretly revelling in a luxury he frowned on in others. The state and his life were inextricably intertwined, and he was prepared to devote all his energies to what he saw as his duty to the Roman world. Perhaps misguidedly, he expected and demanded the same of his family.[5]

History may have been very different if Livia and Octavian had produced healthy, surviving sons early in their marriage. According to Suetonius only one child was conceived and was born prematurely, by which he presumably means that the infant died at birth or was stillborn. There were never to be any heirs of Augustus other than those he promoted or finally adopted, and the fact that the ultimate heir was Tiberius, Livia's first son by her previous marriage, has led to speculation that she was behind the unfortunate deaths of all the others. Tiberius was clearly not Augustus' first choice, and awareness of that cannot have been encouraging to Livia's son. Whether it caused family squabbles between Augustus and Livia can never be substantiated except via unreliable gossip. When Augustus returned to Rome in 19 one of his first acts was to bestow the rank of ex-praetor upon Tiberius, to allow him to reach higher offices so much the faster, and Tiberius' brother Drusus was permitted to stand for office five years before the usual age. It was apparent that their careers were to be promoted and that they had special status, but there was still the knowledge that they both held second place after direct heirs of Augustus himself. His daughter Julia, widowed by the death of Marcellus and given in marriage to Agrippa, had given birth to a son in 20. Her second son was born in 17. The boys were marked out as successors from the start. Augustus eventually adopted both his grandsons, the elder named Gaius Caesar, and the younger Lucius Caesar. The adoptions cannot have stemmed from a decision made on the spur of the moment after the birth of the two boys; it is much more likely that it derived from long-term planning and was part of a pact made with Agrippa before he had even married Julia, to produce heirs that were doubly acceptable, almost as if Agrippa and Augustus had fathered them. Julia's feelings were probably not consulted; her *raison d'être* was to bear children, nothing more. The future held great promise for the establishment of a dynasty, and with that came a sense of security. In addition there were many satellites whose relationship to the family could be utilised. Marriages were kept as far as possible within the tight family circle. Agrippa divorced his wife Marcella, the elder daughter of Octavia and sister of Marcellus, in order to marry Julia. The abandoned Marcella was then married to Iullus Antonius, son of Marcus Antonius and Fulvia, but brought up by Octavia in her household; so he and Marcella could not have been strangers to each other. It did not matter whether they were happy so long as they were playing their parts in the scenario that Augustus was writing for them. A year or so after Augustus returned to Rome, Tiberius was married to Agrippa's daughter Vipsania, who was the woman he truly adored; if he had been allowed to remain in this happy state the story of his reign might also have been happier. Duty to the state came before personal contentment, but by disallowing freedom of choice Augustus brought undeniable misery to his family and friends. He attended carefully to the psychological needs of the Romans, Italians and the provincials more assiduously than he ever considered the needs of his relatives.[6]

As yet the future cast no shadow. It may have been obscured by the sheer enormity of the administrative tasks that lay ahead, but the outlook cannot have seemed so bleak as it probably did on several occasions in the past. For the first time the benefits of peace could be put to good use; in the foundations which were laid now the nascent Empire is already visible, moulded out of older forms, tested by experiment, and remoulded now and then until most of the administrative machinery worked with varying degrees of success. There was some innovation but it was seldom startlingly spectacular. Most legislative and administrative measures went through evolutionary stages until they reached maturity, and some were still evolving after Augustus' death. It was perhaps impossible to arrive at the solutions all at once, even if it was obvious what those solutions should be. By opting for a gradual evolution instead of impatiently executed radical changes, Augustus allowed failures and defects to be revealed, with the result that amendments seemed vitally necessary rather than arbitrarily imposed. The evolutionary process naturally has its darker side. Augustus stands accused by Tacitus of encroaching on power, gathering it into his own hands until he held everyone and everything in his grasp. It cannot be denied that such was the end result, and any judgement formed from that standpoint cannot help but be influenced by it, but it may be a little too cynical to suppose that the result fitted an original master plan formed after the Ides of March 44. It presupposes that Augustus had no other end in view, and denies his flexibility; it suggests that he did everything purely for self-gratification and ignores the devotion to duty and unremitting hard work. If liberty was denied to some people because Augustus took over the state, it is well to remember that what that liberty actually meant was freedom to exercise power among the restricted few, not liberty for all. Whole classes of people were subject to this liberty without sharing in it. There was now a limit to ambition, because no one could rise to a pre-eminence equal to and certainly not superior to that of Augustus, and to arrive anywhere near the top of the scale it seemed that one must curry favour with the master. Most contemporaries may have shrugged and remembered worse times in the past; writers like Tacitus and Pliny only knew that Augustus' achievements had very quickly led to domination by men such as Nero and Domitian. Their resentment coloured their perception of the era that preceded Imperial rule, an era through which they had not lived and which seemed sweeter for being further away and unattainable, so they needed someone to blame for the loss of what they came to see as the innocent Golden Age, and the substitution of tyranny as they experienced it. If Augustus stifled ambition and initiative then he also stifled the constant turnover of supreme military leaders with private armies, whose short-term plans did not include a strategy for Rome and Italy and the provinces, and whose long-term plans, if they entertained any, never had the chance to come to fruition before they were overturned by the next general.[7]

Like Caesar, Augustus had seen most of the provinces of the Empire, and thought in terms of the whole Roman world. He has been accused of thinking only of Rome and Italy, but this perhaps requires modification. He saw himself at the head of all things, Rome as the mistress of the world and Italy in a favoured position; but he also thought of the provinces and their welfare. How he or any other Emperor conceptualised the world without the aid of maps and atlases, rapid transport, and enhanced communications via E-mail and satellites remains a mystery, but at least Augustus knew where there were strengths and weaknesses. He may not have formulated precise plans for the integration and Romanisation of the various peoples of the Empire, but neither did he plan for murderous exploitation at the expense of the provinces for the exaltation of Rome. Policy is difficult to discern at this distance in time and without all the fine details. Augustus did not have to prepare an election manifesto, nor did he have to account for himself in public debates on Imperial television programmes. His retrospective account in the *Res Gestae* is carefully phrased and its purpose was to assess in the most positive fashion what had already happened. Intentions and hopes which came to nothing are absent, and very few of his contemporary thoughts or ideas are on record. Historians can only assess events and developments and extrapolate from them some consistency of purpose and planning, which is the wrong way round as well as haphazard. Current opinion favours a series of *ad hoc* decisions made on the spur of the moment rather than the existence of a 'blue-print for Empire'. The one extreme makes Augustus seem irresponsible to the point of vacillation and inconsistency, continually reactive with never the chance to be proactive, always running just to stand still. The other extreme imbues him with a foresight bordering on the clairvoyant. Most probably the truth lies somewhere between the two, depending on each individual circumstance. Although he would be occupied for much of his time with day-to-day minutiae, it is at least likely that he devoted some attention to the Empire and the directions and ideals he would have liked to follow. Perhaps he arrived in some cases at a broad general outline containing more than one option, so as not to be too rigid or inflexible. The Roman world in 19 was far from homogeneous or pacified. Italy was in some areas still tribal, and was certainly not unified. Rome did not yet govern all the Alpine region, and so her communications with the Rhine and Danube were not everywhere secure. It would require another three or four years before Tiberius and Drusus, following on from the achievements of other generals, would finally subdue the area and bring the Alpine passes under Roman control. Gaul had been fought over continually and Agrippa was there in 19, but the tribes were not fully pacified and it was felt that there could be no such peace until Roman control extended to the Rhine – hence the campaigns that began in the next decade. Spain, especially the northern part, was rebellious and unstable. Augustus' campaigns in 26–25 had failed to subdue the Cantabri, who were brought to heel by Agrippa in 19, but even then, after huge Roman losses, the spirit of the tribesmen remained proud and free. Agrippa was awarded a triumph, which he refused. One reason for his refusal may have been that he never wished to place himself above his master and friend Augustus, but the more compelling reason why he did not hold his triumph was that victory in Spain was nowhere near complete.[8]

The provinces of Africa, comprising a strip of territory bordering on the Mediterranean, had been handed to the Senate in 27. The younger Balbus extended Roman control over the nomadic tribes on the borders of the province and subdued the Garamantes, for which he was allowed a triumph in 19, the last to be celebrated by a provincial governor not part of the Imperial family. Henceforth triumphs were reserved for the favoured few in the Imperial household; for others, triumphal processions were converted into the less ostentatious insignia and titles, minus the pomp and ceremony. Egypt remained Augustus' own preserve, jealously guarded from senatorial influence and governed by equites with the title Prefect. The borders with Ethiopia were stable, secured by the Prefect Publius (or Gaius, according to Dio) Petronius in a campaign conducted in 25 or 24 and again in 22 to subdue a rebellion by the Ethiopian queen Candace. When she submitted she was allowed to send representatives to Augustus on the island of Samos, where he granted her favourable terms and magnanimously abolished or perhaps reduced the tribute exacted in the past. The East had already claimed much of Augustus' and Agrippa's attention. Where there was stability, Augustus left matters as they were, but kept a vigilant eye on developments. His recent diplomatic success in retrieving the lost standards from the Parthians assured a temporary peace. Armenia was in the hands of a king favourable to Rome, and for the time being Rome and Parthia had reached a temporary balance. Elsewhere Augustus interfered when he felt it necessary to do so, sometimes deposing unsuitable monarchs, installing new ones, and on occasion annexing the territory of deceased rulers – for instance, when Amyntas of Galatia was killed Augustus converted most of the territory into a Roman province and installed a governor. The key to the East was Syria, one of the provinces assigned to Octavian in 27. It was the base for military operations both internal and external, surrounded by client kingdoms and facing Rome's most co-ordinated and organised potential enemy, Parthia. In 19 it was still under the supervision of Agrippa, via his deputies, and perhaps because of the recent tours of duty by both Agrippa and Augustus, it was quite secure. Judaea was as stable as Herod could make it, backed by Augustus; he played the game shrewdly and so did Augustus, and the balance was maintained until 4, when Herod's death undid some of the stability.[9]

The arrangements for provincial government in 27 were not immutable, and there were some adjustments, according to circumstances, as time went on. Gallia Narbonensis was given back to the Senate in 22, but Illyricum, previously senatorial, was converted to an Imperial province when there was military activity in Pannonia. Technically the government of the senatorial provinces was separate from that of the Imperial ones. Augustus appointed legates to govern his provinces, so there was always control over who was sent out, and the governors were answerable to Augustus, who answered for them to the Senate. Senatorial governors were chosen by lot and were directly answerable to the Senate, but it was not so simple or clear cut as that in reality. Augustus' influence extended to all parts of the Roman world and beyond. Embassies came to him personally, effectively relegating the Senate to second place, but Augustus dealt very tactfully with such matters. When the Parthians sent an embassy to him he referred the ambassadors to the Senate, but the senators immediately referred them back again for his decision. The scene was set for him to take over all embassies in future, but he knew that the concept of the state was deeply embedded in the senatorial psyche, so that in dealing with and receiving embassies his actions could be interpreted as a usurpation of the powers of the state, and a slight to Rome herself. None the less he did not flinch from the task, nor did he delegate it. Similarly he did not delegate command of the armies, except in so far as those in the senatorial provinces were not under his direct control. But he was the paymaster, because he controlled state finances, and in any case the armies swore an oath of loyalty to him in person. There could be no doubt about who really commanded the armies. Eventually, Augustus was authorised to make treaties in his own name, which was bowing to the inevitable rather than honouring him. Outsiders, subject for generations to monarchs or chieftains, would not find this unusual; they were accustomed to dealing with a person rather than a state. The Paphlagonians, for instance, and those Romans who had businesses in the country, took an oath of allegiance to Augustus and his family and descendants, swearing to hold the same friends and enemies and risking death and destruction if they should break their oath, which they swore at the altars and shrines of Augustus. In contrast to Octavian's insistence twenty-seven years earlier that various temples in the East should be set up to himself in conjunction with Rome, this time Rome received no mention, as though the concept of Augustus now subsumed Rome. During the Empire, tribesmen who had made a treaty with Rome considered that their allegiance was invalidated when the Emperor with whom they had made the treaty died, or the last of his family expired. This privilege of making treaties, in conjunction with command of the armies, gave Augustus control of foreign policy, with the implied ability to control expansion of the Empire, and rationalisation of its boundaries. It was not long before he embarked on the conquest of new territories, to take in the lands between Italy and the Danube, and the lands beyond the Rhine. In all senses and nuances, Augustus really was the head of state. Such continuity, central direction and wide-ranging powers had not been a feature of the Republic. It has been contested whether this continuity and central direction led to an increasing specialism and professionalism in government both at home and abroad. Senatorial governors chosen annually by lot were not given the opportunity to develop any professional expertise except in a very general sense, but it can also be argued that Augustus did not necessarily choose the best man for the task when he made appointments to magistracies or to provincial commands. His criteria for adminstrative and military posts alike was not ability but suitability – loyalty to the regime and compatibility being the foremost attributes that he would look for. Mistakes were unavoidable even in a carefully scrutinised selection made for all the right reasons, but mistakes teach as much as successes, and if a species of professionalism did not grow up immediately among the administrative personnel, the continuity of the administration of Rome and the provinces would gradually build up into a corpus of knowledge that could be drawn upon by all, and the experience gained by one man provided a basis for Imperial rule thereafter.[10]

Augustus could not sustain the entire government without the co-operation, or the complete subjection, of the Senate, and of the two options the first was by far the better method of working with the senators. A balance was difficult to achieve, because by reaching such a supreme position he had intimidated many people and thereby squashed initiative. He needed intelligent, talented and self-sufficient men in the top-ranking posts in the administration and as provincial governors, but not too talented and definitely minus over-weening self-importance and ambition. No one else should be allowed to rise to power as he had done, but on the other hand men must be encouraged to take up administrative posts and play their part in government. There were to be rewards, but they were in his gift, and he had blocked all avenues to personal advancement except through his patronage, so one of the most serious results was apathy. It was a persistent problem that although they dearly liked to retain their rank, with all its privileges, senators were not so enthusiatic about the duties that went with the rank and privilege, and had become disinterested in attendance at the Senate. Over the years the quorum for passing the *senatus consultum* had to be reduced, and penalties for non-attendance were revived and enforced. The problem was still not solved ten years later, for according to

Dio, Augustus rationalised the Senate meetings in 9, substituting two regular days per month for the irregular timetable that had been in operation in the past. On these two specific days there were to be no court sittings and no other meetings, leaving no valid excuse for non-attendance. In order to inculcate interest in the state and devotion to duty Augustus had to appeal to the stern old standards of the ancient Romans, employing a combination of conciliation and influence, example and legislation. By opening up the consulship to the nobles, he gave senatorial careers an impetus and a purpose, but there was a price to pay in the form of the *lectiones*. There is scant mention in the *Res Gestae* where Augustus passes over them with a terse notice that he overhauled the Senate three times (*Senatum ter legi*). In 18, instead of ejecting men himself, and thus becoming too closely involved on a personal level, he tried a novel way of remodelling the Senate. His ideal was a Senate of 300 members, which would have been more manageable and at the same time would have elevated the chosen senators to a very elite status. He tried to achieve this low figure by delegation. He chose thirty senators himself who were to swear on oath that they were the fittest men to be senators, then each of the thirty were to choose a further five men, and of these five one was to be selected by lot to name another five. This would have produced a neatly interlocked list of 300 men, all of whom owed their selection to the goodwill of another senator, but the method was too cumbersome and complicated and broke down without reaching completion. Augustus had to draw up the final list himself and could not reduce the Senate to the manageable numbers he desired. The remodelled Senate was twice the size that he had originally aimed for, with a final total of 600 members. Augustus began to work more closely with the senators and to involve them in decision-making by means of the *consilium principis* which was formally constituted at some time between 27 and 18. Dio describes it as part of the settlement of 27, as though it was fully operative by then. This may be anachronistic, or perhaps there were rudimentary traces of it which developed further over the next few years. The *consilium* grew out of the normal gathering of family and friends that surrounded any noble, and whose advice he would take on important issues. In its fully evolved form, Augustus' *consilium* comprised one or both of the consuls, a praetor, an aedile and a quaestor, and fifteen senators drawn by lot. It is not certain whether any of the tribunes of the plebs were invited to attend. The personnel were not permanently appointed; Dio says that they were changed every six months, but this causes problems because the consuls held office for the entire year until the introduction of six-monthly suffect consulships in AD 2. It is possible that only the junior magistrates and the fifteen senators chosen by lot were rotated on a six-monthly basis. The advantages and disadvantages of this procedure have been succinctly outlined: there was no better way of obtaining a cross section of senatorial opinion, and no worse way to achieve any degree of expert advice. The latter did not concern Augustus, who did not rely on such a system for advice; the *consilium* was an exercise in psychology. On really important matters advice would be taken from a much smaller, select group of *amici*, and business would be well prepared before it came anywhere near the *consilium*. The main tasks of the latter would be to prepare business for discussions in the Senate, and Augustus could deduce from the preliminary meeting how the full Senate might react. He listened to opinions and on occasion changed his mind on certain issues, for instance in drafting some of the laws, where he would reword passages, or amend them in accordance with the recommendations of the *consilium*. In turn the members of the *consilium* would feel that they had a part to play in government, and even though they may never have been allowed to discuss very serious matters before they had been thoroughly scrutinised by Augustus and his closest associates, they would still be left with a considerable share in the routine administration. Augustus was assiduous in cultivating favourable perceptions, and for most of the time he managed to make the Senate appear to be, in Brunt's description, 'the great organ of the state'. The important point was that there should be no feeling of exclusion from policy decisions and legislative business, and no suspicion that senators were being hoodwinked, cheated, or imposed upon. The *consilium* was no safeguard against absolute rule, but it was important that it should appear that the senators had a voice that was heard by the Princeps and that their opinions were given due consideration.[11]

Almost as soon as Augustus arrived home in 19 he was asked to take on the supervision of laws and morals. The recommendation that he should be appointed *curator legum et morum* came from the people and the Senate, and was repeated in 18, and again in 11. The requests are securely dated, for in the *Res Gestae* Augustus took care to mention the names of the consuls for each of the three years in question. He refused each request because he would not take up an office which would have been inconsistent with the ancient customs, especially since it was offered with the highest powers (*summa potestate*) and without a colleague, which was too reminiscent of the turbulence of the past, and could be construed as the Dictatorship dressed up in different terminology. The ancient sources diverge quite widely on this issue. Suetonius makes the *cura morum et legum* into a permanent appointment and links it with the census, while Dio separates the supervision of morals and the censorial power, both of which he says that Augustus took for five years; but in a later passage Dio throws everything into confusion by placing the renewal of the *cura morum* in 12, when strictly speaking, if it ran for five years from 19, the renewal ought to have occurred in 14, unless there was a two-year gap when Augustus did not have this responsibility. Adding to the confusion, Dio also says in another passage that Augustus was censor, which is almost certainly an error. To a modern audience, 'the supervision of morals' has sinister undertones, but in the Roman world of 19 the need for moral and social reforms had become acute in the aftermath of the civil war between Pompeius and Caesar, and the situation had not been improved by the unhappy years of the Triumvirate. Roman values and virtues had given way to self-interest, lack of scruple, and moral degeneration. It has to be admitted that Octavian had set the example for the first two of these. It was now time to set the state on a more positive course. In his *Res Gestae* Augustus was proud to announce that he led by example, by which he presumably meant to describe his post-Triumviral attitudes and behaviour. He could explain most of his Triumviral actions by claiming that he had been driven by *pietas* in avenging Caesar, but there were certain elements that were not susceptible to this positive interpretation. In general his example was not always detrimental. He had always lived simply, despite his access to wealth. He reserved pomp and ceremony for state occasions and could maintain that what he did was for Rome, not himself. Simplicity and lack of ostentation was suited to his character; it was genuine rather than a calculated act designed to deceive, so when he introduced his sumptuary laws as part of the social legislation beginning in 18, he was immune from the charge of hypocrisy. In other respects, though, he could not escape the charge entirely. His marriage was outwardly stable, but childless, and his adulteries were not denied even by his friends, so the marriage laws and the legislation concerning adultery cast a dubious light on his integrity. At best the social legislation can be seen as a cosmetic exercise, or a response to a perceived set of problems. The principal question concerns whose perception prompted the legislation. Before he introduced his laws designed to increase the population, Augustus read out in the Senate the speech of Quintus Metellus on exactly same social problems. He wished to demonstrate that the situation was not new and the measures he was about to propose were in no way novel. As usual, he called upon the cushioning effects of tradition, and tried and tested customs, as a background for his acts in case he should be accused of dictatorial innovation. He also insisted that he had not acted alone on his own initiative; for posterity, he was careful to explain that he carried out the measures that the Senate asked for, but he does not specify which measures. It is an acknowledged technique in management that instead of forcing through new and unaccustomed ideas it is better to allow people to imagine that the new ideas are their own. Augustus subscribed heavily to this concept, waiting for permission to act and then taking the proposals a little further than had perhaps originally been envisaged. It is also debatable whether Augustus truly believed that he could reform morals and the general social situation by legislation. It is not entirely out of the question that it was just as important to be seen to attempt to improve matters as it was to succeed. The fact that the request that Augustus should be made *curator legum et morum* was repeated, seven years after the social legislation was put into effect, would seem to indicate that it had not been as successful as had been hoped, or that it had not gone far enough for some people's tastes.[12]

The social legislation evolved over a period of time. Just how much time cannot always be documented since Augustus chose to use his family name Julius to denote authorship of his laws, with the result that in some cases they cannot be distinguished from those of Julius Caesar. It is suggested that there was an abortive attempt to begin this programme as far back as 28, or at least before 23, but this rests mainly on a literary reference and has been discounted. Most of the legislation probably belongs to 18 or 17, but the evidence is not complete so it is not possible to date it all accurately, nor is it possible to document the exact course that it took. The ideology behind it seems to be consistent, in that overall it was designed to restore the old Roman virtues of *dignitas* and *gravitas*, to encourage thrift and stamp out corruption, to define the various social orders and keep them distinct but not mutually exclusive, and to propagate an active participation on the part of the upper classes in state affairs. Augustus' task was to weed out undesirable elements from the Senate and to ensure that worthy men remained in its ranks. Secondly he wished to elevate the Senate to a deservedly elite position and then to preserve it in that state, which entailed regulation of its morals and encouraging a legitimate increase in its numbers. Below the ranks of the Senate there were other groups of people who needed to be given a sense of identity and position in the state. The various orders required closer definition as part of a descending hierarchy beginning with the senatorial body and extending downwards through the equestrians, the free citizens, the freedmen of varying status, down to the slaves and the unfree. It was not quite so clinical as it sounds, though Augustus' ideology can fairly be described as a place for everyone and everyone in his place. Social mobility was not prevented, but it was well regulated, so promotion when it came was theoretically deserved. Men of Roman or Italian stock were given preferential treatment, but care was taken to ensure that the lower orders did not swamp the upper classes, and Italians were always slightly behind the Romans, with the provincials ranking after the Italians. The upper classes were the main focus of Augustus' attentions in his social legislation. The restructuring of the Senate was a continuous process, and though reshuffling was carried out at various intervals it never seems to have been successful in pruning away the undesirables in their entirety. Financial qualification for entry to the Senate was increased to 1,000,000 sesterces, which served to elevate the senatorial class to a reasonably exclusive level, though it must be admitted that there were many equestrians and freedmen whose fortunes greatly exceeded this figure, and who could probably have bought and sold any number of senators quite happily without so much as noticing the turnover in their account books. If Augustus had been able to reduce membership of the Senate to his desired total of 300 men, that too would have made the body even more of an elite than it was already, but he had to be content with a more broad-based Senate of 600 members. The exclusive status once established required constant monitoring, since unsuitable men gained entry to the Senate, or on occasion existing members degenerated. The dwindling numbers of the nobility had given cause for concern in the recent past, and in consequence Augustus had been granted the right to create patricians. But these measures did not fill all the gaps. Whenever it came to his notice that worthy men could no longer maintain the expenses of the senatorial class Augustus would help them out financially, but once again this partial remedy merely solved the problem for one generation only. Posterity loomed large in Augustus' social legislation, especially in his attempts to encourage the nobles to replicate themselves. The laws concerning marriage and adultery were primarily directed to this end, though they were designed to address several other moral and social problems as well. There was no lack of Roman population in general, as the rising census figures show, but it was a question of the right sort of population. The Roman world in general and the city of Rome in particular were rapidly filling up with citizens of the lesser sort, while the nobles were beginning to shun legitimate marriage and turn their backs on family life. It was much more attractive to live the single life, take pleasures where and when required, and meanwhile to cultivate rich relatives and friends while waiting for the legacies to materialise. The marriage laws, comprising the *Lex Julia de maritandis ordinibus* of 18, and the amendments of AD 9, the *Lex Papia Poppaea* (passed by two consuls who were not married!) were designed to enforce the proper order of things. The various clauses of the two sets of legislation are impossible to distinguish. Later jurists usually quoted both laws together, without affording modern scholars the opportunity to unravel the various stages of the process. Amendments were made in AD 9 in response to objections raised by the people most affected by the marriage laws. According to Suetonius the equestrians made use of their prerogative to make demonstrations in the theatres and at the games, and did so vociferously. The amendments reduced the penalties on citizens who were married but childless, and may also have incorporated changes made because of practical difficulties in enforcing the laws. It is possible that there were intermediate amendments that have since been lost to sight between the two main laws of 18 BC and AD 9.[13]

The laws of 18 seem to have comprised a straightforward attempt to regulate marriage and the production of children. It was held that men between the ages of 25 and 60, and women between the ages of 20 and 50, had a duty to marry and to procreate. Even after divorce or the death of the husband or wife, people were expected to remarry within a specified period. Quicker promotion was offered to married men with children, and it was enacted that unmarried men and women were ineligible to inherit legacies. Marriages among the classes below senatorial level were not set about with too many restrictions, but senators were forbidden to marry beneath themselves, and were especially prevented from marrying their freedwomen. The prohibition extended to the next two generations. This meant that in future all senators must think very carefully about their choice of wives, not least because the women in question would be the mothers of their children. The purity of the upper classes must be preserved down the generations. Intermarriage between senators and freedwomen had become uncomfortably common, and was attributed to the rise in status of Roman women, who had achieved considerable influence and wealth. They were on the verge of enjoying as much freedom of action as men and worse still had begun to voice their opinions. Fulvia of infamous memory had had the temerity to lead armies and meddle in politics. The more chaste Hortensia had confronted the Triumvirs with well-reasoned objections to the taxation of women, and moreover she had won the day. It seemed that women as well as men preferred a life of freedom of choice, and they too were turning their backs on family life, thus ignoring the one purpose that they were designed for – namely, the production of children and the prop-agation of the human race. A reaction to this dreadful state of affairs was bound to occur as soon as there was time to think of matters other than war. The new generation of Roman women were intractable and difficult to live with, so men who were unable to cope with all this chose instead to marry their favourite ex-slaves who owed everything to them and there-fore remained docile, biddable and probably faithful. Even Augustus was unable to answer for himself when asked by the senators how to curb the influence of women. According to Dio he could offer no practical advice, and simply muttered about decent dress and chaste behaviour. In private he was no doubt extremely thankful that Livia played by the rule book and set the required example to the women of Rome. This newly established liberty for women threatened the very existence of the nobility, so having set up laws to enforce legitimate marriage there was now a need to protect and preserve it. This was embodied in the *Lex Julia de adulteriis coercendis*. Adultery was henceforth a punishable offence. Loopholes were closed as far as possible. Husbands could turn a blind eye to the affairs of their wives, but if they did so they could be prosecuted themselves, risking the same penalties as men who lived off immoral earnings, which reduced them to the status of pimps and their wives to that of prostitutes. A husband or father was allowed sixty days to bring about a prosecution himself, and thereafter anyone over the age of 25 could do so independently. The wronged husband must divorce his wife as a matter of course. Naturally, given the circumstances, a profitable trade in domestic spying grew up; a sort of Roman neighbourhood watch with a slightly different slant. Woman were not granted the same rights as men. They could not prosecute unfaithful husbands, and could only resort to undercover activities to make sure that their errant spouses were punished by the relatives of the 'other woman'.

Morality was not the most important issue that the adultery laws were intended to reform. It was not extra-marital sex that was frowned upon. The crucial factor was the legitimacy of offspring. A man needed to be certain that the child that his wife was carrying was his own, and the only way to ensure that the husband and no one else had access to her was to lock her up and keep her immune from contamination by other men. If that did not work, there was the deterrent of recourse to law, and the draconian penalties that attached to condemnation. The mildest form of punishment was banishment from Rome. There is evidence to suggest that laws on marriage and adultery were in operation by 17, which gives some indication of the importance attached to them by Augustus, who obviously thought there was no time to be lost. He probably reflected with some satisfaction that he had set the senatorial class on its feet and prepared the ground for its future growth along the lines that he had laid down for it. Apart from a periodic readjustment here and there, he had only to wait for the next generation to grow up, schooled in the service of Rome. It is unlikely that he could foresee that sixteen years later he would have to exact the penalties that his laws demanded in the case of his own daughter. It was more than ironic that while he was busily ensuring the legitimacy of offspring for the entire senatorial classs, doubts were already being engendered as to the exact origins of his beloved grandsons, Gaius and Lucius, adopted as his own sons. There was of course no doubt that Julia was their mother, but however chaste and well guarded she had been while she was married to Agrippa, her later behaviour gave plenty of scope for widespread, if silent, speculation as to whether Agrippa really was the father of these two boys. Julia's wide-ranging sexual activities were no secret to anyone except her father, who had no choice when he was informed of it in 2 but to apply the full rigour of the law and banish his only daughter, his only child in fact, to the island of Pandateria.[14]

All forms of unnatural vice among free citizens were prohibited by the adultery laws. Instead of trying to stamp out aberrant sexual practices altogether, the laws permitted such behaviour as long as it was perpetrated upon people other than the nobles and the upright free citizens of Rome. There was a large population who received no protection from the sexual attentions of the upper classes and freeborn citizens, because the principle behind the laws was the preservation of Roman dignity, which did not really extend to the lower orders. This class did not have a voice except by resort to rioting and violence, reserved mostly for life-threatening crises such as food shortages. The most voluble opposition to the social legislation came from the equestrian class. When they expressed their feelings at the theatre, Augustus brought out the sons of Germanicus and put them on display to demonstrate that his laws were designed to produce stalwart citizens like these. The brother of Germanicus, and therefore the uncle of these children, was the future Emperor Claudius who, with his stutter and his limping gait, was not exactly a prime example of Roman manhood, and the irony would not go unnoticed. Claudius had the last laugh, of course. Augustus was as attentive to the equestrians as he was to the senators. He defined the class more closely, establishing the property qualification at 400,000 sesterces. He tried to limit the use of the term *eques* to those men who were eligible to receive the public horse. This was an antiquated right that originated during the early Republic, when the need for cavalry had been met by providing mounts at public expense; hence the title 'equestrians' for the class of men who formed the early cavalry. The military functions had fallen into abeyance, but Augustus revived the ceremonial and formal display. His main purpose seems to have been to recreate the processsion of socially acceptable, physically fit young men, which at one and the same time proclaimed the glory and strength of Rome and provided him with an opportunity to review the equestrians and make adjustments. He excused the physically infirm from taking part in the procession, and eventually he extended this to all those over the age of 35. He desired quality not quantity, and above all else appearances mattered. Though there was an element of charlatanism, the display served its purpose as a cohesive link for the class as a whole, and as a source of pride and self-respect. The equestrians were also distinguished by their right to wear a gold ring, and by the broad purple stripe on their togas. They sat at specially designated seats in the theatre. All these distinctions and privileges served to mark the equestrians as a distinct class, second in line after the senators, whose sons were members of the equestrian class until they entered the Senate. Augustus established and strengthened an unequivocal civic hierarchy, but did not erect rigid barriers between the classes. He monitored the equestrians as he monitored the senators. There were reprimands and punishments for notorious behaviour, and rewards for co-operation. Administrative and military posts were opened up to those equestrians who wished to avail themselves of the opportunities. Eventually, over a long period of time, the four great prefectures were established and came to represent the summit of an equestrian career; the Prefect of Egypt was an early innovation dated to the post-Actium phase in 30; the Praetorian Prefects were established probably in 2; while the prefectures of the Vigiles and the corn supply (*annonae*) were developed somewhat later in AD 6 and 8. Aspiring equestrians could rise even further, though it might require time to do so. The aquisition of the necessary wealth, accompanied by Imperial approval, could ensure entry to the Senate. Perhaps the most famous example is that of Vespasian, whose grandfather and father were equestrians; by means of the accumulated wealth of their immediate family, Vespasian and his brother Sabinus became senators, and the rest, as they say, is history. Such startling social mobility did not flourish immediately under Augustus, but it took root in the ground that he prepared for it.[15]

Probably in 17, by means of the *Lex Junia*, Augustus began to address the problem of the massive increase in the numbers of freed slaves in Rome. In part the problem arose from the easy options available to a master who wished to free his slaves without incurring the 5 per cent tax on manumissions. The formal method of freeing slaves required the presence of a magistrate to witness the proceedings; the manumission tax was levied at the same time. The advantage to the freedman was that this legal procedure entitled him to Roman citizenship. The effect on the administration of the city was to add yet another potential name to the lists of those who received the corn dole. On the other hand the less formal method of freeing slaves avoided this particular complication, but created a different one in its place. All that the master had to do was to assemble his household and make an announcement to them that certain of the slaves, or all of them, were now technically free. This meant that a whole category of ex-slaves were thrust into the wide world without the means to support themselves, nowhere specific to go, no employment, and lacking the advantage of citizenship. Between 17 BC and AD 4, the *Lex Junia*, the *Lex Fufia Caninia*, and the *Lex Aelia Sentia* were successively put into operation to try to stem the flow of manumissions, and to cater for those already freed by the informal processes. A specific category was created by the Junian law, whereby the slaves freed informally were recognised. They were technically free, but their property reverted to their original master when they died and they were not allowed to bequeath it to anyone else. This category of ex-slaves became known as Junian Latins, and they were granted rights that were similar to those of the Latin cities, regarded as the preliminary to Roman citizenship. The provisions of the subsequent laws illustrate the loopholes that had been detected in the previous legislation. First there was a limit to the number of slaves that could be freed at the same time, based on a percentage of the total number of slaves owned by the master in question. Then the ages of both the master and the slaves to be freed were stipulated. No one under 20 could free his slaves without good reason, and slaves had to be aged 30 or more to be eligible for the status of a freedman. Some of the legislation was designed to prevent a young man from freeing slaves in order to swell the ranks of his *clientelae*, which provides a sidelight on the political activity of the upper classes. Life was not as dire as it may seem for many freedmen, who amassed great fortunes and lived well, owning slaves themselves. They were not necessarily passionately interested in Roman citizenship or in politics, though social mobility was not completely denied to them. Suetonius says that Augustus gave dinner parties with great regard for rank. His liberality did not extend beyond the first few classes, and he never invited an ex-slave to dinner, wishing always to preserve that distance of caste which he thought necessary to good government. He instructed Tiberius to maintain a distinction between himself and his subjects. Modern society condemns such inflexible class distinction, but this attitude is a phenomenon of relatively recent lineage, and it is unfair and ineffective to judge Augustus by modern standards. Where slaves were concerned he was at least conscious of basic humanitarian principles. When he was at a dinner party given by Vedius Pollio, a slave accidentally broke a cup which the master of the house valued highly. Pollio ordered the slave to be thrown to the lampreys in the garden pool, which would have been a particularly horrible death, similar to, but slower than, being eaten by piranhas. The slave appealed to Augustus, who asked to see the rest of the set of valuable cups. Deliberately he smashed every one of them. In one destructive act he managed to express both his disgust at Vedius Pollio's cruelty, and his disapproval of the unwarranted display of wealth and luxury, which ran counter to his sumptuary laws. Almost incidentally he saved the life of the slave, but of course no one has recorded what perhaps happened to the unfortunate slave on the morning after the dinner party; there may still have been one or two over-fed lampreys in Vedius' pool. What has gone down in history, and has lost nothing in the retelling, is that Augustus thought it inhuman to value a cup more highly than a slave.[16]

As for the populace at large, Augustus did not curry favours or indulge the people unnecessarily. He catered for them in his administrative measures, most of which came to fruition at a much later stage in his careeer. The rudiments of many of his later achievements had already been laid, revealing that he was conscious of the problems. Administratively the burden of work was increasing, so he created more praetors to deal with it in 23. The lack of a fire brigade has already been noted, and the exploits of Egnatius Rufus underlined the need for a regular system of dealing with fires in the city, so in 21 Augustus gave the aediles charge of 600 public slaves, who formed the prototype *vigiles*, but that body was not fully formed until AD 6. Mindful of the need for rapid communications and of a properly organised scheme for road building and repair, in 20 Augustus appointed men of praetorian rank to the new posts of *curatores viarum*. The food supply required constant attention, and was of first priority if riots were to be avoided. Until the elevation of Gaius Turranius to the post of *Praefectus annonae* the corn supply was administered by the *Praefecti frumenti dandi ex SC* whose title indicates that the Senate had been consulted in their appointment. Julius Caesar had regulated the numbers of recipients of the corn dole, and had tried out a novel way of enumerating and listing them, street by street and block by block, no doubt in an attempt to weed out cheats and the inevitable claimants of dead men's rations. He seems to have established the names of those who had died and ordered the praetors to insert new names as substitutes for them. Augustus inherited the same problems that Caesar had experienced, and dealt with them in a similar fashion. The number of citizens receiving the corn dole exceeded 200,000 in 2, when Augustus was consul for the thirteenth time; at various times the numbers were revised, and the task of keeping track of the names of those eligible for free corn was entrusted to two ex-praetors in 22; in 18 they received two further colleagues. In the city of Rome, building was going on all the time; Augustus' boast that he found a city of brick and left one of marble must be allied to the old adage that Rome was not built in a day, particularly Augustan Rome. The populace benefited from these improvements, and the world looked on. Rome was entering a new age, which Augustus chose to proclaim by the ancient ceremony of the Secular Games. These had been held for the first time after the war with Carthage in 249, and again in 149. They were held at intervals of 100 years, or some said every 110 years. They were meant to be witnessed only once in a lifetime, and as such had achieved a very special nature, but by what convoluted reckoning Augustus arrived at 17 for the next celebration is unknown. He bent the rules somewhat, but it hardly mattered, and no one was likely to contradict him. The poet Horace was commissioned to write the *Carmen Saeculare*, a hymn to Apollo, sung or recited by boys and girls whose parents were still alive. During the sacrifices conducted by Augustus and Agrippa, the state prayers specifically mentioned Augustus and his household alongside the Roman people. Self-advertisement had so far been restricted to individual successes gained on Rome's behalf; now there was an element of supremacy and guardianship, ever present but now fully acknowledged. The difference is subtle but indicative of how far he had come since 44. The games, races, theatrical performances, religious ceremonies and sacrifices that constituted the whole festival of the Secular Games laid emphasis on the greatness of Rome, peace and prosperity, and behind it all the genius and achievements of Augustus.[17]

Though there was still much to accomplish, Augustus probably allowed himself a brief glow of satisfaction with progress so far in 17. In that year Agrippa and Julia presented him with a second grandson, immediately adopted by Augustus himself and named Lucius Caesar. There were now two heirs, and if Augustus himself were to die Agrippa could be entrusted to continue his policies and government until Gaius and Lucius were old enough to take over. Livia's sons Tiberius and Drusus were both of them proving themselves more than capable in the military and administrative spheres. Augustus' world was as secure as he could make it. It seems that his social legislation and the adoption of heirs was not welcome to everyone, but that is only to be expected, given the diversity and perversity of human nature. To paraphrase another famous head of state with a reputation for realism, it was simply not possible to please all of the people all of the time. The question is how far were men prepared to go in expressing their discontent? Dio places the first of the plots against Augustus in this context in 17. There is little evidence that such plots ever existed, or if they did that they were very deep-seated or serious. It is true that the adoptions of Gaius and Lucius revealed dynastic tendencies that were not confined to purely domestic or personal affairs. Augustus had fostered the myth that he held only those offices that were authenticated by hallowed tradition, but it was becoming increasingly obvious that despite the built-in safeguards of adherence to traditional forms and the temporal limits on his various offices, Augustus had monopolised power on a permanent basis, and moreover the situation was not going to change with his death. In 16 his grip was still tight on affairs. The consuls were Publius Cornelius Scipio, the son of Augustus' ex-wife Scribonia by her former marriage, and Lucius Domitius Ahenobarbus, who was married to one of the daughters of Octavia and Antonius. Half way though the year Scipio was replaced for reasons unknown by Lucius Tarius Rufus, and thereafter, as has been noted, the consulship was opened up to the nobles. Augustus may have felt that there was a certain insecurity in allowing the nobility access to high office, especially when he was absent from the city. In 16, both Augustus and Agrippa left Rome, each going their separate ways: Augustus to Gaul and Agrippa to the East. Perhaps as a precautionary measure to safeguard his interests while he and Agrippa were absent, Augustus appointed his loyal and trustworthy friend Statilius Taurus to the post of prefect of the city and of Italy, according to Dio. The post is not specifically named, but Dio's language will bear the interpretation that city prefect is meant. Unfortunately it cannot be said with any certainty that this is the exact origin of the city prefect of later times. It is a forerunner, but not necessarily a prototype, and if Taurus was also in charge of Italy then his office was probably more extensive than that of the normal, later city prefect. The crucial point is that while he was not in Italy Augustus ensured that he had reliable deputies on the spot. Some said that his leaving Rome in 16 was a shrewd move because he had become unpopular after the social legislation. It is quite true that familiarity breeds contempt, and this may be one of the reasons why Augustus never stayed in Rome for protracted periods, always keeping on the move throughout the Empire as long as he was physically able to travel. There were many other reasons why he travelled round the Empire, of course; it cannot have been simply to prevent himself from becoming stale that he journeyed to various provinces, and nor can it have been to enjoy repose. Dio inserts the scurrilous story that he left Rome to enjoy the charms of Maecenas' wife Terentia more fully, but this is nonsense. He could enjoy those in Rome perfectly adequately, and probably had already done so many times. Crisis theorists, then as now, claim that he went to Gaul on account of the so-called disaster incurred by Lollius on the Rhine. Troops had been mauled, certainly, but it was hardly a disaster, or at least if the Romans of the day thought of it as such then they were in for a rude awakening twenty-five years later as to the true nature of disasters. Lollius was an enemy of Tiberius, so his activities on the Rhine have been labelled disastrous to discredit him. There was no full-scale war when Augustus reached Gaul, and seemingly not much for him to do. In fact the full-scale offensive did not begin until 12, so it is possible to interpret his presence in Gaul for the next years as thorough preparation for the Rhine campaigns. One of his measures was to establish a mint at Lugdunum (modern Lyons) to enable him to pay the soldiers without convoying money from Rome. He also conducted a census in Gaul and levied taxes. The question must be asked what were his plans for the province of Gaul, and for the lands beyond the Rhine, and for that matter the Danube? From 15 onwards, Tiberius and Drusus fought to subdue the Alpine tribes, thus opening up communications through northern Italy to the Danube, and most important providing access via a land route from there to the Eastern provinces, all of which can be seen as practical necessities. It would have constituted a completely nonsensical situation to administer the growing Empire to the west and east of Italy without being certain of communications through the Alps. On the other hand the campaigns beyond the Rhine have attracted considerable controversy because they do not fall into the same category as the subjugation of the Alps and the establishment of Roman control over essential routes. No one can be certain of what was in Augustus' mind. The idea that he was bent on total conquest has been rejected by modern scholars, and Gruen makes a nice distinction between appearances and reality which fits the facts very well. In his view, there was never any master plan for world conquest. Augustus probably recognised very clearly that total subjection of Free Germany was not possible, nor even desirable, but what *was* desirable was to foster the idea of world conquest, to tranquilise the Roman populace into thinking that it was possible, that it was going to be carried out, and that success was just around the corner. Ever onward, ever upward, ever greater is an inspiring concept, and it is perhaps possible that Augustus thought he could sustain this ideology for ever, relinquishing it only after the disaster of Varus and the loss of three legions. In contrast, the practical school of thought merely imbues Augustus with the rather more down-to-earth desire to search out and establish secure frontiers, either by grand design, which is no longer a popular concept among modern scholars, or by lurching without direction from one reactive response to another, making a series of *ad hoc* decisions, tailored to the particular set of circumstances and needs that obtained at the time. The theory that Augustus was searching for secure frontiers to the provinces may contain a germ of truth, though it is anachronistic to talk of frontiers until much later, when demarcation of territories became much more pronounced. It was all a question of finding the best place to stop, balanced against Roman resources and the ability to administer the territories so far taken in. One reason for campaigning across the Rhine in the next few years may have been to secure the province of Gaul, always subject to Germanic influence and disruption. Caesar had crossed the Rhine, building his famous bridge and then destroying it again; some years later Agrippa had also campaigned across the river and received honours for doing so. These campaigns had not solved the problem, so now it was time to pick up the pieces and do the job thoroughly. That was the official story, but an additional and perhaps more compelling reason was that Augustus needed an army, and moreover one that was fully trained, properly equipped and ready to move. Caesar had dominated Italy from Gaul, and Antonius had followed suit, but their timing was flawed and the political situation weighed against them. They both fell under suspicion because their motives were personal rather than for the benefit of the state. More subtle than either of them, Augustus bided his time until the ideology of Rome's world mission was firmly established, and he was accepted as the selfless leader who could direct that mission. Security of the Gallic provinces and the glory of conquest beyond the Rhine was the noble aim that he fostered, but at the same time he just happened to have found the perfect excuse, sanctioned moreover by the Roman people, for keeping a sizeable number of men under arms, all of whom swore an oath of loyalty to himself.[18]

He attended to the needs of the army assiduously all through his reign, without appearing to indulge the soldiers too much. He noted in his *Res Gestae* that he paid cash for lands upon which to settle his veterans in 14, in the consulship of Marcus Crassus and Gnaeus Lentulus. Settlements and the creation of colonies for veterans had never ceased, but the significance of the settlements of 14, singled out for specific mention by Augustus, may derive from the fact that these were men recruited to fill gaps after Actium, who had thus served for sixteen years. This is the term of service that he fixed in 13 for legionaries, who were to serve for four years as reserves after the initial sixteen, while the Praetorians were to serve for twelve years. Another significant factor is that after 14 land settlements ceased, and henceforth veterans were pensioned off with cash payments. There were no land settlements in Italy for another fifty years, and at first the soldiers, mainly Italians, found it hard to adjust to the new arrangements because they had been expecting land grants upon retirement. The evidence suggests that Augustus devoted considerable attention to all aspects of the army at this period, making regular arrangements for recruitment, terms of service and rewards on completion of service. Recruitment during the civil wars had been for a cause, or for the support of a leader, and soldiers would fight until the enemy was defeated and then go home or to new lands designated for them by their leader, but now conditions had changed. A standing army, distributed over the provinces of the Empire, regularly recruited and kept up to strength as far as possible, regularly paid and properly pensioned, was now a fact of life. The enemy was outside the Empire, often far from Rome. Motives for joining the army were different, and had to be encouraged by means of a 'package deal' which outlined the terms and promised rewards. There was comfort for the soldiers in that they knew where they stood and could expect regular rewards, and reassurance also for the people of Italy and the provinces that they were not under any threat from seizure of their lands, nor from marauding, penniless veterans. The fully evolved military system was not yet in operation, but in 13 it can be seen in its embryonic form. Cash pensions were funded by Augustus himself until AD 6, when he set up the *aerarium militare* as a separate Treasury to cater for discharged veterans. Having placed the terms of service on a regular footing in 13, Augustus extended the number of years later on. The legions and the Praetorians were thus established, while the auxiliary arm had yet to develop, but the use of native levies was already in operation, and it remained for Augustus and his successors to make adjustments of detail and put into effect the fine tuning to the army as a whole. One of the eventual results would be to divorce the soldiery from the populace and create two separate classes, whose interests were not necessarily the same.[19]

Augustus' movements from 16 to 13 are not known, and neither the ancient sources nor modern archaeology can shed very much light on the matter. Dio sums up the three years spent in Gaul, Germany and Spain under an administrative heading, describing in general terms how Augustus spent large amounts of money on some areas and extracted large amounts from others, and granted freedom and citizenship to some and took it away from others. Such anodyne terminology, describing fairly mundane procedures without detailing names, dates and places, implies that Dio had no specific source material to guide him. Similarly, Agrippa's activities in the East are not well documented, except that he was awarded a triumph for his settlement of the kingdom of Bosporus. The five-year term for both Augustus' and Agrippa's powers ran out in 13, so they both returned to Rome. Renewal of their powers in some form or other was no doubt a foregone conclusion, but neither of them wished to seem complaisant or to risk rejection. There was no protracted debate or opposition, but though the renewal was relatively straightforward, it is not without its complications for modern scholars. According to Dio, Agrippa received tribunician powers for five years, which causes few problems, but Dio's following statement is fraught with difficulty. He describes how Augustus sent Agrippa to Pannonia, 'entrusting him with greater authority than the officials outside Italy ordinarily possessed'. Obviously something important was planned for the Pannonian front, requiring a general of Agrippa's calibre to deal with it, but the main point at issue is the nature of Agrippa's command. In the past it was accepted that this is the first time that Dio mentions *imperium maius* in connection with Agrippa; opinions have differed about this matter, especially since this is not precisely what Dio says. The debate has already been described (above, pp. 121–5) with its significance for the powers of Augustus himself. The minimalist view is that there was no such thing as *imperium maius*, which means that some explanation must be found for Agrippa's command in Pannonia in the winter of 13/12. It may be that the intention was to start the Rhine campaigns and the Pannonian offensive at the same time, with Agrippa in overall command of the whole front and Drusus in command in Gaul and Germany; but this is fanciful conjecture, incapable of proof. Suffice it to say that Augustus had implicit trust in Agrippa and was quite prepared to grant him extensive powers, which he knew that his friend would not abuse.[20]

The accent in 13 was definitely on family and friends of Augustus. Drusus was left behind as legate in Gaul, and Tiberius was consul with Quinctilius Varus as colleague. Iullus Antonius was praetor, and gave games on Augustus' birthday, while Tiberius presided over the honours and celebrations for Augustus' return from the Western provinces. True to form, Augustus refused most of the honours, and he foiled the attempts of the people to greet him by entering the city at night. The importance of the family of Augustus, both living and dead, was emphasised in 13 when the Theatre of Marcellus was finally dedicated, but although he wished always to remind people of the solidarity of his family circle, Augustus also liked to pretend that he advanced various relatives only because they were the best men to carry out the tasks that he gave them. Whenever he sought offices for members of his family, according to Suetonius, Augustus invariably added 'If they be worthy', thus subscribing to his own fictional notions that everyone had been granted the opportunity to object, and therefore lack of opposition must necessarily denote agreement. Whilst he actively promoted his relatives he objected to the adulation that the populace was ever-willing to display. He let it be known that he did not approve of the demonstrable favours shown to Gaius Caesar, aged six, at the festivities arranged for his own safe return from Gaul, and yet at the same time he did all in his power to advertise his grandsons and made little secret of their hereditary position. His dual standards perhaps blinded him to the obnoxious behaviour of his spoiled adopted sons, who most likely employed dual standards of their own and behaved perfectly well when he was watching. The solidarity of the family was underlined in several ways, not least in representative art. As part of the honours for Augustus on his return from Gaul it was decided to build the monument that has attracted constant attention and the most intensive study from scholars, namely the Ara Pacis Augustae, or the altar to Augustan peace. It was not finally dedicated until January, AD. 9. Augustus had always attached great importance to the closure of the doors of the temple of Janus, thus promoting himself as the author of universal peace; now the idea was given concrete form, combining portraits of the members of his family with his own, elevating them all into the religious sphere without making them actually divine. It was more permanent than a triumph and more eloquent than a statue, and though the fact that it has survived and can still be seen may have distorted its importance in modern eyes, its significance for contemporaries cannot be underestimated. It epitomised all that Augustus wanted to promulgate in his lifetime and probably gave him immense satisfaction. Modern scholars argue about the identification of the individuals portrayed on the altar, but it is very likely that contemporaries would recognise them, and they would certainly be aware of the family as a corporate entity.[21]

There were few honours or offices that Augustus lacked, save that of the Pontifex Maximus, which he took for himself when Lepidus died in 12. He refused the accompanying honours that the Senate voted to him, which Dio does not enumerate. Since his official functions now stipulated that he had to be accessible to the people, Augustus converted part of his house for public use instead of taking up residence in the official house of the Pontifex Maximus. He had shown admirable restraint in refusing to wrest the priesthood from Lepidus while he still lived, but in contrasting his own election by popular acclaim with what he called Lepidus' usurpation of the office he revealed that there had been no love lost between the two men. Leaving his rival in office and waiting politely for him to expire had not been an entirely benign process; his behaviour brought him credit, which weighed more heavily with him than obtaining the priesthood. He now controlled the whole state, including its religious policy, and his sense of completeness would perhaps have been supreme were it not for a substantial loss that occurred in the same year. Agrippa had left Rome for Pannonia in the winter, but had scarcely begun a campaign. Dio insists that the natives calmed down when they heard of his approach, which sounds far too simple. Having achieved peace without fighting, according to Dio, Agrippa returned home in the early spring of 12 but fell ill in Campania. It is more likely that he fell ill before he had begun operations in Pannonia, and that the campaign was aborted. When he heard the news, Augustus rushed to Campania to meet Agrippa, but by the time he arrived, his life-long friend, his most devoted and reliable assistant, was dead.[22]

7

PROFIT AND LOSS

Following the death of Agrippa, Augustus' next decades were marked by
well-earned successes offset by tragic deaths and misfortunes that beset the
Imperial family. The future had probably looked secure before 12, but from
now on Augustus was forced to adapt to constantly changing circumstances
over which he had very little control. He gave Agrippa a public funeral
and buried him in his own family mausoleum, even though Agrippa had
already prepared a burial place for himself in the Campus Martius. A small
part of the funeral oration has come down to us, preserved on a fragmentary papyrus from the Fayum in Egypt. It is translated into Greek, and
its tantalising contents add to the confusion about Agrippa's powers. The
language is unofficial and imprecise; the occasion would not demand formal
titles or political precision, and the phrase that causes the most problems
is tortuous to say the least: 'it was sanctioned by law that wherever you
were sent, your powers should never be less than those of magistrates in
other provinces'. Then Augustus says that Agrippa reached the supreme
height of power, which refers to *tribunicia potestas*, by dint of Augustus' zeal
and his own superb qualities, with the consent of all men. This last phrase
may have bent the truth a little. Agrippa's popularity was by no means
universal, and the senators did not flock to take part in the funeral celebrations. The oration is revealing for the light that it sheds on Augustus'
opinion of the salient points of Agrippa's career. It demonstrates the importance which he attached to tribunician power and proconsular *imperium*, and
the cautious way in which he described the latter is quite consistent with
his claim that he accepted no office that was at odds with accepted custom;
this claim extended to his friends and subordinates as well.[1]

In his will Agrippa left his gardens to the Roman people, and everything else to Augustus, who distributed 400 sesterces to all citizens,
saying that it was Agrippa's wish. Personal grief scarcely enters the historical record, but it was no doubt there, with all its regrets. Even if he was
unaffected as far as his emotions were concerned, Augustus would certainly
be affected in practical terms. Agrippa's death upset the balance. Augustus
was now left with the full burden of Empire on his own shoulders. One of

his best generals, arguably the best he would ever know, and his acknowledged Eastern specialist, was removed. No one could entirely replace
Agrippa. There were capable men in Augustus' immediate circle who might
have been profitably cultivated. Statilius Taurus, for instance, could have
been elevated to higher rank and schooled to take over some of Agrippa's
official duties. He was a military man, he had been left in charge of Rome
and Italy while Augustus was in Gaul, and he had the necessary administrative experience. He was not the only candidate with some of the requisite
qualifications. Valerius Messalla could easily have been recruited to the
highest office. But no one had undergone the evolutionary education and
companionship that Agrippa had experienced from his earliest years, and
no one else was part of the Augustan family. It was too late now to begin
all over again by suddenly taking into the family circle men who had hitherto been outside it, no matter what their status or compatibility. Dio says
that Augustus was anxious to avoid envy and intrigue, and indeed it would
have given rise to both if he had elevated an outsider, at a time when he
had made peace with the Senate, opened up careers to the nobility, and
established the elements of a hierarchy with himself and his family at the
head of the state. At this potential turning point in history, when Augustus
could have chosen to broaden the base of his power, he chose instead to
continue on his inward course, and 'reluctantly', according to Dio, he
began to cultivate Tiberius as though he had not considered this possibility
before. The portrait of Tiberius that has come down to us is one of an
embittered, resentful man, disliked, even loathed, in his lifetime. Reasons
for his extreme unpopularity have been sought in his early development,
sometimes projected as far back as his youth. An almost certainly fictional
rivalry with his brother Drusus is said to have derived from the fact that
Drusus was the real favourite of both Augustus and the people. This may
not have been true, and although an impression does not have to be true
for a person to feel it very deeply, it is unlikely that Tiberius allowed his
perceptions, whatever they may have been, to colour his relationship with
his brother. He and Drusus remained fond of each other. Another cause
for his supposed discontent is the implication that it was painfully obvious
that he was not Augustus' first choice as successor, and that he was cast in
the role of caretaker while Gaius and Lucius grew to manhood, much as
Agrippa had been. This perception of Tiberius' position leads very easily
to the conclusion that he was resentful because he was fighting all the
battles and doing all the hard work while perpetually relegated to the background. But it is by no means certain that he was ever relegated to the
background. Both he and Drusus had already embarked on distinguished
careers, painstakingly advanced in successive stages to allow for respectable
gaps between offices, which they held at the same age, and even if on occasion they were accorded the rank of a particular office prematurely, Augustus
usually ensured that they also at some time held that office so that they

gained the relevant experience of it. The distortion of Tiberius' image comes about with the death of Agrippa, when it is implied that Augustus was left with no alternative except to choose to promote Tiberius. Agrippa was dead, and Gaius and Lucius were still too young. The 'reluctance' described by Dio may derive from a tortuous form of retrospective reasoning: Tiberius turned out badly; Augustus was good; therefore he must have discerned the true character of Tiberius and cannot possibly have made the error of voluntarily choosing to advance such a man, so of course did so only under duress when he was a victim of circumstance. More credence might attach to this theory if Tiberius had lingered without office or military command until now and then had been suddenly brought out of the closet to find rapid promotion in 12, simply because Augustus needed someone to fill the vacancy left by Agrippa. One glance at Tiberius' career and achievements prior to 12 gives the lie to the theory that he was a mere stop gap, chosen because there was no one else. He had always constituted part of Augustus' training programme for government, but he had not yet held quite such a prominent position because there were others in the limelight who took precedence. It has been suggested that Augustus employed the personnel available to him in a hierarchy of paired colleagues: Augustus himself and Agrippa constituted the first line in the government, next came Tiberius and Drusus, promoted to the same offices at the same relative ages, and after them Gaius and Lucius. The theory is attractive, partially masked, perhaps, by the fact that Augustus resolutely limited his choice of trainees to the immediate family, and to all appearances it was simply coincidental that there were two pairs of brothers in each of the successive generations. What has been interpreted as reluctance to advance Tiberius may have derived from Augustus' innate caution. He did nothing startlingly out of context to bring honours to Tiberius before they were due. True to form, Augustus did not rush things, and continued the promotion of Tiberius in stages, patiently allowing him to grow in stature and experience. He may have regretted the delay, but he did not attempt to create a duplicate Agrippa all at once.[2]

The death of Agrippa left Julia a widow for the second time. She now had three sons; the youngest was born in 12 after the death of his father, and named accordingly Agrippa Postumus. Julia was still young enough for childbearing, and the marriage laws dictated that eligible widows should eventually remarry, so she required an acceptable husband, which to Augustus meant someone within the family circle. His choice was Tiberius, Livia's son; it seemed an ideal way of propagating the Imperial household, to marry his own daughter to his stepson. It was clever, and tidy, and disastrous. Tiberius was very reluctant to divorce his wife. Vipsania was Agrippa's daughter, and no one thought of consulting her feelings. She had lost her father, and then her husband was taken from her – all within a very short time. Tiberius' feelings were not considered either. He probably experienced a wide range of conflicting emotions, including grief because of his enforced separation from Vipsania, gratification of his ambitions which cannot have been entirely absent, and anger at being manipulated in this way for the good of the state. He was no doubt angry at himself for complying. There were few options open to him. For instance, he could not abandon public life altogether and go to live with Vipsania on a remote farm. He clearly possessed a sense of duty to the state, and probably wanted the honours that service to it would bring. Nor could he choose to act the perfect husband in public and carry on seeing Vipsania in private, because the adultery laws must be upheld by the immediate family of the man who had promulgated them. He was forbidden to see Vipsania at all, especially after he had met her by accident one day and followed her around with tears in his eyes. The situation might have been relieved somewhat if he had grown fond of Julia, but there is general agreement in the ancient sources that he never did; quite the opposite in fact. The early years of their marriage were perhaps not fraught with discord; a son was born to them, perhaps in 10, but did not survive. There was probably very little time for the couple to devote to each other, which may in part explain their ultimate estrangement. After the death of Agrippa, Tiberius' energies were directed to wars on the northern front. He subdued the restless tribes of Illyricum, and the province was handed back to Augustus because of its perpetual internal turmoil and its proximity to the new theatre of war in Pannonia. Augustus acknowledged in the *Res Gestae* that it was through the agency of Tiberius that Pannonia was conquered, but he gives himself the credit for bringing it within the rule of the Roman people. Tiberius' Pannonian campaign, taken over from Agrippa, was undertaken in tandem with the Rhine offensive, and has been interpreted as a two-pronged attack, strategically planned by Augustus, perhaps in consultation with Agrippa. The campaigns in Germany have been studied intensively by archaeologists and historians. Many Augustan fort sites are known and have been well documented, and more are coming to light as research progresses, but the dating evidence is not precise enough to be able to allocate the forts to specific campaigns. Agrippa crossed the Rhine and penetrated Germany many years before Drusus repeated the performance with greater intensity, and after Drusus' campaigns Tiberius took over. Some of the military bases would be used only once, some would be occupied repeatedly, and others may have been permanent depots. Archaeologists can define these categories with considerable accuracy, but can only speculate about who used the bases and when. The movements of the various generals within Germany are difficult to trace on the ground, and the ancient authors were not particularly interested in documenting the finer details of the campaigns. Lacking the details, debate centres on what Augustus was hoping to achieve. Argument continues about whether Augustus intended to stop at all, and whether he believed in the proud claim of *imperium sine fine*, power without end, propagated in literature. This claim was probably never more than hyperbole, designed to bolster and encourage the Roman people, since the practicalities of forging ahead as far as the Baltic or the Urals rendered such vast conquest very unlikely. If the intention was not total conquest, then argument descends to the search for a valid frontier, so the previous generation of scholars settled upon the Elbe and the Danube rivers as Augustus' ultimate aim. Drusus reached the Elbe, but did not garrison the territory, and nor did anyone else. The failure to overrun, garrison and annex does not deter those who maintain that the Elbe was the ultimate aim, because the disaster in AD 9, when Varus was defeated and lost three legions, can be pinpointed as the turning point, when the aims were modified and the hopes of distant conquest abandoned. More recent reassessments have been more down-to-earth, reasoning that Augustus upheld the Roman ethos of total conquest but realised only too well the practical difficulties; this leaves us uncertain about his plans for Germany. He never annexed the territory beyond the Rhine, which for much of its length in its lower reaches became the boundary of the Empire. To return to the chronological context of 12 and 11, there were honours for both Tiberius and Drusus, but of a muted kind, compared to the pomp and circumstance of the Republic. Even though they were acclaimed by the soldiers, neither of them was allowed to take the title of Imperator, since they were fighting under the auspices of Augustus. At this time it is possible that Augustus was unwilling to let the army forget that he was the sole commander, and so he appropriated the title Imperator for himself. Tiberius waited five more years to share this honour, by which time his worthiness and military prowess was plain for all to see. For their successes in 12 and 11, neither of the brothers was allowed to hold a triumph. They were granted triumphal insignia instead, a new kind of distinction which Suetonius says that Tiberius was the first to receive, in 12. The following year Drusus was accorded the same honours. While Agrippa was still alive, the question of a triumph did not arise. Augustus had long since renounced the idea for himself, and his colleague followed suit. The Senate consistently voted triumphs for Agrippa, who just as consistently refused them. Honour was thus satisfied on all sides, without the need to parade troops through the city of Rome, with all the connotations of Republican rivalry and jealousy. Tiberius and Drusus had not yet reached the comfortable plateau of acknowledged success that had attended Agrippa. They had yet to establish themselves in that position, so the Roman people needed a reminder of their growing importance, and the brothers themselves needed some form of encouragement that would convince them that they were not exerting themselves for no rewards at all. Denial of honours and distinctions from the outset might discourage them, but on the other hand Augustus could scarcely reverse the policy of renouncing triumphal processions without good cause. Apart from the possibility of opening up avenues for rival claims from other generals, and repeating the problems that Crassus had posed to Octavian when he demanded a triumph for his successes, it would cheapen the distinction to grant Tiberius and Drusus such an honour when it was clear that the campaigns were not yet properly concluded. The invention of new honours signified by the bestowal of the triumphal insignia was a neat way of circumventing the need to hold a real triumph, while still granting the distinction. Augustus knew that appearances very often carry more weight than reality; he had found a suitable compromise.[3]

The marriage of Tiberius and Julia took place in 11. If it could be counted as a gain, it was offset by loss. In the same year, Augustus' sister Octavia died. He accorded her full honours, for she had been loyal and useful to him throughout her life, quite apart from the affection he felt for her. Her body was laid in state in the shrine of Julius, where Augustus delivered his funeral oration. Drusus delivered another from the Rostra. The senators dressed in mourning clothes, and voted many honours for Octavia, most of which Augustus prudently refused. Finally, Octavia was buried in the family mausoleum. Augustus cannot have failed to take stock of his slowly diminishing circle of family and friends; Marcellus had died long before, but now within two years Agrippa and Octavia were interred in the mausoleum. The government of the Empire now devolved upon himself, supported by the family members who remained, but only Livia shared his long experience, and the others would have to be trained and brought to prominence; meanwhile he was alone. For the third time in 11, in the consulship of Paullus Fabius Maximus and Quintus Tubero, Augustus was asked to take on the *cura legum et morum*, with the highest powers, but he refused, as on the other two occasions. It is permissible to ask why morals still needed attention after the rigorous legislation put into operation from 18 onwards. It may have been considered that there were still too many undesirable people enrolled as citizens. No direct evidence proves that Augustus received censorial powers in 11, but Dio says that he conducted a census, registering his own property like any other citizen; it may be erroneous, since Augustus does not mention it in the *Res Gestae*, nor does he mention his review of the Senate, attested by Dio. There may not have been a full-scale revision of the Senate; Dio merely says that he made a list of senators, without implying that he revised the total or ejected anyone. Augustus had obviously devoted some thought to the composition and functioning of the Senate at this time. He reduced the quorum for passing decrees, previously set at 400. Dio does not record that he set a new figure, but says simply that Augustus allowed decrees to be passed if fewer than 400 senators were present. It was no doubt a source of great irritation to Augustus that after having tried to reduce the Senate to a practical, but elite, 300, and being thwarted in the attempt, he then found that of the 600 men who fought to retain their senatorial status over one-third did not take the business of being senators seriously enough to turn up to meetings. Two years later, in 9, he fixed the days for meetings at two per month, and forbade court sessions on those days, to reduce the number of excuses that could be made for non-attendance. The senators had to be encouraged to play their parts in government, but only up to a point. Everyone knew that ambition was capped, even for ardent supporters of the regime. Augustus had not found the incentive which could replace Republican private ambition.[4]

The honours voted to Tiberius and Drusus in 11 did not mark the end of the campaigns. Augustus travelled to Gaul in 10 to keep in touch with the armies, taking Tiberius with him. He was most likely still absent from Rome when the Ara Pacis, voted in 13, was finally dedicated in January 9. This altar is one of the most famous and most meticulously discussed monuments of Augustan Rome. The dedication in 9 may have embraced the whole religious precinct around the altar, as well as the altar itself. It was situated within a public area in the northern sector of the Campus Martius, where the *solarium Augusti*, the huge sundial and astrological clock, was laid out (see Figure 7.1). The whole area had great astronomical significance, orientated in accord with Augustus' conception and his birthday. The gnomon or pointer of the sundial was one of the obelisks brought from Egypt (the other was placed on the *spina* of the Circus Maximus). The Ara Pacis was positioned so that the line of the autumnal equinox, Augustus' birthday, passed through the centre of it. The altar is set within a square enclosure open to the sky, pierced by two doorways before and behind it. On the four panels flanking the doorways, there are relief sculptures representing mythological scenes, and on the two long sides religious processions are depicted. Artistically the altar and its enclosure are of superb quality and the portraits are executed with sensitivity and care. Augustus and his family are depicted on the south side. Some scholars are certain that names can be assigned to most of the persons represented, but others are more cautious, and wonder if even contemporaries could recognise everybody in

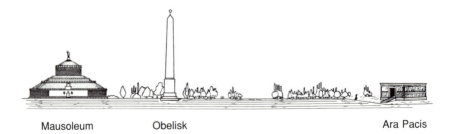

Mausoleum   Obelisk   Ara Pacis

Figure 7.1 The Ara Pacis, the sundial, and the mausoleum of Augustus. Adapted and redrawn from Zanker (1988) and Wallace-Hadrill (1993) by Graeme Stobbs

the processions. Another problem is the nature of the processions. They have been dated to specific events, such as the return of Augustus from Gaul in 13, when the altar was voted by the Senate. One objection to this is that if Augustus is indeed depicted as Pontifex Maximus, then the date ought to be after the death of Lepidus in 12. An additional complication is that Agrippa is shown, veiled as a priest should be in the procession, but he too died in the spring of 12, so if the sculpture commemorates a real event then it ought to have occurred in the early months of 12. Arguably, the procession could have taken place later than 12, and Agrippa was perhaps depicted in the place that he would have occupied had he been alive. Artistic licence in these matters is not unknown; for instance, in 1804 Napoleon's mother refused to attend his coronation as Emperor of the French but she is none the less depicted in David's painting, sitting in the gallery seat that was reserved for her. The planning stages for the decoration of the Ara Pacis would perhaps have been undertaken immediately after the Senate decided upon its creation in 13, and after Agrippa died Augustus would presumably desire that a portrait of him should still be included. An alternative suggestion that obviates the need to date the processions is that they are hypothetical, quite unrelated to any specific events. The ideology of the altar to Augustan peace precluded any reference to military aspects; it is far removed from a triumphal arch, but the peace which it celebrated extended only to Rome and Italy. Wars were going on along the borders of the Empire, but such had been the case when the doors of the temple of Janus were closed in 29 and 25. Foreign wars, comfortably distant from Rome and posing no immediate threat, were not viewed in the same light as civil wars for political supremacy, and principally it was the end of all those years of uncertainty which was being celebrated. The Pax Augusta had subsumed and absorbed the Pax Romana. From now on, Augustus was viewed both as the bringer of peace and as the guardian of it. Confidence in him was such that wars in the distant provinces could be discounted, because he could be relied upon to bring them to successful conclusions.[5]

According to Dio many dire omens presaged the death of Drusus in 9. He was consul in absentia during that year, and embarked upon a campaign against the Chatti and Suebi across the Rhine; he had reached the Elbe and erected a monument, but he did not garrison the territory. Drusus withdrew, warned by a woman of huge stature, so the story goes, that his end was nigh. His horse fell, he was injured, and never properly recovered. Tiberius' famous ride from Ticinum to Germany in a few days is often used as a yardstick for the possibilities of travel in the ancient world, but it was not the norm; it required great endurance and determination. Drusus was barely alive when Tiberius arrived and died very soon afterwards. He was given a magnificent funeral, and his descendants were granted the honorary name Germanicus. The honours granted to his family and the public solemnities of his funeral run counter to the rumours spread about that Drusus intended to force Augustus to restore the Republic, and that he had written to Tiberius to say so. The story may have been a later invention; there may have been no suspicions among contemporaries on this score, save perhaps that Drusus was Republican in attitude, in a way that was acceptable to Augustus, who sometimes reproached Livy for being such a confirmed Pompeian. It was not a serious accusation, so no charges of plotting were laid at Livy's door. The Drusus story is used by accusers of Tiberius to demonstrate the depths to which he would sink; Suetonius says that he produced Drusus' letter in order to compromise his brother because he hated him. The exhausting ride to Germany does not fit in with this theory. The sub-plots are more important than the facts. Drusus emerges as the unsullied hero, but safely dead; Tiberius is cast as the treacherous villain, and Augustus as the autocratic ruler whose grip on Rome strangled freedom. The main point at issue is that Drusus could see the stark truth behind Augustus' claim to have restored the Republic in 27; without actually saying so in as many words, it is implied that it was all false, and Tiberius, by revealing the so-called plot, condoned the perpetuation of autocracy. There is no need to read into the tale any suspicion of plots against Augustus' life, or even of discord in the Imperial house. Augustus immediately transferred Tiberius to the Rhine front, and in that same year he allowed him to share the title Imperator, significantly elevating him from the status of legate to that of a commander in his own right.[6]

Augustus' powers, bestowed upon him for five years in 13, were due to expire in 8. As was by now customary, he returned to Rome to await upon events. With reluctance, he accepted renewed powers for ten years, which extended term was in itself a vote of confidence. This was probably carefully orchestrated, for without Agrippa he perhaps felt the need of a secure tenure for a practical length of time, while Tiberius gained experience and Gaius and Lucius followed in his footsteps. He had been able to rely upon Agrippa, and could have rested secure in the knowledge that if he were to die – for after all he had been the one who was always ailing – then Agrippa would nurture his sons and keep order in the Empire until they took over. Intermediate heirs were Tiberius and Drusus, and now there was only Tiberius. The smooth succession was once again threatened. No one in the Roman world except Augustus himself now possessed the relevant experience or authority. The show of reluctance when his powers were renewed this time may not have been due to play acting; he was 55 years old and was now facing an extended period of almost sole rule, and beginning all over again in creating a colleague with acceptable administrative experience, military prowess, and general all-round credibility. Consistent with his whole approach to Roman politics, he would not elevate Tiberius too rapidly. His policy was to try to ensure that Tiberius, and Gaius and Lucius, earned their promotions. They must be visibly distinguished first, and worthy of the offices to which they were appointed. Too much, too soon would make them stand out in the wrong way, and would leave nothing in reserve, so that future honours would have to be denied altogether, or invented anew, most likely as a departure from hallowed custom. In 9 after the death of Drusus, and certainly in 8, Augustus had no doubt already decided upon the course that he wished Tiberius to follow; significantly, Dio outlines all the honours that were to come to Tiberius, the consulship and triumph of 7, along with the events of the previous year. It was a busy one for Augustus. He records that he completed another census, where 4,233,000 citizens were registered. He carried it out alone, by means of his consular power, which opens up the debate once again as to whether he possessed this power on a permanent basis or whether he now received a special temporary grant in order to conduct the census. Despite the fact that Augustus does not mention any grant of censorial power, bestowed on him at the same time, several scholars are of the opinion that he must have sought some other authority besides the consular power to undertake the census of 8, for although he was undoubtedly very well qualified to conduct a census by means of consular power it would have been an uncharacteristic departure from customary practice if he had neglected to obtain all the properly sanctioned official powers to support his actions, especially since he conducted the census alone. He did not allow Tiberius to share in this power in 8, presumably because he did not yet consider him eligible. It need not constitute any slur on Tiberius' abilities or Augustus' opinion of them. Everything would come to him in its proper time. Augustus attended to other administrative matters, such as strengthening the banks of the Tiber, but without creating any permanent body to take charge of the problem on a regular basis; that was one of Tiberius' contributions to the administration of the city. Electoral corruption was brought to his attention, but he did not undertake a full investigation, merely insisting that prospective candidates should pay a deposit, which was to be forfeited if they were found guilty of bribery. Elections were obviously still held for some of the magistracies in Rome, and they were important enough to incite complaints if there was any evidence of bribery and corruption, but the down-to-earth measures that Augustus adopted suggest that he did not think the matter serious enough to have recourse to legal proceedings. Among his other administrative changes he enlarged the city of Rome by extending the *pomerium*. The city was presumably growing all the time, so the new boundaries probably took in areas already settled rather than new ground which allowed for future expansion. The growth of the citizen body is attested by the rise in the census figures, but this would represent only half the picture because it does not take account of the many groups of people who came under the heading of non-citizens, all of whom required somewhere to live. One administrative change, desired by the people and accepted by Augustus, was a considerable honour. The month Sextilis was renamed August. The people wanted to rename the month of Augustus' birth, September, but he preferred to distinguish the month when he was made consul; besides, it made an innocuous association with the past since it followed the month of July, named after Caesar.[7]

The gains of the year were also attended by losses. Maecenas died, and so did the poet Horace. Augustus seemed destined to reach an old age in isolation, as his contemporaries expired one by one. Dio credits Maecenas with the ability to control Augustus' sometimes violent temper, for which theory there is some support in Augustus' own statement, after he had failed to keep silent at a meeting of the Senate, that if Agrippa or Maecenas had been present he would have been prevented from making an exhibition of his feelings for all to see. Maecenas seems to have been allowed more liberty than many others, and may have been a trusted confidant. Dio illustrates his benign influence by the story of the court session where Augustus seemed intent on passing the death sentence on several people; Maecenas was unable to speak to him, so he sent him a message on a writing tablet, addressing him as 'executioner', which brought Augustus to his senses and stopped the proceedings. Concern for the victims was no doubt peripheral to Maecenas' concern for Augustus' reputation. As an arbiter of public perception Maecenas perhaps fulfilled this role on more than one occasion. Being only human, Augustus presumably at some times required a listener, or a friend with whom to exchange ideas, or a calming influence in times of stress. He had now lost his two closest friends, Agrippa and Maecenas, each of them valuable in completely different ways, who had been with him constantly from his early youth. Their absence created a lacuna in his life that could probably not be filled by anyone else. Practical advice may have been forthcoming from several sources but would not carry the weight of that of his oldest friends, and emotionally perhaps not even Livia could compensate; talented though she undoubtedly was, she was not a soldier or a politician, and had not shared those moments at Apollonia when Caesar's death presented Octavian and his friends with a great opportunity and a momentous challenge. Augustus was surrounded by people all the time, but had probably never felt quite so alone. Grief was becoming a way of life, subordinated to the government of Rome. The show must go on, and the principal actor had to be on stage.[8]

Augustus spent the rest of the year in Gaul, while Tiberius crossed the Rhine. This time they took Gaius with them to broaden his experience and accustom him to warfare. The German campaigns are not well documented, but their conclusion in 8 seems to have been regarded as satisfactory. Velleius, full of admiration for Tiberius, says that he penetrated every corner of Germany, with few losses to his army, and reduced the country almost to the status of a tributary province, but the qualifying 'almost' reveals the incomplete nature of the campaigns. Other than this laudatory general description, Velleius gives few tangible details. According to Dio, all the tribes submitted except the Sugambri, and Augustus refused to make a treaty with any of them unless this recalcitrant tribe could be included in it, probably hoping that by holding them all to ransom in this way the pressure of the majority of the tribesmen would prevail upon the Sugambri. He arrested and imprisoned some of the leaders, who killed themselves, and there the wars seem to have ended, at least for the time being. The army received monetary rewards, distributed in honour of Gaius Caesar. Augustus wanted to ensure that the soldiers should not be in any doubt as to whom they owed their extra cash, and was rather less than subtle in laying foundations for the future. Tiberius entered upon his second consulship in January 7, remaining outside the city until he celebrated his triumph. This was not necessarily a guarantee that Germany was completely conquered, and indeed there was a minor outbreak of trouble later in 7. Tiberius returned briefly to the army, but there seems to have been no serious fighting; Dio dismisses the matter with the brief notice that nothing worthy of mention happened in Germany in 7. The lack of detail implies that there had been no definite gains. Germany had been resolutely invaded, subdued for the time being, and impressed with Roman strength, but as in Spain the native inhabitants had proved just as elusive and determined to remain free. It would be many years before Germany was ready for pacification, and the Romans misjudged both the mood and the moment when they attempted it. Tiberius' triumph was not a definitive celebration of the conclusion of the wars, but it was a signal honour, designed to impress the people with his newly acquired status, and no doubt to extend to him the encouragement and marks of distinction that he needed to boost his morale and compensate him for the sacrifices he had made in his private life. As part of the scheme for promoting him in public life, he embarked upon the repair of the temple of Concord in his own name and that of Drusus, and gave a banquet for the senators on the Capitol. It was the usual round of building work and entertainments such as Agrippa had undertaken, all of which served to advertise the regime and keep the populace well disposed to it. Augustus attended to their well being and safety in his administrative measures in 7; after a serious fire which destroyed many of the buildings around the Forum, he restructured the fire-fighting service, dividing the city into fourteen regions (see Figure 7.2), subdivided into *vici*, each placed in the charge of *curatores viarum*. These men were put in charge of the public slaves, formerly under the supervision of the aediles, who had been trained to put out fires. The division of the city into regions was an intelligent innovation that made administration easier in many departments of life other than fire-fighting and policing; the very longevity of the system is testament to its usefulness and success. It may have been Augustus' own idea, germinating from the previous problems caused by the difficulties in controlling fires without a localised body of trained men, and perhaps also from Caesar's unusual methods of counting those eligible for the corn dole, giving responsibility for collecting names and monitoring

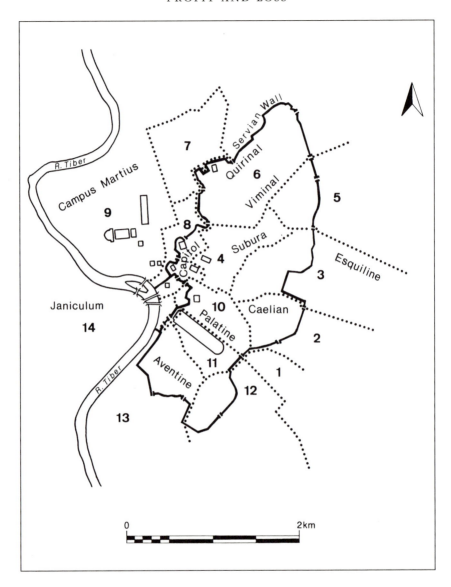

Figure 7.2 The fourteen regions of the city of Rome

deaths to officials who had charge of several groups of houses or entire blocks. Divide and rule is a useful maxim which might be better rendered sometimes as divide and administer.[9]

While Tiberius returned briefly to Germany, Gaius presided over the celebrations held in honour of Augustus' return. Gradually, the Romans were becoming accustomed to seeing Gaius in official roles, minor ones at first, consistent with his age and experience. He and his brother Lucius appeared dressed in black at the funeral games for their father Agrippa, held five years after his death. Such public display of the two boys resulted in notoriety that was not altogether positive. Dio points out that not all the flattery was sincere, because many people were intent only on furthering their careers by means of their supposed attachment to Gaius and Lucius. The people demonstrated their partiality in 6 when they chose Gaius to be consul. He was 14 in that year, and assumed the *toga virilis*, just as Octavian had done. Some scholars think that the election was probably arranged with Augustus' knowledge, and indeed Tacitus accuses him of wanting the consulship for Gaius. It may have been an elaborate way of testing the reactions of the people, or it may have been a spontaneous gesture in response to the fact that Gaius was now legally a man. Augustus was, or pretended to be, very angry at the election, deferring the consulship for Gaius until AD 1 when he would reach the age of 21. Anticipating the obvious charge that he had become consul himself at the age of 19, he made a speech deploring the circumstances which had necessitated that he become consul at such an early age. No one should take up the office before the age of 20, he proclaimed. He bestowed a priesthood on Gaius, and gave him the right to attend meetings of the Senate, which would give him experience of administrative proceedings and of how senators behaved. The management of people was just as important as management of affairs.[10]

There now begins one of the most puzzling episodes of Augustus' reign, when Tiberius retired to Rhodes in 6. He had just been granted *tribunicia potestas* for five years, and everything seemed to be progressing smoothly, then suddenly he announced that he wished to withdraw. His disappearance from Rome is usually interpreted as a self-imposed exile, or even as banishment, but so many conflicting reasons are enumerated for his departure that it is clear that even contemporaries, and the writers who came shortly after, could not penetrate the mystery. Dio's version is that Augustus bestowed the tribunician power on Tiberius in order to elevate him above Gaius and Lucius, the main object being to pull them both up sharply and make them behave properly. It sounds rather extreme as an indirect admonition. The tribunician power was the highest mark of distinction, and not one to be idly distributed to teach someone else a lesson. According to Suetonius, Tiberius let it be known that he required rest and repose, but later he changed his story and attributed his seven-year absence from Rome to his desire to avoid conflict with Gaius and Lucius. From there it is easy to extrapolate further to suggest that his advancement made Gaius and Lucius jealous, and so Tiberius had reason to fear his stepsons. Building upon that, it is assumed that Julia must somehow be implicated, and that there were two factions in the Augustan household – one led by Julia and the other by Livia, who carried the flag for the Claudians. Dio recounts but clearly does not believe the story that Tiberius left Rome because his marriage had irretrievably broken down, nor does he believe the version that claims that Tiberius went to Rhodes to further his education and fill the gaps in his knowledge because he had missed so much while campaigning. The permutations are endless and beyond resolution. That leaves speculation, of which there is a surfeit. The evidence ranged on the side of voluntary exile is in keeping with Tiberius' later development, and naturally invites parallels with his eventual withdrawal to Capri. He is supposed to have refused food for four days when his request to leave Rome was refused, and before he left he read his will to Augustus to prove that he had no nefarious designs on the Empire or his stepsons. Augustus complained in the Senate that Tiberius was deserting him, and he fell ill as a result of the stress. The illness has been construed as genuine, psycho-somatic, or feigned, to induce Tiberius to return. When he heard of it, Tiberius had already embarked from Ostia. He lingered off the Campanian coast until he knew that Augustus was not going to die, then made for Rhodes. He took no large retinue with him, and lived very simply on the island. He retained his tribunician power, but the fact that it was not renewed in 1 BC when the five-year term expired lends support to the theory that he was in disgrace. It was said that he received the title of *legatus*, but only because Livia interceded for him and induced Augustus to grant him something that would disguise the fact that he was out of favour.[11]

There is an obvious parallel with Agrippa's withdrawal in 23, when he left Rome allegedly on account of his rivalry with Marcellus. It has been suggested that Agrippa's mission was an official one, not widely publicised, to watch over the volatile East while Augustus attended to Rome and the Western provinces, and this possibility should not be entirely discounted for Tiberius. The title of legate sounds a note of discord with the theory that Tiberius had been exiled, or had exiled himself. On face value, it means that he was Augustus' deputy, though how wide an area the vague title covered remains obscure; perhaps deliberately so. There are other factors to take into account. In 7 or thereabouts Tigranes II, king of Armenia, installed by Tiberius himself, died or was murdered. The balance between Rome and Parthia, always delicate, was now even more fragile. Dio says that Tiberius was assigned to Armenia; Velleius devotes one line to the fact that the Parthians broke their alliance and laid hold of Armenia. Tiberius had direct experience of Armenian affairs. Modern authors accuse Tiberius of dereliction of duty because he closeted himself in Rhodes and did nothing. Information is next to non-existent. With lapidary simplicity, Augustus records in the *Res Gestae* that he handed over the kingdom to Ariobarzanes the Mede, then after the death of the latter to his son Artavasdes; then Artavasdes died and Augustus gave the kingdom to Tigranes III, of the royal house of Armenia. Dio implies that there was rivalry for the throne between Artavasdes and Tigranes, and when the throne became vacant after the death of Artavasdes, Tigranes made friendly overtures to Rome. In Dio's text it seems as though all this happened when Gaius reached the East, and Augustus encouraged Tigranes to seek an interview with Gaius. The chronology is confused, but it seems that the kingdom of Armenia held its own from the death of Tigranes II to the arrival of Gaius, and there was no heavy fighting to wrest it from the Parthians. It may be that Tiberius did achieve something after all. While he was staying on the island of Rhodes, provincial governors, whether chosen by the Senate or appointed by Augustus, all made a point of visiting him. Velleius says that they all lowered their fasces to him, to acknowledge his superiority, or more specifically 'confessing that his retirement was more worthy of honour than their official position'. The personnel in the provinces around Rhodes have been examined by Levick, all of those attested being associated with Tiberius, if not as close friends then at least not as enemies. Bowersock points out that Tiberius had many clients in the Eastern provinces. These details may be coincidental, or they may point to a coherent policy, never elaborated upon and veiled in secrecy. To take the episode as a whole it is necessary to anticipate events and describe them out of chronological context. In 2 BC, the Parthian king Phraates IV died, and was replaced by the more aggressive Phraates V, who had designs on Armenia. Augustus responded by sending out the 18-year-old Gaius, with advisers and assistants, to lead an armed expedition to the East, with the intention of restoring the balance. He went by way of Arabia and Syria. Tigranes III of Armenia sought and received Roman support, and Phraates and Augustus entered upon a rather high-handed correspondence, in which each addressed the other insolently without the customary flattering series of titles. There was a general expectation of war between Rome and Parthia. Four years went by, until in AD 2 the Parthian king came to terms, significantly renouncing his claims on Armenia. Gaius and Phraates met on an island in the Euphrates, compliments were exchanged, accommodation was reached, and the Armenian question settled. And Tiberius came home.[12]

To suggest that it was all undercover work, and that Augustus had allowed the world to think that Tiberius had gone to Rhodes as an exile, is to invite comments on the over-worked imagination of a manic devotee of espionage films. The problem with the whole episode is that the adoption of any single theory invariably involves rejection or tortuous explanation of some conflicting parts of the so-called evidence, but this undercover observation theory is no more crackpot than some of the ancient ones. It is not entirely impossible that for seven years Tiberius played the part of a finger-on-the-pulse, otherwise innocuous private citizen with no apparent armed force, but none the less a legate of Augustus, situated in the Mediterranean, where communications were fairly rapid in all directions. It provides a reason, other than simple good manners, for the visits of provincial governors, who might have been calling in for briefings and de-briefings on their way to and from their provinces. There are naturally some stories

which conflict with the theory. When Gaius reached the East, a vitriolic
rivalry broke out between him and his stepfather, egged on by Lollius who
was Gaius' principal adviser. Tiberius is said to have become so fearful for
his life that he withdrew even further into Rhodes, and begged for an
observer to be sent out to proclaim his innocence to the world. The tales
may be true, in so far as they were in current circulation at the time, but
this does not necessarily mean that they had any basis in fact. They are
redolent of sensationalism and vindictive glee, as evidenced in the story
that an inhabitant of Nemausus made an offer to Gaius to go to Rhodes
and bring back the head of 'the exile', as Tiberius was called. The unac-
countable factor in these strange tales is that Augustus would surely not
countenance negotiations with Parthia while there was serious dissension
in the Roman presence in the East. Bitterly divided forces, constantly bickering and making accusations of subversion against each other, are not the
best tools with which to set out to impress a potential enemy who has
recourse to the organised strength of an Empire behind him. The best way
to put an end to it would have been to give sole command to Gaius, recall
Tiberius to prevent him from doing any more harm, and then watch
him closely, especially since Tiberius asked to be allowed to come home.
But the story goes that Augustus would not let him come back, and referred
the matter to Gaius, who eventually relented and allowed his stepfather to
return on condition that he took no part in public life. On his return
to Rome, Tiberius lived very quietly as a private citizen without office. It
all sounds like a garbled version of what actually happened, embroidered
by a spiteful audience who loved a scandal. Reality may have been much
more mundane; Augustus could not let Tiberius return to Rome until he
was certain that the Armenian and Parthian problems were settled, and
he would certainly maintain a regular correspondence with Gaius about the
situation, especially as to the question of whether it was safe to let Tiberius
leave the area. Distortion of such a situation would not have been difficult.
The truth will never be known, and each must make his or her own additions and subtractions.[13]

While Tiberius was absent, Augustus took his twelfth consulship in 5
in order to introduce Gaius into public life. He did the same for Lucius
when his turn came three years later. He made each of the boys in turn
princeps iuventutis, one of the stages by which he hoped to accustom them
to leadership. There was no political significance to this titular honour, but
it signalled the fact that Augustus had marked down Gaius and Lucius
as his eventual successors. They were already designated to higher office,
though he made them wait for a suitable interval until they reached the
age that he considered proper. The sources are very slender for the next few
years, rendering a full account impossible. It is known that from 5 onwards
the suffect consulship was introduced to provide a more regular supply of
men with experience to fill the posts in the administration of Rome and

the provinces. In 4, Augustus reformed the procedures allowing provincials to seek redress for extortionate practices of governors, but he made a change which seemed to benefit senators rather than provincials in that the accused men were to be tried by senatorial committee rather than in the old-fashioned way by non-senatorial juries. The years 4 and 3 witnessed further veteran settlements, which Augustus thought worthy of mention in the *Res Gestae* where he says that the soldiers were settled in their home towns with monetary rewards, which he paid himself. This was preparatory to the major reform of AD 6 when he introduced regular pensions paid out of the treasury specially created for the purpose.[14]

There is much more information about the year 2, which was eventful to say the least. Augustus was consul for the thirteenth time, shepherding Lucius into his public role, as he had done for Gaius three years earlier. Administrative measures are the least well documented, perhaps subsumed by the superlative honours and harrowing scandals that occurred during the year. Augustus restructured the corn dole, limiting its distribution to 200,000 recipients according to Dio. Augustus does not mention any limitation on the numbers of recipients, but he corroborates Dio's figure in the *Res Gestae* when he says that in his thirteenth consulship he gave 60 denarii each to the plebs in receipt of the corn dole, who at that time numbered slightly more than 200,000. According to Suetonius, who gives no precise dates, Augustus noted that the monthly distribution took too many men away from their work on a regular basis, so he decided to abolish the monthly system and to substitute instead three distributions per year, each one allowing the plebs to draw four months' supply of corn. Popular discontent made itself felt very clearly, so he dropped the idea. The plebs probably had nowhere to store such a large supply and there would be the problem of rationing it out to last for four months, not to mention the possibility of large-scale thefts. The evolutionary development of the corn supply extended over a long period, and was not complete until the end of Augustus' reign. During this year, the temple of Mars Ultor, the Avenger, was dedicated (see Figure 7.3). It had been vowed forty years earlier, when vengeance for the death of Caesar was paramount. Four decades had changed much of the ideology behind the establishment of the temple, and had hopefully suppressed the memories of how Octavian had started out on his quest for power, finally emerging as Augustus. Perhaps more emphasis was now laid on the Forum of Augustus, where the temple formed the centrepiece, and on the games held in honour of Mars, which Augustus says he was the first to offer. At the beginning of the year, in February, the Senate, the equestrians and the people, voted that Augustus should be granted the title *pater patriae*. It was a tremendous honour, the highest that the Romans had to offer him. It had been voted to him once before, and refused, because Augustus maintained that neither he nor the world was ready for it. He accepted it now, though it seems to have been a long-drawn-out process.

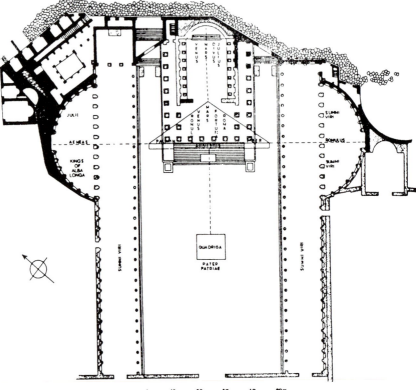

Figure 7.3 The Temple of Mars Ultor, vowed in 42 and dedicated in 2. Plan and suggested reconstruction from Zanker (1988) and Ward-Perkins (1981). Redrawn by Graeme Stobbs

The people came to him at Antium, then demonstrated in the theatre in Rome, and finally Valerius Messalla beseeched him to accept in a speech in the Senate house. The emotion attested in the sources is no doubt accurate; Augustus had tears in his eyes when he made his answering speech, in which he expressed the hope that he would always retain such high esteem and good opinion. He knew very well how fragile it was, and how difficult it could be to avoid falling victim to adverse rumours. From these heights, a descent to the depths was not long in coming. Dio infers that Augustus already knew something of Julia's behaviour, but refused to believe it. When the facts (whatever they really were) came forcibly to his attention in 2, he could not ignore them. On this occasion he gave way to an outburst of violent rage in the Senate, and regretted it immediately, admitting that Agrippa or Maecenas would have prevented him from so far forgetting himself. His image was irretrievably tarnished on two accounts, his own and his daughter's. It was alleged that Julia had taken dozens of lovers, either because she was bored and objected to being used as a political pawn, or because she had entered upon some convoluted political intrigue of her own, though with what ultimate purpose is hard to define. Iullus Antonius, the son of Marcus Antonius and Fulvia, was executed along with a few other men. Their involvement with Julia may have included anything from simple lust to treasonable intentions, but if the latter what were they intending to do? Did they have some scheme to restore the Republic, or remove Augustus in favour of Gaius and Lucius, or remove Gaius and Lucius in favour of Iullus Antonius? Human nature is capable of extreme and dreadful things, but any plot in which Julia was involved surely necessitated doing some harm to one or more members of her family. The search for complicated plots may not be necessary. Augustus had passed laws designed to curb adultery, restore the integrity of the family and establish undoubted paternity. All of that, especially the latter, was now thrown into disarray in his own family. It was not simply a question of her infidelity to Tiberius, but whether she had been unfaithful to Agrippa, and therefore risked the possibility that Augustus' adopted sons may have had unknown fathers. He had no choice except to banish his daughter. It may have been as simple – and as painful – as that. Julia went to the island of Pandateria, and her mother Scribonia chose to accompany her. Tiberius wrote from Rhodes to try to lighten the punishment, which does him credit, even though he very properly divorced her. Modern scholars have interpreted the scandal of 2 as a state crisis, reading into it conspiracies, potential assassinations, restoration of the Republic, or internal palace revolutions. It is suggested that the creation of the two Praetorian Prefects in 2 must somehow be related to the crisis, because Augustus felt the need for greater security. It is not known how the Praetorians were commanded before this date, but Augustus had possessed a bodyguard of troops since his days as consul and Triumvir, so it is very likely that he was quite capable of giving orders directly to the Praetorians. It is difficult to equate the need for greater security with the insertion of two extra men in the line of command, thus providing potential plotters with two more opportunities for subversion. It may be that Augustus was prepared to convert the Praetorians from his own personal guard into a combined bodyguard and city guard, still ultimately commanded by himself but with wider duties and consequently more administration, necessitating intermediate personnel to cope with it.[15]

The situation in the East was becoming more and more dangerous, so in 1 BC, as already described, Gaius was sent on his mission to establish the balance of power with Parthia. He was consul in AD 1, having been designated to the office in 6. The two boys were growing up and relieving Augustus of several tasks. His letter to Gaius, preserved by Gellius, is revealing, for he writes of his two sons taking over from him, in the most benign sense. Lucius was sent to Spain in AD 2. The purpose of his visit is not known, and he never arrived to carry it out. He died at Massilia, perhaps of a contagious disease. Rumours circulated even then that Livia was behind all this, eliminating rivals to Tiberius one by one, but in this case there is probably no reason to doubt that Lucius simply fell ill. Augustus bore the loss stoically. Tiberius returned to Rome, and Gaius was still in the East, after coming to terms with Phraates V. In the following year, AD 3, Augustus' powers were renewed for a further ten years. By now it was probably just a formality. The interesting point is that he took no colleague even at this late date. Gaius had been wounded in a skirmish, and seems to have become slightly deranged; he announced that he wanted to retire. Tiberius was in Rome but still without office. The turning point came about in AD 4. Gaius died in the East. Augustus was alone again in supreme power, and he was not a young man any more. He brought Tiberius back into the government, granted him tribunician power for ten years, and adopted him as his son in June, along with Agrippa Postumus. The conditions were that Tiberius should adopt his nephew Germanicus as companion to his own son Drusus. Thus there were once again two generations of successors, as there had been before in the two pairs of brothers, Tiberius and Drusus and Gaius and Lucius; all that had happened was that the personnel had become Tiberius and Agrippa Postumus, and Germanicus and Drusus. Syme maintains that Germanicus was the preferred candidate, and that all the others, including Tiberius, were peripheral to the scheme, but it could be argued that Augustus had arrived at such an unassailable degree of political influence that if he had wished to do so he could have adopted Germanicus himself, in direct anticipation of his succession. Innate caution for both political and practical reasons may have made Augustus hedge his bets by adopting Tiberius and surrounding himself with potential heirs in a two-tiered arrangement. Whatever his intentions in AD 4, the Imperial family was reconstituted; battered as it had been by fate, and possibly divided by internal quarrels, it was still intact and Augustus was still at the helm.[16]

8

FINALE

The adoption of Tiberius signifies for some authors a capitulation in the face of the inevitable, and for others merely the culmination of the perpetual grand design. Ancient authors assume that there was constant discord and distrust between Augustus and Tiberius, but there is no contemporary record unsullied by retrospective bias, so their relationship cannot be truthfully assessed. There is no doubt that Augustus intended to hand over the government of the Empire to a successor; a return to the Republican system would have negated most of his life's achievement. The only unknown factor is his choice of personnel. Even his own statement on the matter is characteristically ambiguous: 'This I do for reasons of state' he said when he adopted Tiberius and Agrippa Postumus, leaving uncertain and unpronounced his inner thoughts. It is not recorded that he made such a statement when he adopted Gaius and Lucius, so he may have considered that there was a need to excuse himself for adopting someone aged over 30, or he may have wished to explain why he included Agrippa Postumus in his plans, or indeed Germanicus as Tiberius' adopted son. Enemies of Tiberius naturally seized upon the alternative possibilities, that Augustus would not have made the choice from personal reasons but was compelled to do so because there was no one else, and he was not a young man any longer so could not afford to wait.[1]

He was beginning to feel the effects of his age and his labours for the past five decades, but there was no relinquishing of control. What may have seemed like delegation was in fact only delegation of the physical burdens of power. He reduced his exertions gradually. He ceased to attend the courts, but heard judicial cases in the palace from a special tribunal. Eventually he gave up appearing at public banquets as well. In AD 8 he chose three ex-consuls to receive and deal with embassies. Final decisions were referred to him, presumably after he had received writtten or oral summaries of the main business. Opportunities for manipulation of foreign policy by the three senators in question would have been minimal. Augustus would not allow them to deal independently with politically sensitive areas, and in all other circumstances he could ensure that there were no meetings in secret to talk of details which were kept from him. The senators would take on the exhausting but necessary hospitality and entertainment functions. Delegation of the northern wars to Tiberius was nothing new. Although Augustus claimed in the *Res Gestae* that he added provinces to the Empire and led armies, he recognised reality, and recognised that the Roman people would know the truth. He never claimed to be a general; he occupied a position which did not really exist, as commander-in-chief. He was the man who authorised the movements of the armies, who paid the soldiers and ensured that they received rewards on retirement, but he did not direct them in the field. Agrippa's vital contributions were recognised tacitly by the rewards and honours he received, but he was mentioned only once in the *Res Gestae*, not in a military capacity but as consul and colleague in taking the census. Tiberius received acknowledgement for the conquest of Pannonia but was not mentioned in connection with Germany, most likely because no province was ultimately created there. The German campaigns of the years 4 to 6 were successful, suitably lauded by Velleius, who names several tribes subdued by Tiberius. The Elbe was reached once again, and bases set up on the river Lippe. At the end of the campaigning, only the Marcomanni under king Maroboduus remained to be subdued, and preparations were set in motion in AD 5–6 to carry out this task.[2]

While Tiberius was absent, there were sufficient tasks for Augustus to attend to in Rome. This time he did not accompany the armies to Gaul to be near to the theatre of war. There was some discord with Gaius Cornelius Cinna Magnus, accused of plotting against Augustus. This man was a grandson of Pompeius through the female line. Virtually nothing is known about his intentions, or even the date of his so-called plot. Seneca places it somewhere between 16 and 12; Dio recounts it among the events of AD 4, and uses it as the introduction to a long discourse through the mouths of Livia and Augustus himself, about the problems and privileges of monarchy, always threatened, never secure, but better supported by clemency than force. The long scenario is more relevant to Dio's own times than the first century, though there are truisms enough in the speeches of both the main characters. If there was opposition to Augustus in AD 4 it did not make itself keenly felt. Whatever the problems with Cinna, no punishment was meted out, and there seems to have been no widespread circle of accomplices to root out. It was perhaps simply a squabble, overheard and embroidered. Far from falling out of favour, Cinna became consul in the following year. In AD 4, Augustus purged the Senate once again, this time via a watered-down version of the method he had tried to institute once before, to make the senators fulfil the task for him. He chose ten senators, of whom three were appointed by lot to oversee the business. Dio records that there were few problems. Many men resigned voluntarily, and only a few remained to face the erasure of their names from the lists against their will. Augustus was not trying this time to reduce the Senate to a workable but elite 300 members; this was more in the line of quality control. The same could be said perhaps of his census in Italy, recorded by Dio, of all those who possessed fortunes of 200,000 sesterces, or in other words those who had reached the half-way mark to equestrian qualification. He made further adjustments to the freedman problem via the *Lex Aelia Sentia* which tied up most of the loopholes still in evidence after the laws of 17 and 2. Age restrictions were placed both on the slaves to be freed and on the masters who wished to free them; the slaves had to be at least thirty at the time of manumission, otherwise they could not be citizens, and masters had to be at least twenty years old. Those slaves with any sort of criminal record were debarred from citizenship, and not even allowed to reside in Rome. Other grades were properly regulated; young freedmen probably became Latins rather than full citizens. These and the Junian Latins were encouraged to become citizens after they had satisfied the relevant criteria, such as marriage to a Roman and production of children, or service in the *vigiles*. There were reasonable avenues to citizenship, provided that the freedmen made some relevant contribution to the state.[3]

Natural disasters marked the year AD 5, and there were stirrings of the discontents and problems that surfaced repeatedly from the following year onwards. Dio records an earthquake, the flooding of the Tiber, a partial eclipse of the sun and famine in Rome. As if that were not enough, the soldiers were restless and unhappy. These were ongoing problems that caused some discontent. The food supply was only gradually taken in hand; most of the measures adopted up to now were reactive responses to shortages. In 22 Augustus had taken on the *cura annonae* for a few weeks, then later he had handed over the task to two ex-praetors, elected annually to supervise distribution. The number of ex-praetors was increased to four, chosen by lot from among men nominated by the magistrates of the year. When the shortages became acute in AD 6, the praetors were replaced by ex-consuls, but they were still only in charge of distribution. The real need was for centralised organisation of supply, which seems to have remained for some time in the hands of private businessmen, who operated without co-ordination. Eventually, before the end of Augustus' reign, at some unknown date between AD 8 and 14, the system was regularised, and an equestrian *praefectus annonae* was placed in charge of the corn supply. The acute shortages in AD 6 necessitated the removal from Rome of all unnecessary mouths. The gladiators and slaves who were up for sale were sent 100 miles from the city; the courts were allowed to go into recess, and senators allowed to leave. It is assumed that there was sufficient food outside Rome itself for these temporary exiles, and that it was easier to send them away than to bring the food into the city, where fair distribution would probably have been problematic. Suetonius quotes from Augustus' own writings, where he says that he once thought of abolishing the corn dole altogether because dependence on the free distributions had an adverse effect on Italian agriculture, but then he reconsidered on the grounds that the corn distributions would be renewed anyway by men desirous of winning popular favour. So in the long run it was better that he controlled them himself.[4]

The year AD 6 was one of innovation, improvement and organisational changes. It was now that Augustus put the payment of soldiers' pensions on a regular footing. Dio records the first efforts to find a means of financing the army under the events of the previous year. Discontent with the search for revenues was revealed in AD 6, and Augustus dealt with it by asking the senators for ideas on how to raise the necessary cash. By involving them in the process, he encouraged the senators to think for themselves about the magnitude of the problem, and hopefully underlined for them the importance of creating a properly organised system for the settlement of veterans. Perhaps he thought privately that they were too ready to leave the matter to someone else, and moreover that they wanted provincial government and expansion of the Empire at unrealistically low costs. Perhaps also he hoped to promote the idea that the army, especially the care of its veterans, was a communal concern, which would help to disguise the fact that the person who had the most urgent interest in maintaining an army was himself. Dio says that by handing the problem to the senators, Augustus could more easily persuade them to adopt his own plan, which was to institute a 5 per cent tax on inheritances. He endorsed this plan by insisting that he had found the outline of it among Caesar's memoranda. It may be true. The problem of veteran settlement was a perennial one, and it may be that Caesar had discussed with the young Octavius the severity of the matter if ever there were to be a standing army, discharging men at regular intervals. Augustus had thought about the system in some depth. There were to be exclusions for those inheritances which were small, or destined for poor people, or for very close relatives. It had already been revealed at the time when he was pushing through his marriage laws that there was a whole body of men and women in Rome whose main purpose in life was professional legacy-hunting. These were the people who, in the main, would forfeit the tax of 5 per cent. Another source of income was the 1 per cent tax levied on sales of goods at auctions, which was collected not by the tax gatherers as in the case of the inheritance tax, but by the auctioneers. As a class, the auctioneers probably did not suffer too much from the imposition of this tax, except in so far as it made for more paper work. These taxes were destined for the new miltary treasury, the *aerarium militare*, set up for payment of soldiers' pensions. Since the taxes were new, they could not yield sufficient capital for immediate use, so Augustus paid 170,000,000 sesterces into the new treasury to provide a basis for its proper functioning. He also accepted donations from cities and client kings, but not from individuals, though some men said that they had offered contributions.[5]

Finance was also needed for the payment and organisation of the *vigiles*. There had been yet another fire in Rome in AD 6. The prototype fire service, formed originally from Egnatius Rufus' band of 600 slaves, proved inadequate for the control of large fires. The final version of the fire service, also combining an urban police force, was the formation of the seven cohorts, each 1,000 strong, of the *vigiles* in AD 6. A tax of 4 per cent was levied on sales of slaves to pay for the new cohorts. Two of the city's regions were placed in charge of each cohort, and the whole body was commanded by an equestrian prefect. It was a logical development, but it was also indicative of Augustus' state of mind. It was the first time that he had taken personal charge so firmly and decisively of any feature of the administration of the city, without consultation or waiting for evolution to follow a more leisurely pattern. He was on safe ground, of course. Everyone could see the need for an efficient and centrally directed fire service, so he could not be accused too readily of making arrangements that were only of benefit to himself. He perhaps felt that he had little time left, and also that he was secure in his position; like Caesar in the 40s he still had much to do, but by anybody's standards he was an old man, and could no longer be so liberal with time and patience. When there was controversy over the elections of magistrates in AD 8, he simply appointed all of them, to avoid faction, as Dio describes it. The measure was wholly Caesarian, not Augustan. Three years earlier, in AD 5, he had discovered that there was a dearth of men willing to serve as aediles, so he had compelled ex-quaestors and ex-tribunes to serve, selecting them by lot. He had always been an autocrat, but had never acted like one until now. The calm exterior that he strove to maintain, and succeeded in doing so most of the time, seems to have been overcome on occasion with a contempt for dithering subordinates, sorted out at one fell swoop with an impatient gesture.[6]

There was much to try his patience in his last years. Family discord broke out again in AD 6 and seems to have continued sporadically until AD 8. First Agrippa Postumus abdicated from office and was exiled from Rome, eventually being relegated to the island of Planasia in AD 7. The following year saw the banishment of his sister, the younger Julia, and of her lover Iunius Silanus. For some reason her husband L. Aemilius Paullus was accused of treason and exiled as well, though at what date is uncertain. It used to be thought that he was executed, but Syme revealed that he survived. Julia's crime was said to have been adultery, and the child born to her in exile was not allowed to survive. Augustus ordered her house in Rome to be destroyed, which indicates either an explosion of passionate anger, or that her adulteries were not the only problem. Whether there was any connection between the exile of Agrippa and Julia is not known. Attempts have been made to detect a convoluted plot involving all the main characters, and sometimes outsiders unconnected to the family except by their designs of revolution. The exile of Ovid is dated to AD 8, and often allied to the scandal of the younger Julia. Ovid gives tantalising clues in his later works, declaring that the causes of his banishment were a poem and a mistake. Obviously he knew very well what the problem was. Sexual scandal may have been at the root of it, and his *Ars Amatoria* may have been one of the factors which tipped the balance. His books were banned, which is of course an excellent way of ensuring that they would be read and would survive. Rejecting the conspiracy theory, some authors interpret the episode from AD 6 to 8 as a long-term domestic squabble, or indeed two domestic squabbles not necessarily related. Agrippa Postumus is often dealt with as peripheral and unimportant, but it has been pointed out that he possessed quite considerable political worth. It was said that there were plots to liberate both Agrippa and Julia, though there is some confusion as to whether Agrippa's sister or his mother is meant. There was also a story that Augustus visited Agrippa on his island in AD 14. The remarkable point about the conspiracy, if such it was, is that no one among Augustus' contemporaries seemed to know the truth. He never made a statement, and was not called upon to do so; there can be no clearer indication of autocratic rule. The official verdict on Agrippa was that he was brutish and not socially acceptable, but that begs the question as to why he was adopted and promoted from AD 4 and then dropped in AD 6. His trangression may have been simple discontent, too blatantly expressed. He had not been adopted as a young child, like his brothers Gaius and Lucius, and it is not certain what position he would have held if they had both survived. He had never known his father, and from the age of ten he had been deprived of his mother in scandalous circumstances. Little more could have been done to convince him that he was an outsider, and much the same could be said of his sister Julia. It is possible that they both suffered from suspicions on Augustus' part about their true parentage after the adulteries of their mother became public property. On the whole the affair, or affairs, are perhaps best judged as domestic, internal problems rather than attempts at revolution. Some men were punished and exiled, but there was no witch hunt, and nothing like the proscriptions of the Triumvirate. Revolutions and depositions generally do not take place via so few people, and it seems certain that Augustus' life was not endangered. It has been pointed out by more than one author that it was Tiberius who profited from the removal of Agrippa, and that as soon as he came to power he had Agrippa killed, or someone kindly took care of it for him.[7]

Trouble erupted in several different provinces in the same year that famine, fire and family disputes disturbed the Augustan peace in Rome. Dio reports raids by the Isaurian tribesmen in the East, but does not delineate how and by whom they were brought to a halt. In Africa, Cornelius Cossus earned himself triumphal honours and the name Gaetulicus by subduing the rebellious Gaetulians who had risen up against their king, Juba. Herod Archelaus of Judaea was driven out by his brothers and sent by Augustus to Gaul, in permanent exile, and in Sardinia the pirate raids had begun again, necessitating the presence of troops under an equestrian commander, who was appointed by Augustus and left in office for an indefinite term at his discretion, in contrast to the more normal senatorial proconsul chosen annually by lot. Dio adds to this tale the cryptic comment that in the provinces governed by Augustus' appointees, men were left in office for a longer period. This may have been merely an explanatory paragraph to illustrate the fact that the arrangements in Sardinia were perfectly normal while it was governed by the equestrians chosen by Augustus; or it may mean that there was more trouble in other provinces that Dio was not prepared to elucidate. It is true that AD 6 was not a good year. Just as the conquest of Germany seemed to be within reach, and the onslaught against Maroboduus was beginning, Tiberius was recalled to the Pannonian front, where rebellion had broken out and gave him his work to do all over again. It took years of heavy fighting to set it all to rights, and brought Roman armies to the brink of disaster. There was considerable panic in Rome when the news broke. Augustus informed the Senate that the Pannonians could be in Italy in a matter of days, and at the gates of Rome very shortly afterwards. In logistical terms that was probably true, but not necessarily likely. The hyperbole was probably brought on by the difficulties in recruiting men for the army. Augustus had already lengthened the term of service as part of a cost-cutting exercise, but the extra years of service did not solve his problem of manpower. He recruited freeborn men as far as possible, creating the *cohortes civium Romanorum ingenuorum*, but then was forced to buy slaves from their owners and free them for service in the army in the *cohortes civium Romanorum voluntariorum*. Then there was the supposed falling out with Tiberius; Augustus was said to have accused him of not conducting the war vigorously enough. He sent Germanicus, who was only a quaestor, with extra troops; Tiberius sent some of them back, saying he had enough soldiers. Perhaps he was exasperated that he had been given troops who had next to no training, and at this point he was hardly in a position to devote much time to fashioning experienced soldiers out of city dwellers. Augustus travelled to Ariminum to direct the campaigns, or more likely to lend moral support, in AD 8. He had slowed down physically, but Dio says that he showed enough energy when there was need. For a while it was very serious, and Tiberius and Germanicus only began to gain the upper hand after hard fighting. Dio reports that at one point at the siege of Salonae, Tiberius' supply lines were cut. It was difficult terrain, and the locals knew it better than the Romans. Eventually Tiberius was able to make peace on terms favourable to Rome, while Germanicus mopped up resistance. They came home in AD 9 to a rapturous welcome. Tiberius and Augustus were both hailed as Imperator, and voted triumphs; Germanicus received the *ornamenta triumphalia*, the rank of praetor, and the right to stand for the consulship before reaching the correct age. Tiberius' son Drusus had not taken part in the fighting, but was promoted with his father and adopted brother. He was granted the right to attend meetings of the Senate before becoming a senator, and promised that when he should be quaestor he would be given the right to vote before the ex-praetors. Augustus employed the victory to advance his relatives and give them experience. The planned celebrations were to be magnificent, but they never took place. Instead of victory there was resounding disaster. While Tiberius was bringing the Pannonian wars to a successful conclusion, his one-time consular colleague Quinctilius Varus was transforming the recently conquered German tribes into Roman provincials, organising their territories and levying taxes. But the tribesmen were not ready to become Romans, and they demonstrated their reluctance quite unequivocally by wiping out Varus and three Roman legions.[8]

The setback was severe. The major battle in the Teutoburg forest had already been fought by the time the news reached Augustus. The search for the site of this disastrous battle has occupied archaeologists for several centuries, but the problem now seems to have been solved. Claims have been made for a location north of Osnabruck, around Kalkriese, where finds of military equipment and coins support the theory that this was the site of the 'Varusschlacht'. The legions which were wiped out were not named in the ancient sources, but archaeologists and historians deduce that they were the XVII, XVIII, and XIX. These legions disappear from the record and were never reconstituted, nor were their numbers reused, so it is a safe assumption that these were the units annihilated by the Germans in AD 9. The losses could not be taken lightly. Roman armies had been at full stretch since AD 6, recruitment was once again vital, but had to be undertaken from depleted resources; perhaps most important of all, Roman prestige was badly dented. Tiberius was the only man capable of taking command, so after years of campaigning he was sent once again to Germany. Augustus dismissed his German bodyguard, because the men were felt to be untrustworthy. It was a cosmetic operation as much as a prudent safeguard to do so, because public opinion would have turned against them anyway, however loyal they might have been. Freedmen were recruited for the army, and veterans were recalled. The situation was not as bad as was at first believed; some soldiers had survived, and the Germans had not penetrated beyond or even as far as the Rhine. Tiberius retrieved the losses, remaining in Germany for another two years: in AD 10 watching in case the tribesmen penetrated to the Rhine, and in AD 11 campaigning inside German territory – but not too far. Dreams of conquest had faded. Augustus never recovered from the disaster, and turned his back on expansion of the Empire. He was said to give vent to his feelings on occasion by shouting out loud 'Quinctilius Varus, give me back my legions!' and he certainly advised Tiberius not to attempt further conquests. It was probably not necessary to say it; Tiberius had had enough of fighting.[9]

After the German disaster there were no major wars. Augustus concentrated on guaranteeing the succession in so far as he could direct affairs, to clear the path for a seamless join between his own style of government and that of the next Princeps and his entourage. It was obvious that Augustus intended that there should continue to be a group of family members, all of them schooled in Roman administration. Tiberius' son Drusus was quaestor in AD 11, and Germanicus was consul in the following year, and held the office for the whole year even though suffect consuls holding office for half the year were the norm. Germanicus had not been praetor in his turn, so since he had omitted this tour of duty Augustus perhaps wished him to gain the full experience of the consulship and its administrative duties. It was also his intention that Drusus was to be treated in the same fashion, reaching the consulship without having been praetor in AD 15. In the past he had insisted that his adopted sons should as far as possible fill each office in turn, but he desired a streamlined training scheme for his heirs now that he was so much older himself. He wrote a letter commending Germanicus to the Senate, and the Senate to Tiberius, but did not read it out himself because his voice was failing. Germanicus read it 'as usual' according to Dio, which indicates that this had become Augustus' normal method of communicating with the Senate. Augustus' powers were renewed for a further ten years in AD 13; he was in his mid-seventies, and cannot have held out realistic hopes of reaching the stage where he would need to have his powers renewed again. This time he made Tiberius his colleague, with *imperium* equal to his own, and *tribunicia potestas*. At this stage in AD 13 he restructured the *consilium*, perhaps in an attempt to make it more manageable for Tiberius and his successors. He probably realised that personality as well as *auctoritas* counted for a great deal in this respect, and that Tiberius had neither the experience nor the inclination for the looser, more relaxed style of government. The *consilium* certainly became more like an executive council and lost its informal, experimental, advisory capacity. Tiberius, Germanicus, and Drusus were to be regular members of it, with the consuls of the year and twenty senators, who served for a year. Augustus' advisers had previously numbered fifteen, and had served for six months. The *consilium* was given greater powers in that its resolutions were given the same validity as *senatus consulta*. Not that Augustus had any intention yet of retiring. When there was further discontent with the inheritance tax levied for the military treasury he repeated his former offer to the senators to let them find a better way of raising the revenues. Dio adds an interesting note that Augustus instructed Germanicus and Drusus not to say a word about the matter, because if they did speak out then people would seize on the ideas in the expectation that that was what he really wanted. Some written reports reached him, but he ignored them and proposed a land tax instead. He even started to take statistics and make measurements, probably tongue-in-cheek with no intention of carrying out his threat. Knowing that a land tax would hurt far more people, and do it far more deeply than an inheritance tax, he had only to wait until the senators capitulated and settled for his original plan. After all the tribulations of his last years he may have permitted himself a wry smile.[10]

In AD 14 Augustus and Tiberius conducted a census, in which 4,937,000 citizens were registered. The *lustrum* was performed in May, with consular *imperium*, as Augustus states in the *Res Gestae*. If Augustus did not hold this power on a permanent basis, this may have been a special grant made for the specific purpose of conducting the census. Suetonius refers to a law passed by the consuls that Tiberius should govern provinces jointly with Augustus and carry out the census. The problem is that it is not known whether this law was restricted to Tiberius alone, or whether it also applied to Augustus. Some authorities assume that the law could have bestowed consular power on him for the same task of conducting the census. Once again there is no absolute clarity about Augustus' consular power. It has been suggested that Tiberius did not hold consular power in Italy, but the passage recording the census in the *Res Gestae* can be taken as evidence that he did, and so was in all respects the equal of Augustus in AD 14. The debate goes on because there is no proof for what must remain cleverly argued theories. After completing the census, Tiberius set off for Illyricum, and Augustus went to Capri, which he reputedly liked very much, having received it from the city of Naples in return for Ischia. He attended the games at Naples but fell ill. By will-power and determination he reached Nola, where his family owned property. Certain that his end was approaching, he made himself presentable, had his cheeks rouged and sat up in bed to ask the audience gathered around him if they had enjoyed the performance. On 19 August he died, appropriately enough in the month named after him. He had started life as Gaius Octavius, the great nephew of Gaius Julius Caesar. He had gone through several tranformations since then, and now he transformed himself for the last time into an enduring legend and god.[11]

9

THE LEGACY

The Roman world held its breath for a short time, waiting to see what would happen. Augustus had ruled the Empire for a very long time, and the longevity of his rule had lent stability to his regime. There would be many people who had known nothing else except the rule of the Princeps; some people had been born and died while he was still in power, and all the generations born in and after 30 BC would know nothing of the Republic and the turmoil that heralded its end, except for hearsay and their history books. Velleius speaks of the narrow margin between stability and chaos until the accession of Tiberius was assured. One of Tiberius' first acts was to write to the armies spread over the Empire, and to secure the loyalty of the troops in Italy by means of the oath established by Augustus. The secret of Empire, fully revealed after the death of Nero and the civil wars that followed, was already known quite distinctly to Augustus and Tiberius. In his will Augustus had left 300 sesterces to each of the legionaries, with the stipulation that it should be paid out immediately. He knew his men, and the value of money in maintaining loyalty. Even so, the ancient sources record military discontent among the northern legions, quelled by Tiberius' son Drusus and Junius Blaesus. Some of the legions expressed their support of Germanicus, thus compromising his position *vis-à-vis* Tiberius. The soldiers had no high-minded desires to restore the Republic, nor to elevate anyone except a member of Augustus' family; the main thing on their minds was more likely a possible rise in pay and the extraction of privileges from whoever was to be their new paymaster.[1]

After the army, the next hurdle was the Senate. There was little resistance. The consuls, the prefects of the Praetorian Guard and the *praefectus annonae* swore the oath of loyalty to Tiberius, followed by the Senate, the people of Rome, then the soldiers and the people of the provinces. This cannot have happened overnight, but the intention to administer the oath all over the Empire was what counted for immediate purposes. Tiberius summoned the senators by means of his tribunician power, a factor which lends support to the theory that he did not hold consular power in Italy. The context does not necessarily bear this out. The source for the episode

191

is Tacitus, and the passage describing Tiberius' actions should be taken as a whole, since its main point is that Tiberius was anxious not to overstep the mark by too blatant a display of power. He insisted that each first step should be taken by the consuls, as though the Republic still existed, and to indicate that he was not yet certain that he wished to take on the Empire. He wanted to keep a low profile, and so the use of tribunician power to summon the Senate was one of the least provocative ways of doing so. Tacitus accuses him of hypocrisy, because he had already assumed command of the troops and the Praetorian Guard. It could be argued that taking control of the military forces was a prudent step; somebody had to do it to prevent a descent into chaos. Thereafter Tiberius was merely playing Augustus' old game of reluctantly taking on the burden of Empire only after he had been asked to do so, but the main trouble was that Augustus did it better and was more plausible.[2]

Augustus left a will and three other documents which were read out in the Senate after his death. There were written instructions regarding his funeral, the text which is now known as the *Res Gestae*, which he wished to be placed at the entrance to his tomb, and the account of the Empire's resources which Suetonius calls the *breviarium totius imperii*. The will was in two parts, one written in his own hand and one by his freedmen Polybius and Hilarion. His chief heirs were Tiberius and Livia, then Germanicus and Drusus, then members of his extended family. He left a total of 43,000,000 sesterces to the people, 1,000 sesterces apiece to the Praetorians, 500 to the urban troops, and 300 to the legionaries. The account of the Empire contained an enumeration of the soldiers in active service, the money in the public treasuries, and the revenue in arrears. Appended to the document was a list of names of those freedmen and slaves of his household and official staff who could render account of the state finances. Dio adds that there was a fourth document, containing instructions to the people and to Tiberius, to the effect that they should not free too many slaves and thereby risk releasing upon the city an indolent rabble; that they should not enfranchise too many people because to do so would blur the distinctions between the Romans and the rest of the world; that they should entrust public business to those best qualified to understand it, and never allow the whole to fall into the hands of one man, to avoid tyranny or collapse if one man died or was killed; and that they should be content with their gains so far and not try to expand the Empire because it would be too difficult to guard it. Whether this document did once exist is not known, but Dio was on safe ground since all these alleged instructions are in keeping with Augustus' policies as evidenced by his legislation, his use of various members of his family to undertake official tasks, and his later opinions on expansion of the Empire after the disaster of Varus in Germany.[3]

The funeral took place in Rome with suitable pomp and ceremony. Drusus and Tiberius delivered orations as the cortège halted in the Forum near the

Rostra. Augustus' body was burned in the Campus Martius, with the Senate and equites and their families looking on, then the remains were conveyed to the mausoleum. On 17 September, the Senate decreed that Augustus should be deified, and temples set up to his cult; Livia reputedly paid a million sesterces to Numerius Atticus, who said that he had seen Augustus' spirit rising to the Heavens; it sounds like a prearranged scenario, of which Augustus himself would have been proud. After the funeral and the deification came the assessments of Augustus' life and career. Tacitus weighs the pros and cons in two subsequent passages, succinctly summing up the divergent opinions about motives and intentions, and the good and bad effects of the reign. The end results were law and order, centralisation of the administration, a lack of coercion in the later years and the creation of government by the Princeps instead of a dictatorship. On the other hand there were the means by which Octavian had come to power: the proscriptions, the Triumvirate, the civil wars, and the appalling fact that what Augustus had really bequeathed to the Roman world was Tiberius and the unalloyed monarchy (which Tacitus does not mention because he did not need to) that led to the accession of Domitian, everyone's *bête noire* at the time when Tacitus wrote. The significance of Tacitus' assessment of Augustus is that all the positive aspects belong to the later period, and all the negative ones, save for the suppression of a few conspiracies, belong to the death struggles of the Republic. It is hard to escape the conclusion that for the average man in the street the reign of Augustus had not been too detrimental. The positive aspects survived, and with the passage of time became hallowed. Later Emperors had a vested interest in presenting Augustus as the founder of the Empire, and could hardly admit that he might have got it wrong. Dio employs the funeral oration of Tiberius as an assessment of Augustus' life and achievements, echoing more than once the opening, self-justificatory remarks of the *Res Gestae*, claiming that Augustus had put an end to the strife caused by the various warring factions in Rome. Dio's audience had good reason to know at first hand the disruption and despair caused by factions and civil wars; it would strike a curiously modern tone to them to hear how Augustus had faced and overcome the same problems.[4]

The more recent judgements of Augustus have also been influenced by their own particular scholarly environments. The 1930s and 1940s had seen the darker side of political supremacy, and scholars of the period naturally interpreted Augustus' seizure of power and prolonged grasp on it as something less than admirable. More relaxed times have seen a more relaxed version of Augustus, with great attention paid to his use of art and literature to promote his image, or his acquiescence in the undirected developments in these areas. There is still argument about how far his control of these political tools invaded the realm of private initiative; some see him as totally committed to rigid censorship and eradication of the slightest criticism, and to promotion and direction of favourable representations of himself, while others have depicted him as tolerant to a great degree, perfectly willing to let art follow its own course. It cannot be denied that he was aware of and utilised every means of self-advertisement to elevate himself and then maintain his pre-eminence once achieved. A recent author has rightly labelled him an expert showman, which he was, in the sense of being a talented actor, but it is not known who wrote the scripts that he acted out. It may be that there was a person or even an unofficial committee behind the presentation of Augustus to the world. It is important to realise that the constant promotion of the image was not simply to impress the Senate and Roman people, nor the soldiers and the provincials, but also the world outside Rome, where prestige counted for as much as armed force. This promotion of the image was certainly not accidental, but it is not known how, or if, it was co-ordinated and centrally directed. Nameless subordinates have been postulated, acting as ancient versions of publicity agents, not an impossible scenario in the circumstances. Other monarchs have employed the same means, with important parallels for Augustus' reign. A well-researched study by Peter Burke has revealed that the presentation of Louis XIV was orchestrated by his minister Colbert, who glorified and celebrated his master by all the means at his disposal. The process was noted and summed up by Ezechiel Spanheim, a professor of rhetoric from Geneva, who became a diplomat at Versailles; his description could apply equally as well to Augustus as to Louis XIV: 'They present him as the sole author and inspiration of all the successes of his reign, attributed entirely to his wisdom, prudence and courage.' Everything throughout the Roman world was exploited to present Augustus; monuments were adorned with his name and portraits; sculptures of him still abound from all parts of the Empire; coins portrayed his face and the topics of the moment; literature praised his historic and current achievements. There has been argument about the intended audience for these various artistic and literary works, and about how far their influence permeated everyday life. It was certain that the image of the Princeps was constantly before the eyes of almost everyone in the Empire and that, moreover, the presentation of the image was never allowed to lapse. The formality of the portraits was paramount; no evidence has come to light that Augustus was ever depicted in anything other than formal dress, or performing anything other than official tasks, full of Roman *gravitas* and dignity. In everyday life he made jokes and laughed, grew angry from time to time, was frequently ill, and functioned like any other human being, but nothing of this reached the public in visible concrete form. Similarly there was a consistent portrayal of Augustus as an eternal youth who never aged. The image makers of Hollywood would have nothing to teach Augustus. Once having created the legend it is difficult to watch it wither away, and having maintained the youthful image for so long it becomes incongruous to present to the world a sudden dramatic change to the reality of old age. It would have suggested to the Roman world an infirmity that would have contradicted the reliance placed on the self-advertised strength of the ruler.[5]

In the religious sphere, Augustus became Pontifex Maximus only in 12 BC, and so could not be said to stand at the head of the state religion from the very beginning, but there was no threat to his supremacy on this score. He did not suffer from the problems of the medieval kings of Europe, who frequently found themselves in conflict with, and sometimes dominated by, the Church. Religious observances in the Roman world could proceed without the need for Augustus to be chief priest. He was integrated into the system by another means. The growth of the Imperial cult was one of the most remarkable and novel methods of bringing Augustus to the notice of the people. The Eastern provinces subscribed to the notion of his divinity very early, just after the battle of Actium, but Octavian had prudently combined the divinity of Rome with worship of himself. In Rome and the West the process was slower. Rome was a more sensitive area, where proclaiming oneself a living god was not the wisest of courses to follow. When Agrippa wanted to dedicate his new temple as the Augusteum, Augustus refused the honour, and would not allow a statue of himself to be placed inside the temple. Divinity was his at one remove as the son of the deified Caesar. Later in his life, when he had created the fourteen regions of the city, he allowed the *magistri* of the subdivisions of the regions to administer the worship of his *Genius* rather than himself as god on earth. The *Lares Compitales* or local shrines thus became the *Lares Augusti*. The worship of Augustus himself seems to have been more acceptable in the Western provinces, where temples were dedicated to him during his lifetime. These provinces were virgin territories to be moulded into this religious context. The ruler cult had to be manufactured there, and was concentrated on specific sites. At the two main sites there was a sanctuary but no actual temple; the Altar of the Three Gauls was established at Lugdunum, and the Altar of the Ubii at Cologne on the Rhine. These focal points helped to spread the cult throughout the Western provinces. Priests were recruited to officiate at the ceremonies, but beyond the existence of the cult not much is known of the procedures The process would require considerable time to become embedded in public consciousness, and probably yielded more benefits to Augustus' successors than to himself.[6]

His successors built upon the administrative foundations that he had laid, so gradually and seamlessly that at one time it seemed to scholars that the whole system sprang from Augustus' master plan for the government of the Roman Empire. That assessment has been revised in the light of more detailed research which has revealed that only some of the administrative procedures had reached their final form when Augustus died. It has been argued that he took over functions, not powers, especially in the judicial and legislative spheres. He did so very gradually, just as Tacitus says, and without usurpation of anyone's position. He took on judicial functions, attending the courts sometimes as onlooker and sometimes hearing cases himself. As he grew older he heard them in his own house. It was probably inevitable that he or his successors would assume the place of supreme judge, simply because people would look to the Emperor as arbiter, and he would have to make decisions. Eventually the word of the Emperor became law, but this posed a few anomalies, as outlined by Crook; no one seemed to be certain how this had come about, but it was known that it had not always been the case. Augustus promulgated laws through the proper channels, and declined the honour of applying to them the name *Leges Augustae*. It meant that he wanted to remain within the normal range of legislative procedure, calling them instead *Leges Juliae*. None the less he needed to be able to guide the legal process in all its aspects. Similarly he guided administration, but he did not establish anything more than a rudimentary form of centralised bureaucracy. His staff seems to have been quite small, and consisted mostly of freedmen, two of whom are named in the ancient sources, Polybius and Hilarion. The division into specialised departments dealing with incoming and outgoing correspondence, and the career structures of the freedman and equestrian classes, occurred later. Augustus' most important administrative functions embraced the appointment of the important officials in his own provinces, and the subordinate commanders of his own troops. He does not seem to have aimed at total control of the appointments to all magistracies, except at times when there was conflict. The government and administration of the city of Rome evolved empirically, as did the government of some of the provinces, except in one respect which could not be left to chance. By dint of the command of various provinces and his *auctoritas* he controlled foreign policy, and although it could be said that he did so on an *ad hoc* basis without any master plan to guide him, it was vital to ensure that this aspect of Empire never fell into the hands of anyone else. Much of his success came from his government of the Roman Empire, but equally his success depended upon how he dealt with the outside world.[7]

Analysis of Augustus' power and how he came by it and wielded it has produced a vast quantity of literature for many years. The problems have been highlighted, minutely discussed, and acutely dissected, but not unequivocally solved. The most important contributory factors in Octavian's rise were the control of most of the armed forces after the fall of Alexandria, and the sole possession of the wealth of Egypt. Without armies and the private means of remunerating them, he would have failed to make more than a fleeting impression. But the arrival is not as difficult as remaining in power, and he did so through all the vicissitudes of his life for the next forty-four years. As commander of the armed forces and holder of the purse strings he had a head start, but then there other attributes which enabled him to win over the Senate and people. He possessed patience and tact in his dealings with everyone, which masked his real power and gave the impression that the people had a contribution to make almost equal to his own. His position as Princeps, or first citizen, was supported by his modest behaviour and restraint. *Auctoritas* was a concept that he invoked once he was in power to explain to the world how he had arrrived at this position, rather than an ideology that he had set himself to aim for. He could not predict how things would turn out, but he was guided by the knowledge of what people would tolerate and what they found unacceptable, and within that framework he exploited all opportunities that came his way. When he had established peace, he required some reason for control of and access to the armies. He found it by taking on the government of the disruptive half-formed provinces, where promotion of Roman supremacy could be used as the mainstay of his conquests. He did not need to invent for himself a new post equivalent to commander-in-chief of all the armed forces, since proconsular power gave him control of most of the armies. He could afford to allow others to command troops in different parts of the Roman world because he was paymaster of the armies and the soldiers swore an oath of loyalty to him personally. This placed him on the moral high ground; it would not be sufficient to prevent the rise of potential usurpers, but anyone attempting to dislodge him by means of a military coup would probably weigh up the odds and think twice. Augustus was not alone at the head of the state. Agrippa was on hand and would have to be fought as well as Augustus, as second-line defence. When he died there was Tiberius, and Gaius and Lucius, then Germanicus and Drusus. Augustus unashamedly used his family for state and dynastic purposes. He gave important commands to others who were outside the family circle, but reserved the serious wars, and especially the command of troops in sensitive areas or of large numbers of troops, for his family. As time passed, the idea of the Imperial family and its developing court, if such it can be termed at this stage, would become the norm. It may have been questioned whether the relatives of Augustus were the best men to undertake the various campaigns, but behind them all was Augustus himself, whose prestige was almost unassailable. The indefinable quality which he managed to foster was credibility, which scarcely ever wavered. Its component parts are several, including the carefully promoted image, based on tangible successes, but the overriding component is personality. Innate characteristics combined with experience enabled Augustus to rule men; the machinery by which he did so was already available, and all he had to do was recognise how to use it. He saw that men generally distrust innovation, especially if applied by force, and that they usually look back to precedents and procedures that they understand. Proconsular and tribunician power were not too alarming, even if he did have to bend the rules a little to assume the latter. Whether he wielded *imperium maius* has been questioned, and consular power is a constant problem, but all these thorny constitutional questions are in the end somewhat academic. It would be nice to know the answers, but if those particular tools of government had not been available to him he would have adapted what there was; he would never have outlined distinctly what his powers were, and if challenged he would have redefined himself without necessarily inventing anything new. Augustus ruled the Roman world because he had the capacity to make people believe in him, and then make them grateful.[8]

NOTES

ABBREVIATIONS

AE	*L'Année Epigraphique*
ANRW	*Aufstieg und Niedergang der Römischen Welt*, ed. H. Temporini 1972 – date
Appian *BC*	*Roman History: the Civil Wars*
Appian *Ill.*	*Illyrica*
BMC	*Coins of the Roman Empire in the British Museum*: Volume I *Augustus to Vitellius*, ed. H. Mattingly, London, 1923 (reprinted 1965)
BMCR	*Coins of the Roman Republic in the British Museum*, H. A. Grueber, London, 1910
BRGK	*Bericht der Römisch-Germanisch Kommission*
Caesar *BAfr.*	*African War*
Caesar *BC*	*Civil War*
Caesar *BHisp.*	*Bellum Hispanum* (The Spanish War)
CAH	*Cambridge Ancient History*
Cicero *ad Att.*	*Letters to Atticus*
Cicero *ad Fam.*	*Letters to his Friends*
Cicero *ad M. Brut.*	*Letters to Marcus Brutus*
Cicero *ad Q. Fr.*	*Letters to his brother Quintus*
Cicero *Phil.*	*Philippics*
CIL	*Corpus Inscriptionum Latinarum*
CQ	*Classical Quarterly*
EJ²	Ehrenberg, V. and Jones, A.H.M., *Documents Illustrating the Reigns of Augustus and Tiberius*, Oxford, Clarendon Press (2nd edn, 1976)
EPROR	*Etudes Preliminaires aux Religions Orientales dans l'Empire Romain*
ILS	*Inscriptiones Latinae Selectae*, ed. H. Dessau, Berlin (2nd edn 1954–5, 3 vols)
Josephus *AJ*	*Jewish Antiquities*
JRS	*Journal of Roman Studies*
Livy *Epit.*	*Epitome*
OGIS	Dittenberger, W. (ed.), *Orientis Graecae Inscriptiones Selectae*, Leipzig, 1903–5 (2 vols)

PBA	*Proceedings of the British Academy*
PIR	*Prosopographia Imperii Romani*, 1st edn, Berlin 1897–8
*PIR*²	*Prosopographia Imperii Romani*, 2nd edn, Berlin and Leipzig 1933–
Pliny *NH*	*Natural History*
Plutarch *Ant.*	*Life of Antony*
Plutarch *Caes.*	*Life of Caesar*
RE	Pauly-Wissowa (ed.) *Real-Encyclopädie der Classichen Altertums-wissenschaft*
RFIC	*Rivista di Filologia e di Istruzione Classica*
RG	*Res Gestae Divi Augusti*
Seneca *de Benef.*	*de Beneficiis*
Seneca *de Clem.*	*de Clementia*
Suetonius *Aug.*	*Life of Augustus*
Suetonius *Iul.*	*Life of Julius Caesar*
Tacitus *Ann.*	*Annals*
Tacitus *Hist.*	*Histories*
Vell.	Velleius Paterculus *Roman History*
ZPE	*Zeitschrift für Papyrologie und Epigrafik*

1 OCTAVIUS TO OCTAVIAN

1 Suetonius (*Aug.* 5) says that Augustus was born just before sunrise on the ninth day before the Kalends of October in the consulship of Marcus Tullius Cicero and Gaius Antonius; see also Vell. (2.36). The two branches of Octavii are described by Suetonius (*Aug.* 2). Earl (1980, 11) says the connection is not proven, and Suetonius himself admitted (*Aug.* 2.3) that Augustus in his *Memoirs* merely noted that he came from an old and wealthy family, from which his own father was the first to enter the Senate. Carter (1982, 92) points out that Augustus' main concern was to stress his descent from Julius Caesar, and not his municipal origins

2 Suetonius (*Aug.* 7) gives two versions of the origin of the name Thurinus, which was bestowed on Octavius either because his ancestors came from Thurii, or because his father defeated an army of runaway slaves near Thurii and wished to commemorate the victory by naming his son after it. Shuckburgh (1903, 3 n. 1) opts for the ancestral connection, adding that Marcus Antonius used to insult Octavian by asserting that his great-grandfather had a rope-walk or rope factory there; the connection with such low-class activities of course casts aspersions on his ancestry. Carter (1982, 95) prefers the explanation of the battle against the slaves. The history of the Octavii at Velitrae is given by Suetonius (*Aug.* 1).

3 Suetonius (*Aug.* 6) reports the legend that Octavius was born at Velitrae, adding the story that there was a small room in the house of the Octavii, supposedly Augustus' nursery, that no one could remain in without some mishap. The name Oxheads (Suetonius *Aug.* 5) may refer to a street, but it is more likely derived from a house, perhaps with a frieze of carved oxheads around it (Shuckburgh 1903, 2 n. 1). Velleius Paterculus (2.59.2) says that Gaius Octavius senior was a man of dignity, an upright character who led a blameless life and

possessed great wealth. It was considered very ignoble to be poor, so in his own memoirs Augustus would naturally lay great emphasis on wealth: see also Suetonius (*Aug.* 2.3). For the raising of the senatorial census qualification see Wiseman (1971, 66). The sources are very contradictory; see Dio (54.17.3, 26.3, 30.2) and Suetonius (*Aug.* 41.1). Nicolaus of Damascus (*Aug.* 2) refers to ancestors leaving their estates to Octavius. The senior Gaius Octavius' career is documented on an inscription (*ILS* 49). According to Velleius Paterculus (2.59.2), Gaius Octavius was returned first in the poll when he was elected praetor for 61 BC, indicating the extent of his popularity.

4 Suetonius describes M. Atius Balbus whose father was a native of Aricia, fifteen miles south of Rome on the Via Appia. Atius was connected on his mother's side of the family with Pompeius Magnus (Suetonius *Aug.* 4.1). See also Wiseman (1971) for the origins of the Atii.

5 The story of Cicero and Catiline is recounted by Stockton (1971, 110–42). Caesar spoke against execution of the conspirators (ibid. 133–5; Suetonius *Iul.* 14.1). The case of Gaius Rabirius was a political prosecution under the guise of a question of state (Gruen 1974, 277–9; Stockton 1971, 91–7). Caesar's appointment as Pontifex Maximus was significant of his political influence (Gruen 1974, 77, 80–1; Vell. 2.43.1).

6 Gaius Octavius was praetor in 61, then governor *proconsulare* of Macedonia. In letters to his brother, Cicero (*ad Q. Fr.* 1.1.21, 1.2.7) represents Gaius Octavius as a sterling example on which to model himself. Suetonius (*Aug.* 3.2.) refers to these letters of Cicero, adding that Gaius Octavius governed his province with equal justice and courage. Augustus was only 4 years old when his father died (Suetonius *Aug.* 3.1). Tacitus (*Dialogues* 28.5) and Dio (45.1–2) describe the education of the young Gaius Octavius. According to Suetonius (*Aug.* 89.1) Augustus could not speak Greek very well, but Pliny (*NH* 35.91) says that he could; Suetonius contradicts himself in a later passage (*Aug.* 98.4); see also Baldwin (1983, 131).

7 L. Marcius Philippus: *PIR*² M 241a; Syme (1939, 128) describes Philippus as having a disposition towards political neutrality and a fair measure of guile. His background was thoroughly noble.

8 Sulla was the first to seize power by means of an army and not to be punished for murder (Jones 1970, 8). Gruen points out (1974, 43–4) that Pompeius had commanded armies for twelve years, and after such a successful career it was unthinkable to force him to start at the bottom of the political ladder by holding the relevant junior magistracies before proceeding to the consulship.

9 The alliance of Pompeius, Caesar and Crassus, known to modern scholars as the 'first Triumvirate', receives full treatment and discussion from Gruen (1974, 62–120). Velleius (2.44.3) gives Crassus the minor role, in that he is portrayed as using the other two members of the alliance to gain a pre-eminence that he could not have gained single-handed.

10 The events from 59 to the outbreak of the civil war are documented by Appian (*BC* 2.10–23). Both Appian (*BC* 2.19) and Vell. (2.47.2) comment on the fear of the detrimental effects of the death of Julia, because the bonds which held Caesar and Pompeius together were thus broken. Gruen (1974, 450) challenges the usual view that the death of Julia in 54 and that of Crassus in the following year contributed to the breakdown of the alliance and so led directly to war;

but the removal of Crassus upset the balance among the *clientelae* (ibid. 453). The younger Marcus Crassus served with Caesar in Gaul, and remained a staunch Caesarian until he disappeared in 49, 'obviously a victim of the war' (Gruen 1974, 192).

11 Nicolaus states (*Aug.* 3) that when he delivered the funeral oration for Julia, sister of Caesar, Octavius was only 9 years old, but Suetonius (*Aug.* 8) says that he was in his twelfth year, i.e.: the funeral was before 23 September 51, so Octavius was 11 years old. Quintilian (12.6.1) says that Octavius actually was aged 12. The content of the speech that Octavius made is unknown; it would not necessarily be absolutely accurate, since the main purpose was aggrandisement of the family (Carter 1982, 97). Pompeius co-operated with Caesar wholeheartedly (Gruen 1974, 455). With regard to the *Lex Pompeia de iure magistratuum*, Syme (1939, 40) accused Pompeius of hoping that his little deception would not be noticed, and then of making dubious amendments when he was found out, but this seems too far-fetched and credits Pompeius with less intelligence than he possessed. Gruen's suggestion (1974, 456–7) that Pompeius all along regarded Caesar as a legitimate exception to the rule seems much the best interpretation.

12 The *Lex Pompeia de provinciis* has been used as proof that Pompeius meant to disrupt Caesar's future plans, but it can be reassessed: Caesar's command was an extraordinary one, sanctioned by a law, and probably not affected by the Pompeian legislation on provincial government, as indeed Pompeius' own command was unaffected by it (Gruen 1974, 457–60). Vell. (2.47.3) says that Pompeius employed his consulship in correcting electoral abuses.

13 The position of Pompeius in his third consulship was unprecedented and anomalous, and strained precedent in other ways (Gruen 1974, 153–4). The Dictatorship was instituted for times of emergency where a short period of authoritarian government was necessary. Pompeius was the only man eligible, but in order to avoid one-man rule, or even worse the joint rule of Caesar and Pompeius, the Senate agreed to M. Bibulus' suggestion, seconded by Cato, that Pompeius be appointed sole consul. He was to appoint a colleague when peace was restored, and he did so in the person of his new father-in-law Metellus Scipio. The sole consulship was not the only unusual feature of Pompeian politics: Syme (1939, 42) says that Pompeius held Spain in an anomalous and arbitrary fashion; Gruen (1974, 451) describes the position as unorthodox.

14 Appian (*BC* 2.24–37) documents the outbreak of the civil war. Attacks on Caesar by M. Marcellus ultimately devolved upon recalling Caesar from Gaul and refusing to allow him to stand for the consulship *in absentia* (Gruen 1974, 102, 461–3, 466–8, 482–3).

15 On the consular elections in 49 for 48, and voting in the Senate, see Gruen (1974, 475–6). Appian (*BC* 2.27) attests that the people praised Curio for daring to incur the enmity of both Pompeius and Caesar, sacrificing himself for the good of the state. According to Velleius (2.48.1) 'all fair minded men' desired that Caesar and Pompeius should disband their armies. The uproar in the Senate, and the flight of Antonius and Cassius, is described by Appian (*BC* 2.32–3). Vell. (2.48.3–5) blames Curio for 'applying the flaming torch which kindled the civil war'.

16 'They would have it so' is reported in Suetonius (*Iul.* 30.4). To the Romans *dignitas* was far more important than life (Syme 1939, 48). Caesar insisted that he waged wars to protect the sacrosanctity of tribunes, but for a discussion of his real motives see Suetonius (*Iul.* 30.1). Gruen (1974, 494) is of the opinion that Caesar may never have uttered the phrase attributed to him by Suetonius, but if he did it was merely an apologia for the Roman dead at Pharsalus.

17 The seizure of the *aerarium* is described by Appian (*BC* 2.41). Dio (41.17) detects despotic tendencies in Caesar's theft of the Treasury, and he also accuses Pompeius of desertion (41.13). Velleius (2.48.2) laments that if Pompeius' death had occurred two years earlier he would have preserved his high reputation to the grave.

18 'I go to meet an army without a leader' is reported by Suetonius (*Iul.* 34.2). For the full story of the war see Caesar (*BHisp.*); Dio (41.20–25); Appian (*BC* 2.42–3).

19 Cicero (*ad Att.* 10.12a.3) describes anti-Caesarian demonstrations in the theatre. Lepidus as praetor proposed that Caesar should be made Dictator, and in Dio's opinion (41.36) Caesar did not commit any act of terrorism. Scullard (1970, 141) considers that Caesar simply used the Dictatorship to get what he wanted. The ancient authors seem unclear about how old Octavius was when he assumed the *toga virilis*; Nicolaus (*Aug.* 4) says that he was 14 years old; Suetonius (*Aug.* 8) says that he was in his twelfth year (i.e., aged 11) when he delivered the funeral oration for his grandmother, and four years later he assumed the *toga virilis*, which makes him 15 years old. The story of the ripped tunic is recounted by Dio (45.2). Even after the ceremony, Atia insisted that Octavius should remain at home (Nicolaus *Aug.* 4).

20 Octavius' priesthood is mentioned in several ancient sources: Cicero (*Phil.* 2.71, 5.17); Caesar (*BC* 3.99); Suetonius (*Nero* 2); Vell. (2.59.3). According to Nicolaus (*Aug.* 5) Octavius performed all the ceremonies after dark, because he was extremely attractive, a judgement echoed by Suetonius (*Aug.* 79).

21 Heitland (1909, III 32–3) blames Antonius for needless brutality in quelling the riots in Rome, but Gelzer (1968, 261) points out that Antonius acted only when the Senate authorised him to do so. Plutarch (*Ant.* 9.2) reports that the Senate authorised Antonius to act, but by doing so he fell out of favour with Caesar (*Ant.* 10.1). On Caesar's return from Spain, Antonius went to meet him, and travelled with him in the same carriage, so by then it was obvious that he was forgiven (*Ant.* 11.1). The way in which Caesar dealt with the mutinous soldiers is reported by Cicero (*ad Att.* 11.20.2, 21.2, 22.2); by Caesar himself (*BAfr.* 19.3, 28.2); by Appian (*BC* 2.92.3); and by Dio (42.52.1–2).

22 The appointment of Octavius to the post of *praefectus urbi* was quite normal at this period (Dio 49.42; Kienast 1982, 3). In the Greek sources, the terminology for the post of city prefect can be easily confused with that of the master of the horse (*magister equitum*), leading some scholars to assume that Octavius had been given this latter post in 47, at the age of sixteen, which would have been far too responsible a position and would clearly have been anomalous. The confusion arises because some sources state that Caesar designated Octavius *magister equitum*, but the context for this is 44 just as Caesar was about to set out on the campaigns against the Dacians and Parthians: see below, note 31.

23 Caesar proposed to take Octavius to Africa, according to Nicolaus (*Aug.* 6).

24 The battle of Thapsus was fought on 6 April (Caesar *BAfr.* 98). The news of it reached Rome on 20 April (Cicero *ad Fam.* 9.2). Caesar spent a total of 180 days in Africa (Heitland III 1909, 333). Suetonius (*Iul.* 76.1) says that he was made *praefectus morum* on his return. This was a hitherto non-existent office (Meier 1995, 432) which clearly had the powers of the censorship (Gelzer 1968, 288). Dio (43.14) says that he was elected to this office, and Gelzer (1968, 278 n. 1) agrees that there was probably some kind of popular election. The inscription on the base of the statue of Caesar was probably in Latin, and probably declared Caesar *divus* (Gelzer 1968, 278; J.P.V.D. Balsdon, *Historia* 7 1958, 84). According to Taylor (1931, 65 n. 13 and n. 14) Caesar did not notice the statue at first, and had it taken down as soon as he did, but not from motives of modesty or prudence; it is suggested that since he accepted greater honours later on, he thought that the statue was insufficiently glorious, and that the Senate had not discerned what he really wanted. Dio lists only those honours which the great man actually accepted (42.19.4, 43.14.7), thus implying that many more honours were proposed but that Caesar declined them. Suetonius thoroughly disapproves of all the honours, describing them as too great for mortal man (*Iul.* 76.1).

25 Nicolaus (*Aug.* 7–12) expends several chapters on emphasising Octavius' association with Caesar; the information is almost unique to Nicolaus, and most probably derives from Augustus' *Memoirs*. In later life, Augustus played down his connection with the turmoil of the past. It was normal practice for youths such as Octavius to be given *dona militaria* and a prominent place in the triumph of a relative (Kienast 1982, 3). Nicolaus (*Aug.* 8) says that Caesar had now adopted Octavius and regularly conversed with him as if he was his son, so he has either anticipated the date or, less likely, he knew that the adoption was no surprise to Octavius in 44 after Caesar was murdered.

26 The reform of the calendar was long overdue; Suetonius (*Iul.* 40) describes how the seasons were no longer synchronised with the months, and the agricultural year was completely disorientated. Caesar intercalated two months so that the seasons could begin properly at the Kalends of January. Octavius was placed in charge of the theatrical performances and fell ill, thus causing great concern to Caesar (Nicolaus *Aug.* 9). Augustus could not tolerate the strong sunlight and always wore a hat (Suetonius *Aug.* 82). Caesar deferred decisions about who should or should not hold office in his absence probably as a political stopgap (Meier 1995, 451–2).

27 Suetonius (*Aug.* 8) and Velleius (2.59.3) give few details of Octavius' journey to Spain and his stay there. Dio (43.41) is more verbose but just as vague. Both Dio (*loc. cit.*) and Suetonius (*Aug.* 94.11) recount the story of the palm tree which Caesar refused to cut down while preparing his camp at Munda, because he considered it to be an omen of victory. A shoot sprang up from it immediately and within a few days grew taller than the original tree, which Caesar took for a sign that he would be succeeded by none other than his sister's grandson. This can be discerned as retrospective embroidery; if Caesar entertained private thoughts on the matter they would have remained private, and if he went about declaring that the omens revealed that Octavius would succeed him then the events of 44 would probably have taken a very different course. The anti-Caesarians would not have tried to use the young man as a

weapon to rid themselves of Antonius; instead they would have treated him with rather less contempt, and would probably have tried to eliminate him. Octavius may have arrived in Spain in May 45, two months after the battle of Munda; Nicolaus (*Aug.* 10) says that when Octavius joined Caesar, the latter had brought the war to a close in seven months. In the next chapter (*Aug.* 11) Nicolaus emphasises Octavius' wisdom and prudence, and states that he was anxious to gain a good reputation at home.

28 The Saguntine embassy met Octavius at New Carthage (Nicolaus *Aug.* 12). Nicolaus is the sole source for this episode of Augustus' life. Gelzer (1968, 296–8) describes Caesar's administrative measures in Spain, and the founding of colonies, concluding that Caesar's administration had all the elements of monarchic imperialist policy. Marcus Antonius joined the party on its way home (Plutarch *Ant.* 11). Octavius returned to Rome ahead of Caesar (Nicolaus *Aug.* 14). The false Marius was a potential threat to Octavius (Shuckburgh 1903, 13–14; Cicero *ad Att.* 12.49). Cicero implies that Marius had been making a nuisance of himself (*ad Att.* 14.6; 'I thought Caesar had got rid of him'). Marcus Antonius eventually put Marius to death (*ad Att.* 14.8).

29 Caesar did not enter Rome until he held his triumph in October 45, and in the interim he went to one of his estates at Labici where he wrote his will (Suetonius *Iul.* 83.1–2; Gelzer 1968, 306). The will and its relevance to Octavius and the legal aspects are discussed in depth by Schmitthenner (1952); see also Chapter 2 of this book.

30 The honours to Caesar are discussed by Gelzer (1968, 315) and Meier (1995, 473–5). The temple to Freedom (*Libertas*) and the use of Imperator as a hereditary name are reported by Dio (43.44); Suetonius (*Iul.* 76.1) says that Caesar took Imperator as a *praenomen*, and Nicolaus (*Aug.* 8) implies that Caesar had already adopted the name before the date given by Dio, but he may have been referring to the use of the name as a *cognomen*. Dio definitely relates the title to the list of honours bestowed on Caesar after Munda; Suetonius gives no indication of date. Syme ('*Imperator Caesar*; a study in nomenclature', *Historia* 7 1958, 172–88) discusses the hereditary implications of the *praenomen*, which was the normal Imperial title by the time Dio described it. Syme concludes that Octavian adopted the name to enhance his power, to monopolise the glory of the *triumphator*, but not as an official title denoting power *per se*. Caesar appointed magistrates for three years (Dio 43.51.3). In another section (43.51.6) Dio explains that all the magistrates were appointed for the first year, but for the second year only the consuls and tribunes were appointed. Meier (1995, 456–8) accuses Caesar of wanting to abandon the problems of Rome, which had become too onerous, in favour of winning more fame abroad in the Parthian and Dacian wars.

31 Nicolaus (*Aug.* 15) gives the credit for making Octavius a patrician to the Senate, but it was by special decree of the tribune Lucius Cassius that Caesar was enabled to create new patricians. Enrolment of new patricians is mentioned by Tacitus (*Ann.* 11.25), Suetonius (*Iul.* 41), and Dio (43.47.3). The active promotion of Octavius is noted by Suetonius (*Aug.* 2) and Dio (45.2.7), but these authors wrote with the benefit of hindsight, and it is not at all certain that contemporaries of Caesar noticed the advancement of his great-nephew. Shuckburgh (1896, 16) points out that the city of Apollonia was not an

educational centre, so the purpose behind sending Octavius there was more likely to gain military experience. It is attested that Octavius took his own teachers with him (Suetonius *Aug.* 89). According to Appian (*BC* 3.9) Octavian had been appointed Caesar's master of horse (*magister equitum*) for one year, and Dio (43.51.7) says that Octavius had been designated to the post, as though he had not yet taken it up. The Greek terms for *praefectus urbi* and *magister equitum* are very similar, and Schmitthenner (1952, 6) suggested that there may have been some confusion with the appointment of Octavius to the former post in Rome, and that the designation to the post of *magister equitum* was highly unlikely because it was too high an office for a boy of Octavius' age. He is contradicted by Gesche (1973, 470) who points out that Pliny (*NH* 7.147) described the office in Latin, and he would have been familiar enough with the terminology to avoid all confusion. In any case Dio (43.51.8) makes it quite clear that Octavius was to succeed Lepidus as master of horse. Badian (1990, 36) is of the opinion that the public nature of the appointment could have left little doubt among Caesar's contemporaries that he intended to adopt Octavius, but this argument is capable of some refinement. Although it may have drawn attention to the fact that Caesar favoured his great-nephew and was actively promoting him, it is likely that the young man was regarded as merely one among many stronger contenders for a share in Caesar's power. The news of the assassination of Caesar reached Octavius about a month after the event (Suetonius *Aug.* 8; Nicolaus *Aug.* 16; Vell. 2.59; Appian *BC* 3.9; Dio 45.3). After the murder of his great-uncle, according to Appian (*BC* 3.11) Octavius called himself 'Caesar son of Caesar, instead of Octavian son of Octavius, and he continued to do so ever after.'

2 CAESAR, SON OF CAESAR

1 Colleagues urged Octavian to march on Rome at the head of the Macedonian legions to avenge Caesar (Nicolaus *Aug.* 16). High-ranking officers declared themselves ready to protect him (Appian *BC* 3.10). Suetonius (*Aug.* 8.2) says that Octavian toyed with the idea of appealing to the legions but decided against it because it would have been too hasty.

2 The details about the landing at Lupiae instead of Brundisium are related by Appian (*BC* 3.10). Suetonius (*Aug.* 8) and Dio (55.3–4) waste little time or text in getting their hero to Rome. The parental advice to Octavian not to accept the inheritance sounds like common sense in Appian's account (*BC* 3.10), where it is stated that Philippus reminded his stepson that Caesar had been murdered by men whom he counted his friends. This purple prose is most likely an insertion by Appian to make a point about the assassination. Philippus' advice as related by Appian is by no means the 'strong opposition' of Suetonius (*Aug.* 8.3). Cicero reported (*ad Att.* 14.12) that Philippus did not address Octavian as Caesar, even though all the young man's friends did so.

3 The appointment as *magister equitum* underlined Caesar's probable intentions with regard to Octavius (Badian 1990, 36 n. 16). The only other hint that Octavius had been noticed prior to his adoption by Caesar is in the letter from Plancus to Cicero (*ad Fam.* 10.24.5) where it can be interpreted that there had been some association between Plancus and Caesar's heir. Schmitthenner (1952,

1–2, 61) discounts the evidence of this letter, but Kienast (1982, 4 n. 20) thinks his doubts are unfounded and that the letter should be taken at its face value. It was written in July 43, and Plancus admits that he did not see much of the young Octavius. As Heitland observed (1909, III 363), the full meaning of Caesar's promotion of Octavius was probably not clear even to contemporaries. Taylor (1949, 28) suggested that after he came to power, Augustus censored the historical record. Whether it came about by design or by accident, it is a constant lament of historians that Cicero's letters to Atticus written after November 44 have not been preserved. It is assumed that their correspondence did not actually cease altogether at that point, and that the letters must have been lost or deliberately destroyed. The result is that for one of the most crucial periods of Roman history, the potentially most illuminating source is lacking. When Octavian arrived in Italy, Cicero wondered whether there may have been an attempt at a *coup d'état* (*ad Att.* 14.5), then learned that Octavian had decided to accept Caesar's inheritance (*ad Att.* 14.10). He met Octavian while the latter was staying at his stepfather's house; he reported to Atticus 'he is devoted to me' (*ad Att.* 14.11) and that 'he is here on terms of respect and friendship' (*ad Att.* 14.12).

4 Opinion is divided about Caesar's intentions to become king of Rome. Gelzer (1968, 318 n. 4) discusses the problem in detail, agreeing with K. Kraft in his conclusion that any attempt on Caesar's part to win the crown and title of king 'would have been utter political madness'. Dio (44.9.1) says that it was Caesar's enemies who began the rumours and fuelled the flames in order to discredit him. Plutarch (*Ant.* 12) implies that Caesar really wanted the people to make him king at the Lupercalia; he is at least consistent since he also states (*Caesar* 61) that Caesar used the incident as a test case, which failed. Gelzer (1968, 321–2) thinks that the Lupercalia episode was an attempt on Caesar's part to put an end to speculation. Badian (1990, 35) says that 'the chances are that he really preferred to remain Caesar and not demean himself by becoming *rex*'.

5 Most modern authors agree that monarchy was inevitable whether or not Caesar wanted it. Heitland (1909, III 335, 367) considered that the only way to oppose senatorial misrule was to become an autocrat, and that Caesar had no intention of giving up power or sharing it. Meier (1995, 471) thinks that if Caesar wanted to establish a monarchy 'he went about it very ineptly' but elsewhere admits that Caesar was a *de facto* monarch (1995, 475). Syme (1939, 53) realistically states that there can be opinion but no certainty on the problem of Caesar's monarchy. Gelzer (1968, 306) states that Caesar so appreciated the talents of his great-nephew that he increasingly hoped to find in him his political heir, but the possibility that Caesar could bequeath political power is generally denied; Syme (1939, 96) says that 'Caesar could leave no heir to his personal rule', and Meier (1995, 471) agrees that Octavian could not inherit Caesar's special position in politics. Kienast (1982, 4–5) discusses this in connection with the general problems raised by Caesar's will, together with Dio's statement (43.44.3) that the Senate bestowed on Caesar the title Imperator as a hereditary name, and that the office of Pontifex Maximus was heritable 'if Caesar should beget a son or even adopt one' (Dio 44.5.3). Syme (1939, 114) assumes that Octavian knew nothing of the adoption until he arrived in Italy, and only then began to conceive high hopes for his destiny.

6 Caesar's impatience led him to push through decrees without authentic signatures (Gelzer 1968, 290). Cicero wrote to Papirius Paetus (*ad Fam.* 9.15.4) 'Here I am at Rome and in constant attendance in the Forum, and all the while decrees of the Senate are being drafted in the house of my dear friend who dotes on you. Whenever it occurs to him my name is put down as witness to the drafting.' Cicero goes on to say that he sometimes receives letters from various kings of whom he has never heard, thanking him for his part in their elevation, when all the while it is Caesar who has accomplished the deeds single-handed. Dio (43.27.1) relates the facts differently; he says that Caesar planned undertakings for the common weal, and did not carry them out on his own authority but brought the matters before some of the senators, sometimes even before the entire body. The problem here is that by the time that Dio wrote, he was accustomed to two centuries of Imperial rule, but when Caesar was busily drafting good ideas and impatiently pushing them through, the concept was quite novel; clearly the idea of senatorial autonomy and free debate of all issues was lost on Dio. Caesar's vision of the Roman world was broader than the average: he had visited nearly all the provinces and saw the emerging Empire as a whole instead of a collection of subject countries to be exploited (Gelzer 1968, 272, 330). No one knew how to behave during Caesar's Dictatorship, as attested by Cicero's letters; to Paetus he wrote (*ad Fam.* 9.16.5) 'It remains for me to do nothing stupid or rash in opposition to those in power; this too I think is part of wisdom.' Cicero felt that he was being watched when he wrote to Servilius Isauricus (*ad Fam.* 13.68.2) 'I do not write often about high affairs of state; such letters are dangerous.' Nicolaus of Damascus (*Aug.* 19) listed the different groups of men who opposed or feared Caesar for one reason or another. The acceptance of the title *Dictator perpetuo* put an end to the ostensibly provisional character of Caesar's *de facto* monarchy (Meier 1995, 475). The date when he adopted it is disputed, and the alternatives are discussed by Gelzer (1968, 320 n.3).

7 Alföldi (1976, 24) debates whether the initiative in accepting the inheritance was entirely due to Octavian himself, or whether Caesar's intimates who knew something of the Dictator's plans also had a part to play. According to Nicolaus of Damascus (*Aug.* 28) Octavian was the only one to whom power had been bequeathed but he alone had no authority, and the soldiers were ready to defend his 'inherited rights' (ibid. 31). It is a theme which Nicolaus constantly harps upon, no doubt following the party line with promptings from Augustus himself. 'From the beginning his [Octavian's] sense for realities was unnerving, his ambition implacable' (Syme 1939, 113). Octavian's letters to Cicero were duly reported to Atticus (*ad Att.* 16.8.9).

8 Jones (1970, 113) enumerates the supporters of Caesar who rallied to Octavian, such as Balbus, Oppius, Matius, Saserna and Rabirius Postumus. Of these men, Balbus and Oppius were the most important, the ones who prepared the ground for Octavian's rise to power. Their services are not widely known or documented. More is known of Balbus than of Oppius, but no one can have known Caesar's intentions better than these two men (Alföldi 1976, 31–54). Syme (1939, 130–1) discusses the sources of Octavian's money. The Parthian war chest and the year's tribute from Asia are documented by Nicolaus (*Aug.* 18). Dio (45.3.2) gives no indication of the source of Octavian's large sums of

money; presumably he did not know, because by his day the truth may have undergone some alteration and adaptation. Alföldi (1976, 82–4) interprets Dio's statement about large sums of money to mean that Octavian brought Caesar's war chest with him, under guard; Alföldi also suggests that the forward planning for gathering and despatching the cash to finance Caesar's coming war was all due to Balbus. Kienast (1982, 13 n. 58, 23 n. 100) thinks that the money from the war chest cannot have arrived before October 44, when Octavian recruited soldiers by paying them bounties, which means that from April to October his supplies must have come from a different source. Cicero (*ad Att.* 16.8) attests that Octavian recruited men from Casilinum and Capua, paying them 500 denarii each, and in the same letter he says that Octavian asked him for advice about what to do, one of his options being to come to Rome with 3,000 veterans. This was probably not the total number of those he had recruited, and if this surmise is correct then it gives some idea of the huge amounts of money involved.

9   Syme (1939, 77, 130–2, 381) sums up the importance and enormous wealth of Balbus, whose career is summarised by Alföldi (1976, 36–43). As a protégé of Pompeius Magnus and a friend and secretary of Caesar, Balbus knew men from both camps (Alföldi 1976, 32–3). A man with such connections and such wealth was bound to attract enemies; Cicero defended Balbus in court and his published text survives (*pro Balbo*), and in a letter to Atticus, he describes him as Caesar's crony (*ad Att.* 2.3.3). Relations between Cicero and Balbus fluctuated; in January 47 there was a definite coolness, but by August 46 Balbus was cultivating Cicero on Caesar's behalf. While Caesar was in Spain, Balbus and Oppius managed his affairs in Rome, and when Cicero wrote a letter of advice to Caesar it had to be vetted by Balbus (*ad Fam.* 6.8.1; Stockton 1971, 265, 271, 275). It required a leap of faith to discern Augustus behind Octavian (Baker 1937, 206).

10 The conspirators had not planned anything beyond the murder of Caesar; Cicero was very disillusioned, and said that they had planned with the courage of men but the understanding of boys (*ad Att.* 14.12.1, 14.2, 21.3). They had not fully understood what made Caesar's power possible, and in their high-minded rejection of naked power backed up by armed force they somehow forgot to substitute an alternative method of government, so they created chaos (Meier 1995, 481). Antonius stepped into the breach and did not perform badly; Syme's judgement (1939, 105) is that Antonius 'displayed consummate skill as a statesman'. Kienast (1982, 18 n. 81) lists the works on Antonius, most of which are aimed at the more popular market; the full academic assessment of Antonius has yet to be written.

11 Appian (*BC* 3.25) says that Antonius still controlled the Macedonian legions. The *Lex de permutatione provinciarum* was passed to allow Antonius to exchange provinces, probably with effect from 1 January (Syme 1939, 15; Rice-Holmes 1928, 192). Appian (*BC* 3.14–20) invents speeches for both Octavian and Antonius when the two finally met; the content of this dialogue enables Appian to present both points of view, but principally allows him to justify the actions of his hero, Antonius. Syme points out (1939, 107, 130) that Antonius had to find cash to settle Caesar's veterans on their allotments, so the charge that he misappropriated most of the cash for himself is perhaps unjust.

12 Antonius sneered that Octavian owed everything to his name, perhaps more than once; he is quoted by Cicero: '*et te, O puer, qui omnia nomina debes*' (*Phil.* 13.11.24). Caesar's property was sold and the proceeds distributed to the people (Appian *BC* 3.23; Nicolaus *Aug.* 28).

13 Vengeance for Caesar's death is laconically described in *RG* 2: 'I drove into exile the murderers of my father, avenging their crime through tribunals established by law; and afterwards when they made war on the Republic I twice defeated them in battle.' In 42 Octavian vowed that he would build a temple to Mars Ultor (Mars the Avenger); it was finally dedicated forty years later in 2 BC. Octavian tried to display the golden chair at the *Ludi Ceriales* (Syme 1939, 116–17). Antonius blocking Octavian is attested in more than one source: Plutarch (*Ant.* 16) is hostile to Antonius, and compresses events into a manageable narrative without the minute detail. Appian (*BC* 3.28) describes at greater length Antonius' manoeuvres to prevent Octavian from displaying the golden chair, but admits that Antonius began to lose favour because it seemed that he was denouncing Caesar himself, a fact of which Octavian took immediate advantage. Appian tells how the military tribunes intervened to restore harmony (*BC* 3.29) and then he invents a speech in which Antonius vindicates himself; see also Dio (45.4) and Cicero (*ad Att.* 15.3). The comet or star is described by Dio (45.7); it appeared in the north in the evenings during each day of the games, and some people declared that Caesar was now immortal and included in the heavens as a god. Pliny (*NH* 2.94) relates how Octavian thought privately that the star was a sign for him, presaging a great future. See also Kienast (1982, 24–5) and Alföldi (1976, 69).

14 Dio (45.5.4) tells how Antonius appeared to do his best to have the adoption ratified but blocked it in reality by using his tribunes; there is disagreement among modern scholars as to whether it was Lucius or Gaius Antonius who effectively stopped the proceedings. Syme declared that testamentary adoption simply did not exist ('Clues to testamentary adoption', *Epigrafia e Ordine Senatorio* I, 1982, 397ff. = *Roman Papers* IV 1988, 159ff.). Schmitthenner (1952, 40–1) points out that the legal sources for testamentary adoption are of no use; he gathers together all the known examples and discusses the problems (ibid. 39–64). The soldiers and Caesar's *amici* accepted Octavian (Kienast 1982, 6–7). The problem with Caesarion may have been exacerbated by the fact that Antonius recognised him as the son of Caesar (Plutarch *Ant.* 54; Shuckburgh 1903, 121). More important, the boy shared the throne of Egypt with his mother Cleopatra, with the title king of kings (*rex regum*) (Dio 49.41; 50.1.5; 50.3.5). For discussion see Kienast (1982, 33 n. 220; Syme, *Historia* 29, 1980, 422ff.). According to Suetonius (*Aug.* 17) Octavian put to death not only Caesarion but the son of Antonius by Fulvia as well. Taylor (1931, 104) interprets Cleopatra's references to 'father' in Caesarion's titles as a definite link with Caesar, and therefore an attack on Octavian's position as heir.

15 Cicero wrote to Atticus (*ad Att.* 15.12) that he did not know whether to trust Octavian, but whatever happened he must be kept away from Antonius. The soldiers preferred to see an alliance between Antonius and Octavian, according to Appian (*BC* 3.42), who also describes their vacillation between the two leaders (*BC* 3.46, 47). The tribunes tried on two occasions to reconcile the two (*BC* 3.29; 32). After the first reconciliation, Octavian assisted Antonius in

urging the people to pass the law to give him Cisalpine Gaul (*BC* 3.30). This gave rise to the fear that Antonius was planning to emulate Caesar; 'They knew what the last extended command in Gaul had meant' (Syme 1939, 115).

16 The sources are unhelpful and confused on Octavian's attempt to become tribune. Plutarch (*Ant.* 16) merely says that Antonius opposed Octavian when he canvassed for the tribuneship. Appian (*BC* 3.31) puts the emphasis on the action of the people. Despite the fact that Octavian favoured the election of Flaminius, the populace decided that Octavian really wanted the post for himself and were perfectly prepared to vote for him. Suetonius is more realistic (*Aug.* 10.2): in his view Octavian wanted to be tribune simply in order to carry out his plans. There is probably more truth in this than in any of the other sources, and Octavian perhaps felt at this juncture that he could not rely on any other tribune even though he could afford to pay well. The plot to assassinate Antonius is generally dismissed as rubbish, but it has never been satisfactorily explained (Kienast 1982, 25); Syme (1939, 124) doubts the story because Octavian would not eliminate a potential ally. At Brundisium Antonius punished some of the legionaries and offered bribes to persuade the soldiers to give him the names of Octavian's agents, but he could not discover who they were (Appian *BC* 3.43). Octavian recruited among Caesar's veterans in Campania, as attested in many of the sources (Appian *BC* 3.40; Dio 45.12; Suetonius *Aug.* 10). Nicolaus specifies that Octavian approached the veterans of the Seventh and Eighth legions (*Aug.* 31). After a lacuna of unknown length in the text he goes on to say that Octavian's plans met with the approval of his friends Agrippa and Maecenas, the otherwise unknown Q. Iuventius and M. Modalius, and a certain Lucius, who may be L. Coccieus Nerva, the great-grandfather of the Emperor Nerva. Nicolaus' account places Octavian's troop-raising activities after Antonius had left for Brundisium, which gives some credence to the theory that Octavian was prepared to wait for Antonius to make the first move. Cicero (*ad Att.* 16.8) told Atticus that Octavian was giving each man 500 denarii, and commented 'Evidently he means to make war on Antonius.' The theme of saving the state from Antonius is reiterated several times in the speeches of Cicero (*Phil.* 3.2, 3.11, 4.2; 5.11, 8.2).

17 Appian (*BC* 3.40) describes Octavian's army as 10,000 strong, all fighting under the same banner. Linderski (1984, 78 n. 20) thinks that the army was divided into centuries, taking the text of Cicero's letter to Atticus (*ad Att.* 16.9) as his guide, when Cicero says '*centuriat Capuae*'. The division into centuries would make for easier command structure and administration. When Octavian marched north against Antonius at Mutina and Cicero made his speech proposing that the young Caesar should be made propraetor, the army is described as comprising cavalry, archers and elephants (*Phil.* 5.17.46). Before he marched to Rome with 3,000 veterans, Octavian sent one Caecina of Volaterra to ask Cicero's advice about what to do. He proposed that Cicero should meet him at Capua (probably at a location hosted by Balbus), but Cicero refused because the affair could not be kept secret (*ad Att.* 16.8). Appian (*BC* 3.41–2) portrays Octavian in a quandary after his attempt to rouse the soldiers against Antonius had failed; some soldiers deserted him, but then repented when Octavian was on the way to Ravenna. The abandonment of Rome and the supposed flight to Ravenna has been reinterpreted; Kienast (1982, 25 n. 114) quotes M. Sardi,

Studi Etruschi 40, 1972, 3ff., where the episode is treated as a strategic move to intercept Antonius when he came north.

18 Octavian wrote to Cicero that he wanted to act through the Senate (*ad Att.* 16.9). Antonius convened the Senate for 24 November, and had primed one of the consulars to move that Octavian should be declared *hostis*, but when the two Macedonian legions went over to Octavian, he decided to set off for Gaul (Appian *BC* 3.45–6). Stockton (1971, 296) follows Syme (1939, 125–6) in the assumption that it was Fufius Calenus who had prepared the case against Octavian to have him outlawed.

19 Appian (*BC* 3.48) makes Octavian say that he only pretends to serve the Senate, and Nicolaus (*Aug.* 28) says that Octavian was not ignorant of the reasons why the Senate seemed to support him; he then continues with his usual hobby-horse theme that at the time everyone was fighting for power for himself, whereas Octavian was the only one to whom power had been bequeathed. In the Senate on 1 January, Cicero proposed that Octavian should be given *imperium* (*Phil.* 5.16.45) together with a seat in the Senate and permission to stand for office as if he had been quaestor the previous year (*Phil.* 5.16.46). Cicero claimed to know the young man's inner feelings '*omnes habeo cognitos sensus adulescenti*' (*Phil.* 5.18.50).

20 With regard to the troops, Cicero proposed that the Senate should guarantee to pay whatever Octavian had promised them, and grant land to the veterans and exemption from service once they had been discharged (*Phil.* 5.19.53).

21 Octavian reckoned 7 January as his *dies imperii* (Kienast 1982, 28). The *Res Gestae* opens with an account of the raising of the private army. It was strictly an illegal act, but the main reason for mentioning it was the fact that Octavian had used the army to secure the liberty of the Republic (Brunt and Moore 1967, 38). Cicero tidied up the illegality by explaining that in times of danger, the necessity for defence was more important than the observance of legal niceties (*Phil.* 1.28). Antonius' demands, after the embassy from the Senate reached him, were quite reasonable (Syme 1939, 170) and Cicero had to put a great deal of effort into stirring up hostility to him (Stockton 1971, 300).

22 Thanksgiving to last for fifty days was decreed in the names of the three Imperators after the battle of Forum Gallorum. Since Octavian had taken no real part in the battle, according to Dio (46.38) it was simply to flatter him that his name was included alongside those of the consuls. When the second battle was fought at Mutina, Octavian was dropped and the flattery ceased. He was not included in the land commission to allot land to veterans, as attested in letters between Decimus Brutus and Cicero (*ad Fam.* 11.20, 1.21.2). Cicero wished that he was not on it himself because it was so burdensome. The same letters reveal that Octavian had heard of Cicero's clever pun about raising him up and then removing him, which Cicero did not deny. It was known in May that Octavian was aiming for the consulship, now vacant after the deaths of Hirtius and Pansa (Syme 1939, 185; Kienast 1982, 31).

23 Plancus wrote a long letter to Cicero on 6 June 43 BC explaining all that had happened since Antonius abandoned Mutina and eventually joined up with Lepidus in Gaul (*ad Fam.* 10.23). He complained that Octavian had not marched to his assistance, and even if he could not come himself it would have been useful if he could at least send his troops (*ad Fam.* 10.23.6). His next letter,

written on 28 July, is more resigned since he now knows that Octavian has set his mind on higher things (*ad Fam.* 10.24.4). Appian (*BC* 3.82) recounts the story that Octavian asked Cicero to be his colleague as consul, for which there is little or no evidence (Stockton 1971, 325–6). It is not beyond the bounds of possibility that Octavian would think of such a plan. He had been praised to the skies while he was necessary and then summarily dropped, but Cicero was still an important and influential senator who could be used to advantage, and Octavian would not put personal animosities before ambition.

3 CONSUL AND TRIUMVIR

1 Lepidus had tried to arrange a negotiated peace with Antonius in March but did not gain much credit for doing so (Weigel 1992, 54). At Rome it was thought that Antonius was in a desperate plight, so Lepidus would surely see the folly of joining him (Cicero *ad Fam.* 11.18.2; Stockton 1971, 322–3). In reality 'a succesful future for Lepidus clearly lay only with Antonius' (Weigel 1992, 57). The fraternisation of Lepidus' and Antonius' troops is variously reported in the ancient sources: Appian (*BC* 3.83) says that Antonius camped near Lepidus, but did not surround himself with a wall and ditch, and messengers passed between the two armies. Velleius Paterculus (2.63.1) recounts the tale of Antonius forcing an entry into Antonius' camp through a breach in the walls. The most lurid account of all is to be found in Plutarch's *Life of Antony* (18.1.3) which Weigel (1992, 61) judges mostly fictitious. Lepidus sent a letter to the Senate on 30 May, explaining that it was the will of his troops and the impossible situation in which he found himself that compelled him to join Antonius. He also declared his wish to work for the good of the state as a whole (Cicero *ad Fam.* 10.35); after a month's grace, probably to ascertain whether Lepidus might change his mind (Weigel 1992, 62), he was declared *hostis* (Cicero *ad Fam.* 12.10.1). P. Ventidius Bassus' march to join Antonius was known to Decimus Brutus who wrote to Cicero about it (*ad Fam.* 11.9.1, 1.10; Stockton 1971, 320–1; Syme 1939, 126 n. 3, 176, 178). Asinius Pollio is Syme's champion (1939, 5, 166, 180); Velleius calls Asinius *firmus* (2.63) in that he steadfastly supported the Caesarian cause and was always implacably hostile to the Pompeians; Stockton (1971, 330) casts doubts upon Pollio's integrity, because he always sat on the fence until he discerned who was likely to win, then he joined the stronger party.

2 Dio (47.21) describes how Brutus and Cassius decided to go to the East, and devotes three chapters to an account of the troops which came over to Cassius (47.26–8). Appian (*BC* 4.58–9) says that Cassius gained twelve legions (of which eleven are attested) and some Parthian mounted bowmen. On Cleopatra's contribution to the war effort see Taylor (1931, 105). Cassius reported his successes to Cicero on 7 March (*ad Fam.* 12.11.1). At this stage the Senate would not recognise Cassius as governor of Syria (Cicero *ad Fam.* 12.7.1). The Senate declared war on Dolabella when he was outlawed (Dio 47.29.4; Syme 1939, 172; Stockton 1971, 309).

3 Brutus' take over of Macedonia was violent and illegal (Stockton 1971, 311). He raised troops and enrolled them as legions (Heitland 1909, III 420) and after his successes Cicero proposed that Brutus should take control of Macedonia,

Illyricum and Greece (*Phil.* 10.25–6). Appian (*BC* 4.5) equates the reassign-
ment of Macedonia and Syria to Brutus and Cassius with the declaration of
Antonius and Lepidus as *hostes*, but although these events were related in sentiment they were not contemporary. Cassius had to wait for two months longer
than Brutus to be confirmed as governor of Syria (Dio 47.29), then in one
single act he was placed in charge of all the Roman forces in the East (Syme
1939, 172, 177–8). The Senate voted to recall Brutus to Italy after the battles
of Mutina (Syme 1939, 183) and Cicero wrote to him to endorse the request,
but Brutus realised that while his arrival in Italy might well decide the issue
once and for all, it could also solidify the opposition (Stockton 1971, 315).
Gaius Antonius was unable to gain a foothold in Macedonia before Brutus
attacked him (Dio 47.21.4–7) and locked him up at Apollonia; Cicero advised
Brutus to kill him because a little salutary severity would provide a good
example (*ad M. Brut.* 1.2a.2). Sextus Pompeius was granted the status of *praefectus classis et orae maritimae* (Cicero *Phil.* 13.13), which was really only a belated
recognition of the facts (Kienast 1982, 30). Appian (*BC* 4.60–2) reports the
plight and eventual suicide of Dolabella.

4 Octavian was not necessary to the Senate now that the battles of Forum Gallorum
and Mutina were over, and he had nothing to offer that could elevate him to
a position of importance; he suffered from the lack of a party of his own within
the Senate strong enough to influence opinion (Kienast 1982, 30). Velleius
(2.62.5) makes much of senatorial ingratitude once the immediate danger from
Antonius was removed, and shows that Octavian let the soldiers take up this
theme on his behalf. Plancus wrote to Cicero about Octavian's desire for a 'two-
month consulship' (*ad Fam.* 10.29), which he considered ill-advised compared
to the glory of fighting enemies of the Republic; Shuckburgh (1903, 65 n. 2)
comments that this only shows that Plancus did not understand Octavian's
object or policy. If this is so then he was probably not alone in failing to penetrate the ideology of the 19-year-old Caesar.

5 For Octavian's march on Rome see A. Alföldi, 'Der Einmarsch Oktavian in
Rom August 43 v. Chr.', *Hermes* 86, 1980. The legalisation of his adoption
meant that Octavian would become *patronus* of Caesar's freedmen and clients
(Appian *BC* 3.94). When the first convoys approached the army with cash for
the soldiers, Octavian chased them away (Appian *BC* 3.89); Dio says that the
Senate sent money then changed their minds and forbade the army to come
within 100 miles of Rome (46.44.2). The Senate possibly hoped by this means
to avoid conflict near the city, and this is perhaps the context of their offer to
allow Octavian to stand for the consulship *in absentia* (Appian *BC* 3.90). The
African legions arrived accompanied by 1,000 horse; they went over to Octavian
immediately (Appian *BC* 3.91–2), then the Senate convened because a rumour
started that two legions had deserted Octavian. Manius Aquilius Crassus was
sent to Picenum to raise troops, but he was captured and brought back to
Octavian disguised as a slave (Appian *BC* 3.93)

6 While he was approaching Rome at the head of troops, Octavian's mother and
sister would have made valuable hostages and were accordingly searched for,
but the Caesarians in Rome hid them: they were lodged in the temple of Vesta
(Appian *BC* 3.91–2). The flights of vultures over Rome at various crucial
moments of Octavian's career, such as his entry into the city and his first acts

as consul, are reported with discrepancies in the sources; see Taylor (1931, 95 n. 34), quoting the source for six birds when Octavian entered the Campus Martius and six more when he stepped onto the Rostra to address the people. Dio (46.46.2) opts for six vultures when Octavian entered Rome and then twelve all at once when he harangued the soldiers as consul; Appian reports twelve when the newly elected consul made his first sacrifices (*BC* 3.94). The general impression that the omens were favourable has endured, but the exact details are garbled. The numbers and precise occasions are not important; the salient point is the comparison with Romulus. Octavian's handouts to the troops were unprecedented and very generous. Watson (1969, 113) points out that when the soldiers demanded 2,500 denarii from Severus, they relied on this Augustan precedent, and had probably been reading Appian's *Civil Wars*, published ony about a generation previously. The procedure for conducting the elections in the event of the deaths of both consuls is described by Dio (46.45.3), who then sums up the irony of Octavian's withdrawal from the city while the elections were held (46.45.5). The constitutional anomaly is pointed out by Carter (1982, 120).

7 Pedius can be viewed as Octavian's subordinate (Dio 46.46.1). The first choice as colleague may have been P. Servilius Isauricus (Syme 1939, 182 n. 6). Suetonius (*Aug.* 62.1) is the source for Octavian's betrothal to Servilius' daughter. Appian (*BC* 3.82) explains how Octavian asked Cicero to be his consular colleague, because he was the elder statesman with greater experience; he goes on to say that Octavian only wanted to dismiss his soldiers in the proper fashion, which is a transparent attempt to mislead; it is hardly credible that Octavian should consider such a shabby device, when it was clear that he wanted much more than that. Brutus did not believe that Cicero had become or wanted to be consul, and warned him about the ambitions of Octavian (*ad M. Brut.* 1.3.2, 4.6; Stockton 1971, 325; Cicero *Phil.* 14.15).

8 See note 6 above for the various appearances of birds over Rome. Appian (*BC* 3.94) says that Octavian paid part of the money promised to the soldiers before the elections took place, and hints at Caesar's rich freedmen as a source of the cash; Dio (46.48.2) says that Octavian used public funds collected on the pretext of the war, and labels the conciliation of the soldiers and the payment of the outstanding legacies to the people as a bribe to ensure their compliance when the trials of Caesar's assassins began. Octavian revoked the law declaring Dolabella *hostis* and brought to trial both Caesar's actual murderers and even some men who took no part in the assassination but had been aware of the existence of the plot (Appian *BC* 3.95). Octavian gained a short-lived reputation for clemency: Manius Aquilius Crassus was pardoned for attempting to raise troops (Appian *BC* 3.94) and so was Silicius Corona for speaking up in favour of Marcus Brutus (Dio 46.49.5), but both these men were proscribed shortly afterwards.

9 Suetonius (*Aug.* 61) confirms that Octavian's mother Atia died during his first consulship, and that he gave her a public funeral. Dio (47.17) relates that one of the soldiers had the effrontery to ask for her property after her death; unfortunately he does not record Octavian's response.

10 Pedius revoked the outlawry of Antonius and Lepidus while Octavian marched north (Appian *BC* 3.96). Antonius' letter to Hirtius and Octavian is reported

in Cicero's 13th *Philippic*, quoted in sections interspersed with Cicero's comments, but while the eloquence is entertaining and the vituperation very clever, what we are allowed to hear of the letter reveals that Antonius had a better grasp of reality than Cicero himself (Stockton 1971, 313–14). Octavian treated stragglers from Antonius' army quite leniently; one P. Decius is specifically named as a bearer of messages (Appian *BC* 3.80; Syme 1939, 187–8). The fate of Decimus Brutus is narrated by Appian (*BC* 3.98).

11 All the sources, with the exception of Appian, name Bononia as the meeting place of the Triumvirs; Appian opts for Mutina (*BC* 4.2). Bononia is the more likely venue, since Mutina would retain undertones of conflict (Weigel 1992, 67–8). There are few sources besides Appian and Dio for the formation and method of operation of the Triumvirate (Millar 1973, 51). Gowing (1992) enters into full discussion of these sources, and Bleicken (1990) examines the legal framework and procedural aspects of the Triumvirate. Both Appian (*BC* 4.2) and Dio (44.55.3–4) indicate that the Triumvirate was to last for five years, and the terminal date is known from the *Fasti Colotiani*, from an inscription naming all three men, though Antonius' name was later erased. The restored text runs *III viri rei publicae constituendae ex ante diem V K. Dec. ad pridie K. Ian sextas*. 'These *Fasti*, which the erased name of Antonius shows to have been inscribed before September 30 BC, thus make it clear that the Triumvirate was due to expire on 31st December 38 BC' (Millar 1973, 51 and n. 7). On the absence of the term Dictator in the Triumviral titles, see Kienast (1982, 32 n. 142). The Triumvirs were to have powers equal to the consuls, and were each to govern provinces (Appian *BC* 4.2), which they governed via *legati* (Bleicken 1990, 32–6). In his examination of the basis of the power of the Triumvirs, Bleicken (1990, 21–6) laid the greatest emphasis on the proconsular *imperium*, which gave them power over a wider area than Rome. In Rome itself they presumably held *consularis potestas*, but Lintott in his review of Bleicken (*JRS* 82, 1992, 251–2) points out that this does not explain the apparent superiority of the Triumvirs to the consuls in Rome. Lepidus was to govern Spain through deputies while remaining in Italy (Appian *BC* 4.3). Octavian's provinces were the main corn producing areas (Baker 1937, 96); Kienast (1982, 33 n. 143) quotes R.E.A. Palmer (*Athenaeum* 1973, 315) who considers that Antonius virtually surrendered the administration of the city of Rome to Octavian by granting him Africa, Sicily and Sardinia.

12 The settlement of veterans was always problematic and the Triumvirs had to ensure the loyalty of their troops by showing in advance that they intended to cater for their veterans. Appian (*BC* 4.3) names a few of the eighteen designated cities: Capua, Rhegium, Venusia, Beneventum, Nuceria, Ariminum, Vibo. Some of Octavian's recruits had come from Capua in the first place, so the settlement of veterans there was not a completely novel idea. Dio (47.14.4) reports on the establishment of colonies in conjunction with his account of the depredations made by the soldiers in the countryside around the towns, thus linking the settlement of veterans with the other unacceptable activities of the armies. He implies that even these measures did not ensure the loyalty of all the soldiers, so that the Triumvirs were obliged to go even further in satisfying demands, by offering to the most troublesome men the properties of the proscribed.

13 The consulship was already promised to Ventidius as part of the arrangements made by the Triumvirs (Dio 47.15.2–3). Octavian was to be betrothed to Clodia (Suetonius *Aug.* 62); Dio (46.56.3) implies that it was a promise undertaken lightly and without a sense of restriction upon his future plans, because Octavian knew that Caesar and Pompeius had been bound by marriage ties but this had not prevented them from making war on each other. There may have been another reason for Octavian's caution in not entering into full marriage with Clodia: 'If Clodia had inherited the qualities which characterised both her parents [i.e., Clodius and Fulvia] she would probably have been found a less fitting spouse for Augustus than Scribonia' (Adams 1939, 173). Lepidus was from a high-class family, and Cicero enumerated all his sterling qualities (*Phil.* 5.38–41, 13.8). In grateful thanks for his peace settlement with Sextus Pompeius, the Senate voted Lepidus an equestrian statue, which was a high honour, but the statue was torn down when he was declared *hostis* (Dio 46.51.4). By remaining in Italy while the civil war with the conspirators was fought, Lepidus consigned himself to the minor role, and later to oblivion (Weigel 1992, 70).

14 The proscriptions are reported at great length by Appian (*BC* 4.6, 8–11 for the text of the proscription, 12–30 for harrowing accounts of the sufferings of various individuals, 36–51 for miraculous escapes). Dio adds some different tales (47.9–13). Velleius (2.66) and Plutarch (*Ant.* 21) both blame Antonius for the worst excesses of the proscriptions. Without quoting firm evidence, Dio (47.8) makes excuses for the young Caesar, 'who saved as many as he could', and also for Lepidus, who according to Dio allowed his brother to escape. Not all the sources exonerate Octavian, who is said to have resisted at first but then proved more determined and cruel than either Antonius or Lepidus (Suetonius *Aug.* 27), possibly because he had already compromised himself and may as well make a thorough approach to the proscriptions (Kienast 1982, 34). Adams (1939, 119) considered that Octavian's savagery was merely assumed, in order to achieve his immediate aims. For the destruction of documents after the defeat of Pompeius in 36, see Appian (*BC* 5.132).

15 Heitland (1909, III 415) thought that the Triumvirs were happy to let most men escape while leaving all the properties behind, but the financial gain from the seizure of proscribed victims' property was probably only a secondary motive; the chief purpose was political (Kienast 1982, 35). The text of the Triumviral proclamation authorising the proscriptions is preserved, probably more or less accurately, by Appian (*BC* 4.8); Gowing (1992, 251 n. 12) and Hinard (1985, 228 n. 4) agree that Appian's translation into Greek is a faithful rendition of the original Latin. Weigel (1992, 73, 153 n. 25) and Hinard (1985, 259–318) support the view that the main purpose of the proscriptions was to avenge the death of Caesar and in the process to root out the entire opposition, just as Appian reports in the text of the proscriptions where the Triumvirs declare their intention of sweeping aside their enemies once and for all (*BC* 4.9). Dio (47.9) points out that each Triumvir had a different set of enemies and friends, and each acted purely out of concern for his own ends. No roll call of victims has been preserved and numbers are difficult to estimate. Appian (*BC* 4.5) gives the total number of victims as 300 senators and 2,000 equites, while Livy (*Epit.* 120) gives the number as 130 senators. Shuckburgh (1896, 58; 1903, 73–4)

tries to reconcile the two figures by assuming that only 130 senators actually died, while the rest presumably fled. The Senate numbered about 300 members according to Livy (*Epit.* 60) but Appian (*BC* 1.35) implies that the total of 300 was not always realised. Even when there were 300 actual members, there was rarely a full turnout; Cicero (*ad Q. Fr.* 2.1.1) reckoned that an attendance of 200 senators was excellent. Julius Caesar increased the number of senators to 900 by the *Lex Cassia* (Suetonius *Iul.* 41; Tacitus *Annals* 11.25; Dio 43.47). These new senators were Roman citizens but not members of the proud aristocracy of Rome. A joke circulated in the city that no one would show these new men the way to the Senate House. 'Strange names of alien root and termination now invade and disfigure the *Fasti* of the Roman people' (Syme 1939, 199). The removal of senators and their satellites, including the equites who supported them, is pointed out by Kienast (1982, 35). The inclusion of the Triumvirs' own relatives is consistently reported by both Appian (*BC* 4.12) and Dio (47.5–6); Aemilius Paullus and Lucius Caesar escaped, perhaps by design of the Triumvirs (Weigel 1992, 72; Appian *BC* 4.37–8).

16 The Triumvirs were concerned to have their actions approved and ratified by the traditional organ of the state (Millar 1973, 54). Dio is more forthright: 'they ordered everything just as it seemed good to them' (47.15.3). The *Lex Titia* is documented more fully by Appian (*BC* 4.7) than by Dio who merely alludes to it (47.2.2); see also Keinast (1982, 33 n. 145). Suetonius (*Aug.* 26.1) may have had the Triumvirate in mind when he classified Augustus' offices into those held before the normal age, those of a new kind, and those that were perpetual (Bleicken 1990, 16 n. 33). But Shuckburgh (1896, 56) preferred the interpretation that the new kinds of office referred to the proconsular *imperium* and *tribunicia potestas*. For the *Fasti Colotiani* and the terminal date of the Triumvirate see note 11 above; the agreement was renewed, probably without the benefit of a law; the problems are discussed in the next chapter of this book; see also Bleicken (1990, 14 n. 28). The death of Cicero is described by Appian (*BC* 4.19–20) and Dio (47.7); Velleius champions the cause of Cicero and praises him (2.66). The writers of the Augustan age did not mention Cicero; in general the ones who did write of him were not those held in high Imperial esteem (Heitland 1909, III 414 n. 1, 470 n. 4) .

17 The consuls were chosen for the next five years (Syme 1939, 189). The Triumvirs also designated magistrates in advance (Appian *BC* 4.2; Dio 47.91.4). On the survival of the elections during the Triumvirate and the Principate see Millar (1973, 51–2), quoting Frei-Stolba, *Untersuchungen zu den Wahlen in der romischen Kaiserzeit*, 1967.

18 The taxes of the Eastern provinces were diverted by Brutus and Cassius (Appian *BC* 4.5). Old taxes were reintroduced by the Triumvirs and new ones invented (Dio 47.16). No one dared to buy the properties of the proscribed, because nobody was willing to reveal that he possessed wealth, so in the end only the soldiers gained from the proscriptions (Dio 47.17.3). The Triumvirs taxed wealth and included women in their calculations (Appian *BC* 4.32). The low return on confiscated properties meant that the Triumvirs were far short of their target (Appian *BC* 4.31). Plutarch (*Ant.* 21) reports on the seizure of the savings deposited by citizens and foreigners in the temple of Vesta.

19 Plancus and Lepidus each held a triumph before taking up office as consuls (Weigel 1992, 75). Velleius (2.67.3–4) recounts the scurrilous chants of the soldiers that the triumphs were really over their brothers. Dio (47.18.3) reports that the Triumvirs made everyone swear an oath that all Caesar's acts should be considered binding. On the deification of Caesar see Dio (53.27.2) and Kienast (1982, 192). *Divi filius* was 'a unique form for a Roman' (Nock 1934, 482). It was probably first used in 40, on the coinage (Pollini 1990, 346): the coins issued by Q. Voconius Vitulus and Ti. Sempronius Gracchus bear the legend *DIVI JULI F.* and portray both military standards and agricultural implements, which perhaps links the coins to the distribution of land to the soldiers after Philippi. Alföldi dated the coins to 43 (*Revue Numismatique* 75, 1973, 121); Kienast (1982, 42) prefers the later date and strongly favours the connection with the veteran settlements after Philippi; see also Taylor (1931, 106 n. 10) and Syme (1939, 202). Dio describes the temple in the Forum on the spot where Caesar's body was burned (47.18.4, 47.19.3 for the connection with Romulus, also 51.22.1). The *Lex Rufrena:* see *ILS* 73 and 73a. For the view that Caesar intended to set up a hereditary divine monarchy such as those familiar in the East and in Egypt, see Taylor (1931, 73) and Weinstock (1971), reviewed by North (1975, 171). Syme (1939, 55) pointed out that Cicero, the most likely commentator, never mentioned the scheme, and had it been known to him could hardly have failed to make some mileage out of it. The award of the honours while Caesar was still alive and the deification after his death is treated by Dio as a continuous and logical development (47.18.2, 47.19.2, 56.34.2), and the suggestion made by Gesche (1978, 370) that the whole process was bound up together and planned to take place in stages, some before death and some afterwards, seems the most sensible; the divine honours had as their logical consequence the promise of deification once Caesar had departed life on earth. See also the review of Gesche by J.P.V.D Balsdon (*Classical Review* 1970, 62–4). On divine ancestry in general see Taylor (1931, 103). Antonius was connected with both Hercules and Dionysus, and was almost deified after his fair treatment of the Eastern cities (Plutarch *Ant.* 24; Appian *BC* 5.7; Strabo 14.648, 674; Taylor 1931, 107). Octavian rejected divinity for himself, but used his divine ancestry to great effect (Galinsky 1996, 318; Kienast 1982, 192 n. 88). According to Dio (53.27.3) Agrippa wanted to place the image of Augustus as a god among other gods in the Pantheon, but Augustus refused and installed *Divus Julius* instead.

20 Taylor (1931, 99) argued that Caesar as a god was removed from jealousy and hatred. Caesar the Dictator was divorced from *Divus Julius* (Syme 1939, 317; 1958, 432; 1959, 58 = 1979, 434). Slingbullets at Perusia were inscribed *Divum* or *Divom Julium* (Syme 1939, 211; *CIL* XI 6721.26). The watchword of the army was *Divus Julius* (Syme 1939, 471). After the eradication of his rivals, Augustus relied more on his own image as Princeps rather than on his connection with the divine Caesar (Syme 1939, 318; 1950, 13–14 = 1979, 214).

21 Salvidienus failed to oust Sextus Pompeius from Sicily (Appian *BC* 4.84–5; Dio 47.36) perhaps because he and Octavian had underestimated Pompeius' strength and experience (Shuckburgh 1903, 82). Antonius was the better soldier and the hero of Philippi (Weigel 1992, 77–8; Plutarch *Ant.* 21.4; Appian *BC* 4.3; Dio 46.56.1). Octavian followed Antonius because he could not afford to

allow him to be defeated, nor could he allow him to win the war on his own account (Dio 47.37.3). Plutarch (*Ant.* 22) and Appian (*BC* 4.110) both refer to the statements in Augustus' lost *Memoirs* that he stood in the battle line, even though he was ill, because he had been warned in a dream to do so; Dio (47.41.1–4) repeats the tale but makes no allusion to the *Memoirs*. Even Agrippa and Maecenas did not deny that in reality Octavian lurked in a marsh (Syme 1939, 204–5 n.1; Pliny *NH* 7.148). Accounts of the battle of Philippi, complete with invented speeches of each of the generals to the troops, are given by Appian (*BC* 4.105–38) and Dio (47.37–49).

22 Appian (*BC* 4.137–9) and Dio (47.39) sum up the importance of the battle of Philippi. Gowing (1992, 175–6) compares the two accounts, which coincide on many points. They both saw the battle as a conflict far greater than just a civil war between two factions, for it was nothing less than the end of the Republic and beginning of the Principate, though to contemporaries this far-reaching conclusion may not have seemed quite so obvious; there was still a long way to go. Both Appian and Dio depicted the deaths of Brutus and Cassius as divine retribution for the murder of Caesar. Dio adds that the battle was fought to decide which form of government should be adopted in Rome, and that democracy was impossible and unworkable for the Empire. Octavian's savagery after the battle and the hostile attitude of the soldiers is reported by Suetonius (*Aug.* 13.2). The Senate rejoiced that he was ill on the way back to Rome, prompting him to send messages ahead to reassure everyone (Dio 48.3). Cisalpine Gaul was incorporated into Italy, following Caesar's original plans (Appian *BC* 5.3.12, 22.87; Dio 48.12.5; Syme 1939, 206–7). Lepidus was given Africa (Appian *BC* 5.12), but in reality Antonius controlled the province from the East (Weigel 1992, 79).

23 The numbers of veterans to be settled in Italy are reported as 170,000 in Appian's narrative (*BC* 5.5), which is an impossible figure. Keppie (1983, 60) estimates the total as 46,000, comprising 36,000 men sent back after Philippi and more time-served veterans from the Western provinces and Africa. Octavian's task was 'arduous, unpopular and all but fatal to himself', and he received no help from Lepidus (Syme 1939, 207–8). Appian's statement (*BC* 5.13) that Octavian chose the task because of his health is probably wide of the mark; it was definitely not a sinecure for a convalescent. Dio's comment (48.4.1) on the consulship of Lucius Antonius and his colleague Servilius was that the consuls were in reality Marcus Antonius and Fulvia.

24 Appian (*BC* 5.14) documents the first attempts of Lucius Antonius to stir up trouble for Octavian, whose success in reconciling differences promised to bring him credit, thus detracting from the glory of Antonius. The soldier who sat in the seats reserved for the equites was ejected by Octavian, who was nearly lynched because it was thought that he had ordered the man's execution (Suetonius *Aug.* 14; Appian *BC* 5.15). The first fourteen rows were reserved for equites at the games by a law of 67, passed by the tribune L. Roscius Otho. Since it was a matter of law Octavian could not afford to condone the soldier's behaviour. Dio (48.8.4) commented that armed force has no power to compel affection; see also Gowing (1992, 80–1).

25 Appian (*BC* 5.21) describes how Lucius and Fulvia wrote to Antonius to inform him of events; despite a thorough search, Appian had no success in tracing

Antonius' reply. In a later passage, Appian contradicts himself (*BC* 5.52) by insisting that Antonius was innocent and knew nothing about the problems created by his brother and his wife. Syme (1939, 208) lays all the blame on Fulvia; as Dio pointed out (48.28) all hostilities ceased when she died, and everyone could blame the outbreak of war upon her with impunity. Dio also makes the cynical comment (48.5.4) that Antonius gained whatever the result, either as champion of the veterans or of the dispossessed landowners. 'A studied vagueness suited Antonius' purpose' (Pelling 1996, 15). Octavian sent a mission to Antonius to try to find out what he really wanted (Appian *BC* 5.60), but it was too late and produced nothing positive. Dio (48.10.11) maintains that the initiative for peace came from Octavian; see Gowing (1992, 82–3). The soldiers tried to effect a reconciliation at Teanum (Appian *BC* 5.20) and then at Gabii (Appian *BC* 5.23; Dio 48.12.2–3).

26 The course of the Perusine war is described by Appian (*BC* 27–49) and Dio (48.13–14). Lucius surrendered in February or early March 40; his increasingly desperate situation is fully documented by Appian (*BC* 5.39–48). Perusia went up in flames, possibly accidentally as a result of the action of one of the citizens who immolated himself and his house (Appian *BC* 5.49).

4 THE DECISIVE DECADE

1 The period between Philippi and Actium was the most fertile area of all for Octavian's development, but receives little elucidation in the *Res Gestae* (Eder 1990, 72). The victory over Sextus Pompeius was of great importance, and is described briefly (*RG* 25.1) and obliquely by the phrase 'I made the sea peaceful and freed it of pirates.' Octavian's agents, and especially the careers of Oppius and Balbus, are examined by Alföldi (1976). Augustus' outburst in the Senate was a departure from his usual reticence. Holding his tongue was a self-imposed habit rather than a natural characteristic: he had learned it from his tutor Athenodorus, who taught him to recite the letters of the alphabet before saying anything in anger (Yavetz 1969, 33 nn. 36–7).

2 Marcus Vipsanius Agrippa (*PIR* V 457; Reinhold 1965; Roddaz 1984) was a school friend of Octavian's. He accompanied Octavian to Apollonia (Suetonius *Aug.* 95) and came back with him to Rome in 44 (Appian *BC* 3.10). He was tribune in 43 (Dio 46.49.1) and fought in the Perusine war with an independent command which he discharged with credit (Appian *BC* 5.31–3, 35, 50). He went to Gaul, crossed the Rhine and settled the Ubii in the newly founded *colonia*, the modern Cologne (Appian *BC* 5.92) and was awarded a triumph which he refused (Dio 48.49). When Augustus was seriously ill he gave his signet ring to Agrippa (Dio 53.30.2), and as a further mark of trust he granted him tribunician power for five years (Dio 54.12; Vell. 2.90; Tacitus *Ann.* 3.56). It was renewed for a second term (Dio 54.28). His attitude to Augustus and to their relative positions may well contain an element of Dio's own sentiments about subordinates to the Emperor, but the speech which he invents for Agrippa is not at odds with the latter's character (Dio 49.4). Velleius (2.79.1) says of him 'he was of distinguished character, unconquerable by toil, loss of sleep or danger, well disciplined in obedience, but to one man only'. Reinhold (1965, 151–2) remarks that Agrippa never once thought of supplanting Augustus.

3 Maecenas (*PIR*² M 37) is erroneously called Cilnius in Tacitus' narrative (*Ann.* 6.11.2). He was energetic when called upon to act but at other times his love of leisure predominated. He entertained no lofty ambitions (Vell. 2.88). The story of Terentia is recounted by Suetonius (*Aug.* 66.3) and Dio (54.19, 55.7). Two men, Terentius Varro Murena and Licinius Varro Murena have been confused and treated as one; see Syme (1986, 387–93) and Raaflaub and Samons (1990, 426 n. 32). The literary circle and its use on behalf of the Princeps is examined by Syme (1939, 459–75). Williams (1990, 261) maintains that there was no quarrel between Augustus and Maecenas, but once the literary circle had been established by Maecenas, Augustus gradually took it over and used it to create a new kind of patronage (ibid. 267–8).

4 Octavian began to create a senatorial faction which he had hitherto lacked (Syme 1939, 227; Kienast 1982, 43). His marriage to Scribonia allied him to Pompeius but it was not a success (Suetonius *Aug.* 62.2; Appian *BC* 5.53). Octavian fell in love with Livia Drusilla (*PIR*² L 301), who was well connected to members of the senatorial groups whom Octavian wished to attract to his cause (Suetonius *Aug.* 62.2; Appian *BC* 5.53; Dio 48.44; Kienast 1982, 44; Syme 1939, 229 n. 4).

5 According to Appian (*BC* 5.79) the desire to be sole ruler was common to all the Triumvirs, so they could not allow themselves to relax their vigilance at any time. Octavian's troops would not always fight against Antonius (Appian *BC* 5.53, 56–7, 59). The Triumvirs were forced to negotiate with Sextus Pompeius (Appian *BC* 5.67–8). After Perusia, Octavian can be seen as the aggressor, but of course not overtly (Gowing 1992, 84). On the nature of the marriage, if such it was, between Antonius and Cleopatra, see C. Pelling, note on Plutarch *Ant.* 36, in *Plutarch's Life of Antony*, Cambridge University Press, 1988, 219–20, and the review of the above by J.M. Carter in *JRS* 79 1989, 211–12; Pelling 1996, 30 n. 137; see also this book, note 17, below. The literary feud began long before Actium (Eder 1990, 96). On the feud itself see Fadinger (1969, 180–94). Augustus' maxims *festina lente* and 'a thing is done quickly enough that is done well enough' are reported by Suetonius (*Aug.* 25.4). With patience Octavian manipulated public opinion for war (Meier 1990, 64–5). Actium as a decisive turning does not meet with unanimous acceptance; Eder (1990, 72) does not consider either 31 or 27 as such. Tacitus (*Ann.* 1.3.7) talks of the generation born after Actium, who did not know anything of the *res publica*; in the *Histories* (1.1.1) he notes that after Actium all the power was in the hands of one man. For a survey of the contemporary views of Actium and the debate whether the literary portraits of the battle were centrally orchestrated or spontaneously produced, see Gurval (1995, *passim*); for the monuments and artistic representations, and what has been termed as the dawn of a new style after Actium, see Zanker (1988, 79–100).

6 Lucius Antonius was allowed to go to Spain, but he was watched closely by Octavian's agents (Appian *BC* 5.54). When Calenus died in Gaul, Octavian took over his legions (Appian *BC* 5.51), then he substituted his own military commanders, sent away suspect Antonian sympathisers, and despatched Lepidus to Africa with six legions whose loyalties he did not trust (Appian *BC* 5.53; Dio 48.20.3–4). Antonius allied with Domitius Ahenobarbus and Sextus Pompeius (Appian *BC* 5.55–6; Vell. 2.76.2). Octavian insisted that he had not

ordered Brundisium to close its gates against Antonius. Appian (*BC* 5.65), Velleius (2.76.3), Tacitus (*Ann.* 1.10) and Dio (48.28.30) relate the build up to and the arrangement of the treaty of Brundisium. Dio describes the entertainments afterwards, in Roman fashion by Octavian and in Eastern fashion by Antonius.

7 Antonius was inaugurated as *flamen divi Juli* after the treaty of Brundisium (Plutarch *Ant.* 33). He was appointed *flamen* while Caesar was still alive, and Cicero refers to him as such (*Phil.* 2.110), but Taylor (1931, 69, 96) points out that although he was called *flamen* before Caesar's death, he could not actually become priest until Caesar was dead and deified. Antonius was styled priest of the divine Julius when he became Triumvir in 43, but his inauguration was delayed until after the meeting at Brundisium. Kienast (1982, 42–3) cites the inscription where Octavian calls himself Imperator in 40: *Imp. Caesar ovans quod pacem cum M. Antonio fecit palmam dedit* (*Fasti Triumphales Barberini* = *Inscriptiones Italiae* XIIII 1 343; R. Combes, *Imperator*, Paris, 1966, 134ff.). Eder (1990, 94 n. 110) and Galsterer (1990, 15) agree that the use of the title Imperator as a name (*praenomen*) was intended to strengthen Octavian's position with the army and to demonstrate that the powers of the Triumvirs outweighed that of the people, but they are less sure of the authenticity of the date that has been attached to the inscription. Syme (1939, 113 n. 1) says that Octavian used the title perhaps from 40, but the clearest evidence comes from coins of Agrippa struck in Gaul in 38; see *BMCR* II 411. Balbus became consul presumably as a reward for services to Octavian: Alföldi (1976, 54) thinks that he had been on the consular list since 43. The mystery of Salvidienus is not solved in any of the ancient sources, which simply report the case (Dio 48.33; Appian *BC* 5.66; Vell. 2.64; Suetonius *Aug.* 66.1). Bleicken (1990, 51) affirms that it would have been illegal for the Triumvirs to annihilate a man contesting their power, and this was an emergency situation that lay outside their competence, but Lintott (*JRS* 82, 1992, 252) disagrees, since this may simply have been a case in which the Senate's approval was politically desirable at that particular time. Agrippa's exploits in Gaul are not elaborated upon save for brief references in the sources (Appian *BC* 5.96; Dio 48.49.4).

8 As Pompeius cut off the food supply the mob in Rome began to turn against the Triumvirs and rioted; Octavian was in danger of being stoned to death, but was rescued by Antonius' troops. The Triumvirs were forced to negotiate with Pompeius (Appian *BC* 5.67–8). The terms of the treaty of Misenum are given by Appian, who says that the documents were signed and sealed and deposited with the Vestals (*BC* 5.72–3). The peace was very popular at Rome (Dio 48.36–7). The general amnesty to all those who had taken refuge with Pompeius meant that many men would be returning to Rome who would be useful to Octavian later on (Syme 1939, 227; Kienast 1982, 43). Pompeius refused to take the advice of his admiral to cut the cables and make off with Octavian and Antonius on board (Dio 48.38).

9 All the Triumvir's acts were ratified by the Senate (Dio 48.34). More than two consuls were appointed in 39, even though none had died or been removed from office (Dio 48.35), and in the following year the consuls had two quaestors apiece, and there were no less than sixty-seven praetors (Dio 48.43; Kienast 1982, 43–4). The multiple appointments may have eased the

congestion that would have occurred when the exiles returned, and also may have been used to reward some men for undocumented services or displays of loyalty.

10 Shuckburgh (1903, 102) blamed Antonius for not giving up to Pompeius the Peloponnese as promised, thus instigating the war, but this is a little one-sided. Dio (48.39.1, 46.1) accuses Antonius of plundering the Peloponnese and rendering it worthless, effectively denying it to Pompeius in another fashion, rather than churlishly holding on to it. For Octavian's divorce of Scribonia and the hasty marriage to Livia see Dio (48.15, 44), Syme (1939, 229), Kienast (1982, 43–4). Riots in Rome were as much against Octavian himself, and the war with Pompeius was unpopular because it was thought that Octavian had broken the treaty (Syme 1939, 228–31). The defection of Menas, Pompeius' admiral, was the first of several defections (Dio 48.45). After the first disaster and defeat Octavian is portrayed in heroic terms by Appian (*BC* 5.86). The storm which broke out the next day wrecked the remaining ships (ibid. 5.89). Octavian wrote to his friends and the participating generals, in case plots should be formed against him 'as is often the case in times of adversity' (ibid. 5.91). Antonius came from Athens to meet Octavian but sailed back again, where-upon Maecenas was sent to negotiate; among the terms agreed upon at their eventual meeting at Tarentum, Antonius gave Octavian 120 ships (ibid. 5.92–5). The ships were expensive to keep in operation so it could be said that Antonius was only too glad to get rid of them (*CAH*[1] 54–5). On the date of the treaty there is some controversy: the usual suggestion is that the meeting took place in September or October, but it could just as easily have occurred in June or July, which would still satisfy the sources who say that it was too late for Antonius to begin his Parthian campaign (Pelling 1996, 25 n. 112). The renewal of the Triumvirate is fraught with difficulties which have a tremendous bearing on the events of 32; the expiry date was originally 31 December 38, so renewal in the summer or autumn of 37 meant that the Triumvirs had held power ille-gally for several months (Kienast 1982, 46). Probably no one, even among the contemporaries or the Triumvirs, could be certain whether or not the Triumvirate was illegal (Pelling 1996, 26). It would have required superhuman daring to stand up and say that it was illegal, when virtually all the armed forces of the Roman world were under the command of the Triumvirs. Based on the assertion of Appian (*BC* 5.95) who says that the Triumvirs did not ask for the people's consent, it was considered at one time that the Triumvirs never bothered to ratify the renewal of their powers by law, and suitable astonish-ment was expressed (Shuckburgh 1896, 57–8; 1903, 104; Rice-Holmes 1928, 231–45; Carter 1982, 122–3). It now seems that Octavian did have the neces-sary law passed later on (Eder 1990, 94), and it is possible to reinterpret Appian in the same light (Pelling 1996, 27 n.120 and 130). The new terminal date is still not fully understood, especially since Appian (*Ill.* 28) complicates the issue by stating that the Triumvirate expired in 32: for the debate see Pelling (1996, 25–7, 67–8), who comes down on the last day of 33. Bleicken (1990, 14 n. 28) also favours the end of 33. If this surmise is correct then the posi-tions of Antonius and Octavian in 32 are serious (Dio 50.2.5; Bleicken 1990, 65–82; Brunt and Moore 1967, 48–9). The story is told by Syme (1939, 225) from Antonius' point of view.

11 Shuckburgh (1903, 103) describes the shipbuilding programme and suggests (1896, 33) that the Lucrine Lake must have been dredged to make it deeper. The need for 20,000 freed slaves (Suetonius *Aug.* 16.1) implies that these were desperate times and that there was a chronic shortage of manpower (Carter 1982, 105). Dio (48.50) describes the engineering work required for the harbour, called Portus Julius (Suetonius *Aug.* 16). Agrippa's invention of the grappling hook gave the advantage over the Pompeian ships; Appian (*BC* 5.118–20) describes it in action; see also Reinhold (1965, 34 n. 40). Appian recounts the plan of campaign and the arrival of Lepidus from Africa (*BC* 5.97–8). At the battle of Mylae, Agrippa won the day, but Pompeius fell on Octavian's ships as he was ferrying troops into Sicily (ibid. 5. 106–8). Octavian reached the shore after suffering shipwreck, shattered in both body and mind, and was rescued by Valerius Messalla Corvinus (ibid. 5.112–13); on Messalla see Syme (1986, 200–16). Dio (49.1) represents Lepidus as very reluctant to help at all. The battle of Naulochus was fought as a result of a challenge, on a day fixed for the purpose (Appian *BC* 5.118). The fate of Pompeius and his subsequent double dealing with Antonius and the king of Parthia form the subject matter of the last chapters of Appian's account (*BC* 5.133–44).

12 After Naulochus, Lepidus asserted himself and tried to gain some independent power (Appian *BC* 5.123). The result was the loss of everything except his priesthood; a law passed by Octavian abrogated his powers (Eder 1990, 95 n. 116; Dio 49.12.4). The disappearance of Ofillius is told only by Appian (*BC* 5.128–9). After the mutiny of his troops, Octavian released 20,000 of those who had fought at Mutina and Phillipi as well as at Naulochus (Appian *BC* 5.129).

13 Rejoicing in Rome knew no bounds when news came of the defeat of Sextus Pompeius; all sorts of honours were granted to Octavian (Appian *BC* 5.130). There is endless controversy over the tribunician powers awarded to Octavian; Appian, presumably erroneously, says that Octavian became tribune for life (*BC* 5.132). This is discounted, since as a patrician Octavian could not become tribune at all, but what remains is to decide whether only the sacrosanctity of a tribune was granted as Dio (49.15) affirms, or full tribunician power as stated by the late-Roman author Orosius (6.18.34). Kienast (1982, 48–9 n. 204) opts for only the sacrosanctity, which was also extended some time later to Octavian's wife and sister, irrevocably underlining his dynastic tendencies. Brunt and Moore (1967, 10–13) discuss the problem, along with the potential advantages that full tribunician power offered to Octavian. Dio gives two separate dates when full tribunician power was conferred, in 30 (51.19.6) and again in 23 (53.32.5) which leads to the speculative conclusion that Octavian refused it when offered it in 30 (Pelling 1996, 68), or surrendered it and then took it up again later when he had become Augustus. Surrender of any power seems at odds with his usual tenacity, so another suggestion is that Dio confused some of the elements of tribunician power, namely the *ius auxilii*, as Brunt and Moore discuss (1967, 12–13). Pelling (1996, 69) is not in favour of the elements being split up and awarded in sections, some in 30 and more in 23, so favours the argument that in 30 Octavian was offered it but refused. Bleicken on the other hand (1990, 74–6) strongly suggests that Octavian would neither have refused nor surrendered the very power that he regarded as the foundation of

his political influence and freedom of action. On the *tribunicia potestas* in general see Last (1951). For their successes against Pompeius, Agrippa was awarded a naval crown (Vell. 2.81.3) and Octavian the right to wear a laurel wreath (Dio 49.15.1). Octavian turned his attention to the needs of the people after Naulochus, in a continuing programme of improvements that came under the broad general headings of personal safety, protection of property, and reduced taxation (Nicolet 1984, 111). Agrippa as aedile in 33 took charge of many things in Rome, chiefly the water supply (Reinhold 1965, 46ff.; Kienast 1982, 61; Dio 49.43.1–4).

14 The land settlements after Naulochus were carried out by purchase or by using public lands, and did not involve so much distress as the previous settlements (Keppie 1983, 69–73; Reinhold and Swan 1990, 164). The veterans of the Seventh Legion were settled in Baeterrae (modern Beziers) in Gaul (Dio 49.14.4; Pliny *NH* 3.4; Rice-Holmes 1928, 118). A fresh start was made once the dangers from Sextus Pompeius' fleet were over. Documents were burned, and Octavian promised to restore the *res publica* when Antonius returned from the East. For the time being it seemed as though all civil strife had ended (Appian *BC* 5.132).

15 Octavian promised his soldiers rich rewards in Illyricum, while quelling the near mutiny in Sicily (Appian *BC* 5.128). It was hardly a rich province (Pelling 1996, 37–8). On the begining of the war see Appian (*Ill.* 12–13, 15, 18) and Dio (49.34.2). There was no real excuse for the war (Dio 49.36.1) but it served to train and harden the troops (Vell. 2.78.2). Grand strategies have been attributed to Octavian's campaigns in Illyricum (Gruen 1996, 172–3); it was said for instance that he wished to secure all the territory up to the Danube (Rice-Holmes 1931, 130–1). The campaigns are briefly mentioned by Augustus (*RG* 29.1, 30.1) and described at greater length by Appian, who used Augustus' *Memoirs* (*Ill.* 12–28), and by Dio (49.35–8). It is possible that Agrippa's main contribution was to patrol the Dalmatian coast with the fleet (Reinhold 1965, 45 n. 1).

16 Appian's account of Antonius' campaigns in the East is lost (Gurval 1995, 95), so historians must rely on Plutarch (*Ant.* 37–52) and Dio (49.24–30). Ventidius' contribution is described by Dio (49.19–22) and Plutarch (*Ant.* 34). Syme (1939, 271) admires Antonius' administrative arrangements in the East, which were intelligible and workable, and did not go beyond the brief of a Roman proconsul. Antonius' losses in the Parthian campaign and during the retreat are variously given; Velleius (2.82.3) says that he lost a quarter of his entire army; Plutarch (*Ant.* 50) says he lost 20,000 infantry and 4,000 cavalry by the time he reached Armenia, and 8,000 more in the wintry weather afterwards. Cleopatra set sail in winter when summoned 'to a place between Berytus and Sidon' (Plutarch *Ant.* 51). The distribution of lands and the 'triumph' in Alexandria made no impression in Rome (Syme 1939, 260–1) and no difference to the administration of the East (Pelling 1996, 41); see also Dio (49.32; 41) and Plutarch (*Ant.* 36.2). For Caesarion as *rex regum* see Kienast (1982, 53); Dio (49.41.1); Plutarch (*Ant.* 54).

17 Cleopatra schemed to rule the whole Roman world according to Dio (50.4.1–2) and Plutarch (*Ant.* 58.9–11); she used to say that she would one day issue edicts from the Capitol (Dio 50.5.4). Octavia went to Antonius with 2,000

men (Appian *BC* 5.138; Plutarch *Ant.* 53.1). Antonius wrote a tasteless letter to Octavian, accusing him of having had the same number of, if not more, adulterous relationships as himself (Suetonius *Aug.* 69). The phrase *uxor mea est* used of Cleopatra in this letter has been interpreted in two opposing ways: one a literal translation 'she is my wife' and the other with a question mark added to it to mean 'is she my wife?' Those who insist that Antonius was never married to Cleopatra obviously prefer the second interpretation; see note 5 above. In 33 Antonius still had not moved his legions from their positions (Pelling 1996, 37). For some time envoys went back and forth between Antonius and Octavian carrying complaints and messages of self-justification (Dio 50.1–2; Plutarch *Ant.* 55), but they became openly hostile only at the beginning of 32 (Dio 50.2.2) so it may be that Octavian's speech denouncing Antonius did not belong to the year 33, when the Illyricum campaigns were still not terminated and Octavian could not be certain of his position *vis-à-vis* Antonius (Kienast 1982, 54 n. 223, quoting Fadinger 1969, 125ff. and 180). Syme (1939, 276 n. 1) prefers 33 for Octavian's speech.

18 There were triumphs for Octavian's generals every year from 36 to 33, except for 35 when he himself began the wars in Illyricum. Dio hints that triumphs were so cheap that they were for sale (49.42.3). Velleius states that Octavian induced the triumphal generals to erect new buildings and repair old ones (2.79.4). On the buildings of Octavian and his friends, see Zanker (1988, 73–80). Agrippa as aedile set up a maintenance scheme for the water supply of Rome (Reinhold 1965, 48–52; Dio 49.43.1–4, 54.11.7). Octavian's return to the old traditions included the building of temples to the gods, especially Apollo, possibly as a direct contrast to the frenzies of Antonius' Dionysiac associations (Pelling 1996, 44). Agrippa reinstated the ancient military ritual of the *Lusus Troiae* (Dio 49.43.3; Vergil *Aeneid* 5.545–603) and expelled the astrologers (Dio 49.43.5). Octavian's position in 32 was fragile; retrospective knowledge makes it seem as though his victory over Antonius was assured (Pelling 1996, 49). The ancient sources, and the arguments of various scholars, are summarised in a most useful article by Benario (1975). Some authors believe that Octavian was Triumvir all through 32. Grenade (1961, 28) thought that Octavian could cease to be Triumvir only by formally abdicating, and to do so would invite problems, so he did not abdicate. Gabba (1970, 7) dated the beginning of the second five-year term of the Triumvirate to 1 January 36, which meant that the second term had not expired in December 33. Petzold argued (1969, 339) that the Triumvirate was still formally constituted as long as one of the members remained alive, and that Octavian retained Triumviral powers until after Actium (ibid. 340–6). Fadinger proposed a hybrid argument (1969, 143–5) that the Triumvirate had ended on 31 December 33, so Octavian dropped the title Triumvir but still retained the powers until 27 by dint of never having formally abdicated. Other scholars believe that from 1 January 32 Octavian was merely a *privatus cum imperio* (Benario 1975, 304; Kienast 1982, 55). On the political status of the two remaining Triumvirs in 32 see Bleicken (1990, 65–82). Octavian probably had no powers in Rome and Italy, but his provincial commands presumably did not expire at the same time as the Triumvirate, so that was where his powers lay because he could not be replaced until a successor had been appointed (Bleicken 1990, 68–74), and if

that had occurred then a tribune's veto could easily have prevented the appointment (Benario 1975, 306).

19 Antonius' despatch to Sosius and Domitius is reported by Dio (49.41.6). On 1 January Sosius denounced Octavian, but whatever it was that he proposed it was vetoed by the tribune Nonius Balbus (Dio 50.2.3). Bleicken (1990, 66) says that Octavian primed Balbus to veto the proposal, but the tribune may well have been primed by Sosius himself to rescue him from a dangerous situation (Pelling 1996, 49). Octavian found out about Antonius' will from Titius and Plancus (Dio 50.3.3) and was alone when he opened it (Plutarch *Ant.* 58.3). Syme (1939, 282 n.1) and Crook (1957, 36–8) suggest that Octavian forged or fabricated the contents of the will; see also Pelling (1996, 52). The ritual of casting a spear into a piece of land representing enemy territory derives from Dio (50.4.4–5) who says (50.4.3) that Antonius was not declared *hostis* at this time; Suetonius (*Aug.* 17.2) suggests that he was, but may be referring to another occasion.

20 Octavian dropped the title of Triumvir but Antonius continued to use it (Bleicken 1990, 68). The exact chronology for the reading of Antonius' will, the declaration of war against Cleopatra, and the taking of the oath to Octavian is not established; see Kienast (1982, 59 n. 237). Syme (1939, 284) puts the oath first, then the declaration of war (ibid. 291). The military character of the oath is affirmed by Pelling (1996, 53); Brunt and Moore (1967, 67) reject the military comparison, at least for the later oath to the Emperors which some authors think may have evolved from the one sworn to Octavian. Augustus merely described it as an oath to himself as leader in the war which he won at Actium (*RG* 25.2), which gives no assistance whatsoever in the problem of the actual text of the oath, nor of dating it precisely. The town of Bononia was exempted because many of Antonius' clients lived there (Suetonius *Aug.* 17.2); in the same passage Suetonius doubts the voluntary nature of the oath. Earl (1980, 53) calls it 'the last resource of tyranny'. Valerius Messalla replaced Antonius as consul in 31 (Dio 50.4.3; 10).

21 The Actium campaign is briefly documented by Velleius (2.84–5) and in more depth by Plutarch (*Ant.* 61–3) and Dio (50.10–75), complete with invented speeches for both Octavian and Antonius. Agrippa played a major part in the campaign (Reinhold 1965, 53–8). Antonius occupied the coast of Greece but could not prevent landings by Agrippa and Octavian (Syme 1939, 294–5; Reinhold 1965, 53–4). At Actium Sosius risked battle and lost (Dio 50.14.1–2; Vell. 2.84.2). During the days before the final battle, Antonius ordered the crews to take their sails in case he needed to chase the enemy (Plutarch *Ant.* 64.2), but when the battle was fought he simply followed Cleopatra (ibid. 66.7). Agrippa and Maecenas met with problems in Rome and recalled Octavian, who arrived at Brundisium to be met by senators and people; he stayed for thirty days then left for Greece (Dio 51.4.2–8). The plot formed by the younger Lepidus may have taken place after Actium, or as Velleius says (2.88) after the fall of Alexandria in 30; Syme (1986, 35) dates it to autumn 30. Appian (*BC* 4.50) says that Maecenas sent Lepidus to Octavian at Actium; see also Suetonius (*Aug.* 19.1) and Dio (54.15.4). Alexandria fell on 1 August 30 (Vell. 2.87). The deaths of Antonius and Cleopatra are related by Plutarch (*Ant.* 76–8) and Dio (51.5–10).

5 EMPIRE BUILDING

1 The suicide of Cleopatra was doubted by some of the ancient writers (Suetonius *Aug.* 17; Plutarch *Ant.* 86; Dio 51.14), but there could be no doubt that Octavian ordered the deaths of Antyllus, the son of Antonius, and of Caesarion (Suetonius *Aug.* 17.5). Antonius' remaining children were brought up by Octavia, and Cleopatra Selene, the daughter of Cleopatra and Antonius, was given in marriage to king Juba of Mauretania (Plutarch *Ant.* 36, 54, 87; Dio 51.15.6–7; Suetonius *Aug.* 17.5).

2 Augustus claimed that he was in charge of the state by universal consent (*consensus universorum*) (*RG* 34), which was a wider concept than the oath taken in Italy and the provinces before Actium (Syme 1939, 307), even elevating him to a higher plane than the mere human (Wickert 1974, 71). The *consensus* was unofficial; there was no formal vote of any official powers (Brunt and Moore 1967, 76). Ameling (1994, 25 n. 101) postulates an amended reading of *RG* 34, changing *potitus rerum omnium* to *potens rerum omnium*, which alters the implications in a subtle way, elevating the *consensus* from a single occurrence to an ongoing circumstance. Octavian's powers were still bound up with the Triumvirate, even though he had ceased to use the title (Bleicken 1990, 83). The debate about the terminal date of the Triumvirate could be said to be redundant, since Octavian retained Triumviral powers until he laid them down formally (Lacey 1996, 35).

3 Embassies came to Octavian from Eastern cities, which he dealt with in his capacity as consul, as he was careful to style himself, but none the less the decisions have a monarchical tone and Octavian was acting entirely on his own responsibility (Sherk 1969, no. 58 iii, iv; Millar 1973, 58–9; Lintott 1993, 113–14).

4 Octavian's huge army after Actium required immediate attention; Syme (1939, 304) estimated that there were about seventy legions, which Octavian reduced to about twenty-seven. Some men were sent home soon after the fall of Alexandria, and the rest would be dispersed, but the process would be a long one. For a summary of the army at this period, and on the veteran settlements, see Keppie (1996, 376–87; 1983, 73–82).

5 Octavian had already addressed the problem of policing Rome and Italy after Naulochus when he appointed Sabinus (Shuckburgh 1903, 113; Suetonius *Aug.* 32). Later he would establish the urban cohorts in Rome (Dio 55.24; Tacitus *Ann.* 4.5). He recruited freedmen to form a fire brigade (*vigiles*) (Suetonius *Aug.* 25, 30) which Dio (55.26) dates to AD 6; he says there were seven divisions, usually interpreted to mean that there were seven cohorts each containing 1,000 men. Tact in handling the Senate would be of the utmost importance; Augustus' relations with that body are documented by Sattler (1960) and Brunt (1984). There was a need for increased social mobility to break the dominance of the upper classes, and a need for new men to take on various aspects of the administration (Earl 1980, 83). Syme commented on the lack of consulars among Augustus' subordinates (1939, 328), and how he curtailed the proconsular governors with command of armies without eradicating them altogether (ibid. 310–11). The social changes made themselves felt quite soon; equites could rise to senatorial status within two or three generations if they acquired sufficient wealth (ibid. 352–4).

6 Augustus laid great emphasis on his position as consul, which was the legally acceptable basis of power (*consulem se ferens*: Tacitus *Ann.* 1.2), but this was a charade, as Tacitus implies, since he was much more than simply consul. Most people merely wanted peace, economic stability, and safety of life and limb and of personal property (Nicolet 1984, 111). Dio (52.6.4–5) makes Agrippa outline people's needs in this respect in the long speech invented for him, counter-balanced by the ideas that Maecenas puts forward on how to run the Empire; these speeches occupy almost the whole of Dio 52.

7 Augustus maintained an unclarified position from choice (Petit 1976, 125–6), which involved the careful use of words in describing himself and his achievements. *Imperium* does not appear in the *Res Gestae* very often, though Augustus was not shy about using the name Imperator. *Princeps senatus* and *princeps civitatis* were customary terms denoting the leader of the Senate or the state, but Augustus' concept was much wider, as Horace describes him, '*maxime principum*' (*Odes* 4.14.6; Syme 1939, 311–12). On Princeps in general see Wickert (*RE* XXII 1998ff.), von Premerstein (1937), Beranger (1953). *Auctoritas* defies translation with all its shades of meaning, because modern thinking does not grasp all the nuances. The major study, not yet superseded, is by Magdelain (1947). The word is related to *auctor*, or a counsellor with authority born of experience whose advice was likely to be taken (Galinsky 1996, 13). It conferred influence and power without any legal basis (Kienast 1982, 72–3, Crook 1996b 121–3; Lacey 1996, 6), but Augustus had sufficient legal powers as well as influence to justify all his actions (Brunt and Moore 1967, 80).

8 Opposition to Augustus can be overrated (Crook 1996a, 73). A recent conclusion is that opposition was 'scattered, isolated, ineffective and, overall, minimal' (Raaflaub and Samons 1990, 417–54). Augustus formulated plans but did not insist upon driving them to their conclusion without reference to the political climate; he waited for suitable opportunities to introduce ideas (Lacey 1996, 59) and retreated and regrouped when it was obvious that he had used too much force or tried to move too quickly (Jones 1968, 12–13).

9 The Senate confirmed all Octavian's acts on 1 January (Dio 51.20.1) and the doors of the temple of Janus were closed, which pleased him more than any of the other honours; the fact that wars were going on elsewhere was not counted as a serious threat to Rome (Dio 51.20.4–5). The doors of the temple were closed three times during Augustus' reign (Suetonius *Aug.* 22). Octavian made Egypt into a province, decribing the process in the *Res Gestae* (27.1) 'I added Egypt to the Empire of the Roman people', but the governors of Egypt were answerable only to himself and neither the people nor the Senate had any jurisdiction over the province. Dio (51.17.4) phrases it differently: 'Thus was Egypt enslaved.' The first governor was Cornelius Gallus (*PIR*[2] C 1369), the equestrian commander who had marched from Africa while Octavian marched from Syria on Alexandria. He was an equestrian, and is specifically named as such on an inscription from Philae (*ILS* 8995) which also styles him Prefect of Alexandria and Egypt. The Prefect of Egypt stood in the place of the king, according to Reinmuth (1935, 2). Senators were forbidden to enter Egypt without permission of Augustus (Dio 57.17.1; Tacitus *Ann.* 2.59). Crook (1996a, 74) maintains that the decision to employ an equestrian was made on the spot, because Gallus was there, but it proved an acceptable experiment which was

aways followed thereafter. But it is more likely that Octavian appointed Gallus because as an *eques* he would have owed everything to him and not to the Senate. In the end Gallus was a disappointment and fell from favour; perhaps he thought such a mark of distinction conferred by Octavian should have led to greater honours. Whatever the reason for Gallus' fall, Augustus continued to employ equestrians to fill the post of Prefect of Egypt.

10 The long sojourn in the East allowed time for troublesome elements to calm down (Lacey 1996, 64). The quarrel betwen Tiridates and Phraates of Parthia also worked itself out (Dio 51.18.2), and Octavian gained much credit in Rome for his dealings with the Parthians (Dio 51.20.1). He allowed the Eastern cities to erect temples – to Rome and the divine Julius for Roman citizens, and to Rome and himself for the non-Roman citizens (Dio 51.20.6–9). The long catalogue of honours voted to Octavian is listed by Dio (51.19.1 to 20.6); the arches at Brundisium and Rome, and the triumphs for victory at Actium, portrayed as victory over Cleopatra, and then the fall of Alexandria, portrayed as victory over Egypt, are specifically mentioned (Dio 51.19.1, 19.4). Antonius' name was to be obliterated, and his birthday declared *nefastus* (Dio 51.19.3–5), and Valerius Potitus held public sacrifices, a thing which had not been done before for anyone else, when Octavian returned home (Dio 51.21.2). Octavian had been employing Imperator as part of his name since the Triumviral period (Crook 1996a, 75) and now the Senate confirmed his use of it, 'not as the usual salutation, but the title as it had been granted to Caesar' (Dio 52.41.3); see also Syme (1958, 172–88 = *Roman Papers* I 1979, 361–77) and Galsterer (1990, 14–15) for the use of the title to gain the support of the army. The *Lex Saenia* enabled Octavian/Augustus to create patricians; Augustus says that he did so in response to a request from the Senate and the people during his fifth consulship (*RG* 8.1), but he did not confine the process to one single act. Kienast (1982, 128) says that one-third of the patricians of the Empire owed their elevation to Augustus, and Brunt and Moore (1967, 50) point out that more patricians would be needed to fill the vacant priesthoods.

11 The Senate decreed that the whole populace should go out to meet Octavian when he returned home (Dio 51.19.2), but he declined the honour (Dio 51.20.4). See Lacey (1996, 17–56) on the general significance of coming home and the numbers of people who came out of the city to greet returning generals, and ibid. (40–1) on the possibility that Octavian would feel that he had been compromised by the Senate's decree. The returning hero's friends would organise a triumph if appropriate, and until the details were fixed the prospective *triumphator* remained outside the city (Lacey 1996, 21–2). Octavian never held another triumph, and the last proconsuls to celebrate one were L. Sempronius Atratinus 12 October 21, and the younger Cornelius Balbus (*PIR²* C 1331) *ex Africa*, 27 March 19 (Kienast 1982, 91 n. 94; Brunt and Moore 1967, 43). Dio (54.12.1–2) records the demise of the triumph as far as proconsular governors were concerned and then sneers that in any case they had been awarded on the feeblest of excuses, such as arresting robbers or clearing highways. All credit for military victories went in future to Augustus, no matter who won them. His own legates governing his provinces were of praetorian rank and could not take the auspices on their own account, which made them ineligible for the award of a triumph. The position was made very clear by the treatment of M. Licinius Crassus (*PIR²* L 186)

in 27–26 who claimed more than just the triumph that he was awarded, but was not allowed any further honours and disappeared from the historical record thereafter (see below, note 15). In place of the triumph, the substitute honour of *ornamenta triumphalia* was developed, an award which Tiberius was among the first to receive (Suetonius *Tib.* 9.2; Tacitus *Ann.* 1.72.1). Augustus did not permit him to triumph on the grounds that he had not been fighting under his own auspices, but had acted as the subordinate of the Princeps (Dio 54,31.4; *RG* 30.1). Octavian refused the *aureum coronarium* (Dio 51.21.4), which spared the Italian cities unnecessary expense and also earned him some credit, as did the payment of all his debts and the cancellation of debts owed to him (Dio 51.21.4). The loquacious ravens are described by Macrobius *Saturnalia* 2.4, translated by Chisholm and Ferguson (1981, 73–4). The celebrations and games made people forget the wars, and made it seem that all the vanquished foes had been foreigners (Dio 51.21.4). Octavian paid cash for lands on which to settle his veterans after Actium and in AD 14, as he records in the *Res Gestae* (16.1); the total came to 600 million sesterces for Italian lands and 260 million for holdings in the provinces. Keppie (1983, 74) estimates that about 40,000 to 50,000 veterans were settled after Actium and the fall of Alexandria, but it is not possible to estimate how many men settled in the provinces. There was no recorded protest, so it is permissible to assume that adequate compensation was paid where necessary, and that the Egyptian Treasury funded most if not all of the settlements (Keppie 1983, 82).

12 Octavian shared the *fasces* with Agrippa in his sixth consulship (Dio 53.1.1; Rich 1990, 132). Chilver (1950, 417–19) suggests that the phrase simply means that Octavian was following the normal custom of employing the usual number of twelve *fasces* every alternate month. The dubious Triumviral acts were annulled (Dio 53.2), which Tacitus (*Ann.* 3.28) viewed with his usual scepticism: 'In his sixth consulship, Augustus, feeling secure, cancelled the acts of the Triumvirate and presented us with laws to serve our needs in peace under a prince. Thenceforth our fetters were tightened and sentries set over us.' Augustus boasted of repairing eighty-two temples (*RG* 20.4), and Dio (53.2.4) records that he persuaded other men to repair those with which their families had always been associated. The censorial powers were granted to Augustus and Agrippa, but not the actual office of censor, as Dio (52.42.1) mistakenly claims. They used the powers to weed out undesirables from the Senate in the first *lectio* that they conducted. They completed the census that had been begun in 29 (Dio 52.42.1) followed by the performance of the ancient purification ceremony of the *lustrum* (*RG* 8.2; *ILS* 6123). Dio (53.1.3) connects the award of Augustus' title *princeps senatus* to the completion of the census, but as Rich (1990, 132) points out, he probably already had this title in 29; he kept it until his death (*RG* 7.2), but it fell far short of the title Princeps that he later assumed. The *lectio* and reshuffling of the Senate was not totally one-sided, for Octavian gave money to deserving individuals whose fortunes had fallen far short of the prescribed totals for membership of the Senate (Dio 53.2.2) and he created patricians 'who were indispensable for the perpetuation of traditions' (Dio 52.42.5).

13 Velleius' chapter (2.89) eulogising Augustus should be read in its entirety to facilitate some understanding of the advertised benefits of the Augustan regime.

Dio invents a speech for Octavian in the Senate in January 27 (53.2–12); he thought of the events of the Ides of January as a sham, and recognised in Octavian's restoration of the Republic the beginning of the monarchy (53.17.1, 2.6, 12.1, 19.1; Bleicken 1990, 82–3). Suetonius (*Aug.* 84) records that Augustus used to write everything down so as to ensure that he said no more and no less than he intended. Scholars have debated for centuries on what had changed when 'the Republic was restored'. It has been recognised that the form of words meant very little, and the impression on contemporaries seems to have been negligible, judging by the paucity of surviving references to it as an event (Millar 1973, 63). Suetonius (*Aug.* 28.1) ambiguously states that Augustus twice thought of restoring the Republic: the first time after the defeat of Antonius, because it was a constant taunt of Antonius' that it was all Octavian's fault that it had not been restored; the second time after a lingering illness had wearied him, which can be dated perhaps to 23, when Augustus was so ill that it was expected that he would die. But Augustus thought better of the idea, Suetonius says, because he would not be free from danger if he retired, and it was not safe to entrust the state to the control of more than one person. The implication is that he had not actually restored the Republic at all. It is generally agreed that Octavian had been preparing the way for the so-called settlement for some time, as he says in the *Res Gestae* (34.1) 'in my sixth and seventh consulships I transferred the Republic from my power to the dominion of the Senate and people of Rome' which indicates that he thought of it as an ongoing process (Lacey 1996, 77–98; Crook 1996a, 76–7). It is highly unlikely that Octavian would have risked making his speech without first ensuring that the reception would be favourable to his wishes, so it is to be assumed that there was considerable stage-management beforehand (Crook 1996a, 78). This presupposes that he talked it over with some of his intimates first as Dio affirms (53.2.7) and then approached a wider circle of senators, but whether he had formed the *consilium* at this date is debatable (Bleicken 1990, 90–1). This body later developed into a rotating committee comprising senators and *amici* (Crook 1955; Syme 1939, 408). In effect the restoration of the Republic was a continuation of the Triumviral promises to do so when the time was ripe (Millar 1973, 65). The settlement has been described as launching a programme that befitted reality (Bleicken 1990, 87), and if it was not the Republic as men remembered it, then the new system was at least acceptable and preferable to what had gone before (Lacey 1996, 98). The provinces which Octavian received were the potentially threatened ones which could not be safely governed by annual magistrates (Suetonius *Aug.* 47), but one of the main reasons, or at least by-products of Octavian's settlement, is that the proconsular governors were ousted from these provinces, and he could install men who were suited for the task and would also be subordinate to him; in consequence he did not choose to employ nobles or ex-consulars (Syme 1939, 326–8). Dio (53.13.5–6) explains how the system worked, and how Augustus appointed *legati Augusti pro praetore*. The question of Octavian/Augustus' status is insoluble, but the debate continues; Jones (1968, 5) thought that the question of any grant of *imperium*, consular or otherwise, simply never arose in 27 because Augustus was consul; Eder (1990, 107) notes that the status of *consul proconsule* was a constitutional abomination, so opts for the suggestion that Augustus governed his provinces as consul from 27 to 23, and required proconsular *imperium* only when he gave up the consulship in 23. Syme (1939, 314) decided that Augustus was governor by dint of *imperium proconsulare*, equal to any other proconsular governor at this stage, and so he was supreme only because he held a very large extent of territory containing most of the troops; Kienast (1982, 74–5) also opts for the proconsular *imperium*. One of the arguments in support of this theory is that even if he had every intention of doing so, Octavian could not know in 27 whether he could retain the consulship every year, so it is likely that he would make a watertight case for holding his provinces for the ten years that had been granted to him (Syme, in Schmitthenner 1969, 153–75, esp.162 = *JRS* 36 1946, 149–58). Von Premerstein (1937, 229ff.) argued that Augustus held *imperium proconsulare maius* from 27 onwards, which would give him powers superior to all other governors whatever their rank, and he would possess the legal basis upon which to make decisions for any of the senatorial provinces; but this is not supported by any truly incontestable evidence. It has been pointed out that Dio (53.15.4) says that Augustus gave orders to all provincial governors from 27 onwards, but this can be dismissed as an anchronism because such practice was entirely normal in Dio's time. An inscription from Cyme has been adduced as evidence that Augustus issued orders to the provincial governors as early as 27 (Sherk 1988, no. 2; Brunt and Moore 1967, 83–4; Lacey 1996, 66) because it contains the phrase *iussu Augusti* ('on the orders of Augustus') but even this has been explained away as unofficial phraseology with no legal backing, but written with the support of Augustus' overwhelming influence behind it (Rich 1990, 170).

14 The content of Octavian's speech is unknown; Dio's probably fictitious version (53.2–12) allows him to outline the principles behind the foundation of the Principate. Thus it can be argued that the only business dealt with on 13 January concerned the provinces and nothing more (Bleicken 1990, 85), or that much more was discussed in the day's business (Lacey 1996, 90). It took two more days for the Senate to react; Lacey (1996, 92) points out that the two days after the Ides of January would have been inconvenient for public business, hence the delay in the response to Octavian's speech. Augustus says that he received his name from the Senate (*RG* 34 '*senatus consulto Augustus appellatus sum*'), but the motion was put forward by Munatius Plancus (Vell 2.91.1), whose track record so far was perhaps not of the best quality if Velleius is correct in his earlier assessment (2.83.1). The unsavoury reputation of Plancus may have been the reason for Augustus' neglect of him in his account. The name Augustus was connected to augur and indeed to *auctoritas* and so had religious and influential connotations (Syme 1939, 313). It is said that Augustus first toyed with the idea of assuming the name Romulus (Suetonius *Aug.* 7.2; Dio 53.16.7); the name was revered but was too deeply associated with kingship: see Rich (1990, 149) and J.S. Richardson, '*Imperium romanum*: empire and the language of power', *JRS* 81 1991, 1–9, esp. 8 n. 64. The other honours besides the name Augustus are listed by Dio (53.16.4–8) who goes on to say (53.17.1) that in this way the power of both people and Senate passed entirely into the hands of one man. The coinage was pressed into service in 27, with the legend *Caesar cos VII civibus servateis* indicating that Augustus had saved the lives of citizens (*BMC* 656); the honours awarded to Augustus 'furnished

constant themes for the coinage for the ensuing 15 years' (Kent 1978, 277 no. 125).

15 Privacy was sometimes necessary when Augustus wished to work; according to Suetonius he had an office at the top of the house where he used to retire when he wanted to get away from everyone, which he called his 'Syracuse' (*Aug.* 72.2). The subject of the image of Augustus in art and literature has been covered in depth; only a few of the main sources are listed here, in which further references can be found to periodical articles, conference proceedings, Festschriften and so on: Galinsky (1996), Gurval (1995), Hannestad (1986), Kähler (1959), Powell (1992), Toynbee (1961), Woodman and West (1984), Zanker (1988). Augustus repaired the Via Flaminia and all the bridges except two, as he recorded in the *Res Gestae* (20.5). Building was going on in Rome as he left for his provinces. The temple of Apollo next to his house on the Palatine was already dedicated (*RG* 19, 21.2) and the mausoleum may have been completed (Zanker 1988, 27), even though Dio (53.30.5) implies that when Marcellus was interred there in 23 the building was not yet finished. Agrippa's buildings are grouped together by Dio for literary convenience (53.27.15; Rich 1990, 163), but their construction presumably occupied several years. M. Licinius Crassus, fighting in Moesia, had killed with his own hand the enemy chieftain, and so claimed the honour of *spolia opima*, but according to tradition Augustus unearthed the antiquarian excuse that Cossus, the previous claimant, described in all the other sources as tribune, had been consul and acting under his own auspices, a story which Livy (*Epit.* 32.4) recounted but did not believe. Octavian insisted that Crassus had been acting under his orders, and Dio includes the conquest of Moesia as one of Octavian's victories, listed under that heading in the invented speech delivered in the Senate in January 27. The verity of the actual speech is doubtful, but the classification of Crassus' campaign as one fought under Augustus indicates that history sided with the Princeps. See Syme (1939, 307ff.), Crook (1996a, 80 n. 55), Bleicken (1990, 34, 89–91), Rich (1990, 137), Badian (1982, 38–41), Schumacher, *Historia* 34, 1985, 209–11. The Moesian campaign receives in-depth treatment from Dio (51.23.2 to 53.27), so it is to be presumed that he had access to an account of it. The challenge to the orthodox version of the 'crisis' theory has been made by J.W. Rich, 'Augustus and the spolia opima', *Chiron* 26, 1996, 85–127, esp. 98–9, 109–111, 126–7.

16 Cornelius Gallus campaigned as far as the First Cataract of the Nile, constructed buildings in Alexandria, and left his name on several monuments (*ILS* 8895; *AE* 1964, 255). Dio (53.23.5 to 53.24) says that he spread gossip about Augustus, while Suetonius (*Aug.* 66.2) accuses him of ingratitude. Syme (1939, 309) dated the fall from grace to 27 and the suicide to the end of the year; Dio relates the events under the year 26. Syme also considered the possibility that Gallus had to be sacrificed to conciliate the Senate (1939, 310 n. 1). The Arabian campaign of Aelius Gallus (*PIR*² A 179) has been reassessed and the connection with events in Parthia analysed by Marek, (1993, esp. 151–2); see also note 22 below.

17 On Augustus' campaigns in Spain, see Dio (53.25.2 to 26.5) and W. Schmitthenner, 'Augustus' spanischer Feldzug und der Kampf um den Prinzipat', *Historia* 11, 1962, 29–85. Augustus portrayed the campaign as final

by carefully omitting specific dates and also forgetting to add Agrippa's name in his list of achievements (*RG* 26.2). The projected invasion of Britain can be discounted as rumour (Rich 1990, 156). Strabo (115–16, 200) did not think that it was worth the effort and expense of occupying the island. Messalla Corvinus held his triumph in 27 and was made city prefect in 26, but held the post for only six days and then resigned because 'he did not know the rules of the job' (Tacitus *Ann.* 6.11.3; Syme 1939, 403). One interpretation is that Messalla smelled a rat and resigned before he could be compromised (Syme 1986, 211–12, and on Messalla in general see also chapters 15, 16, and 17, pp. 200–43), but Augustus' purpose behind the 'artful device' as Syme calls it is not elucidated.

18 Agrippa was honoured after Actium with a blue flag (in Latin *vexillum*) (Dio 51.21.3), which Suetonius *(Aug.* 25.3) confuses with the awards after Naulochus. Agrippa's status is not defined; Lacey (1996, 117–31) postulates that he was given command of the fleet and coastal areas (*praefectus classis et orae maritimae*). Augustus was ill at Tarraco, and his fear of premature death may have prompted him to arrange the marriage of Julia and Marcellus (Crook 1996a, 83), but it is equally likely that this had been in his mind all along, and by the time he went to Spain he was accustomed to illness. There was probably no more likelihood that he formulated his plans because of illness than there ever was in the past. In 25 and the beginning of 24, it could be said that Augustus was preparing even then for the so-called settlement of 23 (Eder 1990, 107). He paid 400 sesterces to 250,000 citizens (*RG* 15.1), the same sum that he had paid in 29 (Rich 1990, 164). The Senate confirmed all his acts by an oath on 1 January 24 (Dio 53.28.2); Dio says that Augustus was now dispensed from the laws, but this is erroneous (Rich 1990, 164). Augustus was exempt from the marriage laws, and certain other aspects of the laws but not all of them. Marcellus was given a seat in the Senate among the praetors, and to be considered as holding the rank of praetor so he could be aedile in 23 (Dio 53.28.4, 31.2–2), while Tiberius was permitted to stand for office five years before the legal age and served as quaestor in 23 (Dio 53.28.3; Vell 2.94.3). When Augustus was ill in 23, supposedly suffering from an abcess of the liver (Suetonius *Aug.* 81.1), he gave his signet ring to Agrippa and his papers to his consular colleague Piso (Dio 53.31.1; Suetonius *Aug.* 28.1). Badian (1982, 34) thought that had Augustus died there may well have been civil war. Dio (53.31.4) says of Marcellus that Augustus was not yet confident of the young man's ability and judgement. The only man whom Augustus could trust to run the Empire if he was to die in 23 was Agrippa, even though after his recovery he may well have intended to promote Marcellus until he felt that he was ready to be entrusted with government (Rich 1990, 167; Roddaz 1984, 312–19). Syme suggested (1939, 341) that Agrippa was in league with Livia to prevent the promotion of Marcellus. In order to allay suspicions that he had designated neither Marcellus nor anyone else as his successor, Augustus offered to read out his will in the Senate (Dio 53.31.1) but no one would allow him to do so.

19 The trial of Marcus Primus cannot be dated precisely; some authors date it to late in 24 or early in 23 (Syme 1939, 333, 341), though Dio (54.3.2–3) puts it in 22; Badian (1982) suggests that the trial and the conspiracy should be

dated later than the settlement of 23. The confusion over the conspiracy involving a man of consular rank is now thought to be resolved by the fact that firstly Terentius Varro Murena listed in the Capitoline *Fasti* as consul in 23 perhaps died before he had even taken up his office, and not actually in office (Syme 1986. 388–9), while the conspirator was not this Murena, but L. Licinius Murena who had unsuccessfully defended Primus (Raaflaub and Samons 1990, 425–6, nn. 29–35). Velleius (2.91) reports that 'Lucius' Murena and Fannius Caepio had plotted to kill Augustus. Rich (1990, 168–9) prefers to date the conspiracy to 22 as Dio says, and therefore removes it from one of the causes of Augustus' resignation of the consulship. See also Bleicken (1990, 94) and Kienast (1982, 86). Suetonius (*Aug.* 37.1) says that Augustus asked for a third colleague in the consulship but gives no date for the story; Bleicken (1990, 94) thinks the most likely context for it is 23, when Augustus made an attempt to retain the consulship but failed. Having recovered from his illness, Augustus went to the Alban Mount where he formally resigned the consulship on 1 July, thus freeing the supreme office for other candidates (Dio 53.32.3). Nothing suggests that he was reacting to any sort of crisis (Eder 1990, 107–8 n. 170, quoting Badian 1982 who refutes most of the crisis theories). Augustus now required further powers to compensate for the loss of the consulship. According to Dio (53.32.5) *imperium proconsulare maius* was granted to Augustus by legal enactment, but the nature of the proconsular power is disputed and also it was not likely to have been awarded once and for all, as Dio says; as with everything else the powers that were granted to Augustus were usually for limited terms. If he had been granted *imperium maius*, it would have given him authority over all other provincial governors, thus modifying the basis of his legal authority (Syme 1986, 384); several scholars now deny the existence of *imperium proconsulare maius*; Ameling (1994, 14–15 n. 61) enumerates the references, especially Bleicken (1990, 104). Ameling (1994, 17–18, 22) prefers the comparison with Republican precedent, when extraordinary powers were granted only for specific tasks and did not encompass the whole Roman world. In these respects Augustus went beyond the precedent, and he was also exempted from the necessity of laying down his proconsular powers when he crossed the *pomerium* (Dio 53.32.5; Lintott 1993, 115–16; Richardson, *JRS* 81, 1991, 8; Syme 1939, 336). Augustus did not include this grant in the *Res Gestae* where he refers to himself as *consulari cum imperio* (*RG* 8.3). As Bleicken (1990, 96) points out, no one could possibly think in terms of Imperator Caesar Augustus as a *privatus*.

20 *Tribunicia potestas* was confirmed by a law (*RG* 10.1) which Dio relates to the period of the Latin Festival (53.32.3) held in June or July (Rich 1990, 169). Dio says that the Senate voted that Augustus should be tribune for life (53.32.5), which is unlikely as a vote and definitely not what happened, for as Dio himself points out in his next paragraph (53.32.6) neither Augustus nor any other Emperor ever took the actual title of tribune. Eder (1990, 109) thinks that the final two elements of the tribunician power were granted now: the right to act on behalf of the plebs and the right to convene the Senate (*ius cum plebi agendi* and *ius cum senatu agendi*). The separation of the powers from the office was revolutionary, and the censorial powers conferred upon Octavian and Agrippa were not a direct precedent because they were exercised via the consulship (Eder 1990,

109; Bleicken 1990, 95; Brunt and Moore 1967, 45–6). The tribunician powers provided a balance between the nobles and the plebs; to the nobles it held the threat of a return to *popularis* politics and to the plebs it guaranteed safety from noble oppression (Jones 1968, 11–12; Yavetz 1969, 91). Whilst it was not a major instrument of government on its own and could not be used to run the state (Bleicken 1990, 104), when combined with *imperium proconsulare maius* tribunician power formed the complete basis for government (Eder 1990, 109). Augustus used *trib. pot.* to number his 'regnal' years perhaps because it was innocuous and popular (Jones 1968, 11; Eder 1990, 110). Augustus used the powers to introduce legislation (*RG* 6.2) but did not use the veto, though the threat that he could do so if he wished probably was sufficient to deter the proposal of any measures that would displease him; see Chilver (1950, 433) on the uses of the tribunician powers, and Brunt and Moore (1967, 11 n. 1) on the use that other Emperors made of them. Augustus shared the powers with Agrippa and Tiberius, in each case for a limited term (*RG* 6.5; Dio 53.32.5). The system endured, and became the mark of highest distinction, or the *summi fastigii vocabulum* of Tacitus (*Ann.* 3.56.2), conferred upon the designated heir to the throne. Imperial use of the powers represented the complete integration of the tribunate into the organisation of the state (Galsterer 1990, 14).

21 Dio (53.32.1) says that Augustus sent Agrippa to the East because he realised that his favours to Marcellus had upset him, and implies that Augustus preferred Agrippa; Velleius (2.93.2) and Suetonius (*Aug.* 66.3; *Tib.* 10.1) both state that Agrippa went into voluntary exile because of jealousy of Marcellus; Tacitus (*Ann.* 14.53.3; 55.2–3) concurs. When Marcellus died, despite the fact that there was plague in Rome, Livia was suspected of killing him according to Dio (53.33.4). Augustus sent Agrippa back to Rome when he reached the East himself, and offered him the hand of the widowed Julia in marriage; Maecenas said that Agrippa had been raised so high that the only way to deal with him now was to marry him to Julia or to kill him (Dio 54.6.5). Dio affirms that Agrippa's command was limited to Syria (53.32.1), but Josephus (*AJ* 15.350) says that Agrippa was Caesar's deputy in the lands beyond the Ionian sea, in other words for a vast territory including most of the Eastern half of the Empire. Syme (1939, 338) points out that by basing himself on Lesbos, and governing Syria via deputies, Agrippa could also watch over the Balkans. Agrippa's powers have been debated as much as those of Augustus in 27. In his funeral oration for Agrippa, part of which has been preserved (*EJ*[2] 366), Augustus states that it was decreed that no one should have powers superior to Agrippa's wherever he went, which can be interpreted in different ways; it may mean that Agrippa held powers equal to those of the governors of the senatorial provinces. Reinhold (1965, 175) envisaged a gradual accretion of powers for Agrippa, rising from *imperium* over the Imperial provinces, to *imperium maius* over the senatorial provinces east of the Ionian sea, then to those in the West. Lacey (1996, 117–31) suggested that Agrippa had command of the coasts and the fleet, and was then given more powers in 18. It is simpler to suppose that Agrippa held *imperium maius* from 23 onwards, renewed in 18 and again in 13 (Rich 1990, 168), or as Ameling (1994, 27–8) suggests, that Agrippa was granted *imperium aequum* in 23 and retained it until his death in 12. On Agrippa in the East see Reinhold (1965, 169–75) and Roddaz (1984,

319–28). On the connection with the Parthian situation just before Agrippa was sent to the East, see Marek (1993).

22 On the food crisis see Kienast (1982, 92–3) and Yavetz (1969, 26, 93). Augustus refused the Dictatorship (*RG* 5.1–2; Vell. 2.89) with suitable histrionic gestures (Suetonius *Aug.* 52; Dio 54.1.3–4). He is accused of actually causing the food shortages in the first place (Kienast 1982, 93; Sattler 1960, 76). Augustus encouraged or at least condoned Tiridates' attempt to usurp the throne of Parthia, and ordered Aelius Gallus to march into Arabia at the same time. The failure of both these expeditions enfeebled Rome's position in 24; see Marek (1993). The expedition to Armenia was conducted by Tiberius who gave himself airs afterwards (Dio 54.9.4–6), but to Velleius he was the perfect hero (2.94.4); see also Suetonius (*Aug.* 21.3; *Tib.* 9.1), Tacitus (*Ann.* 2.3), Rich (1990, 184). The returned standards were placed in the Temple of Mars Ultor (*RG* 29.2; Suetonius *Aug.* 21.3; Dio 54.8.3). Augustus treated the return of the standards as though he had conquered Parthia in a great war (Dio 54.8.1–2). The coinage was used to celebrate the event (*signis receptis: BMC* 10–17, 40–2, 56–9, 332, 410, 415–16, 679–81; *Armenia capta BMC* 18–21, 43–4, 671–8). The poets made much of the success (Horace *Epist.* 1.12.27–8; *Odes* 4.15.6–8; Ovid *Fasti* 5.585–6, 593–4). See also Galinsky (1996, 155–8) and Rich (1990, 181). Augustus allegedly suffered from abcesses of the liver in 23 (Suetonius *Aug.* 81).

23 The people assumed that their misfortunes resulted from the fact that Augustus was no longer consul (Dio 54.1.2). They refused to elect a second consul for 21, hoping that Augustus could be persuaded to fill the vacancy (Dio 54.6.1–2). Agrippa was sent to Rome to secure order, which he did for a short time (Dio 54.6.4–5), but in 20 when he had left for Gaul and Spain the people refused to elect a second consul for 19 (Dio 54.10.1–2). Egnatius Rufus had earned fame as aedile when he formed a private fire-brigade from gangs of slaves (Dio 53.24.4–6). When he was elected praetor immediately after his aedileship, the Senate turned a blind eye but could not allow his candidacy for the consulship, since he had violated the regulations for the intervals between magistracies (Eder 1990, 112; Raaflaub and Samons 1990, 418–19). Rufus was executed by the Senate when he persisted; he was accused of conspiracy, which may or may not be true (Vell. 2.92.2–4). Dio does not name him in a passage which probably refers to the incident, dated to the year 18 (54.15.4; Rich 1990, 191).

24 Augustus wrote to the Senate to advise no further expansion in the East (Dio 54.9.1–2). The embassy from India met Augustus while he was in the East (Dio 54.9.8–10); Rome's renown had spread to the Indians and the Scythians, peoples only known by name to previous generations (Suetonius *Aug.* 21.3). Augustus recommended that one of the envoys from Rome, Quintus Lucretius, should become consul to fill the vacant place (Dio 54.10.2). Sattler (1960, 86) sees the appointment as a gesture to appease the Senate. The shrine to Fortuna Redux was the only honour that Augustus would accept (Dio 54.10.3).

6 *TOTUS ORBIS TERRARUM*

1 Augustus was granted proconsular *imperium* for another five years (Dio 54.12.5) and Agrippa received both proconsular and tribunician power for the same period (Dio 54.12.4.). Dio's phraseology (54.12.4, 54.28.1) could imply that

Agrippa had *imperium maius* when he received tribunician power (Brunt and Moore 1967, 47). Augustus enumerates the number of times that he asked for a colleague in tribunician power without naming the recipients (*RG* 6). Dio (54,10.5) says that the people quarrelled while Augustus was absent and while he was present they were afraid, a significant statement in itself. Dio implies that as a result of the disorders that broke out during his absence, Augustus was now asked by the people to take on the supervision of morals for five years, censorial authority for the same period, and that of consul for life. Crook (1996a, 91–2) points out that no other ancient source corroborates the fact that Augustus held consular power for life after 19. In 22 Augustus was offered and refused the consulship every year for life (*RG* 5.3). Though the assumption of consular power fits in well with Augustus' request that whenever he was consul he should have two colleagues (Suetonius *Aug.* 37), Suetonius does not go on to say that a few years after he made this request he was granted consular power for life. The omission does not constitute proof that Dio was mistaken, so the problem is left open to discussion.

2 Those who accept Dio's statement (54.10.5) that Augustus took consular power for life assume that in 23 Augustus gave up far too much when he resigned the consulship, because *tribunicia potestas* and proconsular *imperium* did not sufficiently compensate for the loss of his consular power (Eder 1990, 113). According to some authors he required consular powers to perform certain tasks, such as supervision of the election of magistrates, appointment of the city prefect, and to conduct the census (Kienast 1982, 95–6). Augustus himself says specifically that he undertook the censuses by dint of consular power (*RG* 8). Some scholars suggest that he did not hold consular power on a permanent basis, but was given separate, temporary grants of such power in order to conduct the census (E.T. Salmon, *Historia* 5, 1956, 473ff.; Crook 1996a, 91). Jones (1968, 13–15) considered such *ad hoc* grants unlikely; he accepts the idea that Augustus had consular power on a permanent basis, but Jones reinterprets Dio by suggesting that Augustus was granted power equal to that of the consuls, a subtly different matter. Brunt and Moore (1967, 13–14) accept that after the disturbances in Rome from 22–19 Augustus was encouraged to meet popular demand by acquiring the *imperium* and insignia of a consul so that to all intents and purposes he looked like one, and the people were thereby pacified. As Brunt and Moore point out it is hardly likely that the grant was purely honorific, so Augustus was no doubt able to wield all the necessary power; he did not suggest in the *Res Gestae* that he took consular power in order to conduct the censuses, but merely describes by what authority he carried them out, so it is still not clear whether he had been granted consular power temporarily or permanently (ibid. 13 n. 2). On the supervision of morals Augustus says that he was asked three times to take up the post of *curator legum et morum* (*RG* 6). Suetonius (*Aug.* 27.5) confuses the issue by saying that he took on this task permanently, while Dio says that he took it for five years (54.10.5). Sattler (1960, 88) points out that while Augustus perhaps did not always tell the absolute truth he had no reason to lie, so Suetonius is probably mistaken. Dio may also be mistaken when he says (54.30.1) that the supervision of morals was renewed in 12, when the date should be 14 (Sattler 1960, 89). Tacitus accuses Augustus of insidiously encroaching on power (*Ann.* 1.2.1); on

encroachment as a recurrent theme see Lacey (1996, 210–32). After 19, the consuls were drawn from the ranks of the nobles to a far greater extent than in previous years (Syme 1939, 372–3; Kienast 1982, 96–7) and there was a noticeable Italian element in the new nobility who reached the consulship (Salmon 1982, 147).

3 Augustus now appeared to be a consul without holding the office (Brunt and Moore 1967, 13). Tacitus (*Ann.* 1.2) links Augustus' statement that he called himself consul (*consulem se ferens*) to the end of the Triumvirate, but it may have been intended as an ironic comment in the context of 19 as well.

4 The inscription from Aphrodisias (Reynolds 1982, no. 13) that mentions Livia's interest in the people of Samos is given in translation by Sherk (1988, 7 no. 3) where Livia's previous connections with Samos are noted. Livia asked for citizenship for an eminent Gaul, but Augustus refused the request and remitted taxation instead, on the basis that he did not want to make grants of citizenship too easily but could sustain financial losses (Suetonius *Aug.* 40.3). When he wanted to say anything important Augustus used to write everything down (Suetonius *Aug.* 84.2).

5 All the anecdotes about him listed here derive from Macrobius (*Saturnalia* 2.4, translated in Chisholm and Ferguson 1981, 73–6). Dio (55.4.2) tells substantially the same tale about the soldier who asked for Augustus' assistance, which is probably the origin of Macrobius' story. On his deathbed Augustus asked his assembled friends if they had enjoyed the performance (Suetonius *Aug.* 79.1).

6 Suetonius (*Aug.* 63.1) says that one child was conceived by Livia but was born prematurely. There is no explanation why Augustus and Livia produced no children of their own. On Livia in general see Syme (1939, 385–6). In 19 Augustus obtained for Tiberius the rank of ex-praetor and Drusus was allowed to stand for office five years before the normal age (Dio 54.10.4). Marcella was the elder daughter of Octavia and was given in marriage to Agrippa, who divorced her to marry Julia (Suetonius *Aug.* 63.1). Tiberius truly loved Vipsania (who is called Agrippina by Suetonius). After his divorce and enforced marriage to Julia, Tiberius met his former wife and followed her about with tears in his eyes; as a result, he was forbidden to see her ever again (Suetonius *Tib.* 7.2–3).

7 Augustus gathered all power into his own hands, gradually increasing it by stages (*insurgere paulatim*: Tacitus *Ann.* 1.2.1). His policy was governed by location, circumstances and contingencies (Gruen 1996, 194–5) which provoked different responses according to need, but the one consistent theme that Augustus pursued was promotion of himself as world conqueror (Gruen 1990, 396).

8 Augustus had visited all the provinces except Africa and Sardinia (Suetonius *Aug.* 47). He did not develop a 'blueprint for Empire' (Gruen 1990, 396; 1996, 147). Augustus makes it sound as though he secured the Alpine passes single-handed (*RG* 26.3), but in reality the process was long and drawn out and occupied several generals; the task was not completed until 6 BC. Dio (54.22) recounts the harrassments of the Raeti, who exacted tolls on travellers and not infrequently killed them. Strabo (4.205) labels it brigandage when the Salassi exacted like payments but the Romans followed suit when they gained control of the passes (Brunt and Moore 1967, 71). The gradual conquest and absorption of Italy is described by Salmon (1982). For an account of the conquest of

Gaul see Gruen (1996, 179–82). Agrippa sustained great losses in Spain, and even after the campaign of 19 the province was still not totally pacified (Dio 54.11.2–6; Roddaz 1984, 402–10; Gruen 1996, 166).

9 Africa was allocated as a senatorial province in 27 (Dio 53.12.4). On the expedition of Balbus see Gruen (1996, 167 nn.93–4). Balbus found his way into literature via Vergil's *Aeneid* (6.792–5), and Pliny (*NH* 5.35–7) describes his triumph. The Ethiopian campaign was conducted at the command of Augustus and under his auspices (*RG* 26.5). Dio names the Prefect of Egypt who conducted the campaign as Gaius Petronius (54.5.4–6), while Pliny (*NH* 6.181) calls him Publius. The operations were difficult because Petronius could not penetrate beyond Napata, nor could he sustain himself in the desert; the Ethiopian queen Candace attacked his garrisons but was eventually brought to terms in 22; see Strabo (17.1.53–4). Dio (53.26.3) dates the death of Amyntas of Galicia to 25, and describes the partition of some of his territory, the most part being placed under a Roman governor, and parts of Pamphylia being restored to its own district. Agrippa's command in the East was still current (Josephus *AJ* 16.3.3), but he could not be in all places at once; even from the beginning his command entailed sending legates to govern the provinces (Dio 53.26.3).

10 Illyricum became an Imperial province when there was military activity in Pannonia. Dio (54.34.4) dates Tiberius' campaign to 11, though this is not established beyond doubt. The province (which Dio calls Dalmatia) was given to Augustus because it was felt that it would always require a garrison by reason of its internal unrest and the threat posed by the neighbouring Pannonians. Embassies came to Augustus rather than to the Senate; when the Parthians arrived Augustus referred them to the Senate (Dio 53.33.1), but Augustus also received envoys while he was on Samos (Dio 54.9.7) and there were other missions which he may not have reported to the Senate (Dio 53.21.6). In his own words, Augustus says 'fugitives came to me' (*RG* 32) and he may have dealt with the Indian embassies in person without referring them to the Senate (*RG* 31). The inscription concerning the Paphlagonians mentions only Augustus and his family (*OGIS* 532; English translation in Chisholm and Ferguson 1981, 140–1). The army was always crucial to Augustus' regime, and he never relinquished sole command of it (Crook 1996a, 95–6; Lacey 1996; 212–13). Crook (1996b, 126–7) does not subscribe to the idea that a kind of professionalism arose simply because Augustus chose the right man for the task; in fact he chose men not for their proven ability but for their loyalty and availability, except when there was an emergency, as for instance in Africa when generals were sent out who could best deal with the problem. But this somewhat negates Crook's concept of a lack of professionalism, otherwise there would be no suitable soldiers to send when emergencies arose. Accumulated experience surely counts as a kind of professionalism.

11 Apathy and poverty combined to discourage senators from attending meetings (Dio 54.26.3). Penalties were enforced for non-attendance at Senate meetings (Dio 54.18.3) and the quorum had to be reduced for passing decrees (Dio 54.35.1; Crook 1955, 13). The mechanism for levying fines for non-attendance was not new, but Augustus made a point of enforcing fines (Lacey 1996, 217), and increased them later (Dio 5.3.2–3). He fixed two days per month when the Senate should meet, and declared that no other meetings should be scheduled

for those days (Dio 55.3.1). Restructuring the Senate was not something that Augustus himself wished to dwell upon; he described it very laconically with no frills *'Senatum ter legi'* (*RG* 8). Suetonius (*Aug.* 35) describes two *lectiones* together, and conflates some of the details. Augustus' convoluted method of reducing the Senate in 18 is described by Dio (54.13.1 to 14.1). It did not work and some men fought hard to remain in the Senate (Dio 54.14.3); in one instance Augustus had to concede defeat, when he grew angry that Antistius Labeo had recommended that Lepidus should remain a senator. Labeo asked innocently why it should be considered harmful to recommend the man whom Augustus allowed to hold the office of Pontifex Maximus (Dio 54.15.-7–8). The *consilium principis* is described as fully functioning in 27 by Dio (53.21.4), but Crook (1955, 11) assumes that it was established at some point between 27 and 18, because up to 23 Augustus was not in Rome very often and in 18 it is likely that when the social legislation began the *consilium* would have been allowed to play a significant part in discussions. It was not a very practical way of working, and the *consilium* was never intended to perform as an executive body or to be a council of state. It was the overall appearance that was important (Crook 1955, 9). Suetonius (*Aug.* 35.4) says that the *consilium* met to discuss in advance those matters which were to be brought before the full Senate. On occasion Augustus redrafted some of the proposals for legislation when he listened to members of the *consilium*, in which he liked to encourage freedom of speech (Dio 53.21.3–4). In meetings of the full Senate he kept senators on their toes by asking them for their opinions out of turn, on a whim, to make sure that they were paying attention (Suetonius *Aug.* 35.4). Eder (1990, 114–15) quotes and agrees with Brunt (1984, 423–44) that at all times the Senate was made to appear as the 'great organ of the state' during Augustus' reign.

12 Augustus was asked three times to take on the supervision of laws and morals (*RG* 6). Suetonius (*Aug.* 27) says that he took it on permanently, which directly contradicts Augustus himself, and he links it to the census, which must be mistaken. Dio (54.10.5) insists that for a five-year period from 19, Augustus was officially supervisor of morals and also had censorial power. He says that the supervision of morals was extended for another five years in 12 (54.30.1). Brunt and Moore (1967, 45–6) discuss the ramifications of these conflicting pieces of evidence. Augustus states immodestly that he led by example (*RG* 8.5). He carried out the measures that the Senate asked for by virtue of his tribunician power (*RG* 6.2), which enabled him to introduce new legislation; Augustus does not elaborate further upon the legislation, but since the passage comes immediately after the request that he should take on the supervision of morals it describes the social laws of 18/17. Brunt and Moore (1967, 46–7) suspect that Augustus was not quite truthful when he puts the onus on the Senate for the moral and social legislation. In order to demonstrate the need for increase in the population of Roman citizens, and to underline the fact that it was not necessarily revolutionary, Augustus read out in the Senate the speech of Quintus Metellus 'On increasing the progeny' (Suetonius *Aug.* 89.2).

13 It would have been helpful if Augustus had introduced his legislation under the title *Leges Augustae*, but he chose his family name, as was strictly correct. The possibility that there was an attempt to introduce social legislation before 18, possibly even before 23 (Crook 1996a, 92–3) derives from a reading of

Propertius (1.8.21, 2.7.1–3), and Dio (53.13.1–2); Rice-Holmes (1931, 42) believed that the legislation was enacted but then was repealed very quickly. More recently doubt has been cast on the idea that there was a moral and social programme before 18. On the definition of social orders, and the establishment of clear boundaries between Romans and non-Romans, see Eder (1990, 117) and Nicolet (1984, 98). Dio's description of social classes encapsulates to a large extent the opinions of his own day on social orders, but there is no reason to doubt Augustus' advice to Tiberius (56.33.3) to limit the number of manumissions of slaves, and always to preserve the distinctions between themselves and their subjects. Augustus raised the census qualification for entry to the Senate to 1,000,000 sesterces, and that of the equestrians to 400,000 sesterces, which would help to preserve the distinctions and the hierarchy (Nicolet 1984, 92). Poverty by itself was not necessarily seen as a bar to entry to the Senate. Augustus gave money to deserving men (Nicolet 1984, 95). Dio (52.19.2) makes Maecenas advise Augustus not to eject men from the Senate simply because of lack of money. The census figures are given by Augustus for 28 (4,063,000 citizens); for 8 (4,233,000); and for AD 14 (4,937,000) (RG 8). Carter (1982, 143–4) attempts to distinguish the clauses of the Lex Julia de maritandis ordinibus and the Lex Papia Poppaea, pointing out that the legislation was aimed primarily at the upper classes, those with money or those who were eligible for office. Suetonius (Aug. 34) relates how the equestrians voiced their objections to the marriage laws. A recent in-depth study of the legislation concerning marriage and adultery is by Mette-Dittman (1991). Dio (56.10.3) comments on the two consuls who were neither of them married, promoting the amendments and additions to the marriage laws.

14 On the independence of women see Syme (1939, 445) and CAH X (1934, 445). Dio (54.16.3–5) records Augustus' poor showing when challenged directly on the problem of how to control women; see also Lacey (1996, 188). The marriage and adultery laws were probably in force by 17 (CIL VI 32323, line 57; Horace Carmen Saeculare line 45).

15 Suetonius (Aug. 34) describes the opposition of the equites to the marriage laws, which they expressed by demonstrating at the theatres. The equestrians as a class were monitored, as Suetonius explains (Aug. 38–9) and Augustus rejected men whose conduct was scandalous, allegedly after asking each of them to render an account of his life. Social mobility was not denied to equestrians who provided new blood for the Senate when they were adlected to it (Nicolet 1984, 103–4). On equestrians in general see also Carter (1982, 151–2) and Brunt and Moore (1967, 56–7).

16 The date of the Lex Junia is disputed. Duff (1958, 210–14) narrowed its authorship down to two consuls named Junius who held office in 25 and 17, the former while Augustus was in Spain, and the latter when Augustus was in Rome, which seems to pinpoint the date. See also CAH X (1934, 431 n. 1, 888, n. 9). The Junian Latins are mentioned in later laws (Gaius Institutes 1.17.2.29, 2.195, 3.56; Ulpian 20.14); see also Tacitus (Ann. 13.27). Suetonius (Aug. 74) records the fact that Augustus never invited an ex-slave to dinner. Dio (54.23), among others, tells the story of the slave of Vedius Pollio who broke the cup; he is corroborated by several other authors (Seneca de Ira 3.40.1–4; de Clem. 1.18; Pliny NH 9.23.39, 9.53.78; Tacitus Ann. 1.10, 12.60).

17 Velleius (2.89.3) says that Augustus increased the number of praetors from eight to ten. Julius Caesar attempted to regulate the numbers of those in receipt of the corn dole, and used novel ways of enumerating them (Suetonius *Iul.* 41.3). The date of Turranius' appointment as *Praefectus Annonae* is not established; Rickman (1980, 48, 63–4) places it late in Augustus' reign at some point between AD 8 and 14. See also Velleius (2.94.3), Tacitus (*Ann.* 1.7), Suetonius (*Tib.* 8). By the year 2, despite Caesar's and Augustus' attempts to limit the numbers of recipients, the corn dole had to stretch to feed over 200,000 people (*RG* 15.4). Augustus boasted that he had found a city of brick and left one of marble (Suetonius *Aug.* 28.3). In the *Res Gestae* (22.2) Augustus records with lapidary restraint the celebration of the Secular Games, listed along with the other games and shows that he gave. At the end of his reign their importance may have declined, but at the time he would have felt much more satisfaction; as Brunt and Moore (1967, 64–5) point out, he was celebrating nothing less than the return of the standards captured by the Parthians, the peace and prosperity of the Roman world, the restoration of the old Roman morals and customs, and the revival of religion. The prayers invoking the help of the gods 'for me, my family, and my household' (*mihi, domo, familiae*) are recorded on an inscription (*ILS* 5050); for translation see Sherk (1988, no. 11). On the Secular Games see also Lacey (1996, 182–3); Ehrenberg and Jones (1976, 30–3).

18 Dio (54.15.1) recounts the plots against Augustus and Agrippa, which he says began in 17, when 'many immediately and many later were accused, whether truly or falsely'. On the consuls for 16 see Syme (1986, 53–63) and Crook (1996a, 94). Statilius Taurus was put in charge of the city, together with the rest of Italy (Dio 54.19.6), which probably means that he was appointed city prefect, though it is not certain that he held exactly the same post as the later city prefects. See also Tacitus (*Ann.* 6.11). Jones (1968, 14) points out that Augustus would require consular power to make this appointment. Dio (54.19.1–2) says that Augustus was unpopular in Rome after the social legislation, and compares him to the ancient Greek Solon. Dio insists that the troubles in Gaul were merely used by Augustus as an excuse, which would seem to indicate that the so-called Lollian disaster was not as serious as all that; in a later passage (54.20.5–6) he says that Augustus hurried to the scene but found that there was nothing to do, and indeed the disaster theory is now played down since Lollius seems to have suffered from a bad press, being an enemy of Tiberius; see Syme (1986, 402 n. 116), where the events are dated possibly to 16, not 17. Suetonius (*Aug.* 23.1) calls the affair a disaster (*clades*); see also Velleius (2.97.1). Augustus remained in Gaul for three years, which time (according to Wells 1972, 95) he spent in making preparations for the campaigns across the Rhine in 12. He conducted a census and regulated taxes in Gaul (Crook 1996a, 96); Dio simply describes how Augustus occupied these years on 'arranging other matters' (54.21.1).

19 Augustus paid cash for lands in Italy and the provinces for the settlement of veterans in 30 and in 14 and gives the combined totals for the two settlements (*RG* 16.1). The equation of the two settlements and the later establishment in 13 of the fixed term of service of sixteen years for legionaries (Dio 54.25.6) indicates that the veterans of 14 had probably enlisted after Actium to fill gaps

in the ranks; see Brunt and Moore (1967, 42–3). Settlements and the creation of colonies had never ceased altogether; in 26–25, and again in 19, colonies were established in Spain, and in 21 in Sicily. Elsewhere (*RG* 3.3) Augustus enumerates the numbers of men settled by him at 300,000, who either received lands or cash payments. The Italians who constituted a large part of the legionaries were expecting land grants, and were upset by Augustus' new arrangements in 13 when he instituted cash pensions (Keppie 1983, 82, 208).

20 Dio could not give a specific account of Augustus' activities from 16 to 13 and merely describes how he made colonies in Gaul and Spain (54.23.7), gave money to certain areas, and received money from others (54.25.1). Agrippa in the East earned great credit for his settlement of the rebellious factions in the Bosporus (54.24.4–8). He declined the triumph that was voted to him, in Dio's opinion because none of his peers was allowed to triumph (54.24.8). Agrippa was granted tribunician power in 13, and then sent to Pannonia, where a rebellion had broken out in 14, receiving scant mention by Dio (54.24.3). In the winter of 13/12 Agrippa set out for the area, with powers greater than those normally enjoyed by officials outside Italy (Dio 54.28.1), an ambiguous statement which has caused great debate as to whether Agrippa now held *imperium maius* for the first time, or indeed at all. See above, pp. 237–9 for references.

21 Tiberius as consul presided over the celebrations for Augustus' homecoming (Dio 54.27.1); Augustus rebuked both him and Gaius for the applause that had greeted the boy's appearance at the festivities. The Theatre of Marcellus was dedicated in 13 (Dio 54.26.1). Augustus liked to pretend that his promotion of the various members of his family kept to the rules, and he always added 'If they be worthy' after asking for posts for them (Suetonius *Aug.* 56.2). The Ara Pacis Augustae has been discussed by many authors, notably Toynbee (1953, 1961), Zanker (1988) and Galinsky (1996) to name but three. It was dedicated in 9, and is described more fully in this book in its chronological context.

22 When Lepidus died in 12 Augustus became Pontifex Maximus in his place and made part of his house public so as to conform to the regulations (Dio 54.27.2–3). In the *Res Gestae* (10) Augustus contrasts his election by popular acclaim (modestly describing how the crowds that turned out were unprecedented) with Lepidus' usurpation of the office. In the same year, Agrippa died, of causes unknown. Dio (54.29) gives a résumé of all his sterling qualities and his importance to Augustus. Crook (1996a, 97 n. 139) follows Syme in speculating that there was a plague at this time. If so, it is probable that both Lepidus and Agrippa fell victim to it, since neither of them were old men.

7 PROFIT AND LOSS

1 Dio (54.28–9) relates Agrippa's death, and in a short 'obituary' he lists all his fine qualities. The funeral oration is given in the original Greek in *EJ*² 366, and in translation in Sherk (1988, no. 12). Dio reports that senators were reluctant to attend the funeral ceremonies (54.29.6); see also Kienast (1982, 103; Wiseman 1971, 104). Five years later funeral games were held in honour of Agrippa (Dio 55.8).

2 Augustus distributed 400 sesterces to the people in Agrippa's name (Dio 54.29.4). The choice of Tiberius as the successor is debated. Dio says that Augustus chose him reluctantly (54.31.2), and Tacitus (*Ann.* 2.41.3) indicates that Drusus was the more popular of the two brothers, enjoying the favour of the people (*favor vulgi*), but with his usual twist Tacitus merely uses the popularity of Drusus to illustrate the fact that the favour of the populace was not a guarantee of success. On balance it seems more likely that Tiberius was the first choice for successor all along, and that Augustus always intended to promote him. Levick (1972, 780–6) argues that advancement of Tiberius was part of Augustus' consistent plans for the succession. She agrees with Kornemann's proposal (1930) that Augustus kept within the Republican principles of collegiality, and that to ensure that the government of the Empire continued without a pause Augustus intended that there should be three pairs of *principes* from three generations, in the first rank Augustus and Agrippa, then Tiberius and Drusus, and after them Gaius and Lucius (Levick 1966; 1972, 782–3 n. 4). Kienast (1982, 107 n. 162) does not subscribe to Kornemann's theory, but none the less agrees that Tiberius was Augustus' chosen successor, and not simply a kind of Regent who would hold the reins of government until Gaius and Lucius grew up. See also Corbett (1974).

3 According to Velleius (2.96) Agrippa's death brought Tiberius and Augustus closer, since Tiberius married Augustus' daughter. Velleius' readers would know very well what was the outcome of the marriage, so he concentrated on the positive aspects, but it may not have been so preposterous a statement that Augustus and Tiberius were on good terms in 12–11. It was well known that Tiberius did not want to divorce his wife Vipsania (Suetonius *Tib.* 7.2; Dio 54.31.2). Suetonius tells us that the marriage to Julia was at first reasonably harmonious, but, after the death in infancy of their only child, Tiberius and Julia grew apart (Suetonius *Tib.* 7.3). Sattler (1969, 494–502) discusses the political implications of the marriage and the possible role of Livia in bringing it about. Tiberius subdued the tribes of Illyricum, and the province was returned to Augustus because it was continually restless and it was close to the Pannonian theatre of war (Dio 53.34.4). Syme outlined the importance of Illyricum as the province which bound the Empire together (*CAH*[1] X, 355). The Pannonian campaign and the Rhine offensive can be seen as a joint venture, the strategic conception of Augustus himself (Kienast 1982, 303). Augustus gives Tiberius the credit for the victories in Pannonia but insists that he himself brought the province into the Empire (*RG* 30). For his achievements in Pannonia, Tiberius was acclaimed Imperator by the soldiers (Dio 54.33.5); he was also voted a triumph by the Senate, but Augustus did not allow him to celebrate it, granting him triumphal honours instead (Dio 54.31.4). Drusus was acclaimed by the soldiers in Germany in 11, but Augustus did not allow him to call himself Imperator; he added the two Imperatorial salutations to the total of his own titles on account of the victories of Tiberius and Drusus (Dio 54.33.5). The brothers were not fighting as independent commanders, but under the auspices of Augustus (Brunt and Moore 1967, 73; Kienast 1982, 108 n. 165). Tiberius was *Imperator iterum* by 8 (*ILS* 95); eventually he was to share the title with Augustus seven times (Brunt and Moore 1967, 47). Suetonius says that Tiberius was the first to

receive the new honour of *ornamenta triumphalia*, 'never before granted to anybody else' (*Tib.* 9.2).

4 The marriage of Tiberius and Julia took place in 11 according to Dio (54.35.4), and in the same year Octavia died (54.35.4–5). For the third time in 11 Augustus was asked to take on the *cura morum* (*RG* 6.1; Brunt and Moore 1967, 45–6). Dio adds confusion to the problem by his insistence that Augustus was made supervisor of morals for a second five-year term in 12 (54.30.1), then he says that he conducted a census in 11 (54.35.1), and also drew up a list of the Senate. This renews the debate about whether Augustus held censorial power, or was granted it for specific purposes. Crook (1996a, 97) thinks that Dio mangled the facts, and that Augustus revised the Senate by dint of *censoria potestas* granted to him temporarily for that specific purpose. Augustus had given some thought to the Senate and 'wanted it to function properly' (Talbert 1984, 222). He reduced the quorum for passing decrees to less than 400 (Dio 54.35.1) and later fixed the days for meetings at two per month (Dio 55.3.1–2).

5 While Tiberius campaigned, Augustus stayed in Gallia Lugdunensis, keeping a watch on the Gauls (Dio 54.36.3–4). The Ara Pacis Augustae has a considerable bibliography of its own, covering the artistic, social, religious and political aspects (Toynbee 1953, 1961; Zanker 1988; Elsner 1991; Galinsky 1996). There is little doubt about the identification of the main participants in the processions; Augustus is clearly depicted, resembling the numerous portraits of him, but the identification of many of the people on the friezes is contested. There is controversy about some of the children portrayed on the friezes; for instance, the identification of two small boys, commonly labelled Gaius and Lucius, has been contested because in 9 when the altar was dedicated they were older than the infants depicted in the procession; see also R. Syme, 'Neglected children on the Ara Pacis', *American Journal of Archaeology* 88, 1984, 583–9. Elsner (1991, 60–1) argues that not even contemporaries would be able to identify all the figures; Crook (1996a, 96) disagrees. Zanker (1988, 121) points out that it was the Senate which commissioned the monument, and the principle concern would be to ensure that the priests in the processions were depicted in the correct classifications, so that the correct portrayal of the actual persons took second place. The *solarium Augusti* may have been dedicated in 9, at the same time as the Ara Pacis (Bowersock 1990, 384), but Zanker (1988, 144) dates it to the previous year. The processions depicted on the altar may have been fictional; Bowersock (1990, 392) dates them to 12, but is forced to speculate that Agrippa returned to Rome before he died in Campania.

6 Drusus' campaigns in Germany receive brief mention by Velleius (2.97.2–4) and Dio (55.1–2). Florus (2.30.26) writes of fort building on the Rhine. Despite extensive archaeological excavation and research, which has identified many sites as Augustan or Tiberian in origin, modern authors are hampered by lack of precise dating materials. Wells (1972, 246–8) attempts a classification of forts into two groups, legionary bases and auxiliary forts, and then assigns them to known campaigns by date. The Roman forts along the river Lippe constituted an important line of penetration into Germany, and have been studied by H. von Schnürbein (1981). Schönberger discusses the Augustan campaigns in general (1985, 324–44) and provides a catalogue of sites (ibid. 425–38; and see his map A). He includes marching camps in his list, since more and more

of these camps are coming to light in Germany. The death of Drusus is reported by Suetonius (*Claud.* 1.3), Dio (55.1.4), and Velleius (2.97.3). After his death Drusus' family was honoured with the name Germanicus (Dio 55.2.3). Suetonius (*Tib.* 50.1) illustrates Tiberius' supposed hatred for his brother by the tale that he showed to Augustus the letter discussing the restoration of the Republic. In another passage (*Claud.* 1.4) Suetonius repeats but personally discounts the story that Augustus was suspicious of Drusus. Tiberius was allowed to share the title Imperator with Augustus (Dio 55.6.5). The relaxation of Augustus' personal guidelines on this issue suggests that perhaps Tiberius had special status while fighting under the auspices of Augustus, or much more likely that Augustus had granted him a command of his own, though it has to be admitted that there is no record of Tiberius having been given an independent *imperium* (Brunt and Moore 1967, 73).

7 Augustus returned to Rome in 8, and accepted the renewal of supreme power with reluctance (Dio 55.5.2, 6.1). Tiberius was to be consul in 7, which Dio records (55.6.5) along with the other honours accorded to him in 8. The census was conducted by Augustus alone by dint of his consular power (*solus consulari imperio*) (*RG* 8.3). Augustus gives no hint as to the permanence or otherwise of his consular power, nor of any grant, presumably temporary, of censorial power to enable him to carry out the census (Brunt and Moore 1967, 45–6). Strengthening the banks of the Tiber, attested by inscriptions (*ILS* 5293 a–d) was an intermediate measure; in Tiberius' reign a special board was set up to take charge of the river banks. The charge of bribery and corruption in the elections did not seem to concern Augustus very deeply; he simply made candidates put up a deposit (Dio 55.5.3). He also extended the *pomerium* (Dio 55.6.6).

8 The death of Maecenas and the anecdotes about him are related by Dio (55.7.1). He had been ill for some three years before his death (Kienast 1982, 106 n. 153; Seneca *de Benef.* 6.32.2).

9 Velleius (2.97.4) makes Tiberius into a hero in his campaigns in Germany, but has to admit that the end result was not quite so positive; the territory was *almost* made into a tax-paying province (*paene stipendiariae redigeret provinciae*). Gruen (1990, 406) points out that Germany had been invaded but was nowhere near properly subdued. Dio (55.6.3) recounts the intransigence of the Sugambri and Augustus' treatment of them. In 7, he dismisses Germany where 'nothing worthy of note happened' (55.9.1). At the beginning of the year Tiberius held his triumph, and entered upon his second consulship. He undertook the restoration of the Temple of Concord (Dio 55.8.1). After the serious fire in Rome in 7, Augustus divided the city into fourteen regions (Dio 55.8.6–7). The officials (*vicomagistri*) in charge of the regions were usually freedmen (*CAH*[1], 199).

10 Tiberius was recalled briefly to Germany, so Gaius presided over the celebrations for Augustus' return to Rome (Dio 55.8.3). Then there were the funeral games in honour of Agrippa, where everyone except Augustus wore black, including Gaius and Lucius (Dio 55.6.5). The election of Gaius to the consulship supposedly displeased Augustus (Dio 55.9.2–4), but Tacitus accuses him of wanting the office for Gaius (*Ann.* 1.3) even though he deferred it for several years until the boy reached the age of 20.

11 The withdrawal of Tiberius will probably never be explained. Levick (1972, 790) and Kienast (1982, 109) argue that Tiberius retired because of hurt pride.

Dio (55.9.4–6) says that Augustus granted tribunician power to Tiberius in order to bring Gaius and Lucius to their senses, which had the opposite effect in that it made them jealous and therefore enemies of their stepfather. Velleius (2.99.1–2) insists that Tiberius was full of consideration for Augustus, and left Rome so as not stand in the way of Gaius and Lucius, but of course he also needed rest from his labours in the strenuous German campaigns. Suetonius says (*Tib.* 10.2) that the need for rest was the excuse that Tiberius gave out at the time of his withdrawal, but he changed his mind later on and said that he had retired because he wanted to avoid rivalry with his stepsons (*Tib.* 11.5). Dio disbelieves the story that he left on account of his quarrels with Julia (55.9.7), whereas Velleius (2.100.3–5) lays the blame squarely on Julia, listing her adulterous companions for good measure. Suetonius (*Tib.* 10.1) treats his readers to the whole catalogue of possible reasons for Tiberius' withdrawal, without deciding firmly upon any single cause. He adds another possible factor, that Tiberius wished to underline his prestige by absenting himself, to let the world see how it survived without him. Dio (55.9.7) confuses the issue when he says that Tiberius was annoyed because he had not been designated Caesar, but this is meaningless in the context of the first century (Levick 1972, 782). Sattler (1969, 511) suggests that Tiberius wanted full adoption as Augustus' son, but as Levick points out this would not have been possible 'while Julia remained unemancipated' and it would still merely place Tiberius on an equal footing with Gaius and Lucius (1972, 782 n. 2). Determined to leave, Tiberius refused food for four days (Suetonius *Tib.* 10.2), and when he did leave he took a very small retinue (Dio 55.9.5). He was granted the title and presumably the status of *legatus* when Livia interceded for him (Suetonius *Tib.* 12.1).

12 Tigranes II, king of Armenia, died or was murdered in 7 (Gruen 1996, 160). Dio says that Tiberius was assigned to Armenia (55.9.4), but Gruen accuses Tiberius of failure to fulfil his mission. Tigranes III, son of Tigranes II, was suspected of sympathy with the Parthians (Kienast 1982, 285); he sent gifts to Augustus when Gaius led his expedition to the East (Dio 55.10.20–1). Augustus (*RG* 27.2) says that he subdued the rebellious Armenians through the agency of his son Gaius, giving the kingdom to Artabazus, then to Artavasdes, then to Tigranes. Velleius (2.100.1) merely notes that the Parthians laid hold of Armenia, without giving specific dates or any further details. The statement is made in the context of the world-wide influence that Tiberius wielded, and the dire effects caused by his absence in that the world fell apart because he was not on hand to stop it. Unfortunately, Velleius unconsciously lends support to those who accuse Tiberius of doing nothing to stop the Parthians laying hold of Armenia. The visits of the provincial governors to Rhodes are recorded by Velleius (2.99.4) and Suetonius (*Tib.* 12.2). Levick (1972, 801–9) examined the known personnel who governed the provinces surrounding Rhodes, and Bowersock (1984, 176–9) points out that Tiberius had many clients in the East. Both Dio (55.10.18–19) and Velleius (2.101.1) describe the Eastern expedition of Gaius; Dio says that there was fear in Rome that there would be a war (55.10a.3), but Gaius eventually brought the Parthians to terms when Phraates renounced interest in Armenia; the two of them met on an island in the Euphrates and then entertained each other to dinner (Dio 55.10a.4–5; Vell. 2.101.2–3).

13 A citizen of Nemausus offered to bring the head of 'the exile' to Gaius, according to Suetonius (*Tib.* 13.1). The rivalry between Tiberius and Gaius is recorded by Dio (55.9.5) and Suetonius (*Tib.* 11.5, 12.1). Tiberius' enemy Lollius, whose Rhine disaster may have been exaggerated in importance, was now Gaius' adviser (Vell. 2.102.1). Levick (1972, 810–12) examines the nature of the quarrel, concluding that Tiberius was in real danger and feared for his life.

14 Augustus was consul in 5, and having introduced Gaius into public life he made him *princeps iuventutis* (Dio 55.9.9). Lucius received the same honours when his turn came; Dio says after the lapse of a year, which in the extant text implies the year after Gaius, but it was in reality three years. Presumably the intervening text has been lost (Dio 55.9.20). In the *Res Gestae* (14) Augustus records that Gaius and Lucius were designated consuls when they reached the age of 14 by the Senate and people, with the provision that they took up office after a five-year interval. The suffect consulship was not a completely new idea, but it became common after 5, and provided more men with administrative experience (Kienast 1982, 110; Talbert 1984, 21). Augustus relates the several occasions when he settled veterans and how he paid them cash pensions out of his own funds (*RG* 16.2).

15 The corn dole was limited to 200,000 recipients in 2 (Dio 55.10.1; Rickman 1980, 62–3). Augustus gave the plebs who received the corn dole 60 denarii apiece in his third consulship; they numbered a few more than 200,000 (*RG* 14.4). Suetonius (*Aug.* 40.2) gives details without the benefit of dates about Augustus' plan to introduce three annual distributions of corn, each of four months' supply. The Temple of Mars Ultor was finally dedicated in the same year (Dio 55.10.2), but Dio's narrative is fragmentary at this point so there are few details. At the beginning of the year, on 5 February 2, the people and the Senate voted the title *pater patriae* to Augustus (Suetonius *Aug.* 58.2; *RG* 35). It was the highest honour that any Roman could receive, and Augustus significantly rounds off the *Res Gestae* with the honour (Brunt and Moore 1967, 5, 80), but it was not a political statement (Crook 1996a, 102). When the news about Julia's behaviour was made known to him, Augustus gave way to an outburst of rage in the Senate, and said later that if Agrippa or Maecenas had been alive they would have prevented him from doing so (Seneca *de Benef.* 6.32.3). The scandal involved several men who were executed, including Iullus Antonius, the son of Marcus Antonius (Dio 55.12.10–16; Tacitus *Ann.* 4.13.3, 44.3, 44.5). Some were spared but exiled instead. The Praetorian Guard had been in existence for some time before Augustus gave them two commanders, probably in 2. He adapted Republican forms in creating his bodyguard (Durry 1938, 67), but it is not known how it was commanded before the creation of the first two Prefects, the equestrians P. Ostorius Scapula and P. Satrius Aper. Collegiality can be seen as a safeguard against corruption and plotting (Durry 1938, 158). The Prefects probably accompanied Augustus into the Senate; the machinations of Sejanus seems to have put an end to the practice, but according to Dio (60.23) Claudius revived it, which indicates that Augustus had instituted it (Durry 1938, 177). Purcell (1996, 793) points out that Augustus made available to the magistrates more personnel for the policing of Rome. It is possible that in 2 Augustus decided to widen the scope of the Praetorians, enabling them to provide security for the city as well as himself.

16 Gaius' expedition to the East and his campaigns are recounted by Dio (55.10.16–19) and Velleius (2.101). Augustus relied on the two boys to take the burden from him, as reported in the letter that he wrote to Gaius (Gellius *Attic Nights* 15.7.3; Crook 1996a, 104 n. 71). Lucius died on the way to Spain (Dio 55.10.9). In AD 3 Augustus' powers were renewed; Dio (55.12.2) says that he mellowed in his old age, and forbade people to call him master (*dominus*). Gaius' wound seems to have unhinged him; his retirement was followed soon after by his death (Dio 55.10.9). Tiberius was finally adopted on 24 June AD 4 (Dio 55.13.2), which Velleius calls a day of good omen (2.103.3–5). Agrippa Postumus was adopted by Augustus as well as Tiberius 'for reasons of state' (Vell. 2.104.1). In turn Tiberius was to adopt Germanicus, the son of his brother Drusus, alongside his own son (Dio 5.13.2). Syme (1986, 93–4) opts for Germanicus as the main heir, and suggests that Tiberus was merely slotted into the scheme as a convenience. It is true, as Syme points out, that Germanicus was advanced much more rapidly than Agrippa Postumus or Tiberius' own son Drusus, but this does not necessarily detract from Tiberius' own position, which could still have been second to Augustus. Tacitus implies (*Ann.* 1.3) that everything revolved around Tiberius: '*Nero solus e privignis erat, illuc cuncta vergere.*'

8 FINALE

1 Augustus adopted Tiberius and Agrippa Postumus for reasons of state (Vell. 2.104.1). Dio (55.13.1a) links the adoption with the immediate need for a commander in the German war. Mutual distrust between Augustus and Tiberius is taken as read in the ancient sources; for instance Dio (55.27.5) relates how Tiberius returned frequently to Rome in case Augustus should prefer someone else during his absence.

2 As he aged and became more infirm, Augustus adapted himself and made different arrangements for some of the administrative functions. He gave up appearing at the courts, but instead heard cases from a tribunal within the palace, and he also appointed three senators to receive embassies (Dio 55.33.5). At a later date he tried to prevent too many audiences with well-wishers and ceased to attend public banquets (Dio 56.26.2–3). In the *Res Gestae* (8.2) Augustus mentions Agrippa only as a consular colleague; Tiberius receives the same acknowledgement (*RG* 8.4) and also is described as *legatus meus* (*RG* 30.1) in the Pannonian wars. Tiberius' campaigns in Germany from AD 4 to 6 receive full treatment in Velleius' narrative (2.104.3 to 105.3), which is laudatory and biased, but Velleius was the best qualified to write about the campaigns because he took part in them. Dio is perhaps more realistic (55.28.5) in that the end result was negligible.

3 Syme (1986, 266) points out that Cinna cannot have done anything very serious if he was rewarded with the consulship in the next year. Crook (1996a, 105 n. 182) dismisses the Cinna conspiracy as a moral fiction. Seneca (*de Clem.* 1.9) uses the tale as an illustration of merciful treatment, and Dio (55.14.1) mentions it as the preface to a long dialogue between Livia and Augustus about the problems of monarchical rule. Augustus purged the Senate by means of three senators chosen by lot from an initial panel of ten (Dio 55.13.3) and he took

a census of Italians worth 200,000 sesterces (Dio 55.13.5–6). The details of the *Lex Aelia Sentia* are set out by Carter (1982, 154–5) and in *CAH* II, 895–6.

4 Dio (55.22.3) records floods and famine in Rome, and the discontent beginning to make itself felt among the soldiers (55.23.1). In AD 6 the slaves and gladiators who were for sale were sent 100 miles from Rome (Dio 55.26.1). Suetonius (*Aug.* 42.3) corroborates this story, and adds the note that Augustus left written testimony to the fact that he once considered abolishing the corn dole, but never did so because it would open up avenues to those who wanted speedy popularity. The development of the food supply under Augustus is documented by Rickman (1980, 63–4). In AD 7, according to Dio (55.31.4), Augustus appointed two ex-consuls to take charge of the distribution of the corn; the first *praefectus annonae* was C. Turranius (Tacitus *Ann.* 1.7).

5 The pension scheme for the veterans is described by Dio (55.25): Augustus accepted contributions from cities but not from private individuals (55.25.3); he ordered the senators to think of an alternative plan, but that was to persuade them to adopt his own (55.25.4); the 5 per cent inheritance tax was one of the schemes outlined in Caesar's memoranda (55.25.6). There was also a 1 per cent tax on goods sold at auction; Dio (55.25.9) seems to think that the two taxes went towards paying the soldiers' wages as well, but Brunt and Moore (1967, 60) argue that this was not so. Augustus founded the *aerarium militare* with a huge injection of cash (170 million sesterces) from his own funds (*RG* 17.2).

6 A serious fire destroyed parts of Rome in AD 6 (Dio 55.26.4–5). The *vigiles* were established as fire-fighters in AD 6; they certainly went on night patrols and had some policing functions, but it is not certain to what extent they could intervene to preserve law and order. The juridical competence of their commander provides a clue; they could arrest runaway slaves and oversee building regulations (Nippel 1995, 96–7). Augustus appointed all the magistrates in AD 8, to avoid faction (Dio 55.34.3), and compelled ex-quaestors to put themselves forward for election as aediles (Dio 55.25.1).

7 Agrippa Postumus was said to be surly and to possess a violent temper (Suetonius *Aug.* 65; Dio 55.32.1–2). Raaflaub and Samons (1990, 431) conclude that the affair was just a palace revolution which had gone wrong, and reject the ideas of those who link the exile of Agrippa and Julia with larger plots; see B. Levick, 'Abdication and Agrippa Postumus', *Historia* 21 1972, 674–97. Kienast (1982, 119) blames the unrest caused by the food shortages for the outbreak of attempted rebellion, centring on Agrippa Postumus. Suetonius indicates (*Aug.* 51.1) that a certain Junius Novatus had circulated a most scathing letter about Augustus in the name of the young Agrippa (*Agrippae iuvenis nomine*). The ambiguity is probably not the fault of Suetonius; it may have been just as ambiguous in Augustus' day as it is now. It is thus not clear whether Agrippa had authorised the letter. It is quite possible that Novatus was entirely responsible and the unfortunate Agrippa need not have had anything to do with it. Suetonius also says (*Aug.* 19.1) that Audasius (appropriately named!) and Epicadus planned to take Augustus' daughter Julia and his grandson Agrippa from their islands, but the elder Julia had by this time been allowed to come back to the mainland, still banished from Rome, but no longer on her island. It is thought that there may have been an error, in that Suetonius should have said granddaughter,

meaning the younger Julia; see also B. Levick, 'The fall of the younger Julia', *Latomus* 35, 1976. 307–9. Julia's husband L. Aemilius Paullus was exiled but survived (Syme 1986, 115–27); Decimus Iunius Silanus, her lover, was exiled but allowed back home by Tiberius (Tacitus *Ann.* 3.24, 4.71). The exile of Ovid is generally considered to have occurred in AD 8, and to have been connected in some way with the exile of the younger Julia, though the date had been disputed, and some authorities have linked Ovid with the scandals of 2 when the elder Julia was banished. Syme (1986, 121–2) opts for some involvement with Julia and her husband L. Aemilius Paullus; the double crime that Ovid writes of concerns the publication of his *Ars Amatoria*, and the 'error', according to Syme, meant that Ovid had been foolish, not a criminal: 'He had been a witness to some misdemeanour or other' (ibid. 412).

8 The raids of the Isaurians and the rebellion of the Gaetulians are mentioned by Dio (55.28.3). The pirates had descended on Sardinia, which required troops under an equestrian commander (Dio 55.28.1). The Pannonian revolt broke out when troops were levied for the German war, and they could see their own strength (Dio 55.29.3). It was feared that the tribesmen would invade Italy (Dio 55.30.1), which led to hurried recruitment in Italy; but Augustus did not think that Tiberius was fighting vigorously enough (Dio 55.31.1). Augustus went to Ariminum to be closer to the war zone (Dio 55.34.3). At one point Tiberius' supply lines were cut while he besieged Salonae (Dio 56.12). After the revolt was put down after years of fighting, the rewards extended to Tiberius and Augustus, who were both hailed as Imperator, and allowed to triumph, and to Germanicus and Drusus, whose rewards were scaled down to suitable levels; Germanicus was awarded *ornamenta triumphalia* and allowed to stand for the consulship before the proper age; Drusus was allowed to attend Senate meetings and vote ahead of the ex-praetors as soon as he became quaestor (Dio 56.17.1–3). Meanwhile in Germany, the legions had been wiped out under Varus; Dio (56.18 to 56.22) describes at length the plight of the Romans, and lays the blame squarely upon Varus, who would not listen to his advisers. This is perhaps unfair; Varus was not a military man and his task was to Romanise an area that was thought to be pacified. The error in judgement was not his alone.

9 The battle site is now thought to have been near and around Kalkriese; see Edward Manking (ed.), *Kalkriese: Ort der Varusschlacht*, Regensburg: Verlag Schnell und Steiner GMBH (English edition) 1994; D. Timpe, 'Geographische Faktoren und politische Entscheidungen in der Geschichte der Varuszeit', in Wiegels and Woesler 1995, 13–28; W. Schlüter, 'Neue Erkentnisse zur Örtlichkeit der Varusschlacht: die archäologischen Untersuchungen in der Kalkrieses-Niewedder Senke in Vorland des Wiehengebirges', in Wiegels and Woesler 1995, 67–96. Augustus dismissed his German bodyguard because he considered the men untrustworthy (Dio 56.23); see M.P. Speidel, *Riding for Caesar: the Equites Singulari Augusti*, Batsford 1995. The news from Germany was not as bad as had first been suspected; the tribesmen had made no dash across the Rhine (Dio 56.24). After mopping up, Tiberius and Germanicus watched the Germans for the next two years, AD 10 and 11 (Dio 56.24.6 to 56.25.1), though Germanicus found time to come back to Rome and make a name for himself in the law courts. Suetonius reports (*Aug.* 23.2) that Augustus used to shout 'Quinctilius Varus, give me back my legions!' The losses were

XVII, XVIII and XIX, which were never reconstituted (Watson 1969, 23). Augustus wrote in the *Res Gestae* (26.1) that he pacified Germany to the mouth of the Elbe, passing over in silence the losses of AD 9. As Jones remarks (1970, 77) earlier versions of the *Res Gestae* would probably have stated 'I pacified Germany to the Elbe' omitting 'to the mouth of', but this begs the question of Augustus' intentions towards Germany. The end of expansion of the Empire did not occur until much later, but Augustus instructed Tiberius not to expand any further (Tacitus *Ann.* 1.11; Dio 56.33); see also J. Ober, 'Tiberius and the political testament of Augustus', *Historia* 31, 1982, 306–28; T. Cornell, 'The end of Roman Imperial expansion', in J. Rich and G. Shipley, *War and Society in the Roman World*, London: Routledge 1993, 139–70.

10 Drusus was quaestor in AD 11 (Dio 56.25.4) and Germanicus was consul in the following year (Dio 56.26.1). The renewal of Augustus' powers was accepted by him with reluctance; Tiberius received *tribunicia potestas* and Drusus was permitted to stand for the consulship two years later (in AD 15) without having been praetor (Dio 56.28.1). Velleius maintains that Tiberius' powers were equal to those of Augustus (2.121.1); Suetonius (*Tib.* 21.1) says that the consuls had passed a law that he should govern the provinces jointly with Augustus and conduct the census with him. The *consilium* was reformed in AD 13, ostensibly because Augustus was too old to attend the meetings of the Senate (Dio 56.28.2–3). Crook (1955, 14–15) assumed that Augustus was aware that Tiberius 'had not the temperament to guide successfully a purely senatorial probouleutic body of the old kind'. When discontent arose with the inheritance tax, Augustus offered to let the senators find another means of raising the money; he instructed Germanicus and Drusus not to speak of the matter in case everyone imagined that whatever they said must be what he wanted (Dio 56.28.4–5). He proposed a land tax instead, and started to measure up estates (Dio 56.28.6).

11 Jones (1968, 16; 1970, 77) consistently argued that Tiberius did not possess consular power in Rome and Italy. Brunt and Moore (1967, 51) point out that the text of the *Res Gestae* (8.4) implies that he did, and that the law mentioned by Suetonius (*Tib.* 21.1) empowering Tiberius to take the census may well have included Augustus in the special grant of consular power. Augustus liked Capri, which he had received from Naples (Suetonius *Aug.* 92.2; Dio 52.43.2). He died at Nola (Dio 56.30.5), in the same room as his father Gaius Octavius (Suetonius *Aug.* 100.1), having first assembled his friends to ask if they had enjoyed the performance (Suetonius *Aug.* 99.1). According to Velleius (2.123.2) he conversed with Tiberius and died in his arms; Tacitus (*Ann.* 1.5) admits that no one knows whether Tiberius found Augustus alive or dead when he returned to Nola; Suetonius (*Aug.* 99.1) says that only Livia was present when Augustus died; Dio is full of suspicion and subterfuge, in that Livia was suspected of poisoning her husband by smearing poison over some figs, and she kept his death a close secret until Tiberius safely reached Nola (56.31.1).

9 THE LEGACY

1 Dio (56.44.3–4) points out that the length of Augustus' reign gave the world stability, and that many people would know no other form of government.

After Augustus' death Velleius (2.124.1) describes the near panic, and the 'narrow margin between safety and ruin'. Tiberius may have increased the pay of the Praetorian Guard to make sure of their loyalty; Watson (1969, 98) points out that at an unspecified date between AD 6 and 14 Praetorian pay doubled, and though this may have derived from a measure promoted by Augustus, Watson thought that it was due to Tiberius, 'who as the designated future ruler of Rome would find it desirable to secure the loyalty of what to an emperor was the most important section of the army'. Tiberius bound the soldiers in Italy to himself by administering to them the oath of loyalty established by Augustus (Dio 57.3.2). The soldiers in Germany and Pannonia were restless; some of them hailed Germanicus, who was compromised but quelled the troublemakers, while Drusus and Junius Blaesus quieted the rest (Dio 57.4.1–4, 57.5.1–3).

2 The oath of loyalty to Tiberius was sworn by the consuls, then the prefects, then the Senate and people; Tacitus accuses them of rushing into slavery (*Ann.* 1.7). In the same passage he also accuses Tiberius of hypocrisy because he professed reluctance to take on the Empire, but had none the less taken control of the armies; he 'nowhere manifested the least hesitation except when speaking in the Senate'. When it came to the meeting of the Senate, Tiberius expressed reluctance again, which Tacitus says was more dignified than convincing (*Ann.* 1.11). Velleius becomes emotional when he describes how the Senate and people had to force Empire upon Tiberius (2.124.2), but he took it on in the end because he saw that whatever he did not protect would perish.

3 Augustus' will was read out in the Senate by his freedman Polybius (Dio 56.32.1), who is named by Suetonius as one of the freedmen who wrote part of Augustus' will (*Aug.* 101.4). The other documents produced in the Senate after Augustus' death are described by Suetonius (*Aug.* 101.4); one of them concerned the directions for the funeral, the second was an account of his achievements (*Res Gestae*), and the third was the *breviarium totius imperii*, or the account of the revenues and military strength of the Empire. This document is also briefly described by Tacitus (*Ann.* 1.11). Dio adds that there was a fourth document, instructing Tiberius and the people how to govern the Empire (56.33).

4 The funeral of Augustus is described by Dio (56.34 to 56.42). Livia gave a million sesterces to Numerius Atticus because he had seen Augustus' spirit ascending to Heaven (Dio 56.4.61–2). Tacitus makes an assessment of Augustus' reign, contrasting the good and the bad points (*Ann.* 1.9–10), whereas Dio ascribes it all to Tiberius in his funeral oration (56.35–41), in which he mentions at least three times how Augustus made an end of factions and strife (56.37.1, 41.3, 44.2).

5 The image of Augustus has been extensively and intensively studied in the past few years; see Zanker (1988); Galinsky (1996). As for the monuments and buildings it is not known how much direct involvement Augustus had in their design, nor how much interest he took in them afterwards (Jones 1970, 159), and the coinage as a propaganda tool has been questioned because it is not known who dictated the legends and images appearing on coins (Crook 1996b, 138 and n. 113). The image of Louis XIV was deliberately created and promoted by his minister Colbert, and duly noted by the diplomat Spanheim (Burke

1992, 26, 49). Crook (1996b, 133, 137) describes Augustus as a showman, and is prepared to believe in some faceless assistant who attended to the promotion of Augustus.

6 Taylor studied the early development of the divinity of the Emperors; she describes the worship of the *Genius* of Augustus in Rome (1931, 190–3) and concluded that in the West Augustus was worshipped as a god in his own lifetime (ibid. 244). Temples were established to Augustus himself, and not to his *Genius* alone on an equal basis in the Eastern and Western halves of the Empire (Hanlein-Schafer 1985, reviewed by S. Price, *JRS* 76, 1986, 300–1). Two important evalutions of the divinity of Augustus and the establishment of his cult are by Pollini (1990) and Ostrow (1990). The most in-depth study of the Imperial cult in the West is by Fishwick (1987). Wardman (1982, 67) points out that there was no coronation ceremony where Augustus could rely on the support of the state religion, but it should be remembered that powerful priests were as dangerous as they were helpful to the medieval monarchs. When he at length combined the chief priesthood with all his other powers, Augustus hardly needed the extra authority that this gave him.

7 Crook (1996b, 113) argues that Augustus took on functions, but not powers. The administration of the Empire evolved from the form that Augustus gave it, but without precise dates for the institution of various procedures it is difficult to analyse the full contribution that he made. Millar (1984) analysed the changes brought about by one-man rule, and Nicolet (1984) dealt with the administration in so far as it affected the upper classes. In a series of papers, Lacey (1996) traced the development of the Principate as a system, and Millar (1966) and Lintott (1993) examined provincial government. These are only a few of the main studies of this vast subject.

8 Tacitus' *Annals* should be the starting point for an acute observation of how Augustus controlled the state. Syme (1939) treated Augustus' reign as a revolution; chapters 26 and 27 on the Government and the Cabinet, and chapter 29 on the National Programme, analyse how Augustus worked within the existing framework but took total charge. Jones (1968, 1–26) analysed Augustus' powers, but is not without his critics, such as Ameling (1994) to name one of the most recent. A useful synopsis of Augustus' life and career and the assumption of his powers, which has not been outclassed, can be found in Brunt and Moore (1967).

SELECT BIBLIOGRAPHY

ANCIENT SOURCES

Appian	*Roman History: the Civil War*
	Illyrica
Caesar	*Civil War*
	African War
Cicero	*Letters to Atticus*
	Letters to his Friends
	Letters to Marcus Brutus
	Philippics
Dio	*Roman History*
Florus	
Gaius	*Institutes*
Gellius	*Attic Nights*
Horace	*Carmen Saeculare*
	Epistulae
	Odes
Josephus	*Jewish Antiquities*
Livy	*Epitome*
Macrobius	*Saturnalia*
Nicolaus of Damascus	*Life of Augustus*, translated with commentary by C.M. Hall, Smith College Classical Studies No. IV, Northampton, Mass., 1923.
Orosius	*Historiae Adversus Paganos*
Ovid	*Ars Amatoria*
	Fasti
Pliny	*Natural History*
Plutarch	*Life of Antony*
	Life of Caesar
Propertius	
Quintilian	*Institutio Oratoria*
Seneca	*de Beneficiis*
	de Clementia
	de Ira
Strabo	*Geography*

258

Suetonius　　　　　*Lives of the Caesars*
Tacitus　　　　　　*Annals*
　　　　　　　　　　Dialogues
　　　　　　　　　　Histories
Ulpian　　　　　　*Digest*
Velleius Paterculus *Roman History*
Vergil　　　　　　*Aeneid*
　　　　　　　　　　Eclogues
　　　　　　　　　　Georgics

NB　References cited only once are given in full in the notes to each paragraph of the text. This bibliography covers a selection of the more important works or those cited frequently.

Adams, M. 1939. *C. Suetonius Tranquillus Divi Augusti Vitae.* London: Macmillan.
Alföldi, A. 1976. *Oktavians Aufstieg zur Macht.* Bonn: Antiquitas Reihe 1 Band 25.
Ameling, W. 1994. 'Augustus und Agrippa: Bemerkungen zu P.Köln VI 249', *Chiron* 24, 1–28.
Badian, E. 1982. 'Crisis theories and the beginning of the Principate', in G. Wirth (ed.) *Romanitas–Christianitas: Untersuchungen zur Geschichte und Literatur der Römischen Kaiserzeit: Johannes Straub zum 70 Geburtstag gewidmet.* Berlin, 18–41.
Badian, E. 1990. Review of C. Meier, *Caesar* (1982) (German edition) *Gnomon* 62, 22–39.
Baker, G.P. 1937. *Augustus: the Golden Age of Rome.* London.
Baldwin, B. 1983. *Suetonius.* Amsterdam: Adolf M. Hakkert.
Benario, H.W. 1975. 'Octavian's status in 32 BC', *Chiron* 5, 301–9.
Béranger, J. 1953. *Recherches sur l'Aspect Idéologique du Principat.* Basel: Verlag Friedrich Rheinhardt.
Bleicken, J. 1990. *Zwischen Republik und Principat: zum Charakter des Zweiten Triumvirats.* Göttingen.
Bowersock, G. 1984. 'Augustus and the east: the problem of the succession', in Millar and Segal (eds), 169–88.
Bowersock, G. 1990. 'The Pontificate of Augustus', in Raaflaub and Toher (eds), 380–94.
Brunt, P.A. 1984. 'The role of the Senate in Augustus' regime', *CQ* n.s. 34, 423–44.
Brunt, P.A. and Moore, J.M. 1967. *Res Gestae Divi Augusti: the Achievements of the Divine Augustus.* Oxford.
Burke, P. 1992. *The Fabrication of Louis XIV.* New Haven and London: Yale University Press.
Carter, J.M. 1982. *Suetonius: Divus Augustus.* Edited with introduction and commentary. Bristol Classical Press.
Chilver, G.E.F. 1950. 'Augustus and the Roman constitution, 1939–1950', *Historia* 1, 408–35.
Chisholm, K. and Ferguson, J. 1981. *Rome: the Augustan Age.* Oxford University Press in association with Open University.
Corbett, J.H. 1974. 'The succession policy of Augustus', *Latomus* 33, 88–97.
Crook, J. 1955. *Consilium Principis: Imperial Councils and Counsellors from Augustus to Diocletian.* Cambridge University Press.

Crook, J. 1957. 'A legal point about Mark Antony's will', *JRS* 47, 36–8.

Crook. J. 1996a. 'Political history 30 BC to AD 14', in *CAH²*, Vol. X, 70–112.

Crook, J. 1996b. 'Augustus, power, authority, achievement', in *CAH²*, Vol. X, 113–46.

Dettenhofer, M.H. 1992. *Perdita Iuventus: zwischen den Generationen von Caesar und Augustus*. Vetigia 44. Munich: Beck'sche Verlag.

Duff, A.M. 1958. *Freedmen in the Early Roman Empire*. Cambridge.

Durry, M. 1938. *Les Cohortes Prétoriennes*. Paris: Boccard.

Earl, D. 1980. *The Age of Augustus*. London: Ferndale Editions. First published by Elek, 1968.

Eder, D. 1990. 'Augustus and the power of tradition: the Augustan Principate as binding link between Republic and Empire', in Raaflaub and Toher (eds), 71–122.

Ehrenberg, V. and Jones, A.H.M. 1976. *Documents Illustrating the Reigns of Augustus and Tiberius*. Oxford: Clarendon Press, 2nd edn reprinted with addenda.

Elsner, J. 1991. 'Cult and sculpture: sacrifice in the Ara Pacis Augustae', *JRS* 81, 50–61.

Fadinger, V. 1969. *Die Begrundung des Prinzipats: Quellenkritische und Staatsrechtliche Untersuchungen zu Cassius Dio und der Paralleluberlieferung*. Berlin.

Fishwick, D. 1987. *The Imperial Cult in the Latin West*. I. Leiden: EPROR.

Gabba, E. 1970. 'La data finale de secondo Triumvirato', *RFIC* 98, 5ff.

Galinsky, K. 1996. *Augustan Culture: an Interpretive Introduction*. Princeton University Press.

Galsterer, H. 1990. 'A man, a book, and a method: Sir Ronald Syme's *Roman Revolution* after fifty years', in Raaflaub and Toher (eds), 1–20.

Gelzer, M. 1968. *Caesar: Politician and Statesman*. Oxford: Basil Blackwell.

Gesche, H. 1973. 'Hat Caesar den Octavian zum Magister Equitum designiert?', *Historia* 22, 468–78.

Gesche, H. 1978. 'Die Vergottung Caesars', in A. Wlosock (ed.) *Römische Kaiserkult*. Darmstadt: Wissenschaftliche Buchgesellschaft, (a synopsis of the book published in 1968).

Gowing, A.M. 1992. *The Triumviral Narratives of Appian and Cassius Dio*. Ann Arbor: University of Michigan Press.

Gray, E.W. 1970. 'The imperium of M. Agrippa: a note on P. Colon. inv. nr. 4701', *ZPE* 6, 227–38.

Grenade, P. 1961. *Essai sur les Origines du Principat*. Paris.

Gruen, E.S. 1974. *The Last Generation of the Roman Republic*. Berkeley: University of California Press.

Gruen, E.S. 1990. 'The Imperial policy of Augustus', in Raaflaub and Toher (eds), 395–416.

Gruen, E.S. 1996. 'The expansion of the Empire under Augustus', in *CAH²*, Vol. X, 148–97.

Gurval, R.A. 1995. *Actium and Augustus: the Politics and Emotions of Civil War*. Ann Arbor: University of Michigan Press.

Hammond, M. 1933. *The Augustan Principate*. Cambridge, Mass.: Harvard University Press.

Hannestad, H. 1986. *Roman Art and Imperial Policy*. Aarhus.

Heitland, W.E. 1909. *The Roman Republic*. (3 vols) Cambridge University Press.

Hinard, F. 1985. *Les Proscriptions de la Rome Republicaine*. Rome.

Jones, A.H.M. 1968. *Studies in Roman Government and Law.* Oxford: Basil Blackwell.

Jones, A.H.M. 1970. *Augustus.* New York: W.W. Norton and Co.

Kähler, H. 1959. *Die Augustusstatue von Prima Porta.* Cologne.

Kent, J.P.C. 1978. *Roman Coins.* London: Thames and Hudson.

Keppie, L. 1983. *Colonisation and Veteran Settlement in Italy 47–14 BC.* British School at Rome.

Keppie, L. 1996. 'The army and the navy', in *CAH²*, Vol. X, 371–96.

Kienast, D. 1982. *Augustus: Prinzeps und Monarch.* Darmstadt.

Kornemann, E. 1930. *Doppelprinzipat und Reichsteilung im Imperium Romanum.* Berlin.

Lacey, W.K. 1996. *Augustus and the Principate: the Evolution of the System.* Liverpool: Francis Cairns.

Last, H. 1951. 'On the *tribunicia potestas* of Augustus', in *Rendiconti del Istituto Lombardo di Scienze e Lettere* 84, 93–110 = Schmitthenner 1969, 241–63.

Levick, B. 1966 'Drusus Caesar and the adoptions of AD 4', *Latomus* 25, 227ff.

Levick, B. 1972. 'Tiberius' retirement to Rhodes in 6 BC', *Latomus* 31, 779–813.

Linderski, J. 1984. 'Rome, Aphrodisias and the *Res Gestae*: the *genera militiae* and the status of Octavian', *JRS* 74, 74–80.

Lintott, A. 1993. *Imperium Romanum.* London: Routledge.

Magdelain, A. 1947. *Auctoritas Principis.* Paris.

Marek, C. 1993. 'Die Expedition des Aelius Gallus nach Arabien im Jahre 25 v. Chr.', *Chiron* 23, 121–56.

Meier, C. 1990. 'C. Caesar divi filius and the formation of the alternative in Rome', in Raaflaub and Toher (eds), 54–71.

Meier, C. 1995. *Caesar.* London: HarperCollins.

Mette-Dittman, A. 1991. *Die Ehegesetze des Augustus: eine Untersuchung im Rahmen der Gesellschaftspolitik des Prinzeps.* Historia Einzelschriften LXVII.

Millar, F. 1966. 'The Emperor, the Senate, and the provinces', *JRS* 56, 156–66.

Millar, F. 1973. 'Triumvirate and Principate', *JRS* 63, 50–67.

Millar, F. 1984. 'State and subject; the impact of monarchy', in Millar and Segal (eds), 37–60.

Millar, F. and Segal, E. (eds) 1984. *Caesar Augustus: Seven Aspects.* Oxford: Clarendon Press.

Nicolet, C. 1984. 'Augustus, government and the propertied classes', in Millar and Segal (eds), 89–128.

Nippel, W. 1995. *Public Order in Ancient Rome.* Cambridge University Press.

Nock, A.D. 1934. 'Religious developments from the close of the Republic to the death of Nero', in *CAH¹* Vol. X, 465–511.

North, J.A. 1975. '*Praesens Divus*'. Review of Weinstock 1971, *JRS* 65, 171–7.

Ostrow, G.E. 1990. 'The *Augustales* in the Augustan scheme', in Raaflaub and Toher (eds), 364–79.

Pelling, C. 1996. 'The Triumviral period', in *CAH²*, Vol. X, 1–69.

Petit, P. 1976. *Pax Romana.* London: Batsford.

Petzold, K.-E. 1969. 'Die Bedeutung des Jahres 32 fur die Entstehung der Principats', *Historia* 18, 334–51.

Pollini, J. 1990. 'Man or God: divine assimilation and imitation in the late Republic and early Principate', in Raaflaub and Toher (eds), 334–63.

Powell, A. (ed.) 1992. *Roman Poetry and Propaganda in the Age of Augustus.* Bristol Classical Press.

Purcell, N. 1996. 'Rome and its development under Augustus and his successors', in *CAH*², Vol. X, 782–811.

Raaflaub. K.A. and Samons, L.J. II, 1990. 'Opposition to Augustus', in Raaflaub and Toher (eds), 417–54.

Raaflaub, K.A. and Toher, M. (eds.) 1990. *Between Republic and Empire: Interpretations of Augustus and his Principate*. University of Los Angeles.

Reinhold, M. 1965. *Marcus Agrippa: a Biography*. Rome: Bretschneider.

Reinhold, M. and Swan, P.M. 1990. 'Cassius Dio's assessment of Augustus', in Raaflaub and Toher (eds), 155–73.

Reinmuth, O.W. 1935. 'The Prefect of Egypt from Augustus to Diocletian', *Klio* Beiheft XXXIV n.s. no. 21 (Leipzig).

Reynolds, J. 1982. *Aphrodisias and Rome*. London: Society for the Promotion of Roman Studies.

Rice-Holmes, T. 1928. *The Architect of the Roman Empire*. Oxford: Clarendon.

Rice-Holmes, T. 1931. *The Architect of the Roman Empire 27 BC to AD 14*. Oxford: Clarendon.

Rich, J.W. 1990. *Cassius Dio and the Augustan Settlement (Roman History 53–55.9)*. Warminster: Aris and Philips.

Rich, J.W. 1996. 'Augustus and the spolia opima', *Chiron* 26, 85–127.

Rickman, G. 1980. *The Corn Supply of Ancient Rome*. Oxford: Clarendon.

Roddaz, J.-M. 1984. *Marcus Agrippa*. (BEFAR 253) Rome.

Salmon, E.T. 1982. *The Making of Roman Italy*. London: Thames and Hudson.

Sattler, P. 1960. *Augustus und der Senat: Untersuchungen zur Romischen Innenpolitik zwischen 30 und 17 v. Chr.* Göttingen.

Sattler, P. 1969. 'Julia and Tiberius: Beiträge zur römischen Innenpolitik zwischen den Jahren 12 v. und 2 n. Chr.', in Schmitthenner (ed.), 486–530.

Schmitthenner, W. 1952. *Oktavian und das Testament Caesars: eine Untersuchung zu den Politischen Anfängen des Augustus*. Munich: C.H. Beck'sche Verlag.

Schmitthenner, W. (ed.) 1969. *Augustus*. Darmstadt: Wissenschaftliche Buchgesellschaft.

Schönberger, H. 1985. ' Die römischen Truppenlager der frühen und mittleren Kaiserzeit zwischen Nordsee und Inn', *BRGK* 66, 321–497.

Scullard, H.H. 1970. *From the Gracchi to Nero*. London: Methuen (3rd edn).

Sherk, R.K. 1969. *Roman Documents from the Greek East: Senatus Consulta and Epistulae to the Age of Augustus*. Baltimore.

Sherk, R.K. (ed.) 1988. *The Roman Empire from Augustus to Hadrian*. Cambridge University Press.

Shuckburgh, E.S. 1896. *C. Suetonii Tranquilli: Divus Augustus*. Cambridge University Press.

Shuckburgh, E.S. 1903. *Augustus: the Life and Times of the Founder of the Roman Empire*. London: T. Fisher Unwin.

Stockton, D. 1971. *Cicero: a Political Biography*. Oxford University Press.

Syme, R. 1939. *The Roman Revolution*. Oxford: Clarendon Press.

Syme, R. 1950. 'A Roman post-mortem: an inquest on the fall of the Roman Republic'. Todd Memorial Lecture no. 3 = Syme 1979, 205–17.

Syme, R. 1958 *Tacitus* (2 vols). Oxford University Press.

Syme, R. 1959. 'Livy and Augustus', *Harvard Studies in Classical Philology* 64, 27–87 = Syme 1979, 400–54.

Syme, R .1979. *Roman Papers*. Vol. 1 (ed. E. Badian). Oxford: Clarendon Press.

Syme, R. 1984. *Roman Papers*. Vol. 3 (ed. A.R. Birley). Oxford: Clarendon Press.

Syme, R. 1986. *The Augustan Aristocracy*. Oxford: Clarendon Press.

Syme, R. 1988a. *Roman Papers*. Vol. 4 (ed. A.R. Birley). Oxford: Clarendon Press.

Syme, R. 1988b. *Roman Papers*. Vol. 5 (ed. A.R. Birley). Oxford: Clarendon Press.

Syme, R. 1991. *Roman Papers*. Vol. 6 (ed. A.R. Birley). Oxford: Clarendon Press.

Talbert, R.J.A. 1984. *The Senate of Imperial Rome*. Princeton University Press.

Taylor, L.R. 1931. *Divinity of the Roman Emperor*. American Philological Association: Monograph no. 1.

Taylor, L.R. 1949. *Party Politics in the Age of Caesar*. Berkeley and Los Angeles.

Toynbee, J.M.C. 1953. 'The Ara Pacis reconsidered and historical art in Roman Italy', *PBA* 39, 67–95.

Toynbee, J.M.C. 1961. 'Ara Pacis Augustae', *JRS* 51, 153–6.

von Premerstein, A. 1937. *Vom Werden und Wesen des Prinzipats*. Munich; Verlag der Bayerische Akademie der Wissenschaft.

von Schnürbein, S. 1981. 'Untersuchungen zur Geschichte der römischen Militärlager an der Lippe', *BRGK* 62, 1ff.

Wallace-Hadrill, A. 1993. *Augustan Rome*. Bristol Classical Press.

Wardman, A. 1982. *Religion and Statecraft Among the Romans*. London: Granada.

Ward-Perkins, J.B. 1981. *Roman Imperial Architecture*. Harmondsworth (2nd edn).

Watson, G.R. 1969. *The Roman Soldier*. London: Thames and Hudson.

Weigel, R.D. 1992. *Lepidus: the Tarnished Triumvir*. London: Routledge.

Weinstock, S. 1971. *Divus Julius*. Oxford: Clarendon Press.

Wells, C.M. 1972. *The German Policy of Augustus*. Oxford: Clarendon Press

Wickert, L. 1974. 'Neue Forschungen zur römische Principat', *ANRW* II.1, 3–90.

Wiegels, R. and Woesler, W. 1995. *Arminius und die Varusschlacht*. Paderborn.

Williams, G. 1990. 'Did Maecenas "fall from favour?" Augustan literary patronage', in Raaflaub and Toher (eds), 258–75.

Wiseman, T.P. 1971. *New Men in the Roman Senate*. Oxford.

Woodman, A.J. and West, D. (eds) 1984. *Poetry and Politics in the Age of Augustus*. Cambridge.

Yavetz, Z. 1969. *Plebs and Princeps*. Oxford University Press.

Zanker, P. 1988. *The Power of Images in the Age of Augustus*. Ann Arbor: University of Michigan Press.

INDEX

Entries referring to Octavian and Augustus have been abbreviated to O. and A.

69–70; origins and character, 72–3; designated consul for 37 BC, 82; trains ships' crews, 82; battle of Mylae, 83; awarded *corona navalis*, 85; in Illyricum, 90; water supply in Rome, 93; in Actium campaign, 97; consul in 28 BC with O. in 28 BC, 109; position in 26 BC, 118; A. gives him signet ring when not expected to live, 120; Agrippa goes to the East, 123–5; returns to Rome and takes over in Spain, 128; marriage to Julia, 123–4, 137, 149; role in Secular Games, 153; goes to the East again in 16 BC, 154; awarded triumph for settlement of the kingdom of Bosporus, 157; *tribunicia potestas*, 157, 160; *imperium*, 121–5, 131, 157; Pannonian command, 157, 159; death, 159; A.'s funeral oration, 160–1; portrait on the Ara Pacis, 167